SMALL ENGINE Manual

Martynn Randall

The Haynes Manual for maintaining, fault finding and repairing most small engines up to and including 5.5HP

Haynes Publishing
Sparkford, Nr Yeovil, Somerset BA22 7JJ England

Haynes North America, Inc
861 Lawrence Drive, Newbury Park, California 91320 USA

Haynes Publishing Nordiska AB
Box 1504, 751 45 Uppsala, Sweden

Acknowledgements
Thanks are due to Rochford Garden Machinery Ltd. of Wincanton, Somerset, and Loxton Garden Machinery Ltd. of Barrington, Somerset, for their invaluable assistance. Thanks are also due to Briggs & Stratton UK Ltd (www.briggsandstratton.com) and to Tecumseh UK (www.tecumsehuk.co.uk) for assistance with the provision of technical information.

This manual is not a direct reproduction of any engine manufacturer's data, and its publication should not be taken as implying any technical approval by engine manufacturers or importers.

© Haynes Publishing 2010

A book in the Haynes Service and Repair Manual Series

Printed in the USA

All rights reserved. No part of this book may be reproduced or transmitted in any form or by any means, electronic or mechanical, including photocopying, recording or by any information storage or retrieval system, without permission in writing from the copyright holder.

ISBN 978 1 84425 250 7

British Library Cataloguing in Publication Data
A catalogue record for this book is available from the British Library

While every attempt is made to ensure that the information in this manual is correct, no liability can be accepted by the authors or publishers for loss, damage or injury caused by any errors in, or omissions from, the information given.

(4250-240)

Illegal Copying

It is the policy of Haynes Publishing to actively protect its Copyrights and Trade Marks. Legal action will be taken against anyone who unlawfully copies the cover or contents of this Manual. This includes all forms of unauthorised copying including digital, mechanical, and electronic in any form. Authorisation from Haynes Publishing will only be provided expressly and in writing. Illegal copying will also be reported to the appropriate statutory authorities.

Contents

Introduction	0•4
1 Setting up	1•1
2 Workshop practice	2•1
3 Troubleshooting	3•1
4 Tune-up and routine maintenance	4•1
5 Repairs common to all engines	5•1
6 Briggs & Stratton MAX 4hp 4-stroke engine	6•1
7 Briggs & Stratton Intek/Europa OHV engines	7•1
8 Briggs & Stratton Quantum 55 'L' head engine	8•1
9 Briggs & Stratton I/C horizontal crank 'L' head 5 hp engine	9•1
10 Briggs & Stratton 35 Sprint/Classic 2.6 kW engine	10•1
11 Honda GXV120 OHV 4-stroke engine	11•1
12 Honda GCV 135 OHC engine	12•1
13 Tecumseh 3.5 hp/Vantage 35 4-stroke engine	13•1
14 Tecumseh MV100S 2-stroke engine	14•1
Glossary	GL•1

Introduction

Introduction

There are literally millions of small engines in the garages and sheds of homes all across the country today. They're mounted on lawn mowers, garden rotavators, generators, air compressors, pumps, mini-bikes, karts and various other types of equipment and recreational vehicles...and many of them are badly neglected – in need of some type of maintenance or repair (often both). Since they're required to operate in hostile conditions (dust, heat, overloading and in many cases without proper lubrication), it's a tribute to the designers, as well as those who have a part in the manufacturing processes, that they perform as well and last as long as they do! However, you don't have to be guilty of neglecting the small engines in your possession, now that Haynes, the world's largest publisher of owners workshop manuals, has made available this repair manual covering the most popular and widely used small engines from the leading manufacturers. Its proven approach, featuring easy-to-follow, step-by-step troubleshooting, maintenance and repair procedures, profusely illustrated with photographs taken in our own workshop, has been refined over the years in our do-it-yourself automotive and motorcycle repair manuals.

The purpose of this manual is to help you maintain and repair small petrol engines. It can do so in several ways. It can help you decide what work must be done, even if you choose to have it done by a repair workshop, it provides information and procedures for servicing and routine maintenance and it offers diagnostic and repair procedures to follow when trouble occurs.

It's hoped you'll use the manual to tackle the work yourself. For many jobs, doing it yourself may be quicker than arranging an appointment to get the machinery into a workshop and making the trips to drop it off and pick it up. More importantly, a lot of money can be saved by avoiding the expenses the workshop must pass on to you to cover labour and overhead costs. An added benefit is the sense of satisfaction and accomplishment you feel after doing the job yourself. We also hope that as you gain experience and confidence working on small engines, you'll decide to move on to simple motorcycle, car or truck maintenance and repair jobs. When you do, Haynes can supply you with virtually all the service information you'll need.

How to use this repair manual

The manual is divided into several chapters. Each chapter is sub-divided into well-defined sections, many of which consist of consecutively numbered paragraphs (usually referred to as 'steps', since they're normally part of a maintenance or repair procedure). If the material is basically informative in nature, rather than a step-by-step procedure, the paragraphs aren't numbered.

The first five chapters contain material that applies to all engines, regardless of manufacturer. The remaining chapters cover specific material related to the individual brand engines only. Since most people are initially exposed to practical mechanics working on small engines, comprehensive chapters covering tool selection and usage, safety and general workshop practices have also been included. *Be sure to read through them before beginning any work.*

The term 'see illustration', is used in the text to indicate that a photo or drawing has been included to make the information easier to understand (the old cliché 'a picture is worth a thousand words' is especially true when it comes to how-to procedures). Also, every attempt is made to position illustrations near the corresponding text to minimize confusion.

The terms 'Note', 'Caution' and 'Warning' are used throughout the text with a specific purpose in mind – to attract the reader's attention. A 'Note' simply provides information required to complete a procedure properly or information which will make the procedure easier to understand. A 'Caution' outlines a special procedure or special steps which must be taken when completing the procedure where the Caution is found. Failure to pay attention to a Caution can result in damage to the component being repaired or the tools being used. A 'Warning' is included where personal injury can result if the instructions aren't followed exactly as described.

Even though extreme care has been taken during the preparation of this manual, neither the publisher nor the author can accept responsibility for any errors in, or omissions from, the information given.

Introduction

Engines covered

The information in this repair manual is restricted to single-cylinder, air-cooled engines rated up to 5.5 horsepower, normally used to power lawn mowers, garden rotovators, generators, air compressors, pumps and other types of commonly available equipment. The following manufacturers' engine types are included.

Briggs & Stratton single-cylinder four-strokes (side valve and OHV)
Tecumseh single-cylinder four-strokes (side valve only)
Tecumseh single-cylinder two-strokes
Honda single-cylinder four-strokes (OHV and OHC)

The following is a list of popular applications for the engines covered by this manual. Please note that due to model and engine supply changes, you may have an application that is not listed. If in doubt contact your local horticultural engineering dealer to assist with engine identification.

AL-CO
Engines: E-31, E-41, E-36, E-46, E-56
Tecumseh 3.5 hp/Vantage 35

AL-CO 42/48
Engine: GJAF
Honda OHC GCV135 4.5 hp (3.3 kW)

AL-CO Euroline 4200/4700
Engine: GJAF
Honda OHC GCV135 4.5 hp (3.3 kW)

Allen 216/218
Model/spec. number of engine: E-16
Tecumseh MV100S

Ariens LM series
Engines: 128802, 127702, 12H802, 12F802
Briggs & Stratton Quantum 55 'L' Head

Atco
Engines: 110700, 111700, 112700, 114700
Briggs and Stratton MAX 4hp

Atco Admiral
Engines: 128802, 127702, 12H802, 12F802
Briggs & Stratton Quantum 55 'L' Head

Atco Club
Engine: 135232
Briggs and Stratton I/C horizontal crank 'L' Head 5 hp

Atco Royale
Engine: 135232
Briggs and Stratton I/C horizontal crank 'L' Head 5 hp

Atco Viscount
Engines: 128802, 127702, 12H802, 12F802
Briggs & Stratton Quantum 55 'L' Head

Bearcat BC series
Engines: 128802, 127702, 12H802, 12F802
Briggs & Stratton Quantum 55 'L' Head

BRILL Hattrick
Engines: 128802, 127702, 12H802, 12F802
Briggs & Stratton Quantum 55 'L' Head

Castel
Engines: E-31, E-41, E-36, E-46, E-56
Tecumseh 3.5 hp/Vantage 35

Efco LR series
Engines: 9D902, 10D902, 98902
Briggs & Stratton 35 Sprint/Classic 2.6 kW
Engines: E-31, E-41, E-36, E-46, E-56
Tecumseh 3.5 hp/Vantage 35

Efco LR/MR series
Engines: 128802, 127702, 12H802, 12F802
Type: Briggs & Stratton Quantum 55 'L' Head

Flymo
Engines: 110700, 111700, 112700, 114700
Briggs and Stratton MAX 4hp

Flymo 42cm/46cm
Engines: E-31, E-41, E-36, E-46, E-56
Tecumseh 3.5 hp/Vantage 35

Flymo L50/L38/L47/L470
Engine: E-16
Tecumseh MV100S

Harry
Engines: E-31, E-41, E-36, E-46, E-56
Tecumseh 3.5 hp/Vantage 35

Harry 302/C48/322/C49C50/424
Engines: 128802, 127702, 12H802, 12F802
Briggs & Stratton Quantum 55 'L' Head

Harry 313
Engines: 9D902, 10D902, 98902
Briggs & Stratton 35 Sprint/Classic 2.6 kW

Hayter
Engine: GXV120
Honda GXV120

Hayter Harrier
Engines: 110700, 111700, 112700, 114700
Briggs and Stratton MAX 4hp

Hayter Harrier 2
Engines: 110700, 111700, 112700, 114700
Briggs and Stratton MAX 4hp

Hayter Harrier 41
Engines: 128802, 127702, 12H802, 12F802
Briggs & Stratton Quantum 55 'L' Head

0•5

Introduction

Hayter Harrier 48
Engine: 121602
Briggs and Stratton Intek/Europa OHV

Hayter Hawk
Engines: 110700, 111700, 112700, 114700
Briggs and Stratton MAX 4hp

Hayter Hayterette
Engines: 128802, 127702, 12H802, 12F802
Briggs & Stratton Quantum 55 'L' Head

Hayter Hobby
Engines: E-31, E-41, E-36, E-46, E-56
Tecumseh 3.5 hp/Vantage 35

Hayter Hunter 48
Engines: 110700, 111700, 112700, 114700
Briggs and Stratton MAX 4hp

Hayter Jubilee
Engines: 128802, 127702, 12H802, 12F802
Briggs & Stratton Quantum 55 'L' Head

Hayter Ranger
Engines: 128802, 127702, 12H802, 12F802
Briggs & Stratton Quantum 55 'L' Head

Honda HR194
Engine: GXV120
Honda GXV120

Honda HRA214
Engine: GXV120
Honda GXV120

Honda HRB425C
Engine: GJAF
Honda OHC GCV135 4.5 hp (3.3 kW)

Honda HRG415C
Engine: GJAF
Honda OHC GCV135 4.5 hp (3.3 kW)

Honda HRG465C
Engine: GJAF
Honda OHC GCV135 4.5 hp (3.3 kW)

HondaHR214
Engine: GXV120
Honda GXV120

Husqvarna
Engines: 110700, 111700, 112700, 114700
Briggs and Stratton MAX 4hp

IBEA 4221/4237/4238/4204/4704/4721
Engines: 128802, 127702, 12H802, 12F802
Briggs & Stratton Quantum 55 'L' Head

IBEA 5361
Engine: 121602
Briggs and Stratton Intek/Europa OHV

IPU 400 series
Engine: GXV120
Honda GXV120

Kompact 90
Engines: E-31, E-41, E-36, E-46, E-56
Tecumseh 3.5 hp/Vantage 35

Kompact 90S
Engine: 135232
Briggs and Stratton I/C horizontal crank 'L' Head 5 hp

Lawn-Boy 400
Engines: 128802, 127702, 12H802, 12F802
Briggs & Stratton Quantum 55 'L' Head

Lawnflite by MTD 383
Engines: 9D902, 10D902, 98902
Briggs & Stratton 35 Sprint/Classic 2.6 kW

Lawnflite by MTD 384
Engines: 128802, 127702, 12H802, 12F802
Briggs & Stratton Quantum 55 'L' Head

Lawnflite by MTD 991 SP6
Engines: 128802, 127702, 12H802, 12F802
Briggs & Stratton Quantum 55 'L' Head

Lawnflite by MTD GE40
Engines: 9D902, 10D902, 98902
Briggs & Stratton 35 Sprint/Classic 2.6 kW

Lawnflite by MTD GES 45 C
Engines: 128802, 127702, 12H802, 12F802
Briggs & Stratton Quantum 55 'L' Head

Lawnflite by MTD GES 53
Engines: 128802, 127702, 12H802, 12F802
Briggs & Stratton Quantum 55 'L' Head

Lawn-King NG series
Engines: 9D902, 10D902, 98902
Briggs & Stratton 35 Sprint/Classic 2.6 kW

Lawn-King PA/NP/T484 series
Engines: 128802, 127702, 12H802, 12F802
Briggs & Stratton Quantum 55 'L' Head

McCulloch ML857
Engines: 128802, 127702, 12H802, 12F802
Briggs & Stratton Quantum 55 'L' Head

Mountfield Emblem
Engines: E-31, E-41, E-36, E-46, E-56
Tecumseh 3.5 hp/Vantage 35

Mountfield Emblem 15
Engines: 9D902, 10D902, 98902
Briggs & Stratton 35 Sprint/Classic 2.6 kW

Mountfield Emperor
Engines: 110700, 111700, 112700, 114700
Briggs and Stratton MAX 4hp
Engines: 128802, 127702, 12H802, 12F802
Briggs & Stratton Quantum 55 'L' Head

Introduction

Mountfield Empress
  Engines: 110700, 111700, 112700, 114700
  Briggs and Stratton MAX 4hp
  Engines: E-31, E-41, E-36, E-46, E-56
  Tecumseh 3.5 hp/Vantage 35

Mountfield Empress 16
  Engines: 128802, 127702, 12H802, 12F802
  Briggs & Stratton Quantum 55 'L' Head

Mountfield Empress 18
  Engines: 128802, 127702, 12H802, 12F802
  Briggs & Stratton Quantum 55 'L' Head

Mountfield Laser
  Engines: E-31, E-41, E-36, E-46, E-56
  Tecumseh 3.5 hp/Vantage 35

Mountfield Laser Delta 42/46
  Engines: 9D902, 10D902, 98902
  Briggs & Stratton 35 Sprint/Classic 2.6 kW

Mountfield M3
  Engines: E-31, E-41, E-36, E-46, E-56
  Tecumseh 3.5 hp/Vantage 35

Mountfield MPR series
  Engine: 121602
  Briggs and Stratton Intek/Europa OHV

Oleomac G43
  Engines: 9D902, 10D902, 98902
  Briggs & Stratton 35 Sprint/Classic 2.6 kW
  Engines: E-31, E-41, E-36, E-46, E-56
  Tecumseh 3.5 hp/Vantage 35

Oleomac G47
  Engine: GJAF
  Honda OHC GCV135 4.5 hp (3.3 kW)
  Engines: 128802, 127702, 12H802, 12F802
  Briggs & Stratton Quantum 55 'L' Head

Oleomac MAX 53
  Engines: 128802, 127702, 12H802, 12F802
  Briggs & Stratton Quantum 55 'L' Head

Partner 431
  Engines: 9D902, 10D902, 98902
  Briggs & Stratton 35 Sprint/Classic 2.6 kW

Qualcast Quadtrak 45
  Engines: E-31, E-41, E-36, E-46, E-56
  Tecumseh 3.5 hp/Vantage 35

Qualcast Trojan
  Engines: E-31, E-41, E-36, E-46, E-56
  Tecumseh 3.5 hp/Vantage 35

Rally 21/MR series
  Engines: 128802, 127702, 12H802, 12F802
  Briggs & Stratton Quantum 55 'L' Head

Rover
  Engine: GXV120 – Honda GXV120

Rover 100
  Engines: 9D902, 10D902, 98902
  Briggs & Stratton 35 Sprint/Classic 2.6 kW

Rover 100/200/260
  Engines: 128802, 127702, 12H802, 12F802
  Briggs & Stratton Quantum 55 'L' Head

Rover 200 18"
  Engine: GJAF
  Honda OHC GCV135 4.5 hp (3.3 kW)

SARP 484
  Engine: GJAF
  Honda OHC GCV135 4.5 hp (3.3 kW)

Stiga Multiclip Pro 48
  Engine: GJAF
  Honda OHC GCV135 4.5 hp (3.3 kW)
  Engines: 9D902, 10D902, 98902
  Briggs & Stratton 35 Sprint/Classic 2.6 kW

Stiga Turbo 48/55
  Engines: 128802, 127702, 12H802, 12F802
  Briggs & Stratton Quantum 55 'L' Head

Suffolk Punch P16
  Engines: 9D902, 10D902, 98902
  Briggs & Stratton 35 Sprint/Classic 2.6 kW

Suffolk Punch P19
  Engines: 128802, 127702, 12H802, 12F802
  Briggs & Stratton Quantum 55 'L' Head

Suffolk Punch P19S
  Engines: 128802, 127702, 12H802, 12F802
  Briggs & Stratton Quantum 55 'L' Head

The Club 470 T35/40
  Engines: E-31, E-41, E-36, E-46, E-56
  Tecumseh 3.5 hp/Vantage 35

TORO Re-cycler 20776
  Engines: 128802, 127702, 12H802, 12F802
  Briggs & Stratton Quantum 55 'L' Head

TORO Re-cycler 26637/20791/20789/20826/20827
  Engine: 121602
  Briggs and Stratton Intek/Europa OHV

Tracmaster Camon
  Engine: GXV120
  Honda GXV120

Valex Daytona
  Engines: E-31, E-41, E-36, E-46, E-56
  Tecumseh 3.5 hp/Vantage 35

Viva PB seies
  Engines: 128802, 127702, 12H802, 12F802
  Briggs & Stratton Quantum 55 'L' Head

Yardman by MTD YM series
  Engines: 128802, 127702, 12H802, 12F802
  Briggs & Stratton Quantum 55 'L' Head

Introduction

How to identify an engine

To determine what repair information and specifications to use, and to purchase replacement parts, you'll have to be able to identify accurately the engine you're working on. Every engine, regardless of manufacturer, comes from the factory with a model number stamped or cast into it or a tag attached to it somewhere *(see illustration)*.

The most common location is on the shroud used to direct the cooling air around the cylinder (look for the recoil starter – it's normally attached to the shroud as well). On some engines, the model number may be stamped or cast into or attached to the main engine casting and may not be visible, especially if the engine is dirty. To identify an engine from a known manufacturer covered in this manual, refer to the chapter with the specific repair information for the particular manufacturer.

If you can't find a model number or tag, you can determine if the engine is a two or four stroke (which will help a dealer decide what engine model you're dealing with) using one or more of the following quick checks:

Look for a cap used to check the oil level and add oil to the engine – if the engine has a threaded or friction fit cap or plug that's obviously intended for adding oil to the crankcase *(see illustration)*, it's a four-stroke (the cap may be marked 'Engine oil' or 'Oil fill' and may have an oil level dipstick attached to it as well).

Look for instructions to mix oil with the petrol – if the engine requires oil in the petrol *(see illustration)*, it's a two-stroke.

Look for a silencer near the cylinder head – if the silencer (usually a canister-shaped device with several holes or slots in the end) is threaded into or bolted to the engine near one end, it's a four-stroke. Two-stroke engines have exhaust ports on the cylinder itself, near the centre.

Use the recoil starter to feel for compression strokes – detach the wire from the spark plug and earth it on the engine, then slowly operate the recoil starter. If you can feel resistance from cylinder compression every revolution of the crankshaft, the engine is a two-stroke. If compression resistance is felt every other revolution, the engine is a four-stroke.

The engine model/serial number is usually located on the cooling shroud (as shown here), but it may be located on the main engine casting

Four-stroke engines will have an oil level check/fill plug like this one somewhere on the lower part of the engine

Two-stroke engines require oil to be mixed with the petrol for lubrication

Introduction

Buying parts

The best place (and sometimes the only place) to buy parts for any small engine is the dealer that sells and repairs the engine brand or the equipment the engine is mounted on. Some motor factors also stock small engine parts, but they normally carry only service and maintenance items. Look in your telephone directory, or under 'Lawnmower & garden machinery dealers' in Yellow Pages, for a list of dealers in your area.

Always purchase and install name-brand parts. Most manufacturers market new, complete replacement engines and also what is termed a 'short block'. A short block is a brand new engine sub-assembly that includes the main crankcase casting, piston, rings and connecting rod, valves and related components, cylinder and camshaft. If you purchase one, you'll have to bolt on the external parts, such as the cylinder head, magneto, carburettor, fuel tank and starter/cooling shroud. A short block typically costs about half as much as a complete new engine and approximately twice as much as a new crankshaft. If you have an engine that's worn out, severely damaged or that requires more work than you're willing to invest, a short block – or an entire new engine – may be the best alternative to an overhaul or major repairs

Be sure to have the engine model and serial number available when buying parts and, if possible, take the old parts with you to the dealer. Then you can compare the new with the old to make sure you're getting the right ones. Keep in mind that parts may have to be ordered, so as soon as you realize you're going to need something, see if it's in stock and allow extra time for completing the repair if parts must be ordered

You may occasionally be able to purchase used parts in usable condition and save some money in the process. A reputable dealer won't sell substandard parts, so don't hesitate to inquire about used components.

Notes

Setting up   1

Finding a place to work

Tools and equipment needed

Special factory tools

Finding a place to work

Before considering what tools to collect, or how to use them, a safe, clean, well-lit place to work should be located. If anything more than routine maintenance is going to be done, some sort of special work area is essential. It doesn't have to be particularly large, but it should be clean, organized and equipped especially for doing mechanic work. It's understood, and appreciated, that many home mechanics don't have a good workshop or garage available and end up servicing or repairing an engine out of doors; however, an overhaul or major repairs should be completed in a sheltered area with a roof (the main reason is to prevent parts from collecting dirt, which is abrasive and will cause wear if it finds its way into an engine).

The workshop building

The size, shape and location of a workshop building is usually dictated by circumstances rather than personal choice. Ideally, every do-it-yourselfer would have a spacious, clean, well-lit building specially designed and equipped for working on everything from small engines on lawn and garden equipment to cars and other vehicles. In reality, however, most of us must be content with a corner of the garage or a small shed in the backyard.

As mentioned above, anything beyond minor maintenance and adjustments in nice weather should be done indoors. The best readily-available building would be a normal one or two car garage, preferably one that's detached from the house. A garage provides ample work and storage space and room for a large workbench. With that in mind, it must be pointed out that even the most extensive job possible on the typical small engine could, if necessary, be done in a small shed or corner of a garage. The bottom line is you'll have to make do with whatever facilities you have and adapt your workshop and methods of work to it.

Whatever the limitations of your own proposed or existing workshop area are, spend some time considering its potential and drawbacks, even a well established workshop will benefit from occasional re-organisation. Most do-it-yourselfers find that lack of space causes problems; this can be overcome to a great extent by carefully planning the locations of benches and storage facilities. The rest of this Section will cover some of the options available when setting up or re-organising a workshop. Perhaps the best approach when designing a workshop is to look at how others do it. Try approaching a local repair workshop owner and asking to see his workshop; note how work areas, storage and lighting are arranged, then try to scale it down to fit your own space, finances and needs.

General building requirements

A solid concrete floor is probably the best surface for any area used for mechanic work. The floor should be as even as possible and must also be dry. Although not absolutely necessary, it can be improved by applying a coat of paint or sealer formulated for concrete surfaces. This will make oil spills and dirt easier to remove and help cut down on dust – always a problem with concrete. A wood floor is less desirable and may sag or be damaged by the weight of equipment and machinery. It can be reinforced by laying sheets of thick plywood or chipboard over the existing surface. A dirt floor should be avoided at all costs, since it'll produce abrasive dust, which will be impossible to keep away from internal engine components. Dirt floors are also as bad as gravel or grass when it comes to swallowing up tiny dropped parts such as ball bearings and small springs.

Walls and ceilings should be as light as possible. It's a good idea to clean them and apply a couple of coats of white paint.

Chapter 1

The paint will minimize dust and reflect light inside the workshop. On the subject of light, the more natural light there is the better. Artificial light will also be needed, but you'll need a surprising amount of it to equal ordinary daylight.

A normal doorway is just wide enough to allow all but the biggest pieces of machinery and equipment through, but not wide enough to allow it through easily. If possible, a full-size garage door (overhead or hinged at each side) should allow access into the workshop. Steps (even one of them) can be difficult to negotiate – make a ramp out of wood to allow easier entry if the step can't be removed.

Make sure the building is adequately ventilated, particularly during the winter. This is essential to prevent condensation problems and is also a vital safety consideration where solvents, petrol and other volatile liquids are being used. You should be able to open one or more windows for ventilation. In addition, opening vents in the walls are desirable.

Storage and shelving

All the parts from a small engine can occupy more space than you realise when it's been completely disassembled – some sort of organised storage is needed to avoid losing them. In addition, storage space for hardware, lubricants, solvent, rags, tools and equipment will also be required.

If space and finances allow, install metal shelf units along the walls. Arrange the shelves so they're widely spaced near the bottom to take large or heavy items. Metal shelf units are expensive, but they make the best use of available space. An added advantage is the shelf positions are not fixed and can be changed if necessary.

A cheaper (but more labour intensive) solution is to build shelves out of wood *(see illustration)*. Remember that wooden shelves must be much heftier than metal shelves to carry the same weight and the shelf positions are difficult to change. Also, wood absorbs oil and other liquids and is obviously a much greater fire hazard.

Small parts can be stored in plastic drawers or bins mounted on metal racks attached to the wall. They're available from most do-it-yourself shops as well as hardware stores. The bins are available in various sizes and normally have slots for labels.

Other containers can be used to keep storage costs down, but try to avoid round tubs, which waste a lot of space. Glass jars are often recommended as cheap storage containers, but they can easily get broken. Cardboard boxes are adequate for temporary use, but eventually the bottoms tend to drop out of them, especially if they get damp. Most plastic containers are useful, however, and large ice cream tubs are invaluable for keeping small parts together during a rebuild or major repairs (collect the type that has a cover that snaps into place).

Electricity and lights

Of all the useful workshop facilities, electricity is by far the most essential. It's relatively easy to arrange if the workshop is near to or part of a house and it can be difficult and expensive if it isn't. It must be stressed that safety is the number one consideration when dealing with electricity; unless you have a very good working knowledge of electrical installations, any work required to provide power and lights should be done by an electrician.

You'll have to consider the total electrical requirements of the workshop, making allowances for possible later additions of lights and equipment. Don't substitute extension leads for legal and safe permanent wiring. If the wiring isn't adequate or is substandard, have it upgraded.

Careful consideration should be given to lights for the workshop (two 150-watt incandescent bulbs or two 1.2 m (48-inch) long, 40-watt fluorescent tubes suspended approximately 1.2 m (48-inches) above the workbench would be a minimum). As a general rule, fluorescent lights are probably the best choice for even, shadow-free lighting. The position of the lights is important; for example, don't position a fixture directly above the area where the engine (or equipment it's mounted on) will be located during work – this will cause shadows even with fluorescent lights. Attach the light or lights slightly to the rear of or to each side of the workbench or work area to provide even lighting. A portable inspection light is very helpful for use when overhead lights are inadequate. Note that if solvents, petrol or other flammable liquids are present, which is usually the case in a mechanic's workshop, special fittings should be used to minimize the risk of fire. Also, don't use fluorescent lights above machine tools (like a drill press). The flicker produced by alternating current is especially pronounced with this type of light and can make a rotating chuck appear stationary at certain speeds – a very dangerous situation.

Since they're relatively inexpensive and can be designed to fit available space, home-made wooden shelves may be the best choice for storage – however, keep in mind the obvious fire hazard they will become

Setting up

Equipment needed

Fire extinguisher

Since the use, maintenance and repair of any petrol engine requires fuel to be handled and stored, buy a good-quality fire extinguisher before doing any maintenance or repair procedures *(see illustration)*. Make sure it's rated for flammable liquid fires, familiarize yourself with its use and be sure to have it checked/recharged at regular intervals. Refer to Chapter 2 for safety-related information – warnings about the hazards of petrol and other flammable liquids are included there.

Workbench

A workbench is essential – it provides a place to layout parts and tools during repair procedures, which means they'll stay clean longer, and it's a lot more comfortable than working on a floor or the driveway. This very important piece of equipment should be as large and sturdy as space and finances will allow. Although many types of benches are commercially available, they're usually quite expensive and don't necessarily fit into the available space as well as custom-built ones will. An excellent free-standing bench frame can be fabricated from slotted angle-iron or good quality softwood (use 50 x 150's rather than 50 x 100's) *(see illustration)*. The pieces of the frame can be cut to any required size and bolted together. A 760 or 910 by 2000 mm (30 or 36 by 80-inch) wood, solid-core door with hardboard surfaces, available at any do-it-yourself shop, makes a nice bench top and can be turned over to expose the fresh side if it gets damaged or worn out.

If you're setting up in a garage, a sturdy bench can be assembled very quickly by attaching the bench top frame pieces to the wall with angled braces, effectively using the wall studs as part of the framework. Regardless of the type of frame you decide to use for the workbench, be sure to position the bench top at a comfortable working height and make sure everything is level. Shelves installed below the bench will make it more rigid and provide useful storage space.

One of the most useful pieces of equipment – and one that's usually associated with the workbench – is a vice. Size isn't necessarily the most important factor to consider when shopping for one; the quality of materials used and

Always have a fire extinguisher handy, and know how to use it. Make sure it's rated for flammable liquid fires, and that it meets the relevant British Safety Standard

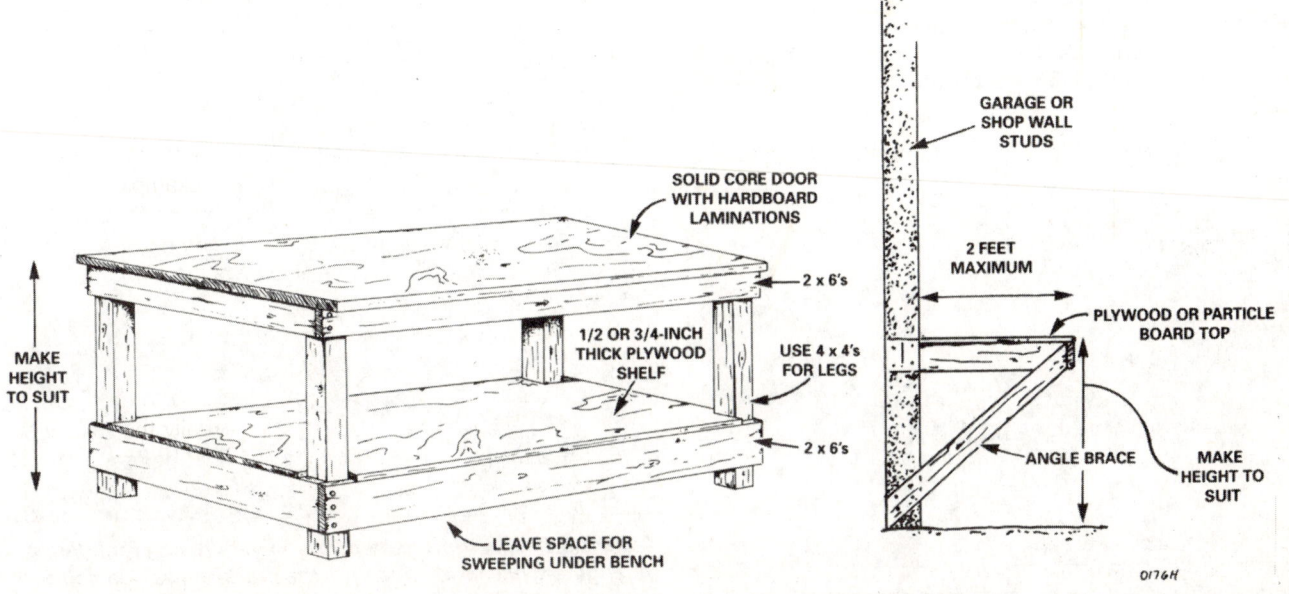

A sturdy, inexpensive workbench can be constructed from 50 x 150 mm (2 x 6 inch) lengths of wood

Chapter 1

A bench vice is one of the most useful pieces of equipment you can have

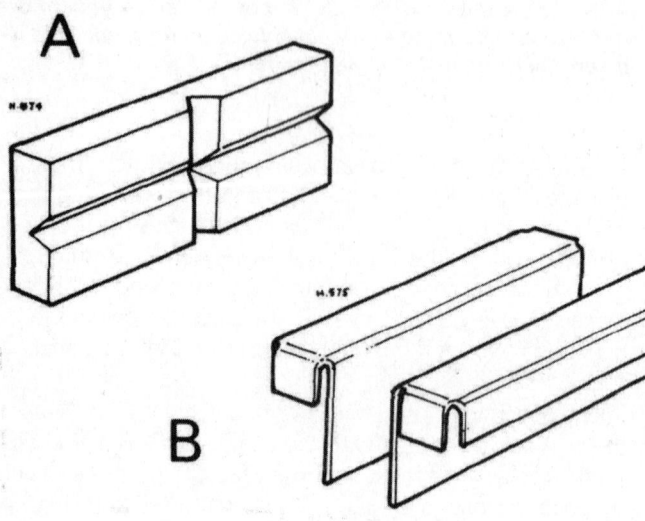

Some jobs will require engine parts to be held in the vice – to avoid damage to the parts from the hardened vice jaws, use commercially available fibreglass or plastic 'soft jaws' (A) or fabricate inserts from 3.0 mm thick aluminium to fit over the jaws (B)

A handy engine stand can be made from short lengths of 50 x 100 mm timber and coach bolts or nails

workmanship is. Good vices are very expensive, but as with anything else, you get what you pay for. Buy the best quality vice you can afford and make sure the jaws will open at least 100 mm (4 inches). Purchase a set of soft jaws to fit the vice as well (they're used to grip engine parts that could be damaged by the hardened vice jaws) *(see illustrations)*.

Engine stands

Many small engine manufacturers also distribute a special fixture to hold engines during disassembly and reassembly. Equipment of this type is undoubtedly very useful, but outside the scope of most home workshops. In practice, most do-it-yourselfers will have to make do with a selection of wood blocks that can be used to prop the engine up on a bench. They can be arranged as required so the engine is supported in almost any position. An engine stand can also be fabricated from short lengths of 50 x 100 mm timber and coach bolts, screws or nails *(see illustration)*. When using wood blocks or a home made engine stand, it's a good idea to have a helper available to assist in steadying the engine while fasteners are loosened or tightened. In some situations, the engine can be clamped in a vice, but be very careful not to damage the crankcase or cylinder castings.

Adjustable workbenches, like the Black & Decker Workmate, can also be very useful for holding an engine while it's being worked on *(see illustration)*. You probably won't want to buy one just for working on a lawn mower engine, but if you already have one, it can easily be adapted for use as a holding fixture.

Air compressor

Although it isn't absolutely necessary, an air compressor can make many tasks much easier and enable you to do a better

A Black & Decker Workmate comes in very handy for holding an engine while working on it – the quick-release clamping feature makes it easy to change the engine's position quickly

Setting up

job. (How else can you easily remove debris from the engine's cooling fins, dry off parts after cleaning them with solvent or blow out all the tiny passages in a carburettor?) If you can afford one, you'll wonder how you ever got along without it. In addition to supplying compressed air for cleaning parts, a compressor (if it's large enough) can also be used to power air tools, which are now widely available and quite inexpensive and can take much of the drudgery out of mechanical repair jobs *(see illustration)*. For example, an impact spanner (and special impact sockets) can be invaluable when it comes time to remove the large nut that holds a lawn mower blade or the magneto flywheel to the end of the crankshaft. On the down side, the cost involved, the need for maintenance on the equipment and additional electrical requirements must be considered before equipping your workshop with compressed air.

Tools

A selection of good mechanic's tools is a basic requirement for anyone who plans to maintain and repair small petrol engines. For someone who has few tools, if any, the initial investment might seem high, but when compared to the spiralling costs of routine maintenance and repairs, it's a wise one; besides, most of the tools can also be used for other types of work. Keep in mind that this chapter simply lists the tools needed for doing the work – Chapter 2 explains in greater detail what to look for when shopping for tools and how to use them correctly.

To help the reader decide which tools are needed to perform the tasks detailed in this manual, two tool lists have been compiled: *Routine maintenance* and *minor repair and Repair and overhaul.* A separate section related to special factory tools is also included, but only the most serious do-it-yourselfers will be interested in reading about, purchasing and using them. Illustrations of most tools on each list are also included.

Although it's not absolutely necessary, an air compressor can make many jobs easier and produce better results, especially when air-powered tools are available to use with it

The newcomer to mechanic work should start off with the Routine maintenance and minor repair tool kit, which is adequate for simple jobs. Then, as confidence and experience increase, you can tackle more difficult tasks, buying additional tools as they're needed. Eventually the basic kit will be built into the Repair and overhaul tool set. Over a period of time, the experienced do-it-yourselfer will assemble a set of tools complete enough for most repair and overhaul procedures and may begin adding special factory tools when it's felt the expense is justified by the frequency of use or the savings realized by not taking the equipment in to a shop for repair.

Routine maintenance and minor repair tools

The tools on this list should be considered the minimum required for doing routine maintenance, servicing and minor repair work *(see illustrations)*. Incidentally, if you have a

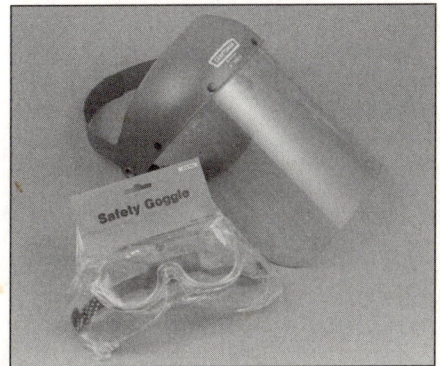

One of the most important items you'll need is a face shield or safety goggles – fortunately, it'll also be one of the least expensive

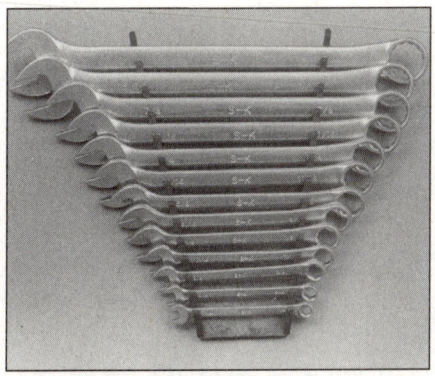

Combination spanners – buy a set with sizes from 1/4 to 7/8-inch or 6 to 21 mm

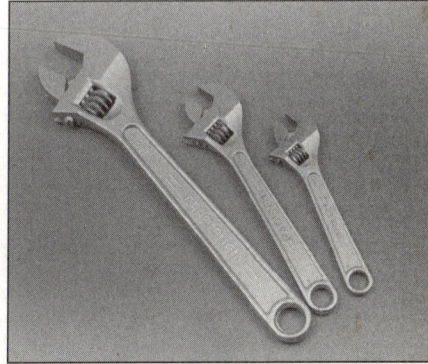

Adjustable spanners are very handy – just be sure to use them correctly or you can damage fasteners by rounding off the hex head

1•5

Chapter 1

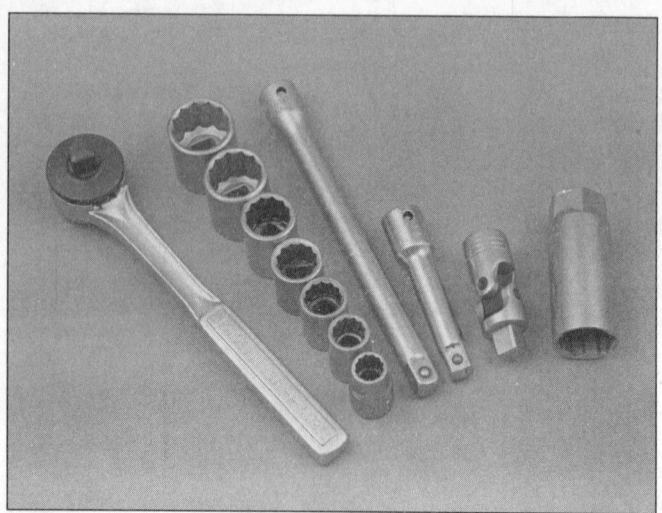

A 3/8-inch drive socket set with interchangeable accessories will probably be used more often than any other tool(s) (left-to-right; ratchet, sockets, extensions, U-joint spark plug socket) – don't buy a cheap socket set

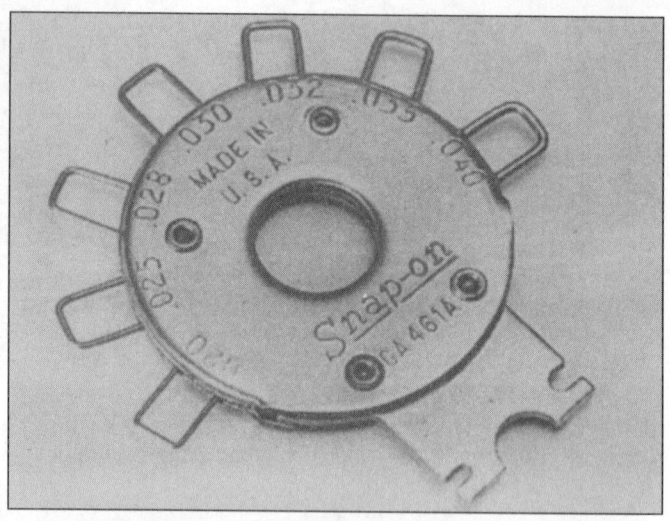

A spark plug adjusting tool will have several wire gauges for measuring the electrode gap and a device used for bending the side electrode to change the gap – make sure the one you buy has the correct size wire to check the spark plug gap on your engine

Feeler gauge sets have several blades of different thicknesses – if you need it to adjust contact breaker points, make sure the blades are as narrow as possible and check them to verify the required thickness is included

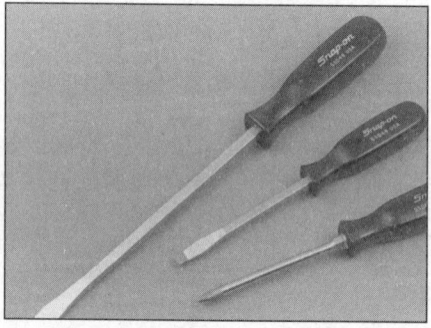

The routine maintenance tool kit should have 8 x 150 mm and 10 x 250 mm standard screwdrivers, as well as a no. 2 x 150 mm Phillips screwdriver

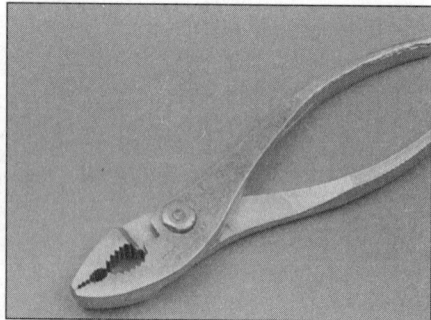

Common slip-joint pliers will be adequate for almost any job you end up doing

A shallow pan (for draining oil, cleaning parts with solvent), a wire brush and a medium size funnel should be part of the routine maintenance tool kit

To remove the starter clutch used on some Briggs & Stratton engines, a special tool (which is turned with a spanner) will be needed

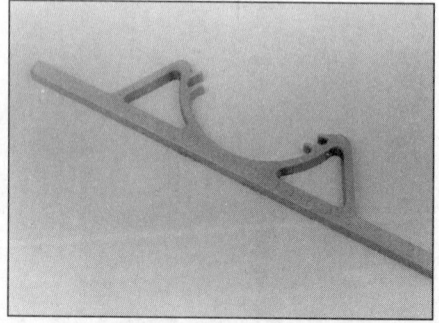

Briggs & Stratton also sells a special flywheel holder for use when loosening the nut or starter clutch

Setting up

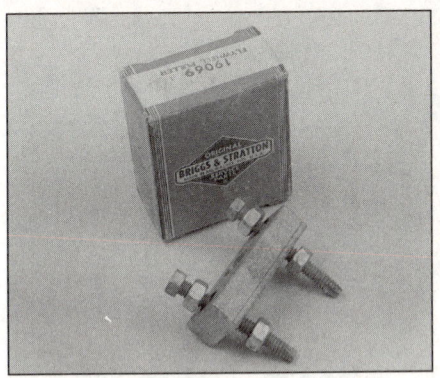

The flywheel on a Briggs & Stratton engine can be removed with a puller (shown here) . . .

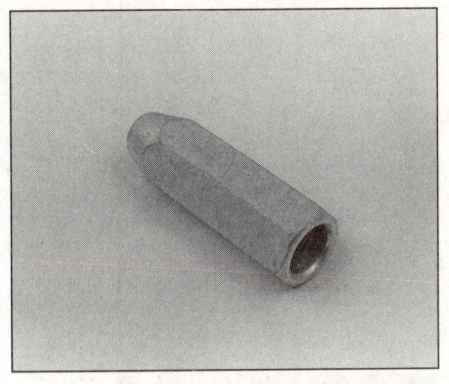

. . . or, although it's not recommended by the factory, a knock-off tool, which fits on the end of the crankshaft (Tecumseh flywheels can also be removed with one of these tools)

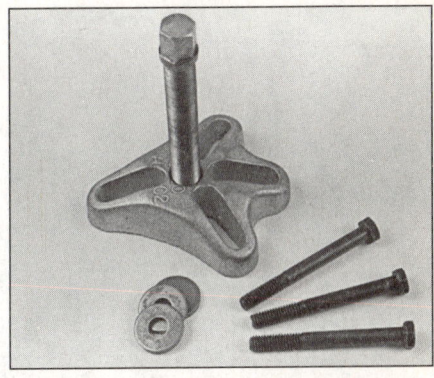

Many Tecumseh and Honda engines require a three jaw puller like the one shown here for flywheel removal

choice, it's a good idea to buy combination spanners (ring and open-end combined in one spanner); while more expensive than open-end ones, they offer the advantages of both types.

Also included is a complete set of sockets which, though expensive, are invaluable because of their versatility (many types of interchangeable accessories are available). We recommend 3/8-inch drive over 1/2-inch drive for general small engine maintenance and repair, although a 1/4-inch drive set would also be useful (especially for ignition and carburettor work). Buy 6-point sockets, if possible, and be careful not to purchase sockets with extra thick walls – they can be difficult to use when access to fasteners is restricted.

Safety goggles/face shield
Combination spanner set (1/4 to 7/8-inch or 6 to 19 mm)
Adjustable spanner – 250 mm
Socket set (6-point)
Reversible ratchet
Extension – 150 mm
Universal joint
Spark plug socket (with rubber insert)
Spark plug gap adjusting tool
Feeler gauge set
Standard screwdriver (8 mm x 150 mm)
Standard screwdriver (10 mm x 250 mm)
Phillips screwdriver (no. 2 x 150 mm)
Combination (slip-joint) pliers – 150 mm
Oil can
Fine emery cloth
Wire brush
Funnel (medium size)
Drain pan
Starter clutch spanner *
Flywheel holder*
Flywheel puller or knock-off tool *

* Although these tools are normally available exclusively through distributors/dealers (so technically they're 'special factory tools'), they are included in this list because certain tune-up and minor repair procedures can't be done without them (specifically contact breaker points and flywheel key replacement on most older Briggs & Stratton and Tecumseh engines). The factory tools may also be available at hardware and lawn and garden centres and occasionally you'll come across imported copies of the factory tools – examine them carefully before buying them.

Repair and overhaul tools

These tools are essential if you intend to perform major repairs or overhauls and are intended to supplement those in the *Routine maintenance and minor repair* tool kit *(see illustrations)*.

The tools in this list include many which aren't used regularly, are expensive to buy, or which need to be used in accordance with their manufacturer's instructions. Unless these tools will be used frequently, it's not very economical to purchase many of them. A consideration would be to split the cost and use between yourself and a friend or neighbour.

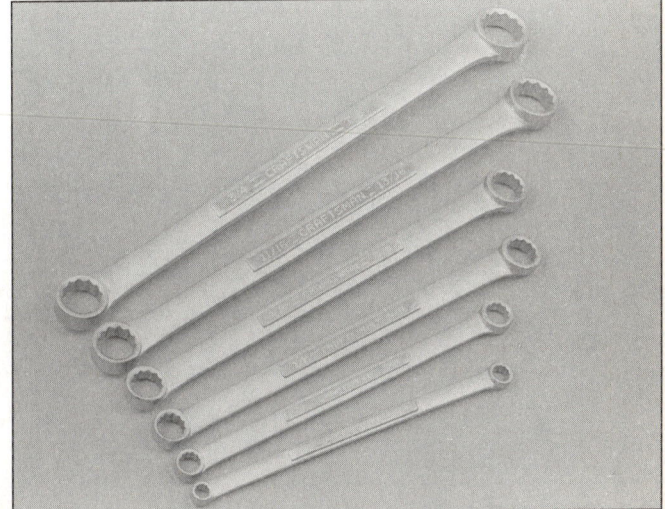

A set of ring spanners will complement the combination spanners in the routine maintenance tool kit

1•7

Chapter 1

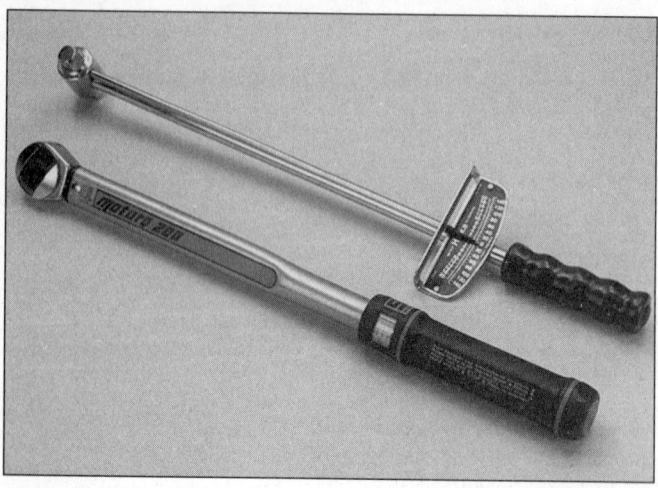

A torque wrench will be needed for tightening head bolts and flywheel nuts (two types are available click type – left; beam type – right)

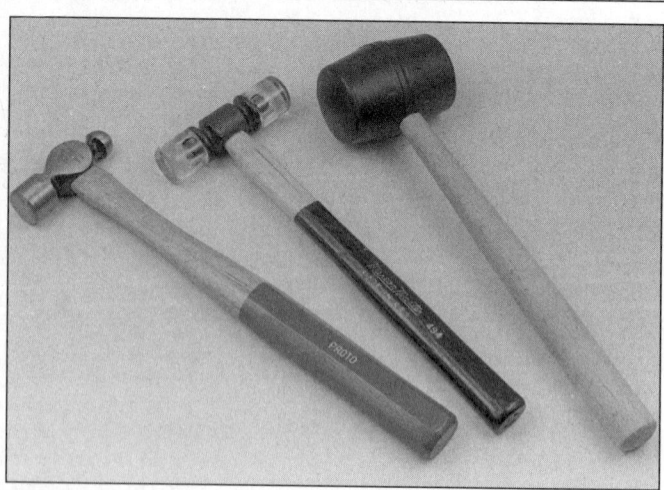

A ball-pein hammer, soft-face hammer and rubber mallet (left-to-right) will be needed for various tasks (any steel hammer can be used in place of the ball-pein hammer)

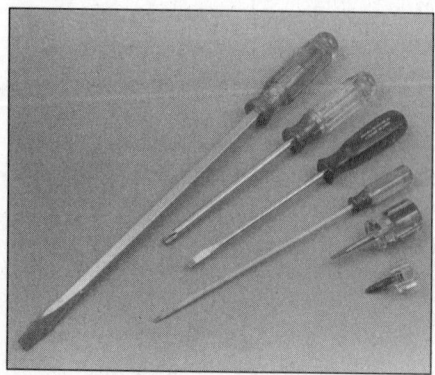

Screwdrivers come in many different sizes and lengths

A hand impact screwdriver (used with a hammer) and bits can be very helpful for removing stubborn, stuck screws (or screws with deformed heads)

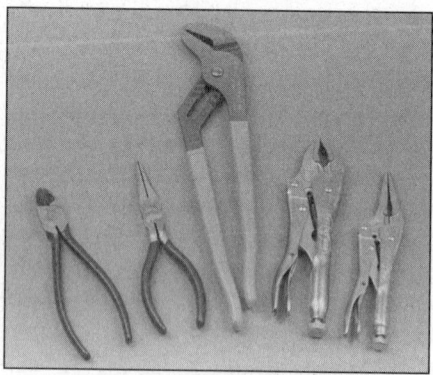

As you can afford them, water-pump, needle-nose, self-locking and wire cutting pliers should be added to your tool collection

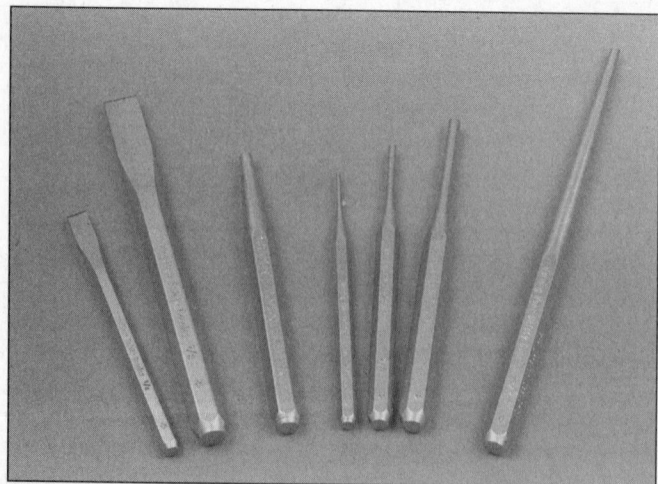

Cold chisels, centre punches, pin punches and line-up punches (left-to-right) will be needed sooner or later for many jobs

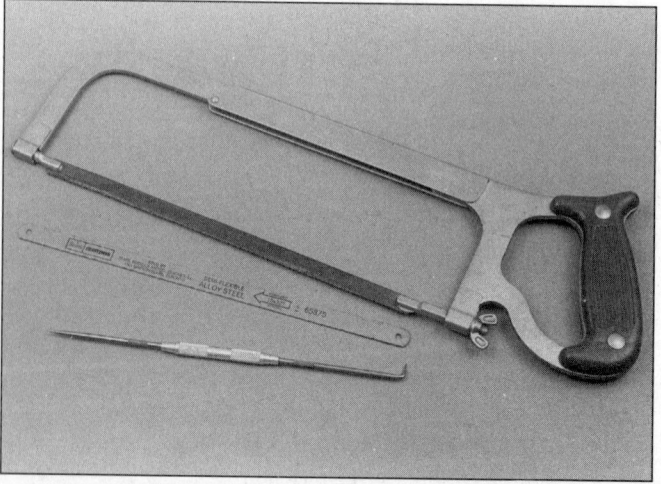

A scribe is used for making lines on metal parts and a hacksaw and blades will be needed for dealing with fasteners that won't unscrew

Setting up

A gasket scraper is used for removing old gaskets from engine parts after disassembly – scouring pads can be used to rough up the gasket surfaces prior to reassembly

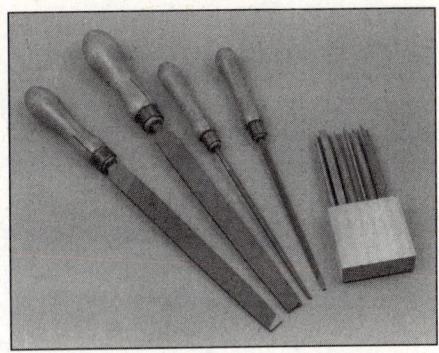

Files must be used with handles and should be stored so they don't contact each other

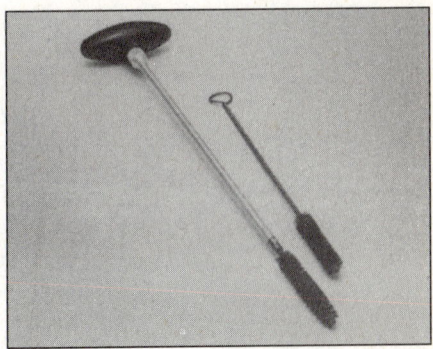

A selection of nylon/metal brushes is needed for cleaning passages in engine and carburettor parts

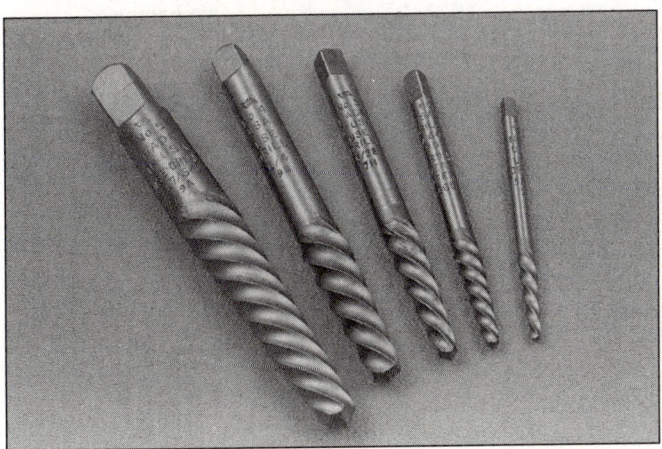

Special tools called screw extractors are used to remove broken-off screws and bolts from engine parts

A spark tester (for checking the ignition system) can be purchased at a motor factor's (left) or fabricated from a block of wood, a large crocodile clip, some nails, screws and wire and the cap end of an old spark plug (right)

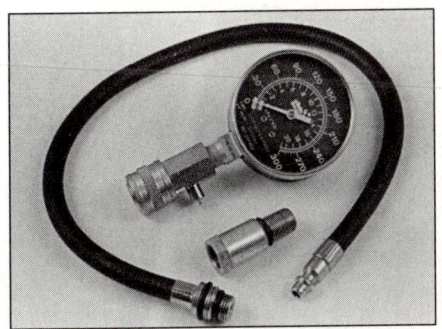

Although not required by most small engine manufacturers, a compression gauge can be used to check the condition of the piston rings and valves (two types are commonly available the screw-in type – shown here – and the type that's held in place by hand pressure)

A ridge reamer is needed to remove the carbon/wear ridge at the top of the cylinder so the piston will slip out

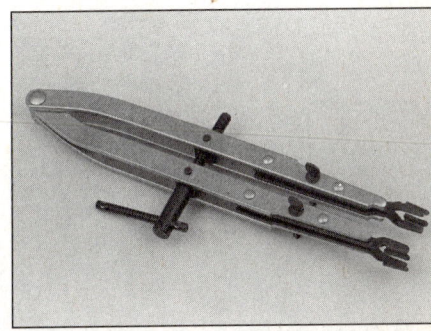

A valve spring compressor like this is required for side valve Briggs & Stratton engines

Chapter 1

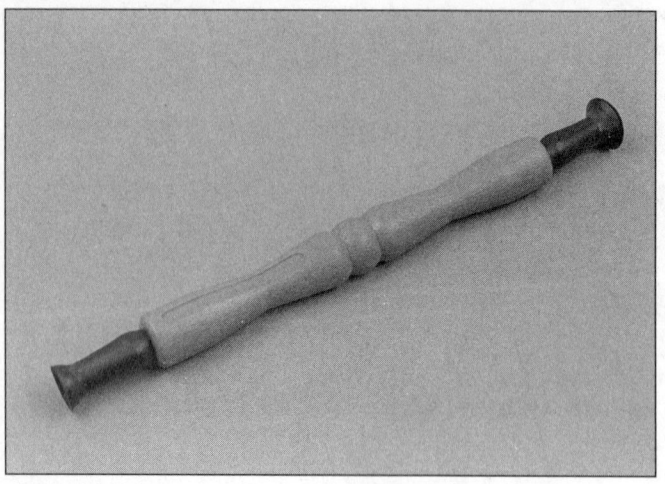

A valve lapping tool will be needed for any four-stroke engine overhaul

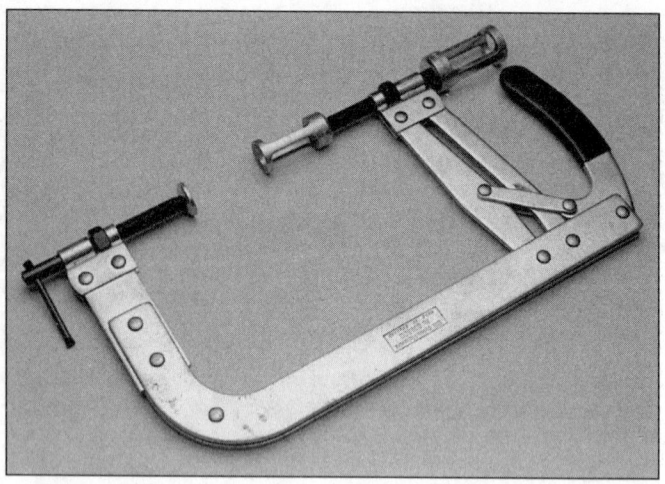

Some overhead valve (OHV) four-stroke engines require a tool like this to compress the springs so the valves can be removed

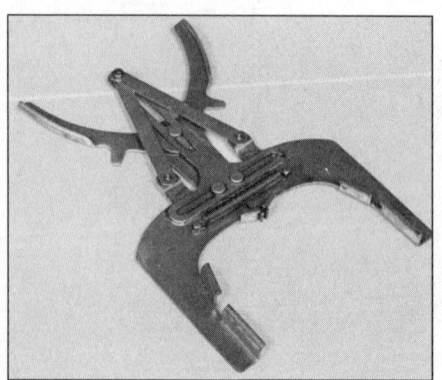

A special inexpensive tool is available for removing/installing piston rings

Piston ring compressors come in many sizes – be sure to buy one that will work on your engine

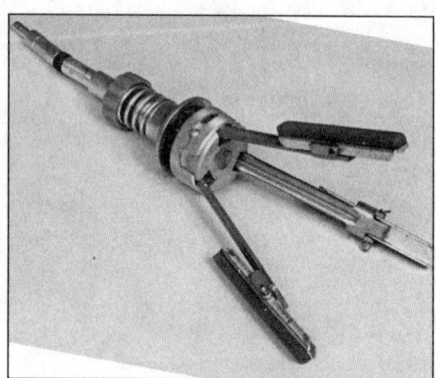

A cylinder surfacing hone can be used to clean up the bore so new rings will seat, but it won't resize the cylinder

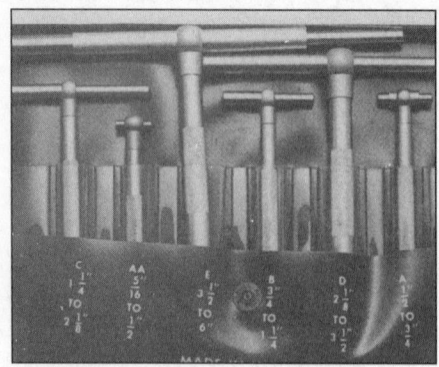

Telescoping gauges are used with micrometers or calipers to determine the inside diameter of holes (like the cylinder bore) to see how much wear has occurred

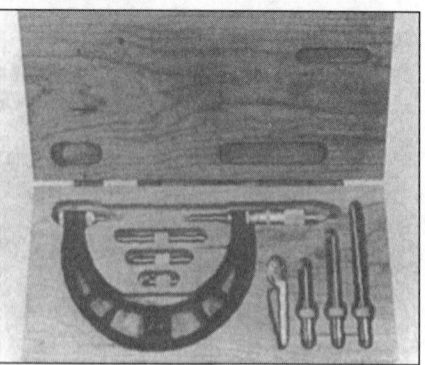

Micrometers are needed for precision measurements to check for wear – they're available in two styles the mandrel type, shown here, which has one frame and interchangeable mandrels which allow for measurements from 0 to 100 mm, and . . .

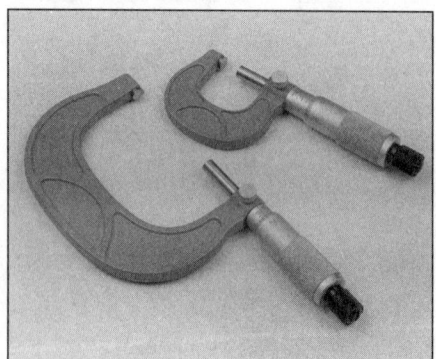

. . . individual fixed-mandrel micrometers that are capable of making measurements in 25 mm increments (0 to 25, 25 to 50, 50 to 75 mm, etc.)

Setting up

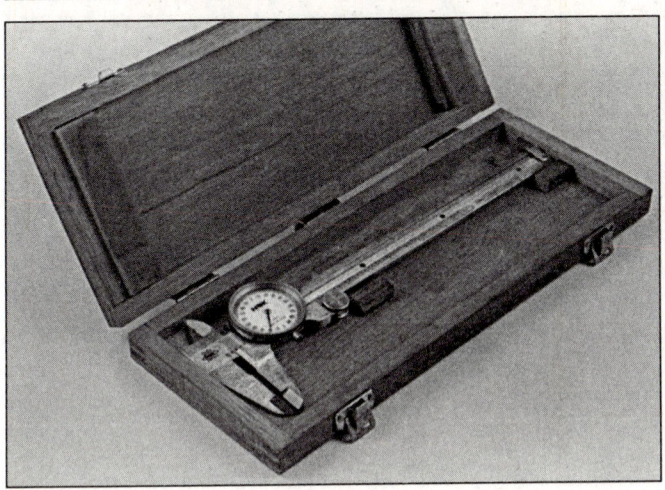

Vernier or dial calipers (shown here) can be used in place of micrometers for most checks and can also be used for depth measurements

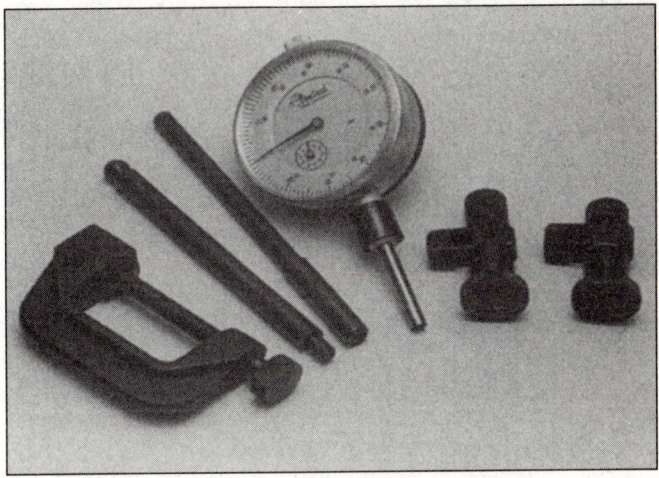

A dial indicator can be used for end play checks on crankshafts and camshafts

Ring spanners
Torque spanner (same size drive as sockets)
Ball pein hammer – 300 g (any steel hammer will do)
Soft-face hammer (plastic/rubber)
Standard screwdriver (6 mm x 150 mm)
Standard screwdriver (stubby – 8 mm)
Phillips screwdriver (no. 3 x 200 mm)
Phillips screwdriver (stubby – no. 2)
Hand impact screwdriver and bits
Pliers – self-locking
Pliers – needle-nose
Wire cutters
Cold chisels – 6 mm and 12 mm
Centre punch
Pin punches (1.5, 3.0 and 4.5 mm)
Line up tools (tapered punches)
Scribe
Hacksaw and assortment of blades
Gasket scraper
Steel rule/straight edge – 300 mm
A selection of files
A selection of brushes for cleaning small passages
Screw extractor set
Spark tester
Compression gauge
Ridge reamer
Valve spring compressor
Valve lapping tool
Piston ring removal and installation tool
Piston ring compressor
Cylinder hone
Telescoping gauges
Micrometer(s) and/or dial/Vernier callipers
Dial indicator
Tap and die set
Torx socket(s)**
Tachometer, or strobe timing light with rpm scale

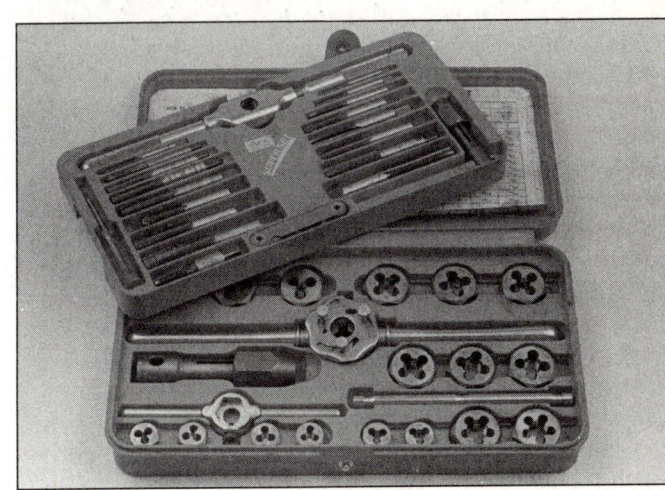

A tap-and-die set is very handy for cleaning and restoring threads

** Some Tecumseh two-stroke engines require a Torx socket (size E6) to remove the connecting rod cap bolts (see illustration). If you're overhauling one of these engines, purchase a socket before beginning the disassembly procedure.

Some Tecumseh two-stroke engines require a no. 6 Torx socket for removal of the connecting rod bolts during an engine overhaul

1•11

Chapter 1

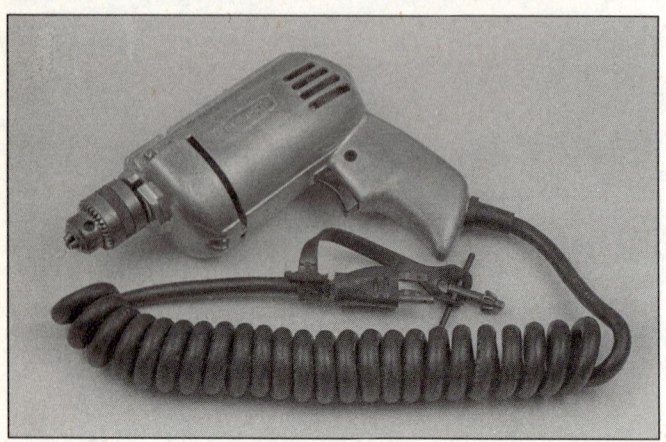 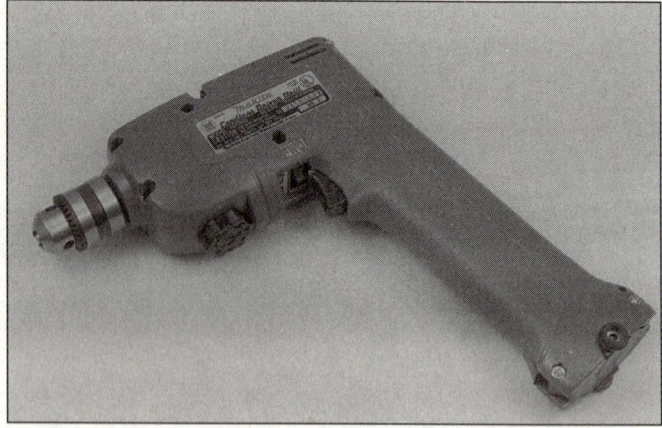

An electric drill (both 220-volt AC and cordless types are shown here) . . .

One of the most indispensable tools around is the common electric drill *(see illustration)*. One with a 10 mm capacity chuck should be sufficient for most repair work – it'll be large enough to power a cylinder surfacing home. Collect several different wire brushes to use in the drill and make sure you have a complete set of sharp bits (for drilling metal, not wood) *(see illustration)*. Cordless drills, which are extremely versatile because they don't have to be plugged in, are now widely available and relatively inexpensive. You may want to consider one, since it'll obviously be handy for non-mechanical jobs around the house and workshop.

Another very useful piece of equipment is a bench-mounted grinder *(see illustration)*. If a wire wheel is mounted on one end and a grinding wheel on the other, it's very handy for cleaning up fasteners, sharpening tools and removing rust from parts. Make sure the grinder is fastened securely to the bench or stand, always wear eye protection when using it and never clean up aluminium parts on the grinding wheel.

Buying tools

For the do-it-yourselfer just starting to get involved in small engine maintenance and repair, there are a number of options available when purchasing tools. If maintenance and minor repair is the extent of the work to be done, the purchase of individual tools is satisfactory. If, on the other hand, extensive work is planned, it would be a good idea to purchase a modest tool set. A set can usually be bought at a substantial savings over the individual tool prices (and they often come with a tool box). As additional tools are needed, add – on sets, individual tools and a larger box can be purchased to expand the tool selection. Building a tool set gradually allows the cost to be spread over a longer period

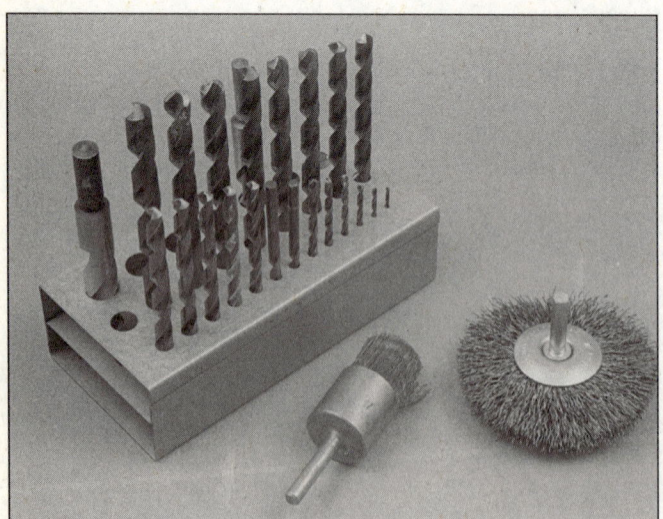

. . .a set of good-quality drill bits and wire brushes of various sizes will find many uses

Another almost indispensable piece of equipment is a bench grinder (with a wire wheel mounted on one arbor) – make sure it's securely bolted down and never use it with the tool rests or eye shields removed!

of time and gives the mechanic the freedom to choose only tools that will actually be used.

Tool stores and small engine distributors or dealers will often be the only source of some of the overhaul and special factory tools needed, but regardless of where tools are bought, try to avoid cheap ones (especially when buying screwdrivers, spanners and sockets) because they won't last very long. The expense involved in replacing cheap tools will eventually be greater than the initial cost of quality tools. Read Chapter 2 for an in-depth, detailed look at choosing and using tools.

Storage and care of tools

Good tools are expensive, so it makes sense to treat them with respect. Keep them clean and in usable condition and store them properly. Always wipe off dirt, grease and metal chips before putting them away. Never leave tools lying around in the work area.

Some tools, such as screwdrivers, pliers, spanners and sockets, can be hung on a panel mounted on the garage or workshop wall, while others should be kept in a tool box or tray. Measuring instruments, gauges, cutting tools, etc. must be carefully stored where they can't be damaged by weather or impact from other tools.

When tools are used with care and stored properly, they'll last a very long time. However, even with the best of care, tools will wear out if used frequently. When a tool is damaged or worn out, replace it; subsequent jobs will be safer and more enjoyable if you do.

Special factory tools

Each small engine manufacturer provides certain special tools to distributors and dealers for use when overhauling or doing major repairs on their engines. The distributors and dealers often stock some of the tools for sale to do-it-yourselfers and independent repair shops. A good example would be tools like the starter clutch spanner, flywheel holder and flywheel puller(s) supplied by Briggs & Stratton, which are needed for relatively simple procedures such as contact breaker points and flywheel key replacement (they're required to get the flywheel off for access to the ignition parts). If the special tools aren't used, the repair either can't be done properly or the engine could be damaged by using substitute tools. Fortunately, the tools mentioned are not very expensive or hard to find.

Other special tools, like bushing drivers, bushing reamers, valve seat and guide service tools, cylinder sizing hones, main bearing repair sets, etc. are prohibitively expensive and not usually stocked for sale by dealers. If repairs requiring such tools are encountered, take the engine or components to a dealer with the necessary tools and pay to have the work done, then reassemble the engine yourself.

Chapter 1

Workshop practice

Safety first!
How to buy and use tools
Precision measurements

Basic maintenance and repair techniques
How to remove broken bolts and repair stripped threads
Small engine lubricants and chemicals

Safety first!

Like it or not, a workshop can be a dangerous place. Electricity, especially if it's misused or taken for granted, is potentially harmful in an environment that's often damp. Hand and power tools, if misused, present opportunities for accidents, and stored petrol, solvents, lubricants and chemicals are a very real fire risk.

There's no way to make a workshop totally safe (as long as people and potentially hazardous equipment/materials are involved) – the topic of safety really must focus on minimizing the risk of accidents by following safe practices (primary safety) and using the correct clothing and equipment to minimize injury in the event of an accident (secondary safety). The subject of safety is large and could easily fill a chapter on it's own. To keep the subject within reasonable bounds -and because few people will bother to read an entire chapter on safety – it's been confined here, initially, to a set of rules. (Additional notes appear in the text and captions, where necessary, throughout the manual.)

The rest of this section covers some of the more important and relevant safety topics, but isn't intended to be definitive. Read through it, even if you've done mechanic work for years without scraping a knuckle. It should be emphasized that the most important piece of safety equipment of all is the human brain – try to get into the habit of thinking about what you're doing, and what could go wrong. A little common sense and foresight can prevent the majority of workshop accidents.

Safety rules

Professional mechanics are trained in safe working procedures. Regardless of how eager you are to start working on an engine or piece of equipment, take the time to read through the following list. As mentioned above, lack of attention, no matter how brief, can result in an accident. So can failure to follow certain simple safety precautions. The possibility of an accident will always exist, and the following points aren't intended to be a comprehensive list of all dangers; they are intended, however, to make you aware of the risks involved in mechanic work and encourage a safety conscious approach to everything you do.

DON'T start the engine before checking to see if the drive is in Neutral (where applicable).

DON'T turn the blade attached to the engine unless the spark plug wire has been detached from the plug *(see illustration)* and positioned out of the way!

Before doing any checks or maintenance on a small engine that require you to turn the blade attached to the crankshaft, detach the wire from the spark plug and position it out of the way!

2•1

Chapter 2

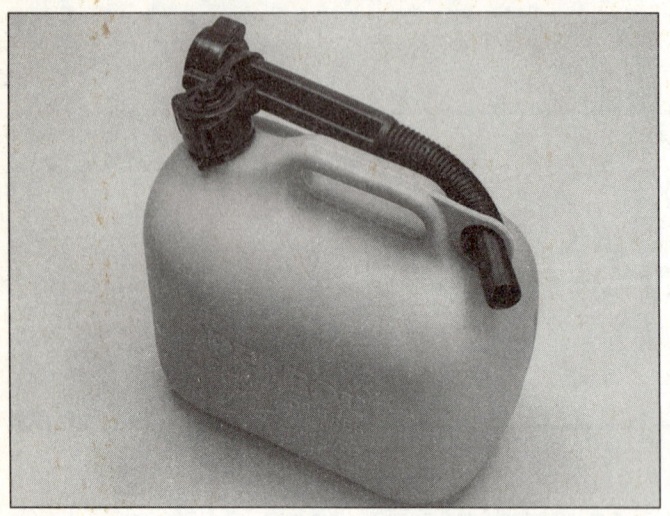

Store and transport petrol only in an purpose-made metal or plastic jerry can, which meets the relevant British Safety Standard – never use a glass bottle.

Don't try to clear a flooded engine by removing the spark plug and cranking the engine – the petrol vapour coming out of the plug hole could be ignited

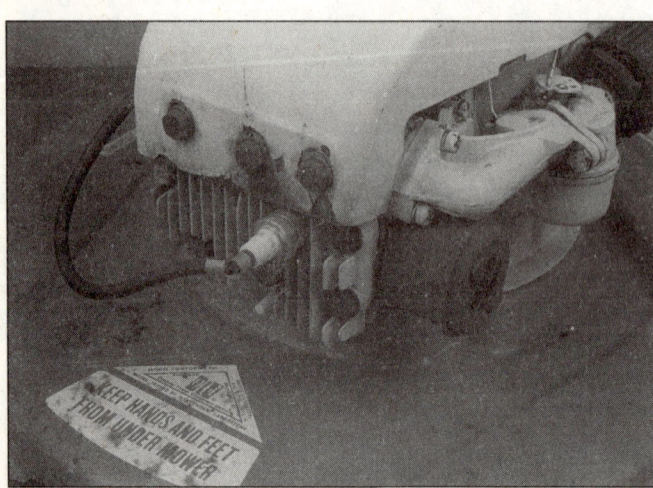

The cooling fins and silencer can get extremely hot!

Spanners that don't fit snugly on the fastener can result in skinned knuckles, cuts and bruises

DON'T use petrol for cleaning parts – ever!

DON'T store petrol in glass containers – use an approved metal or high-impact plastic petrol container only *(see illustration)*!

DON'T store, pour or spill petrol near an open flame or devices such as a stove, furnace, or water heater which utilises a pilot light or devices that can create a spark.

DON'T smoke when filling the fuel tank!

DON'T fill the fuel tank while the engine is running. Allow the engine to cool for at least two minutes before refueling.

DON'T refuel equipment indoors where there's poor ventilation. Outdoor refueling is preferred.

DON'T operate the engine if petrol has been spilled. Move the engine away from the spill, and don't start the engine until the petrol has evaporated.

DON'T crank an engine with the spark plug removed *(see illustration)*. If the engine is flooded, open the throttle all the way and operate the starter until the engine starts.

DON'T attempt to drain the engine oil until you're sure it's cooled so it won't burn you.

DON'T touch any part of the engine or silencer *(see illustration)* until it's cooled down enough to avoid burns.

DON'T siphon toxic liquids, such as petrol, by mouth, or allow them to remain on your skin.

DON'T allow spilled oil or grease to remain on the floor – wipe it up before someone slips on it.

DON'T use loose fitting spanners *(see illustration)* or other tools that may slip and cause injury.

DON'T push on spanners when loosening or tightening nuts or bolts. Always try to pull the spanner towards you *(see*

Workshop practice

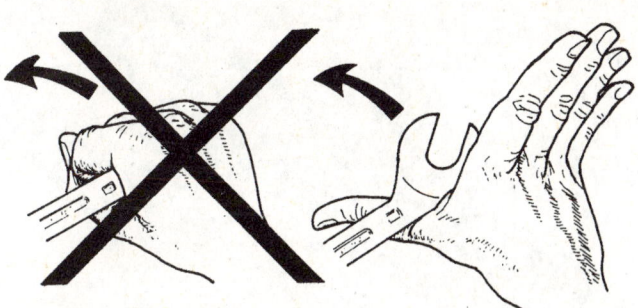

Always pull on a spanner when loosening a fastener – if you can't pull on it, push with your hand open as shown here

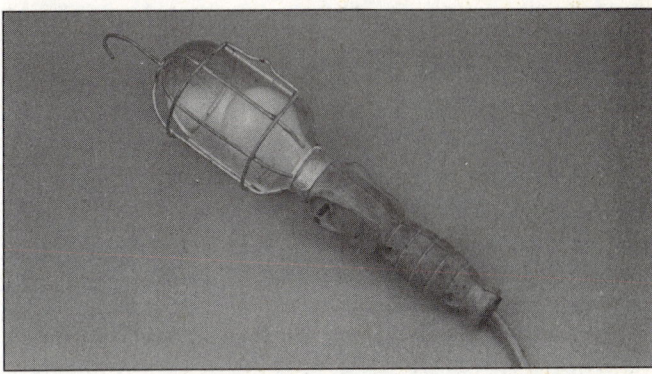

Never use an unshielded light bulb in the workshop – special inspection lights designed to prevent broken bulbs and the accompanying safety hazards are commonly available

illustration). If the situation calls for pushing the spanner away, push with an open hand to avoid scraped knuckles if the spanner slips.

DON'T use unshielded light bulbs in the workshop, especially if petrol is present. Use an approved inspection light only *(see illustration)*.

DON'T grind aluminum parts on a grinding wheel – the aluminum can load up the wheel and cause it to come apart!

DON'T attempt to lift a heavy piece of equipment which may be beyond your capability -get someone to help you.

DON'T rush or take unsafe short cuts to finish a job.

DON'T allow children on or around equipment when you're working on it.

DON'T run an engine in an enclosed area. The exhaust contains carbon monoxide, an odourless, colourless, deadly poisonous gas.

DON'T operate an engine with a build-up of grass, leaves, dirt or other combustible material in the silencer area.

DON'T use equipment on any forested, brush-covered, or grass-covered unimproved land unless the engine has a spark arrester installed on the silencer.

DON'T run an engine with the air cleaner or cover (directly over the carburetor air intake) removed *(see illustration)*.

DON'T store lubricants and chemicals near a heater or other sources of heat or sparks.

DO wear eye protection when using power tools such as a drill, bench grinder, etc. *(see illustration)*.

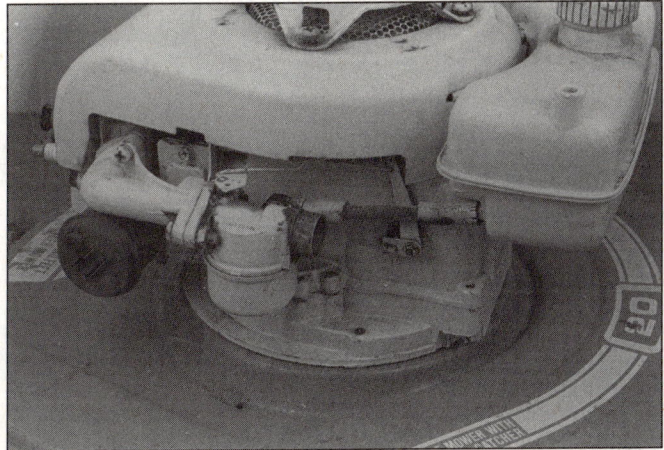

Do not run the engine with the air cleaner removed

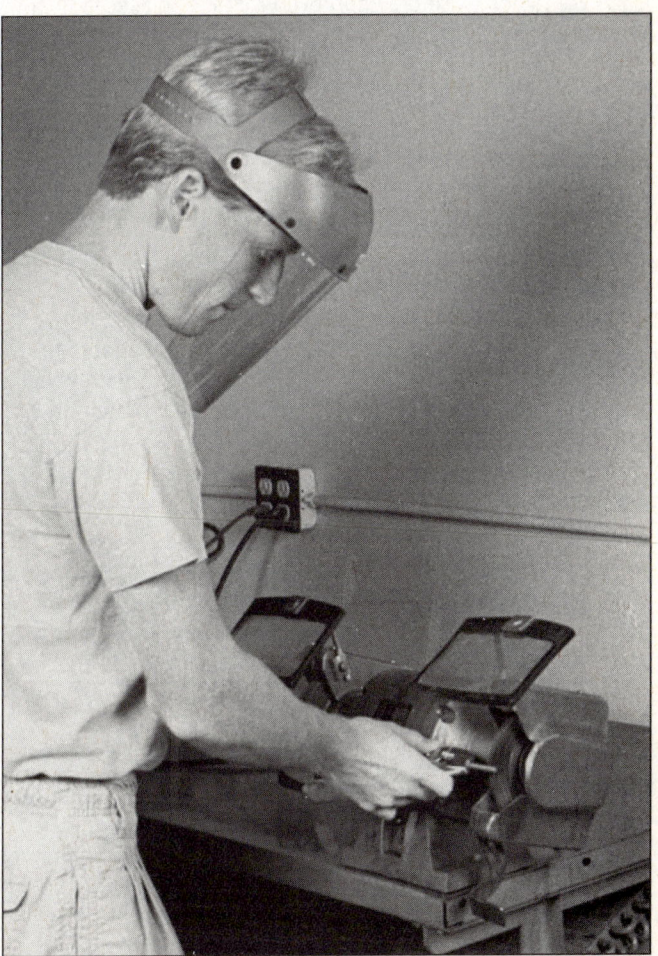

Always wear eye protection when using power tools

2•3

Chapter 2

DO keep loose clothing and long hair well out of the way of moving parts.

DO wear steel-toe safety shoes when working on equipment on a bench. If heavy parts are dropped or fall, they won't crush your toes.

DO get someone to check on you periodically when working alone.

DO carry out work in a logical sequence and make sure everything is correctly assembled and tightened.

DO keep lubricants, chemicals and other fluids tightly capped and out of the reach of children and pets.

Petrol

Remember – petrol is extremely flammable! Never smoke or have any kind of naked flames or unshielded light bulbs around when working on an engine. The risk doesn't end there however -a spark caused by an electrical short-circuit, by two metal surfaces striking each other, or even static electricity built up in your body under certain conditions, can ignite petrol vapour, which in a confined space is highly explosive. As mentioned above, DO NOT, under any circumstances, use petrol for cleaning components – use an approved degreaser only. Also, DO NOT store petrol in a glass container – use only approved metal or plastic containers.

Fire

Always have a fire extinguisher suitable for use on fuel and electrical fires handy in the garage or workshop. Never try to extinguish a petrol or electrical fire with water!

Fumes

Certain fumes are highly toxic and can quickly cause unconsciousness and even death if inhaled to any extent. Petrol vapour falls into this category, as well as vapours from some cleaning solvents. Draining and pouring of such volatile fluids should be done in a well-ventilated area, preferably outdoors.

When using cleaning fluids and solvents, read the instructions on the container carefully. Never use materials from unmarked containers.

Don't run the engine in an enclosed space such as a garage; exhaust fumes contain carbon monoxide, which is extremely poisonous. If you need to run the engine, always move it outside.

Household current

When using an electric power tool, inspection light, etc., which operates on household current, always make sure the lead is correctly connected to the plug and properly earthed *(see illustration)*. Don't use such items in damp conditions and, again, don't create a spark or apply excessive heat in the vicinity of fuel or fuel vapour. Never string extension leads together to supply electricity to an out of the way place.

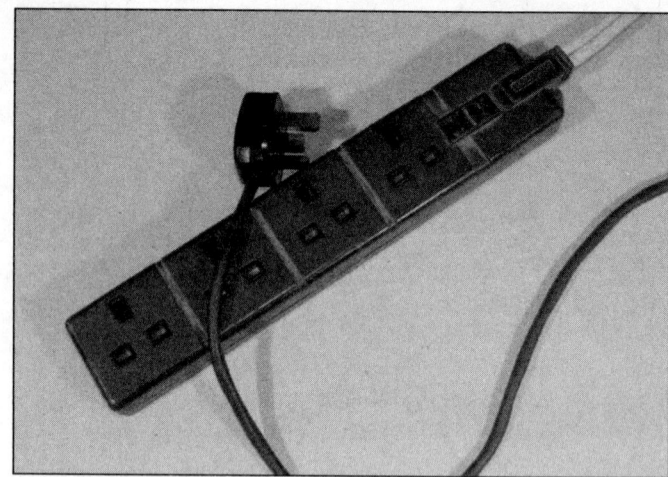

Check the plugs on power tools and extension leads to make sure they're securely attached, with no burned or frayed wires

Spark plug voltage

A severe electric shock can result from touching certain parts of the ignition system (such as the spark plug wire) when the engine is running or being cranked, particularly if components are damp or the insulation is defective. If an electronic ignition system is involved, the secondary system voltage is much higher and could prove fatal.

Keep it clean

Get in the habit of taking a regular look around the workshop, checking for potential dangers. The work area should always be kept clean and neat – all debris should be swept up and disposed of as soon as possible. Don't leave tools lying around on the floor.

Be very careful with oily rags. If they're left in a pile, it's not uncommon for spontaneous combustion to occur, so dispose of them properly in a covered metal container. Check all equipment and tools for security and safety hazards (like frayed leads). Make necessary repairs as soon as a problem is noticed – don't wait for a shelf unit to collapse before fixing it.

Accidents and emergencies

These range from minor cuts and skinned knuckles to serious injuries requiring immediate medical attention. The former are inevitable, while the latter are, hopefully, avoidable or at least uncommon. Think about what you would do in the event of an accident. Get some first aid training and have an adequate first aid kit somewhere within easy reach.

Think about what you would do if you were badly hurt and incapacitated. Is there someone nearby who could be summoned quickly? If possible, never work alone just in case something goes wrong.

Workshop practice

If you had to cope with someone else's accident, would you know what to do? Dealing with accidents is a large and complex subject, and it's easy to make matters worse if you have no idea how to respond. Rather than attempt to deal with this subject in a superficial manner, buy a good First Aid book and read it carefully.

Environmental safety

Be absolutely certain that all materials, especially volatile liquids, are properly stored, handled and disposed of. Store all volatile liquids in sealed containers – do not allow them to evaporate and produce harmful fumes. When disposing of used or leftover engine oil or solvents, give due consideration to any detrimental environmental effects. Do not, for instance, pour engine oil or solvents down drains into the general sewage system, or onto the ground to soak away. If a commercial oil disposal service is not available, consult your local authority to find the location of your nearest waste disposal point.

Note: It is antisocial and illegal to dump oil down the drain. To find the location of your local oil recycling bank, call this number free.

How to buy and use tools

Chances are you already own some of the tools in the lists included in Chapter 1. Many of them are the same ones needed for home maintenance and simple car repairs. This chapter will cover the types of tools to buy, assuming you'll need more, and how to use them properly so the repairs you tackle will be enjoyable and successful.

It's easy to fall into the trap of thinking you should only purchase individual, high-quality tools, gradually expanding your tool set as needs change and finances allow. This is good advice on the subject, and is normally suggested in how-to books and magazine articles, but it's difficult to follow through on. For starters, a glance through any mechanic's tool collection will reveal a very mixed assortment of tools. You'll usually find top-quality, lifetime guaranteed items alongside cheap tools purchased on the spur of the moment from many sources.

There seems to be a law governing the contents of tool boxes that dictates that any expensive, well-made and indispensable tool will get lost or 'disappear' very quickly, but during your short ownership of it, it'll never break, slip or damage fasteners. Conversely, a cheap, ill-fitting and poorly made tool will be with you for life, even when you thought you had thrown it away. It'll never quite fit properly and will probably drive you crazy.

Although this is a broad generalisation, it does happen in the real world. There are some very methodical and organized people out there who unfailingly clean and check each tool after use, before hanging it back up on the pegboard hook or placing it in its special drawer in the tool box. While there are few who practise this disciplined treatment of tools, there's no denying it's the correct approach and should be encouraged.

There are also those to whom the idea of using the correct tool is completely foreign and who will cheerfully tackle the most complex overhaul procedures with only a set of cheap open-end spanners of the wrong type, a single screwdriver with a worn tip, a large hammer and an adjustable spanner. This approach is undeniably wrong and should be avoided – but while it often results in damaged fasteners and components, people sometimes get away with it.

It's a good idea to strive for a compromise between these two extremes and, like most mechanics, cultivate a vision of the ideal workshop that's tempered by economic realities. This will inevitably lead to a mixed assortment of tools and seems to end up as the controlling factor in most workshops.

In this chapter we'll also try to give you some kind of idea when top-quality tools are essential and where cheaper ones will be adequate. As a general rule, if tools will be used often, purchase good quality ones – if they'll be used infrequently, lower quality ones will usually suffice.

If you're unsure about how much use a tool will get, the following approach may help. For example, if you need a set of combination spanners but aren't sure which sizes you'll end up using most, buy a cheap or medium-priced set (make sure the jaws fit the fastener sizes marked on them). After some use over a period of time, carefully examine each tool in the set to assess its condition. If all the tools fit well and are undamaged, don't bother buying a better set. If one or two are worn, replace them with high-quality items – this way you'll end up with top-quality tools where they're needed most and the cheaper ones are sufficient for occasional use. On rare occasions you may conclude the whole set is of poor quality. If so, buy a better set, if necessary, and remember never to buy that brand again.

The best place to buy hand tools is a motor factor's, car accessory shop or hardware shop. You may not find cheap tools, but you should have a large selection to choose from and expert advice will be available. Take the tool lists in Chapter 1 with you when shopping for tools and explain what you want to the salesperson. Sources to steer clear of, at least until you have experience judging quality, are mail order suppliers (other than those selling name-brands) and car boot sales. Some of them offer good value for the money, but most carry cheap, imported tools of dubious quality. The resulting tools can be acceptable or, on the other hand, they might be unusable. Unfortunately, it can be hard to judge by looking at them.

Finally, consider buying second hand tools from garage sales or used tool outlets. You may have limited choice in sizes, but you can usually determine from the condition of the tools if they're worth buying. You can end up with a number of unwanted or duplicate tools, but it's a cheap way of putting a basic tool kit together, and you can always sell off any surplus tools later.

Chapter 2

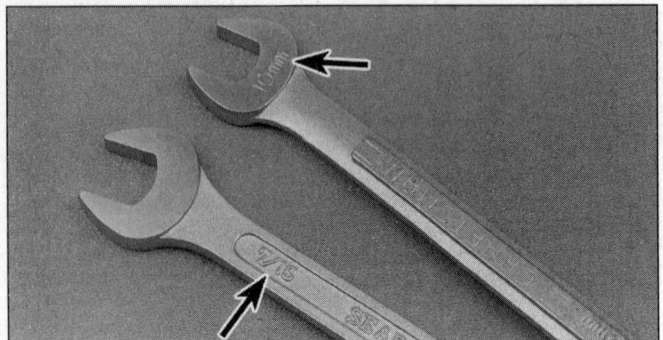

Spanner sizes are clearly stamped on the ends or handle

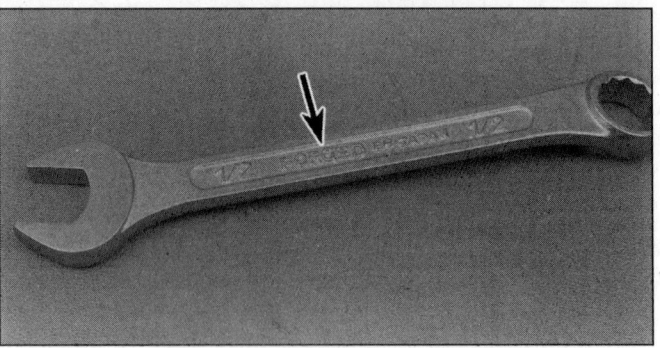

Look for the words 'chrome vanadium' or 'forged' when trying to determine spanner quality

Buying spanners and sockets

Spanners of varying quality are available and cost is usually a good indication of quality – the more they cost, the better they are. In the case of spanners, it's important to buy high-quality tools. Your spanners will be some of the most often used tools, so buy the best you can afford.

Buy a set with the sizes outlined in Chapter 1. The size stamped on the spanner *(see illustration)* indicates the distance across the nut or bolt head (or the distance between the spanner jaws), in inches or millimetres, not the diameter of the threads on the fastener. For example, a 1/4-inch bolt will almost always have a 7/16-inch hex head – the size of the spanner required to loosen or tighten it. In the case of metric tools, the number is in millimetres. At the risk of confusing the issue, it should be mentioned that the relationship between thread diameter and hex size doesn't always hold true; in some applications, an unusually small hex may be used, either for reasons of limited space around the fastener or to discourage over-tightening.

Conversely, in some areas, fasteners with a disproportionately large hex-head may be encountered.

Spanners tend to look similar, so it can be difficult to judge how well they're made just by looking at them. As with most other purchases, there are bargains to be had, just as there are overpriced tools with well-known brand names. On the other hand, you may buy what looks like a good set of spanners only to find they fit badly or are made from poor-quality steel.

With a little experience, it's possible to judge the quality of a tool by looking at it. Often, you may have come across the brand name before and have a good idea of the quality. Close examination of the tool can often reveal some hints as to its quality. Prestige tools are usually polished and chrome-plated over their entire surface, with the working faces ground to size. The polished finish is largely cosmetic, but it does make them easy to keep clean. Ground jaws normally indicate the tool will fit well on fasteners.

A side-by-side comparison of a high-quality spanner with a cheap equivalent is an eye opener. The better tool will be made from a good-quality material, often a forged/chrome-vanadium steel alloy *(see illustration)*. This, together with careful design, allows the tool to be kept as small and compact as possible. If, by comparison, the cheap tool is thicker and heavier, especially around the jaws, it's usually because the extra material is needed to compensate for its lower quality. If the tool fits properly, this is not necessarily bad – it is, after all, cheaper – but in situations where it's necessary to work in a confined area, the cheaper tool may be too bulky to fit.

Open-end spanners

The open-end spanner is the most common type, due mainly to its general versatility. It normally consists of two open jaws connected by a flat handle section. The jaws usually vary by one size, with an occasional overlap of sizes between consecutive spanners in a set. This allows one spanner to be used to hold a bolt head while a similar-size nut is removed.

A typical spanner set might have the following jaw sizes: 6, 8, 10, 11, 13, 14 mm and so on.

Typically, the jaw end is set at an angle to the handle, a feature which makes them very useful in confined spaces; by turning the nut or bolt as far as the obstruction allows, then turning the spanner over so the jaw faces in the other direction, it's possible to move the fastener a fraction of a turn at a time *(see illustration)*. The handle length is generally determined by the size of the jaw and is calculated to allow a nut or bolt to be tightened sufficiently by hand with minimal risk of breakage or thread damage (though this doesn't apply to soft materials like brass or aluminum).

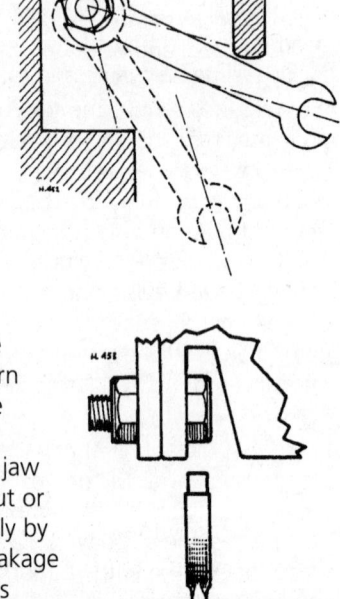

Open-end spanners are the most versatile for general use

2•6

Workshop practice

Common open-end spanners are usually sold in sets and it's rarely worth buying them individually unless it's to replace a lost or broken tool from a set. Single tools invariably cost more, so check the sizes you're most likely to need regularly and buy the best set of spanners you can afford in that range of sizes. If money is limited, remember that you'll use open-end spanners more than any other type – it's a good idea to buy a good set and cut corners elsewhere.

Ring spanners

A ring spanner consists of a ring-shaped end with a 6-point (hex) or 12-point (double hex) opening *(see illustration)*. This allows the tool to fit on the fastener hex at 15 (12-point) or 30-degree (6-point) intervals. Normally, each tool has two ends of different sizes, allowing an overlapping range of sizes in a set, as described for open-end spanners.

Although available as flat tools, the handle is usually offset at each end to allow it to clear obstructions near the fastener, which is normally an advantage. In addition to normal length spanners, it's also possible to buy long handle types to allow more leverage (very useful when trying to loosen rusted or seized nuts). It is, however, easy to shear off fasteners if not careful, and sometimes the extra length impairs access.

As with open-end spanners, ring spanners are available in varying quality, again often indicated by finish and the amount of metal around the ends. While the same criteria should be applied when selecting a set of ring spanners, if your budget is limited, go for better quality open-end spanners and a slightly cheaper set of ring spanners.

Combination spanners

These spanners combine a ring-end and open-end of the same size in one tool and offer many of the advantages of both. Like the others, they're widely available in sets and as such are probably a better choice than ring spanners only. They're generally compact, short-handled tools and are well suited for small engine repairs, where access is often restricted.

Adjustable spanners

These tools come in a wide variety of shapes and sizes with various types of adjustment mechanisms. The principle is the same in each case – a single tool that can handle fasteners of various sizes. Adjustable spanners are not as good as single-size tools and it's easy to damage fasteners with them. However, they can be an invaluable addition to any tool kit – if they're used with discretion. Note: If you attach the spanner to the fastener with the movable jaw pointing in the direction of spanner rotation *(see illustration)*, an adjustable spanner will be less likely to slip and damage the fastener head.

The most common adjustable spanner is the open-end type with a set of parallel jaws that can be set to fit the head of a fastener. Most are controlled by a threaded spindle, though there are various cam and spring-loaded versions available. Don't buy large tools of this type; you'll rarely be able to find enough clearance to use them. The sizes specified in Chapter 1 are best suited to small engine repair work.

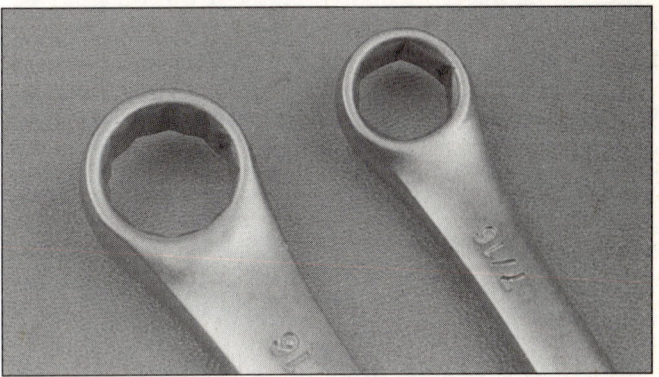

Open end spanners are available in both 6 and 12-point openings – if you have a choice, buy 6-point spanners

Socket sets

Interchangeable sockets consist of a forged steel alloy cylinder with a hex or double hex formed inside one end. The other end is formed into the square drive recess that engages over the corresponding square end of various socket drive tools.

Sockets are available in 1/4, 3/8, 1/2 and 3/4-inch drive sizes. Of these, a 3/8-inch drive set is most useful for small engine repairs, although 1/4-inch drive sockets and accessories may occasionally be needed.

The most economical way to buy sockets is in a set. As always, quality will govern the cost of the tools. Once again, the 'buy the best' approach is usually advised when selecting sockets. While this is a good idea, since the end result is a set of quality tools that should last a lifetime, the cost is so high it's difficult to justify the expense for home use. Go shopping for a socket set and you'll be confronted with a vast selection, so stick with the recommendations in Chapter 1.

As far as accessories go, you'll need a ratchet, at least one extension (buy a 75 or 150 mm length extension), a spark plug socket and maybe a T-handle or swivel-drive handle. Other desirable, though less essential items, are a speed handle, a U-joint, extensions of various other lengths and

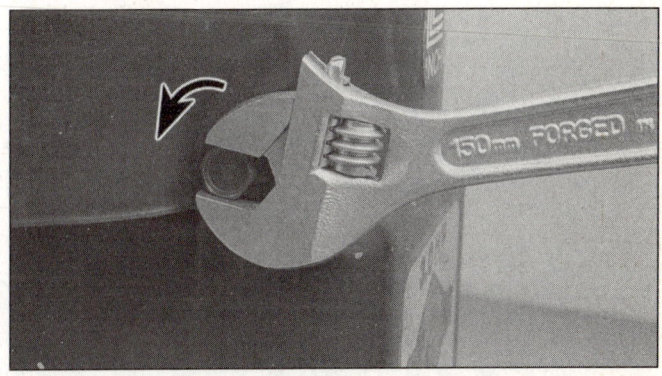

When using an adjustable spanner, the movable jaw should point in the direction the spanner is being turned (arrowed) so the spanner doesn't distort and slip off the fastener head

2•7

Chapter 2

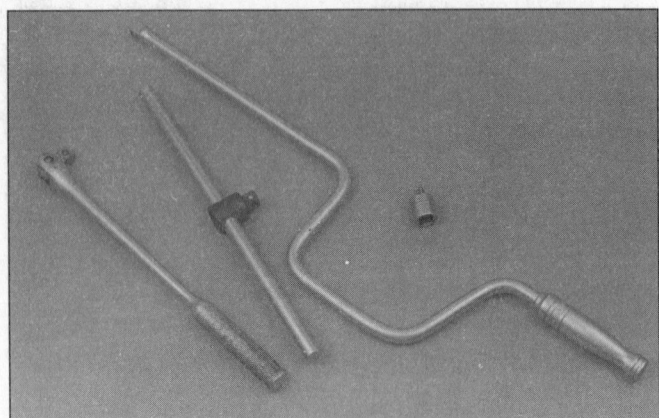

Many accessories are available in each drive size for use with sockets (left to right Swivel-drive handle, sliding T-handle, speed handle and a 3/8 to 1/4-inch drive adapter)

Deep sockets are handy for loosening/tightening recessed bolts and nuts threaded onto long bolts or studs

adaptors from one drive size to another *(see illustration)*. Some of the sets you find may combine drive sizes; they're well worth having if you find the right set at a good price, but avoid being dazzled by the number of pieces.

Above all, be sure to completely ignore any label that reads '86-piece Socket Set'; this refers to the number of pieces, not to the number of sockets (and in some cases even the metal box and plastic insert are counted in the total!).

Apart from well-known and respected brand names, you'll have to take a chance on the quality of the set you buy. If you know someone who has a set that has held up well, try to find the same brand, if possible. Take a few nuts and bolts with you and check the fit in some of the sockets. Check the operation of the ratchet. Good ones operate smoothly and crisply in small steps; cheap ones are coarse and stiff – a good basis for guessing the quality of the rest of the pieces.

One of the best things about a socket set is the built-in facility for expansion. Once you have a basic set, you can purchase extra sockets when necessary and replace worn or damaged tools. There are special deep sockets for reaching recessed fasteners or to allow the socket to fit over a projecting bolt or stud *(see illustration)*. You can also buy screwdriver, Allen and Torx bits to fit various drive tools (they can be very handy in some applications) *(see illustration)*. Most socket sets include a special deep socket for 14 millimetre spark plugs. They have rubber inserts to protect the spark plug porcelain insulator and hold the plug in the socket to avoid burned fingers.

Torque wrenches

Torque wrenches complement the socket set, since they require the use of a socket so a fastener can be tightened accurately to a specified torque figure. To attempt an engine overhaul without a torque wrench is to invite oil leaks, distortion of the cylinder head, damaged or stripped threads or worse.

The cheapest type of torque wrench consists of a long handle designed to bend as pressure increases. A long pointer is fixed to the drive end and reads off a scale near the handle as the fastener is tightened *(see illustration)*. This type of torque wrench is simple and usually accurate enough for most jobs. Another version is the pre-set or 'click' type. The torque figure required is dialled in on a scale before use *(see illustration)*. The tool gives a positive indication, usually a loud

Standard and Phillips screwdriver bits, Allen-head and Torx drivers are available for use with ratchets and other socket drive tools

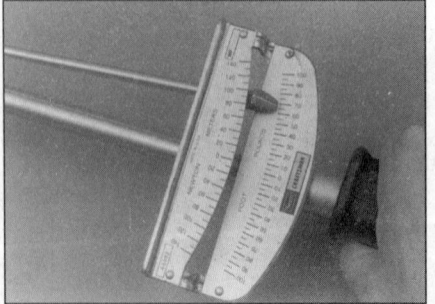

A simple, inexpensive, deflecting beam torque wrench will be adequate for small engine repairs – the torque figure is read off the scale near the handle

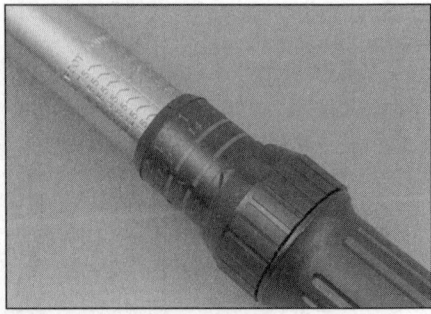

'Click' type torque wrenches can be set to 'give' at a pre-set torque, which makes them very accurate and easy to use

Workshop practice

click and/or a sudden movement of the handle, when the desired torque is reached. Needless to say, the pre-set type is far more expensive than the beam type – you alone can decide which type you need. For occasional use, go for the cheaper beam type.

Torque wrenches are available in a variety of drive sizes and torque ranges for particular applications. For small engine use, the range required is lower than for cars or trucks; 0 to 100 Nm (0 to 75 ft-lbs) should be adequate. However, if you anticipate doing car repairs in the future, you may want to take that into consideration when buying a torque wrench – try to settle on one that'll be usable for both.

Impact drivers

The impact driver belongs with the screwdrivers, but it's mentioned here since it can also be used with sockets (impact drivers normally are 3/8-inch square drive). An impact driver works by converting a hammer blow on the end of its handle into a sharp twisting movement. While this is a great way to jar a seized fastener loose, the loads imposed on the socket are excessive. Use sockets only with discretion and expect to have to replace damaged ones occasionally.

Using spanners and sockets

In the last section we looked at some of the various types of spanners available, with a few suggestions about building up a tool collection without bankrupting yourself. Here we're more concerned with using the tools in actual work. Although you may feel it's self-explanatory, it's worth some thought. After all, when did you last see instructions for use supplied with a set of spanners?

Before you start tearing an engine apart, figure out the best tool for the job; in this instance the best spanner for a hex-head fastener. Sit down with a few nuts and bolts and look at how various tools fit the bolt heads.

A good rule of thumb is to choose a tool that contacts the largest area of the hex-head. This distributes the load as evenly as possible and lessens the risk of damage. The shape most closely resembling the bolt head or nut is another hex, so a 6-point socket or box-end spanner is usually the best choice *(see illustration)*. Many sockets and ring spanners have double hex (12-point) openings. If you slip a 12-point box-end spanner over a nut, look at how and where the two are in contact. The corners of the nut engage in every other point of the spanner. When the spanner is turned, pressure is applied evenly on each of the six corners *(see illustration)*. This is fine unless the fastener head was previously rounded off. If so, the corners will be damaged and the spanner will slip. If you encounter a damaged bolt head or nut, always use a 6-point spanner or socket if possible. If you don't have one in the right size, choose a 12 point spanner or socket that fits securely and proceed carefully.

If you slip an open-end spanner over a hex-head fastener, you'll see the tool is in contact on two faces only *(see illustration)*. This is acceptable provided the tool and fastener are both in good condition. The need for a snug fit between the spanner and nut or bolt explains the recommendation to buy good-quality open-end spanners. If the spanner jaws, the bolt head or both are damaged, the spanner will probably slip, rounding off and distorting the head. In some applications, an open-end spanner is the only possible choice due to limited access, but always check the fit of the spanner on the fastener before attempting to loosen it; if it's hard to get at with a spanner, think how hard it will be to remove after the head is damaged.

The last choice is an adjustable spanner or self-locking plier/spanner. Use these tools only when all else has failed. In some cases, a self- locking spanner may be able to grip a damaged head that no spanner could deal with, but be careful not to make matters worse by damaging it further.

Bearing in mind the remarks about the correct choice of tool in the first place, there are several things worth noting about the actual use of the tool. First, make sure the spanner head is clean and undamaged. If the fastener is rusted or coated with paint, the spanner won't fit correctly. Clean off the head and, if it's rusted, apply some penetrating oil. Leave it to soak in for a while before attempting removal.

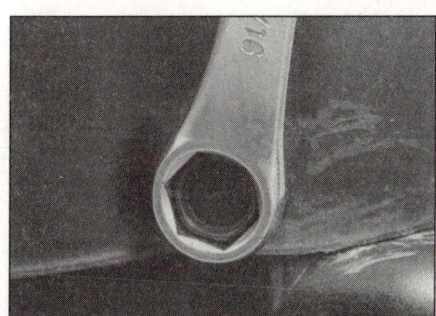

A 6-point ring spanner contacts the nut or bolt head entirely, which spreads out the force and tends to prevent rounded-off corners

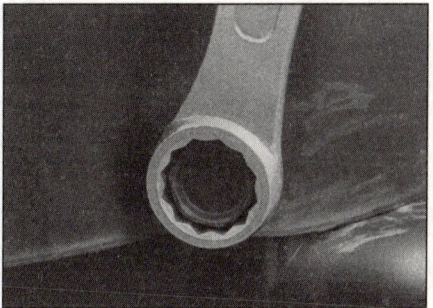

A 12-point ring spanner only contacts the nut or bolt head near the corners and concentrates the force at specific points, which leads to rounded-off fasteners and a frustrated mechanic

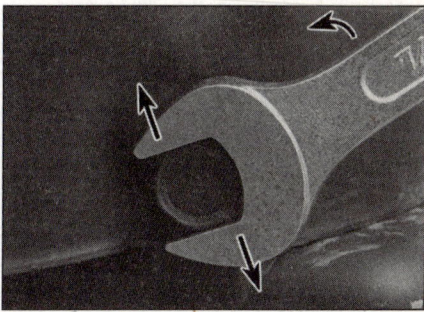

Open-end spanner jaws tend to spread apart when loosening tight fasteners and will quickly damage a nut or bolt

Chapter 2

It may seem obvious, but take a close look at the fastener to be removed before using a spanner. On many mass-produced machines, one end of a fastener may be fixed or captive, which speeds up initial assembly and usually makes removal easier. If a nut is installed on a stud or a bolt threads into a captive nut or tapped hole, you may have only one fastener to deal with. If, on the other hand, you have a separate nut and bolt, you'll have to hold the bolt head while the nut is removed. In some areas this can be difficult, particularly where engine mounts are involved. In this type of situation you may need an assistant to hold the bolt head with a spanner, while you remove the nut from the other side. If this isn't possible, you'll have to try to position a ring spanner so it wedges against some other component to prevent it from turning.

Be on the lookout for left-hand threads. They aren't common, but are sometimes used on the ends of rotating shafts to make sure the nut doesn't come loose during engine operation. If you can see the shaft end, the thread type can be checked visually. If you're unsure, place your thumbnail in the threads and see which way you have to turn your hand so your nail 'unscrews' from the shaft. If you have to turn your hand anti-clockwise, it's a conventional right-hand thread.

Beware of the upside-down fastener syndrome. If you're loosening an oil drain plug on the underside of a mower deck, for example, it's easy to get confused about which way to turn it. What seems like anti-clockwise to you can easily be clockwise (from the plug's point of view). Even after years of experience, this can still catch you once in a while.

In most cases, a fastener can be removed simply by placing the spanner on the nut or bolt head and turning it. Occasionally, though, the condition or location of the fastener may make things more difficult. Make sure the spanner is square on the head. You may need to reposition the tool or try another type to obtain a snug fit. Make sure the engine you're working on is secure and can't move when you turn the spanner. If necessary, get someone to help steady it for you. Position yourself so you can get maximum leverage on the spanner.

If possible, locate the spanner so you can pull the end towards you. If you have to push on the tool, remember that it may slip, or the fastener may move suddenly. For this reason, don't curl your fingers around the handle or you may crush or bruise them when the fastener moves; keep your hand flat, pushing on the spanner with the heel of your thumb. If the tool digs into your hand, place a rag between it and your hand or wear a heavy glove.

If the fastener doesn't move with normal hand pressure, stop and try to figure out why before the fastener or spanner is damaged or you hurt yourself. Stuck fasteners may require penetrating oil, heat or an impact driver or air tool.

Using sockets to remove hex-head fasteners is less likely to result in damage than if a spanner is used. Make sure the socket fits snugly over the fastener head, then attach an extension, if needed, and the ratchet or swivel-drive handle. Theoretically, a ratchet shouldn't be used for loosening a fastener or for final tightening because the ratchet mechanism may be overloaded and could slip. In some instances, the location of the fastener may mean you have no choice but to use a ratchet, in which case you'll have to be extra careful.

Never use extensions where they aren't needed. Whether or not an extension is used, always support the drive end of a swivel-drive handle with one hand while turning it with the other. Once the fastener is loose, the ratchet can be used to speed up removal.

Pliers

Generally speaking, three types of pliers are needed when doing mechanic work: slip-joint, 'water pump', and self-locking pliers. Although somewhat limited in use, needle-nose pliers and wire cutters should be included if your budget will allow it.

Slip-joint pliers (which are not widely available now, but may feature in an existing tool kit) have two open positions. A figure-eight shaped elongated slot in one handle slips back and forth on a pivot pin on the other handle, to change the open position. Good quality pliers have jaws made of tempered steel and there's usually a wire-cutter at the base of the jaws. The primary uses of slip-joint pliers are for holding objects, bending and cutting throttle wires and crimping and bending metal parts, not loosening nuts and bolts.

'Water pump' pliers are similar to the slip joint type, but are usually larger, and have more open positions. Since the tool expands to fit many size objects, it has countless uses for small engine and equipment maintenance.

Self-locking pliers come in various sizes – the medium size with curved jaws is best for all-round work. However, buy a large and small one if possible, since they're often used in pairs. Although this tool falls somewhere between an adjustable spanner, a pair of pliers and a portable vice, it can be invaluable for loosening and tightening fasteners – they're the only pliers that should be used for this purpose. The jaw opening is set by turning a knurled knob at the end of one handle. The jaws are placed over the head of the fastener and the handles are squeezed together, locking the tool onto the fastener *(see illustration)*. The design of the

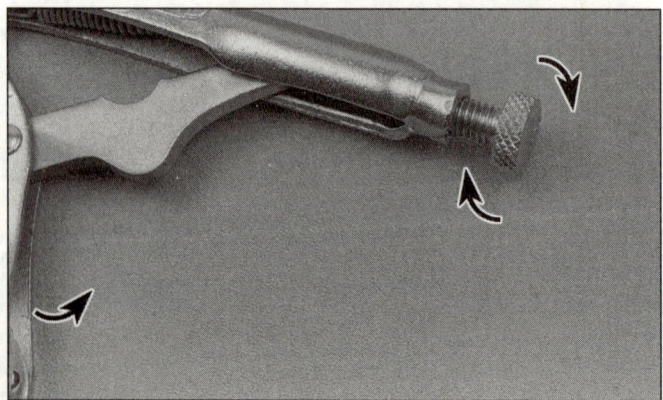

Self-locking pliers are adjusted with the knurled bolt, then the handles are closed to lock the jaws on the part

Workshop practice

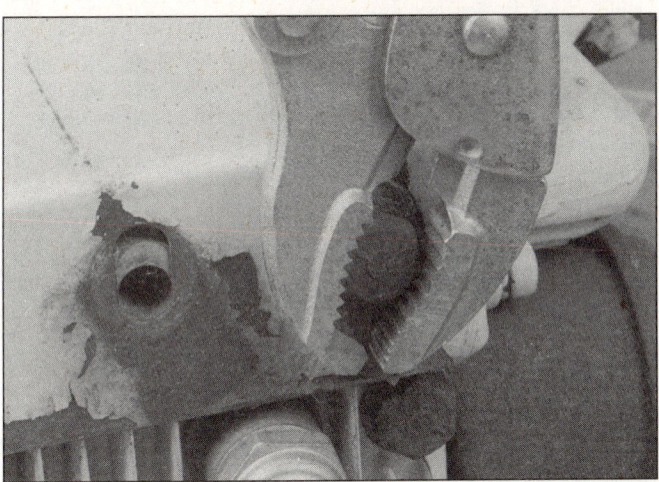

As a last resort, you can use locking pliers to loosen a rusted or rounded-off nut or bolt

tool allows extreme pressure to be applied at the jaws and a variety of jaw designs enable the tool to grip firmly even on damaged heads (see illustration). Self-locking pliers are great for removing fasteners rounded off by badly-fitting spanners.

As the name suggests, needle-nose pliers have long, thin jaws designed for reaching into holes and other restricted areas. Most needle-nose, or long-nose, pliers also have wire cutters at the base of the jaws.

Look for these qualities when buying pliers: smooth operating handles and jaws, jaws that match up and grip evenly when the handles are closed, a nice finish and the word 'forged' somewhere on the tool.

Screwdrivers

Screwdrivers come in innumerable shapes and sizes to fit the various screw head designs in common use. Regardless of the tool quality, the screwdrivers in most tool boxes rarely fit the intended screw heads very well. This is attributable not only to general wear, but also to misuse.

Screwdrivers make very tempting and convenient crowbars, chisels and punches, uses which in turn make them very bad screwdrivers.

A screwdriver consists of a steel blade or shank with a drive tip formed at one end. The most common tips are standard (also called straight slot and flat-blade) and Phillips/Posi-Drive. The other end has a handle attached to it. Traditionally, handles were made from wood and secured to the shank, which had raised tangs to prevent it from turning in the handle. Most screwdrivers now come with plastic handles, which are generally more durable than wood.

The design and size of handles and blades vary considerably. Some handles are specially shaped to fit the human hand and provide a better grip. The shank may be either round or square and some have a hex-shaped bolster under the handle to accept a spanner to provide more leverage when trying to turn a stubborn screw. The shank

diameter, tip size and overall length vary too. As a general rule, it's a good idea to use the longest screwdriver possible, which allows the greatest possible leverage.

If access is restricted, a number of special screwdrivers are designed to fit into confined spaces. The 'stubby' screwdriver has a specially shortened handle and blade. There are also offset screwdrivers and special screwdriver bits that attach to a ratchet or extension.

Standard screwdrivers

These are used to remove and install conventional slotted screws and are available in a wide range of sizes denoting the width of the tip and the length of the shank (for example: a 10 x 250 mm screwdriver is 10 mm wide at the tip and the shank is 250 mm long). You should have a variety of screwdrivers so screws of various sizes can be dealt with without damaging them. The blade end must be the same width and thickness as the screw slot to work properly, without slipping. When selecting standard screwdrivers, choose good quality tools, preferably with chrome moly, forged steel shanks. The tip of the shank should be ground to a parallel, flat profile (hollow ground) and not to a taper or wedge shape, which will tend to twist out of the slot when pressure is applied (see illustration).

All screwdrivers wear in use, but standard types can be reground to shape a number of times. When reshaping a tip, start by grinding the very end flat at right angles to the shank. Make sure the tip fits snugly in the slot of a screw of the appropriate size and keep the sides of the tip parallel. Remove only a small amount of metal at a time to avoid overheating the tip and destroying the temper of the steel.

Phillips/Posi-drive screwdrivers

Some engines have screws that are installed during initial assembly with air tools and are next to impossible to remove later without ruining the heads, particularly if the wrong size screwdriver is used. Be sure to use a screwdriver with a tip profile that closely matches the cross-profile of the screw.

The only way to ensure the tools you buy will fit properly is to take a couple of screws with you to make sure the fit between the screwdriver and fastener is snug. If the fit is good, you should be able to angle the blade down almost

Misuse of a screwdriver – the blade shown is both too narrow and too thin and will probably slip or break off

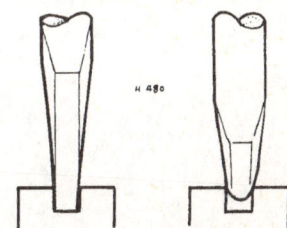

The left-hand example shows a snug-fitting tip. The right-hand drawing shows a damaged tip which will twist out of the slot when pressure is applied

Standard screwdrivers – wrong size (left), correct fit in screw slot (centre) and worn tip (right)

Chapter 2

vertically without the screw slipping off the tip. Use only screwdrivers that fit exactly – anything else is guaranteed to chew out the screw head instantly.

The idea behind all cross-head screw designs is to make the screw and screwdriver blade self-aligning. Provided you aim the blade at the centre of the screw head, it'll engage correctly, unlike conventional slotted screws, which need careful alignment. This makes the screws suitable for machine installation on an assembly line (which explains why they're usually so tight and difficult to remove). The drawback with these screws is the driving tangs on the screwdriver tip are very small and must fit very precisely in the screw head. If this isn't the case, the huge loads imposed on small flats of the screw recess simply tear the metal away, at which point the screw ceases to be removable by normal methods. The problem is made worse by the normally soft material chosen for screws.

To deal with these screws on a regular basis, you'll need high-quality screwdrivers with various size tips so you'll be sure to have the right one when you need it. Phillips/Posi-Drive screwdrivers are sized by the tip number and length of the shank (for example: a number 2 x 6-inch Phillips screwdriver has a number 2 tip -to fit screws of only that size recess -and the shank is 6-inches long). Tip sizes 1, 2 and 3 should be adequate for small engine repair work *(see illustration)*. If tips get worn or damaged, buy new screwdrivers so they don't destroy the screws they're used on *(see illustration)*.

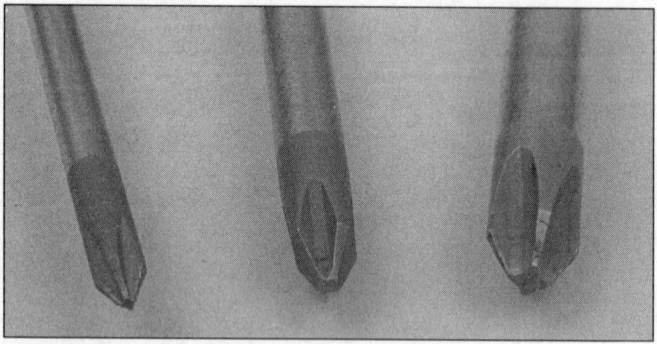

The tip size on a Phillips screwdriver is indicated by a number from 1 to 4, with 1 being the smallest (left – no. 1; centre – no. 2; right – no. 3)

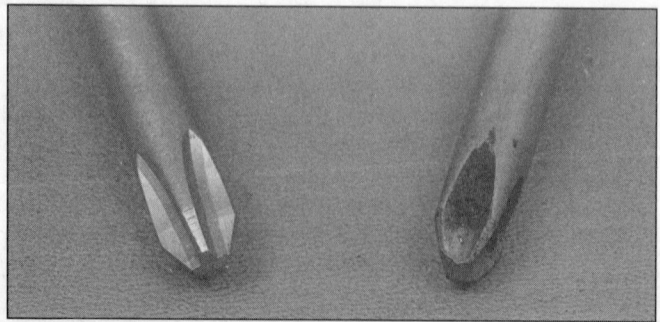

New (left) and worn (right) Phillips screwdriver tips

Here's a tip that may come in handy when using Phillips screwdrivers -if the screw is extremely tight and the tip tends to back out of the recess rather than turn the screw, apply a small amount of valve lapping compound to the screwdriver tip so it will grip better.

Hammers

You'll need at least one ball-pein hammer, although almost any steel hammer will work in most cases. A ball-pein hammer has a head with a conventional cylindrical face at one end and a rounded ball end at the other and is a general-purpose tool found in almost any type of workshop. It has a shorter neck than a claw hammer and the face is tempered for striking punches and chisels. A fairly large hammer is preferred over a small one. Although it's possible to find small ones, you won't need them very often and it's much easier to control the blows from a heavier head. As a general rule, a single 340 or 450 gram (12 or 16-ounce) hammer will work for most jobs, though occasionally larger or smaller ones may be useful.

A soft-face hammer is used where a steel hammer could cause damage to the component or other tools being used. A steel hammer head might crack an aluminium part, but a rubber or plastic hammer can be used with more confidence. Soft-face hammers are available with interchangeable heads (usually one made of rubber and another made of relatively hard plastic). When the heads are worn out, new ones can be installed. If finances are really limited, you can get by without a soft-face hammer by placing a small hardwood block between the component and a steel hammer head to prevent damage.

Hammers should be used with common sense; the head should strike the desired object squarely and with the right amount of force. For many jobs, little effort is needed – simply allow the weight of the head to do the work, using the length of the swing to control the amount of force applied. With practice, a hammer can be used with surprising finesse, but it'll take a while to achieve. Initial mistakes include striking the object at an angle, in which case the hammer head may glance off to one side, or hitting the edge of the object. Either one can result in damage to the part or to your thumb, if it gets in the way, so be careful. Hold the hammer handle near the end, not near the head, and grip it firmly but not too tightly.

Check the condition of your hammers on a regular basis. The danger of a loose head coming off is self-evident, but check the head for chips and cracks too. If damage is noted, buy a new hammer – the head may chip in use and the resulting fragments can be extremely dangerous. It goes without saying that eye protection is essential whenever a hammer is used.

Punches and chisels

These tools are used along with a hammer for various purposes in the workshop. Drift punches are often simply a length of round steel bar used to drive a component out of a

Workshop practice

bore in the engine or equipment it's mounted on. A typical use would be for removing or installing a bearing or bushing. A drift of the same diameter as the bearing outer race is placed against the bearing and tapped with a hammer to drive it in or out of the bore. Most manufacturers offer special drifts for the various bearings in a particular engine. While they're useful to a busy dealer service department, they are prohibitively expensive for the do-it-yourselfer who may only need to use them once. In such cases, it's better to improvise. For bearing removal and installation it's usually possible to use a socket of the appropriate diameter to tap the bearing in or out; an unorthodox use for a socket, but it works.

Smaller diameter drift punches can be purchased or fabricated from steel bar. In some cases, you'll need to drive out items like corroded engine mounting bolts. Here, it's essential to avoid damaging the threaded end of the bolt, so the drift must be of softer material than the bolt. Brass or copper is the usual choice for such jobs; the drift may be damaged in use, but the thread will be protected.

Punches are available in various shapes and sizes and a set of assorted types will be very useful. One of the most basic is the centre punch, a small cylindrical punch with the end ground to a point. It'll be needed whenever a hole is drilled. The centre of the hole is located first and the punch is used to make a small indentation at the intended point. The indentation acts as a guide for the drill bit so the hole ends up in the right place. Without a punch mark the drill bit will wander and you'll find it impossible to drill with any real accuracy. You can also buy automatic centre punches. They're spring loaded and are pressed against the surface to be marked, without the need to use a hammer.

Pin punches are intended for removing items like roll pins (semi-hard, hollow pins that fit tightly in their holes). Pin punches have other uses, however. You may occasionally have to remove rivets or bolts by cutting off the heads and driving out the shanks with a pin punch. They're also very handy for aligning holes in components while bolts or screws are inserted.

Of the various sizes and types of metal-cutting chisels available, a simple cold chisel is essential in any mechanic's workshop. One about 150 mm (6-inches) long with a 12 mm (1/2-inch) wide blade should be adequate. The cutting edge is ground to about 80-degrees *(see illustration)*, while the rest of the tip is ground to a shallower angle away from the edge. The primary use of the cold chisel is rough metal cutting – this can be anything from sheet metal work (uncommon on small engines) to cutting off the heads of seized or rusted bolts or splitting nuts. A cold chisel can also be useful for turning out screws or bolts with messed up heads.

All of the tools described in this section should be good quality items. They're not particularly expensive, so it's not really worth trying to save money on them. More significantly, there's a risk that with cheap tools, fragments may break off in use – a potentially dangerous situation.

Even with good quality tools, the heads and working ends will inevitably get worn or damaged, so it's a good idea to maintain all such tools on a regular basis. Using a file or bench grinder, remove all burrs and mushroomed edges from around the head. This is an important task because the build-up of material around the head can fly off when it's struck with a hammer and is potentially dangerous. Make sure the tool retains its original profile at the working end, again, filing or grinding off all burrs. In the case of cold chisels, the cutting edge will usually have to be reground quite often because the material in the tool isn't usually much harder than materials typically being cut. Make sure the edge is reasonably sharp, but don't make the tip angle greater than it was originally; it'll just wear down faster if you do.

The techniques for using these tools vary according to the job to be done and are best learned by experience. The one common denominator is the fact they're all normally struck with a hammer. It follows that eye protection should be worn. Always make sure the working end of the tool is in contact with the part being punched or cut. If it isn't, the tool will bounce off the surface and damage may result.

Hacksaws

A hacksaw consists of a handle and frame supporting a flexible steel blade under tension. Blades are available in various lengths and most hacksaws can be adjusted to accommodate the different sizes. The most common blade length is 250 mm (10-inches).

Most hacksaw frames are adequate and since they're simple tools, there's not much difference between brands. Try to pick one that's rigid when assembled and allows the blade to be changed or repositioned easily.

The type of blade to use, indicated by the number of teeth

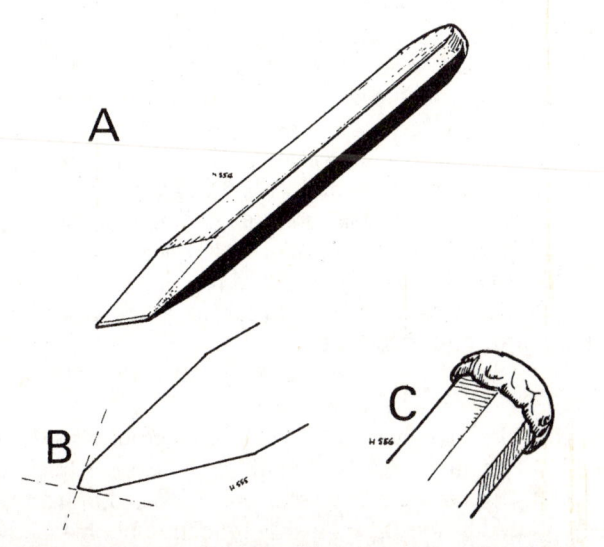

A typical general purpose cold chisel – note the angle of the cutting edge (B), which should be checked and resharpened on a regular basis; the mushroomed head (C) is dangerous and should be filed to restore it to its original shape

Chapter 2

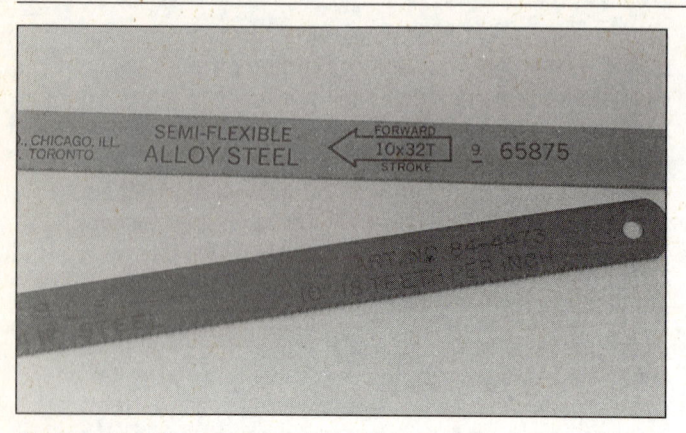

Hacksaw blades are marked with the number of teeth per inch (TPI) – use a relatively course blade for aluminum and a fine blade for steel

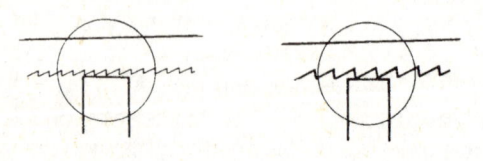

When cutting thin materials, check that at least three teeth are in contact with the workpiece at any time. Too coarse a blade will result in a poor cut and may break the blade. If you do not have the correct blade, cut at a shallow angle to the material.

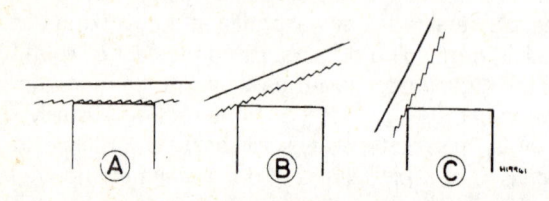

The correct cutting angle is important. If it is too shallow (A) the blade will wander. The angle show at (B) is correct when starting the cut, and may be reduced slightly once under way. In (C) the angle is too steep and the blade will be inclined to jump out of the cut.

Correct procedure for use of a hacksaw

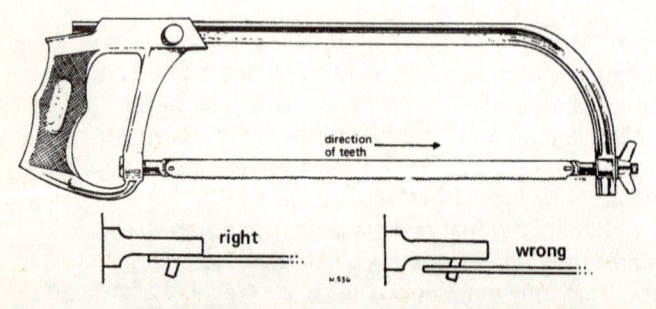

Correct installation of a hacksaw blade – the teeth must point away from the handle and butt against the locating lugs

per inch, (TPI) *(see illustration)*, is determined by the material being cut. The rule of thumb is to make sure at least three teeth are in contact with the metal being cut at anyone time *(see illustration)*. In practice, this means a fine blade for cutting thin sheet materials, while a coarser blade can be used for faster cutting through thicker items such as bolts. It's worth noting that when cutting thin materials it's helpful to angle the saw so the blade cuts at a shallow angle. This way more teeth are in contact and there's less chance of the blade binding and breaking or teeth being broken off. This approach can also be used when a fine enough blade isn't available; the shallower the angle, the more teeth are contacting the workpiece.

When buying blades, choose a reputable brand. Cheap, unbranded blades may be perfectly acceptable, but you can't tell by looking at them. Poor quality blades will be insufficiently hardened on the teeth edge and will dull quickly. Most reputable brands will be marked 'Flexible High Speed Steel' or something similar, giving some indication of the material they're made of. It is possible to buy 'unbreakable' blades (only the teeth are hardened, leaving the rest of the blade less brittle).

In some situations, a full-size hacksaw is too big to allow access to a frozen nut or bolt. Sometimes this can be overcome by turning the blade 90-degrees – most saws allow this to be done. Occasionally you may have to position the saw around an obstacle and then install the blade on the other side of it. Where space is really restricted, you may have to use a handle that clamps onto a saw blade at one end. This allows access when a hacksaw frame would not work at all and has another advantage in that you can make use of broken off hacksaw blades instead of throwing them away. Note that because only one end of the blade is supported, and it's not held under tension, it's difficult to control and less efficient when cutting.

Before using a hacksaw, make sure the blade is suitable for the material being cut and installed correctly in the frame *(see illustration)*. Whatever it is you're cutting must be securely supported so it can't move around. The saw cuts on the forward stroke, so the teeth must point away from the handle. This might seem obvious, but it's easy to install the blade backwards by mistake and ruin the teeth on the first few strokes. Make sure the blade is tensioned adequately or it'll distort and chatter in the cut and may break. Wear safety glasses and be careful not to cut yourself on the saw blade or the sharp edge of the cut.

Files

Files come in a wide variety of sizes and types for specific jobs, but all of them are used for the same basic function of removing small amounts of metal in a controlled fashion. Files are used by mechanics mainly for deburring, marking parts, removing rust, filing the heads off rivets, restoring threads and fabricating small parts.

File shapes commonly available include flat, half-round, round, square and triangular. Each shape comes in a range

Workshop practice

Files will be either single-cut (left) or double-cut (right) – generally speaking, use a single cut file to produce a very smooth surface; use a double-cut file to remove large amounts of material quickly

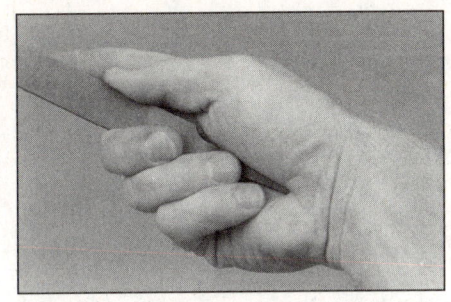

Never use a file without a handle – the tang is sharp and could puncture your hand

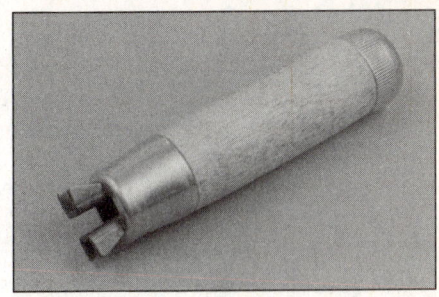

Adjustable handles that will work with many different size files are also available

of sizes (lengths) and cuts ranging from rough to smooth. The file face is covered with rows of diagonal ridges which form the cutting teeth. They may be aligned in one direction only (single cut) or in two directions to form a diamond-shaped pattern (double-cut) *(see illustration)*. The spacing of the teeth determines the file coarseness, again, ranging from rough to smooth in five basic grades: Rough, coarse, bastard, second-cut and smooth.

You'll want to build up a set of files by purchasing tools of the required shape and cut as they're needed. A good starting point would be flat, half-round, round and triangular files (at least one each – bastard or second-cut types). In addition, you'll have to buy one or more file handles (files are usually sold without handles, which are purchased separately and pushed over the tapered tang of the file when in use) *(see illustration)*. You may need to buy more than one size handle to fit the various files in your tool box, but don't attempt to get by without them. A file tang is fairly sharp and you almost certainly will end up stabbing yourself in the palm of the hand if you use a file without a handle and it catches in the workpiece during use. Adjustable handles are also available for use with files of various sizes, eliminating the need for several handles *(see illustration)*.

Exceptions to the need for a handle are fine swiss pattern files (needle files), which have a rounded handle instead of a tang. These small files are usually sold in sets with a number of different shapes. Originally intended for very fine work, they can be very useful for use in inaccessible areas. Swiss files are normally the best choice if piston ring ends require filing to obtain the correct end gap.

The correct procedure for using files is fairly easy to master. As with a hacksaw, the work should be clamped securely in a vice, if needed, to prevent it from moving around while being worked on. Hold the file by the handle, using your free hand at the file end to guide it and keep it flat in relation to the surface being filed. Use smooth cutting strokes and be careful not to rock the file as it passes over the surface. Also, don't slide it diagonally across the surface or the teeth will make grooves in the workpiece. Don't drag a file back across the workpiece at the end of the stroke –

lift it slightly and pull it back to prevent damage to the teeth.

Files don't require maintenance in the usual sense, but they should be kept clean and free of metal filings. Steel is a reasonably easy material to work with, but softer metals like aluminium tend to clog the file teeth very quickly, which will result in scratches in the workpiece. This can be avoided by rubbing the file face with chalk before using it. General cleaning is carried out with a file card or a fine wire brush. If they're kept clean, files will last a long time – when they do eventually dull, they must be replaced; there is no satisfactory way of sharpening a worn file.

Twist drills and drilling equipment

Drills are often needed to remove rusted or broken off fasteners, enlarge holes and fabricate small parts.

Drilling operations are done with twist drills, either in a hand drill or a drill press. Twist drills (or drill bits, as they're often called) consist of a round shank with spiral flutes formed into the upper two-thirds to clear the waste produced while drilling, keep the drill centred in the hole and finish the sides of the hole.

The lower portion of the shank is left plain and used to hold the drill in the chuck. In this section, we will discuss only normal parallel shank drills *(see illustration)*. There is

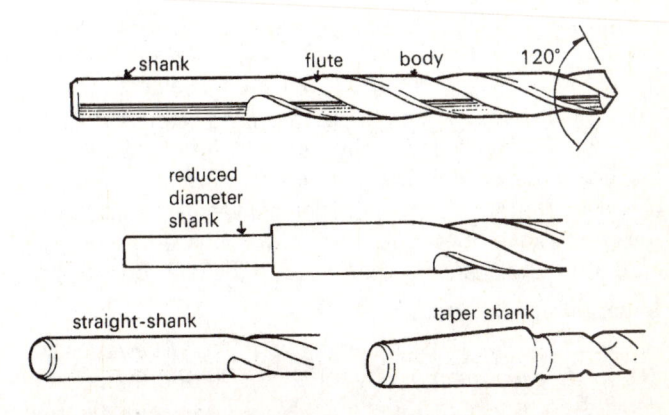

A typical drill bit (top), a reduced shank bit (centre) and a tapered shank bit (bottom right)

Chapter 2

Drill bits in the range most commonly used are available in metric or imperial sizes (left) and number sizes (right) so almost any size hole can be drilled

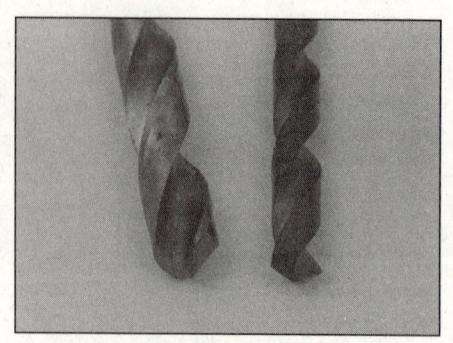

If a bit gets dull (left), it should be discarded or resharpened so it looks like the one on the right

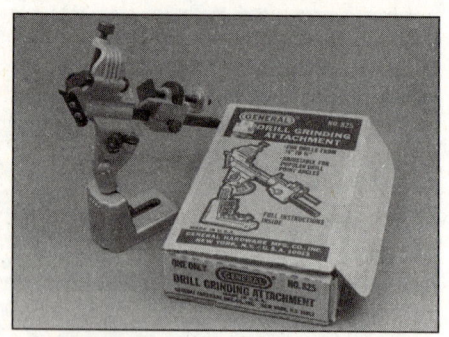

Inexpensive drill bit sharpening jigs for use with a bench grinder are widely available. Even if you use it infrequently it'll pay for itself quickly

another type of bit with the plain end formed into a special size taper designed to fit directly into a corresponding socket in a heavy-duty drill press. These drills are known as Morse Taper drills and are used primarily in machine shops.

At the cutting end of the drill, two edges are ground to form a conical point. They're generally angled at about 60-degrees from the drill axis, but they can be reground to other angles for specific applications. For general use the standard angle is correct – this is how drill bits are sold.

When buying bits, purchase a good-quality set (sizes 1.5 to 10 mm 1/16 to 3/8 in). Make sure they're marked 'High Speed Steel' or 'HHS'. This indicates they're hard enough to withstand continual use in metal; many cheaper, unmarked bits are suitable only for use in wood or other soft materials. Buying a set ensures the right size bit will be available when it's needed.

Twist drill sizes

Twist drills are available in a vast array of sizes, most of which you'll never need. There are four basic sizing systems: metric, imperial, number and letter *(see illustration)*.

Metric sizes usually start at 1.5 mm, and go up in increments of 0.5 mm, while imperial size drills start at 1/64-inch, and go up in 1/64-inch steps. Number drills range in descending order from 80 (0.34 mm or 0.0135-inch), the smallest, to 1 (5.79 mm or 0.2280-inch), the largest. Letter sizes start with A (5.94 mm or 0.234-inch), the smallest, and go through Z (10.49 mm or 0.413-inch), the largest.

This bewildering range of sizes means it's possible to drill an accurate hole of almost any size within reason. In practice, you'll be limited by the size of chuck on your drill (normally or 10 or 12 mm). In addition, very few stores stock the entire range of possible sizes, so you'll have to shop around for the nearest available size to the one you require.

Sharpening twist drills

Like any tool with a cutting edge, twist drills will eventually get dull *(see illustration)*. How often they'll need sharpening depends to some extent on whether they're used correctly. A dull twist drill will be obvious in use. A good indication of the condition of the cutting edges is to watch the waste emerging from the hole being drilled. If the tip is in good condition, two even spirals of waste metal will be produced; if this fails to happen or the tip gets hot, it's safe to assume that sharpening is required.

With smaller size drill bits – under about 3.0 mm (1/8-inch) – it's easier and more economical to throw the worn drill away and buy another one. With larger (more expensive) sizes, sharpening is a better bet. When sharpening twist drills, the included angle of the cutting edge must be maintained at the original 120-degrees and the small chisel edge at the tip must be retained. With some practice, sharpening can be done freehand on a bench grinder, but it should be noted that it's very easy to make mistakes. For most home mechanics, a sharpening jig that mounts next to the grinding wheel should be used so the drill is held at the correct angle *(see illustration)*.

Drilling equipment

Tools to hold and turn drill bits range from simple, inexpensive hand-operated or electric drills to sophisticated and expensive drill presses. Ideally, all drilling should be done on a drill press with the workpiece clamped solidly in a vice. These machines are expensive and take up a lot of bench or floor space, so they're out of the question for many do-it-yourselfers. An additional problem is the fact that many of the drilling jobs you end up doing will be on the engine itself or the equipment it's mounted on, in which case the tool has to be taken to the work.

The best tool for the home workshop is an electric drill with a 10 mm (3/8-inch) chuck. As mentioned in Chapter 1, both cordless and AC drills (that run off household current) are available. If you're purchasing one for the first time, look for a well-known, reputable brand name and variable speed as minimum requirements. A 6.0 mm (1/4-inch) chuck single-speed drill will work, but it's worth paying a little more for the larger, variable speed type.

Most drills require a key to lock the bit in the chuck. When removing or installing a bit, make sure the lead is unplugged to avoid accidents. Initially, tighten the chuck by hand, checking to see if the bit is centred correctly. This is especially

Workshop practice

important when using small drill bits which can get caught between the jaws. Once the chuck is hand tight, use the key to tighten it securely – remember to remove the key afterwards!

Drilling and finishing holes

Preparation for drilling

If possible, make sure the part you intend to drill in is securely clamped in a vice. If it's impossible to get the work to a vice, make sure it's stable and secure. Drill bits often catch during drilling – this can be dangerous, particularly if the work suddenly starts spinning on the end of the drill. Obviously, there's not much chance of a complete engine or piece of equipment doing this, but you should make sure it's supported securely.

Start by locating the centre of the hole you're drilling. Use a centre punch to make an indentation for the drill bit so it won't wander. If you're drilling out a broken-off bolt, be sure to position the punch in the exact centre of the bolt (see 'Removing broken-off bolts' section).

If you're drilling a large hole (above 6.0 mm or 1/4-inch), you may want to make a pilot hole first. As the name suggests, it will guide the larger drill bit and minimize drill bit wandering. Before actually drilling a hole, make sure the area immediately behind the bit is clear of anything you don't want drilled.

Drilling

When drilling steel, especially with smaller bits, no lubrication is needed. If a large bit is involved, oil can be used to ensure a clean cut and prevent overheating of the drill tip. When drilling aluminum, which tends to cling to the cutting edges and clog the drill bit flutes, use paraffin as a lubricant.

Wear safety goggles or a face shield and assume a comfortable, stable stance so you can control the pressure on the drill easily. Position the drill tip in the punch mark and make sure, if you're drilling by hand, the bit is perpendicular to the surface of the workpiece. Start drilling without applying much pressure until you're sure the hole is positioned correctly. If the hole starts off centre, it can be very difficult to correct. You can try angling the bit slightly so the hole centre moves in the opposite direction, but this must be done before the flutes of the bit have entered the hole. It's at the starting point that a variable-speed drill is invaluable; the low speed allows fine adjustments to be made before it's too late. Continue drilling until the desired hole depth is reached or until the drill tip emerges from the other side of the workpiece.

Cutting speed and pressure are important – as a general rule, the larger the diameter of the drill bit, the slower the drilling speed should be. With a single-speed drill, there's little that can be done to control it, but two-speed or variable speed drills can be controlled. If the drilling speed is too high, the cutting edges of the bit will tend to overheat and dull. Pressure should be varied during drilling. Start with

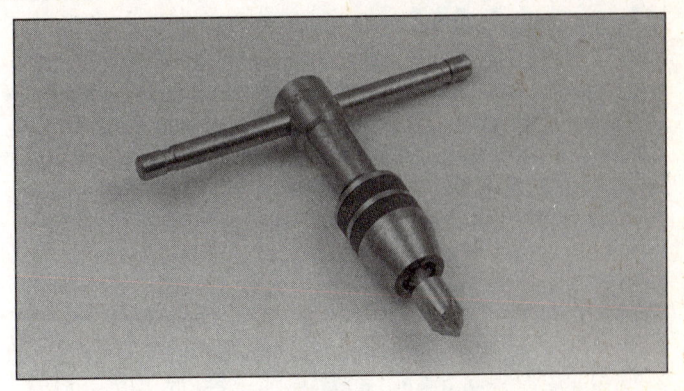

Use a large drill bit or a countersink mounted in a tap wrench to remove burrs from a hole after drilling or enlarging it

light pressure until the drill tip has located properly in the work. Gradually increase pressure so the bit cuts evenly. If the tip is sharp and the pressure correct, two distinct spirals of metal will emerge from the bit flutes. If the pressure is too light, the bit won't cut properly, while excessive pressure will overheat the tip.

Decrease pressure as the bit breaks through the workpiece. If this isn't done, the bit may jam in the hole; if you're using a hand-held drill, it could be jerked out of your hands, especially when using larger size bits.

Once a pilot hole has been made, install the larger bit in the chuck and enlarge the hole. The second bit will follow the pilot hole – there's no need to attempt to guide it (if you do, the bit may break off). It is important, however, to hold the drill at the correct angle.

After the hole has been drilled to the correct size, remove the burrs left around the edges of the hole. This can be done with a small round file, or by chamfering the opening with a larger bit or a countersink *(see illustration)*. Use a drill bit that's several sizes larger than the hole and simply twist it around each opening by hand until any rough edges are removed.

Enlarging and reshaping holes

The biggest practical size for bits used in a hand drill is about 12 mm (1/2-inch). This is partly determined by the capacity of the chuck (although it's possible to buy larger drills with stepped shanks). The real limit is the difficulty of controlling large bits by hand; drills over 12 mm (1/2-inch) tend to be too much to handle in anything other than a drill press. If you have to make a larger hole, or if a shape other than round is involved, different techniques are required.

If a hole simply must be enlarged slightly, a round file is probably the best tool to use. If the hole must be very large, a hole saw will be needed, but they can only be used in sheet metal and other thin materials.

Large or irregular-shaped holes can also be made in relatively thin materials by drilling a series of small holes very close together. In this case the desired hole size and shape must be marked with a scribe. The next step depends on the size bit to be used; the idea is to drill a series of almost

Chapter 2

touching holes just inside the outline of the large hole. Centre punch each hole location, then drill them out. A cold chisel is used to knock out the waste material at the centre of the hole, which can then be filed to size. This is a time consuming process, but it's the only practical approach for the home workshop. Success is dependent on accuracy when marking the hole shape and using the centre punch.

Taps and dies

Taps

Taps, which are available in imperial and metric sizes, are used to cut internal threads and clean or restore damaged threads. A tap consists of a fluted shank with a drive square at one end. It's threaded along part of its length – the cutting edges are formed where the flutes intersect the threads *(see illustration)*. Taps are made from hardened steel so they'll cut threads in materials softer than what they're made of.

Taps come in three different types: Taper, plug and bottoming. The only real difference is the length of the chamfer on the cutting end of the tap. Taper taps are chamfered for the first 6 or 8 threads, which makes them easy to start but prevents them from cutting threads close to the bottom of a hole. Plug taps are chamfered up about 3 to 5 threads, which makes them a good all around tap because they're relatively easy to start and will cut nearly to the bottom of a hole. Bottoming taps, as the name implies, have a very short chamfer (1/2 to 3 threads) and will cut as close to the bottom of a blind hole as practical. However, to do this, the threads should be started with a plug or taper tap.

Although cheap tap and die sets are available, the quality is usually very low and they can actually do more harm than good when used on threaded holes in aluminum engines. The alternative is to buy high-quality taps if and when you need them, even though they aren't cheap, especially if you need to buy two or more thread pitches in a given size. Despite this, it's the best option – you'll probably only need taps on rare occasions, so a full set isn't absolutely necessary.

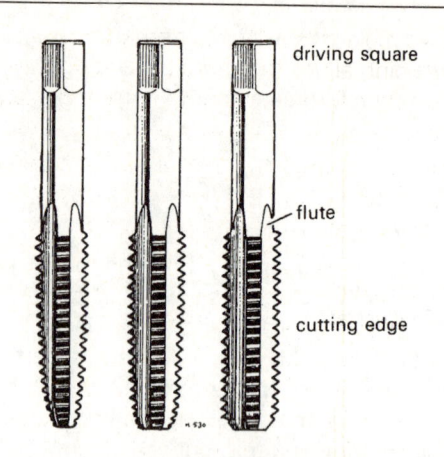

Taper, plug and bottoming taps (left-to-right)

Taps are normally used by hand (they can be used in machine tools, but not when doing engine repairs). The square drive end of the tap is held in a tap spanner (an adjustable T-handle). For smaller sizes, a T-handled chuck can be used *(see illustration)*. The tapping process starts by drilling a hole of the correct diameter. For each tap size, there's a corresponding twist drill that will produce a hole of the correct size. This is important; too large a hole will leave the finished thread with the tops missing, producing a weak and unreliable grip. Conversely, too small a hole will place excessive loads on the hard and brittle shank of the tap, which can break it off in the hole. Removing a broken off tap from a hole is no fun!

The correct tap drill size is normally marked on the tap itself or the container it comes in *(see illustration)*.

Dies

Dies are used to cut, clean or restore external threads. Most dies are made from a hex-shaped or cylindrical piece of hardened steel with a threaded hole in the centre. The threaded hole is overlapped by three or four cutouts, which equate to the flutes on taps and allow waste to escape during the threading process. Dies are held in a T-handled

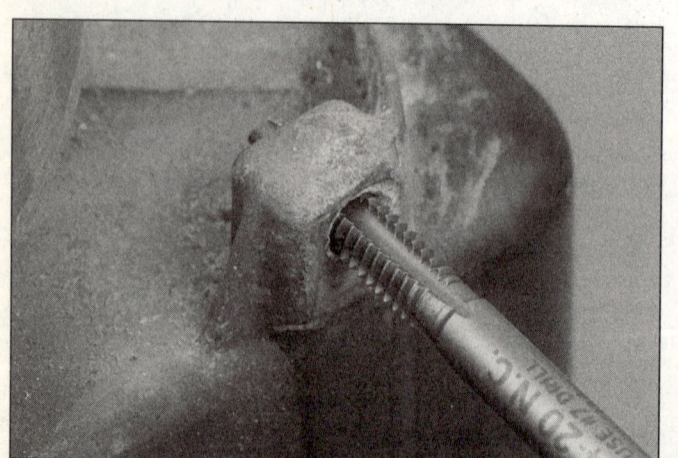

You'll run into many situations where a tap is needed to clean up or restore threads when working on small engines

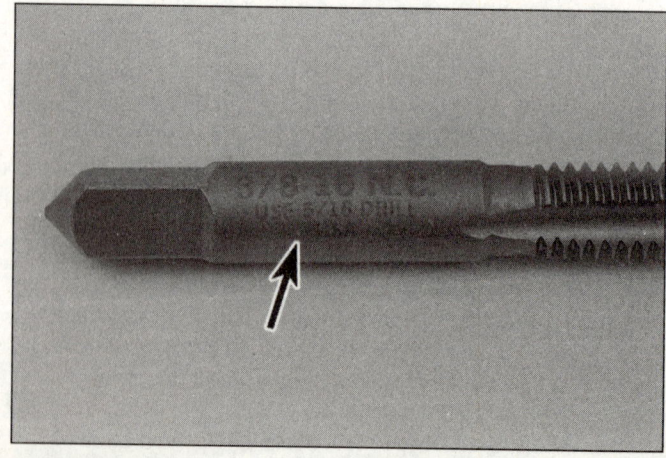

If you need to drill and tap a hole, the drill bit size to use for a given bolt (tap) size is marked on the tap

Workshop practice

holder (called a die stock) *(see illustration)*. Some dies are split at one point, allowing them to be adjusted slightly (opened and closed) for fine control of thread clearances.

Dies aren't needed as often as taps, for the simple reason it's normally easier to install a new bolt than to salvage one. However, it's often helpful to be able to extend the threads of a bolt or clean up damaged threads with a die. Hex-shaped dies are particularly useful for mechanic work, since they can be turned with a spanner *(see illustration)* and are usually less expensive than adjustable ones.

The procedure for cutting threads with a die is similar to the one for taps. When using an adjustable die, the initial cut is made with the die open as far as possible. The adjustment screw is then used to reduce the diameter of successive cuts until the desired finished size is reached. As with taps, cutting oil should be used, and the die must be backed off every few turns to clear waste from the cutouts.

Pullers

During every engine overhaul, and many simple repairs, you'll often need some type of puller. The most common pullers are required for removal of the magneto flywheel from the end of the crankshaft. Other less common tasks that'll require some sort of puller include the removal of bushings and bearings.

Common to all of these jobs is the need to exert pressure on the part being removed while avoiding damage to the surrounding area or components. The best way to do this is with a puller specially designed for the job.

As mentioned in Chapter 1, it's a good idea to have procedures that require a puller (other than flywheel removal) done by a dealer or repair workshop, then you won't have to invest in a tool that won't be used very often.

Special pullers

A good example of a special puller is the one needed for removal of the magneto flywheel. On most engines, the flywheel fits over the tapered end of the crankshaft, where it's secured by a large nut and located by a Woodruff key. Even after the nut has been removed, you have to exert lots of pressure to draw the flywheel off the shaft. This is because the nut draws the tapered faces on the shaft and the inside of the flywheel hub together very tightly during assembly.

The method normally used to remove the flywheel requires a specially designed puller that fits over the crankshaft end and has bolts that thread into holes in the flywheel hub. After the bolts are threaded into place (they often will have to cut their own threads in the holes, but they're designed to do so), the lower nuts are tightened in 1/4-turn increments until the flywheel pops loose *(see illustration)*.

Flywheel 'knock-off' tools are also available for Briggs & Stratton and Tecumseh engines. **Note:** *Briggs and Stratton does not endorse or recommend the use of flywheel knock-off tools on their engines, while Tecumseh does. A knock-off*

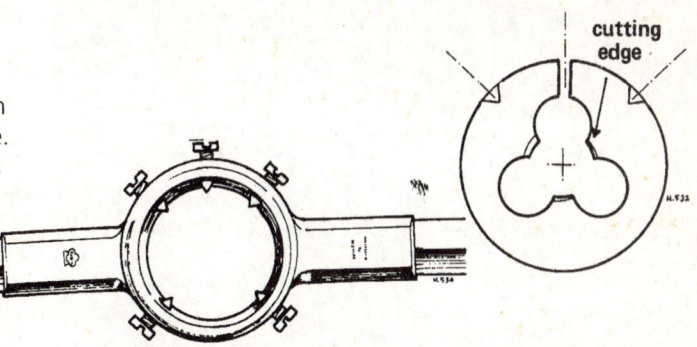

A die (right) is used for cutting external threads (this one is a split-type/adjustable die) and is held in a tool called a die stock (left)

Hex-shaped dies are especially handy for mechanic work because they can be turned with a spanner

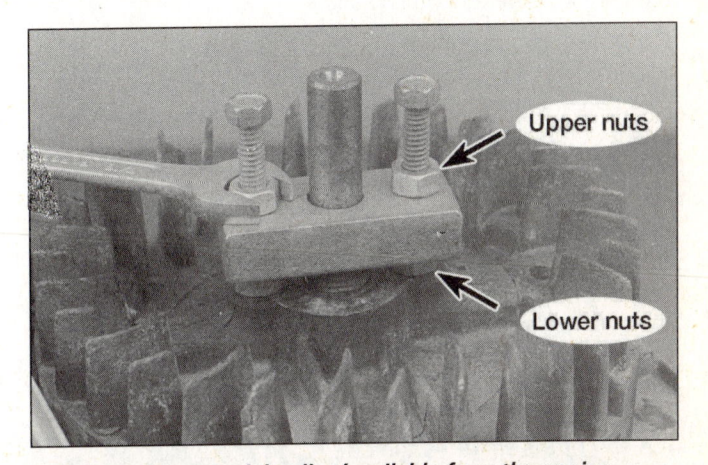

In most cases, a special puller (available from the engine manufacturer) will be needed for removing the flywheel – in this example (Briggs & Stratton engine shown), the puller body is slipped over the end of the crankshaft, the bolts are threaded into the flywheel holes (they may have to cut their own threads if the flywheel has never been removed before), the lower nuts are tightened against the flywheel and the upper nuts are tightened in 1/4-turn increments until the flywheel pops off the shaft taper

Chapter 2

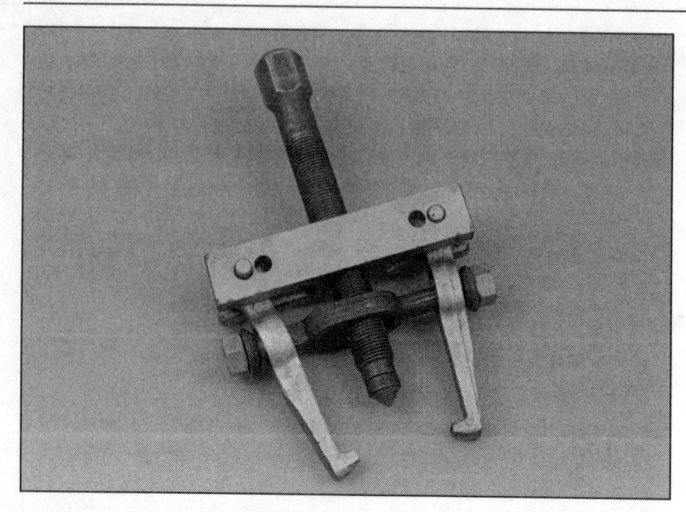

A two or three-jaw puller will come in handy for many tasks and can also be used for working on other types of equipment

tool should not be used on any engine that has a ball bearing on the flywheel side of the crankshaft. The tool is slipped over or threaded onto the end of the crankshaft until it contacts the flywheel, than it's backed off one or two turns. Moderate pressure is applied to the flywheel with a large screwdriver and the end of the knock-off tool is struck with a hammer – the blow from the hammer will usually pop the flywheel loose.

Using a puller means the pressure on the flywheel is applied where it does the most good – at the centre of the hub, rather than at the edge, where it would be more likely to distort the flywheel than release the hub from the shaft taper. Read Chapter 1 to find out about specific pullers for the engines covered in this manual.

General-purpose pullers

You're likely to need some sort of general-purpose puller at some point in most overhauls, often where parts are seized or corroded, or where bushings or bearings nuts be removed. Universal two and three-jaw pullers are widely available in numerous designs and sizes.

These tools generally have jaws attached to a large centre boss, which has a threaded hole to accept the puller bolt. The ends of the jaws have hooks which locate on and grip the part to be pulled off *(see illustration)*. Normally, the jaws can be reversed to allow the tool to be used on internal bushings and bearings as well. The jaws are hooked over the part being removed and the puller bolt is positioned against the end of the shaft. As the bolt is tightened, the component is drawn of the shaft.

It's possible to adapt pullers by making special jaws for specific jobs, but it'll take extra time and may not be successful. If you decide to try this approach, remember that the force should be concentrated as close to the centre of the component as possible to avoid damaging it.

When using a puller, it should be assembled and a careful check should be made to ensure it doesn't snag on anything and the loads on the part to be removed are distributed evenly. If you're dealing with a part held on a shaft by a nut, loosen the nut, but don't remove it entirely. It will help prevent distortion of the shaft end under pressure from the puller bolt and will also stop the part from flying off the shaft when it comes loose.

Pullers of this type should be tightened gradually until moderate pressure is applied to the part being removed.

> **Caution:** *The puller bolt should never be tightened excessively or damage will occur!*

Once it's under pressure, try to jar the component loose by striking the puller bolt head with a hammer. If this doesn't work, tighten the bolt a little more and repeat the procedure. The component should come off the shaft with a distinctive 'pop'. The puller can then be detached, the nut removed from the shaft (if applicable) and the part pulled off.

If the above approach doesn't work, it's time to stop and reconsider what you're doing. Proceed with caution – at some point a decision must be made whether it's wise to continue applying pressure in this manner. If the component is unusually tight, something will probably break before it comes off. If you find yourself in this situation, try applying penetrating oil around the joint and leaving it overnight, with the puller in place and tightened securely. In some cases, the taper will separate and the problem will resolve itself by the next morning.

If you have the necessary equipment, are skilled in its use and take the necessary safety precautions, you can try heating the component with a propane or gas welding torch. This can be a good way to release a stubborn part, but isn't recommended unless you have experience doing it.

> **Caution:** *This approach should be used with extreme caution on a flywheel – the heat can easily demagnetize it or cause damage to the coil windings.*

The heat should be applied to the hub area to the component to be removed, keeping the flame moving to avoid uneven heating and the risk of distortion. Keep pressure applied with the puller and make sure you're able to deal with the resulting hot component and the puller jaws if it does come free (wear gloves to protect your hands). Be very careful to keep the flame away from aluminum parts.

If all rational methods fail, don't be afraid to give up an attempt to remove something; it's cheaper than repairing a badly damaged engine. Either buy or borrow the correct tool or take the engine to a dealer and ask him to remove the part for you.

Drawbolts

A simple drawbolt extractor is easy to make and invaluable in many situations. There are no standard, commercially

Workshop practice

available tools of this type; you simply make a tool to suit a particular application. You can use a drawbolt to pull out stubborn piston pins and to remove bearings and bushings.

To make up a drawbolt extractor, you'll need an assortment of threaded rods in various sizes (available at hardware stores), along with nuts to fit them. In addition, you'll need assorted washers, spacers and pieces of pipe. Don't forget to improvise where you can. A socket set can provide several sizes of spacers for short parts like bushings. For things like piston pins you'll usually need a longer piece of pipe.

Some typical drawbolt uses are shown in the accompanying illustration – they also reveal the order of assembly of the various pieces. The same arrangement, minus the spacer, can usually be used to install a new bushing or piston pin. Using the tool is quite simple – the main thing to watch out for is to make sure you get the bushing or pin square in the bore when it's installed. Lubricate the part being pressed into place, if appropriate.

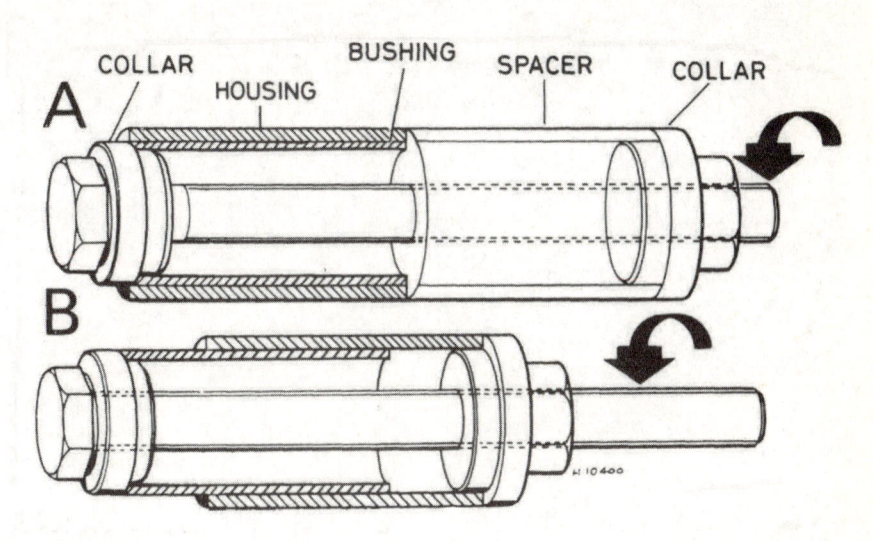

Typical drawbolt uses – in A, the nut is tightened to pull the collar and bushing into the large spacer; in B, the spacer is left out and the drawbolt is repositioned to install the new bushing

Pullers for use in blind holes

You may encounter bushings or bearings installed in blind holes in almost any engine; there are special pullers designed to deal with them as well. In the case of engine bearings, it's sometimes possible to remove them without a puller if you heat the engine or component evenly (in an oven) and tap it face down on a clean wooden surface to dislodge the bearing. If you use this method, be careful not to burn yourself when handling the heated components – wear heavy gloves! If a puller is needed, a slide-hammer with interchangeable tips is your best bet. They range from universal two or three jaw puller arrangements to special bearing pullers. Bearing pullers are hardened steel tubes with a flange around the bottom edge. The tube is split at several places, which allows a wedge to expand the tool once it's in place. The tool fits inside the bearing inner race and is tightened so the flange or lip is locked under the edge of the race.

A slide-hammer consists of a steel shaft with a stop at the upper end. The shaft carries a sliding weight, which is moved along the shaft until it strikes the stop. This allows the tool holding the bearing to drive it out of the bore *(see illustration)*. A bearing puller set is an expensive and infrequently-used piece of equipment – to avoid the expense of buying one, as mentioned in Chapter 1, take the engine to a dealer and have the bearings/bushings replaced.

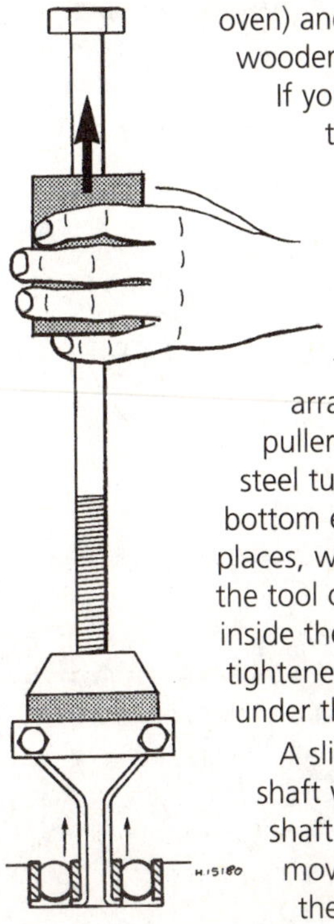

A slide hammer with special attachments can be used for removing bearings and bushings from blind holes

Precision measurements

During any overhaul or major repair job, you'll need certain precision measuring devices to determine the amount of wear that has occurred and whether or not a component can be reused in the rebuilt engine. In addition, some of the more basic tools, like feeler gauges, are needed for routine service and tune-up work. In this section we'll look at the most commonly-needed tools, starting with those that are considered essential, and working up to more specialized and expensive items. Some of them, such as vernier calipers and micrometers, are specialized pieces of equipment, but – unless you have someone else do the measuring for you – no substitutes are available.

Feeler gauges

These are an essential purchase for work on almost any machine. If it's a four-stroke, or has contact breaker points, you'll need feeler gauges to check/set the valve or contact breaker point clearances.

Feeler gauges normally come in sets. In the smaller sets, different feeler gauges must be combined to make up thicknesses not included separately. Larger sets have a wider range of sizes to avoid this problem. Feeler gauges are available in both imperial and metric sizes; they're usually

Chapter 2

Feeler gauges are usually marked with inch and metric equivalents

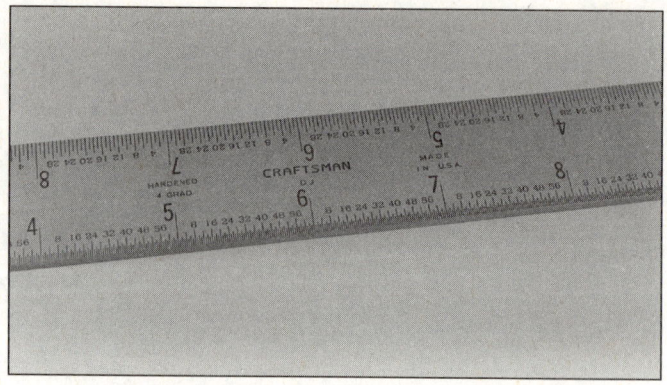

A steel rule will come in handy in any workshop – if it's a good-quality tool, it can be used for checking engine components (like the cylinder head) for distortion

marked both ways *(see illustration)*. Blade-type feeler gauges are thin steel strips and are the best choice for most purposes. There are also wire-type feeler gauges, which may be preferable in some circumstances.

You'll need feeler gauges whenever you have to make an accurate measurement of a small gap (typical applications are checking valve clearances on four-stroke engines and endplay in crankshafts or camshafts). You can also use feeler gauges when checking for distortion of gasket surfaces. The cover or casting is placed, gasket surface down, on a flat plate and any gap (which indicates distortion) can be measured directly with feeler gauges.

To measure a gap with feeler gauges, slide progressively thicker blades into the gap until you find the size that fits with a slight drag as it's moved back-and-forth.

Rulers

A basic steel rule is another essential workshop item. It can be used for measurements and layout work and as a straightedge for checking warpage of gasket surfaces *(see illustration)*. Buy the best quality tool you can afford and keep it out of your tool box or it'll soon get bent or damaged.

Dial indicators (DTI)

The dial gauge, or dial test indicator (DTI) as it's more commonly known, consists of a short stem attached to a clock-type dial capable of indicating small amounts of movement very accurately (generally in 0.025 mm or 1/1000-inch increments). These test instruments are generally useful for checking runout in shafts and other rotating components. The gauge is attached to a holder or bracket and the stem positioned so it rests on the shaft being checked. The rotating face of the dial is set to zero in relation to the pointer, the shaft is turned and the movement of the needle noted.

Vernier calipers

Although not strictly essential for routine work, a vernier caliper is a good investment in any workshop (if you're willing to learn how to read it accurately). The tool allows for fairly precise internal and external measurements, up to a maximum of about 150 mm or 6-inches or so. The object to be measured is positioned inside the external jaws – or outside the internal jaws – and the size is read off the main scale *(see illustration)*. The vernier scale allows it to be narrowed down even more, to about 0.025 mm or 1/1000-inch. A vernier caliper allows reasonably precise measurements of a wide variety of objects, so it's a versatile piece of equipment. Even though it lacks the absolute accuracy of a micrometer, it's much cheaper to buy and can be used in more ways.

Micrometers

The micrometer is the most accurate measuring tool likely to be needed in the home workshop, and you could successfully argue that the cost of the tool, weighed against

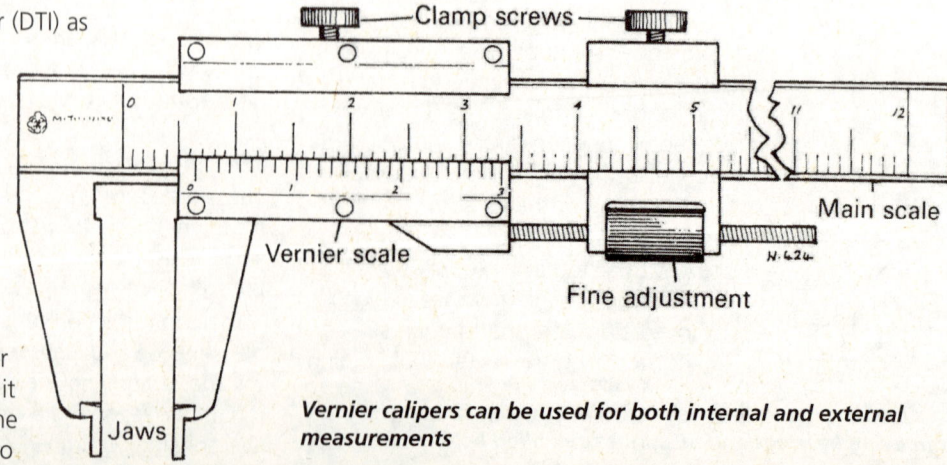

Vernier calipers can be used for both internal and external measurements

Workshop practice

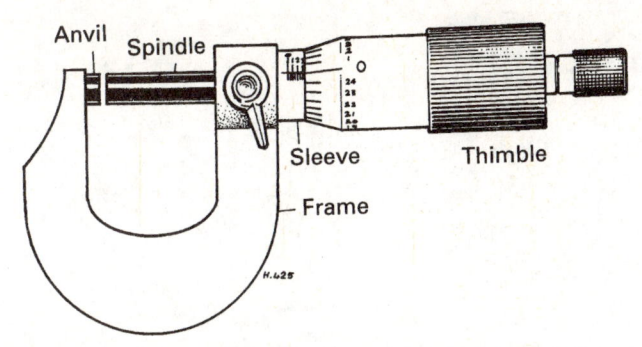

Micrometers, though expensive, are very accurate and almost indispensable when checking engine parts for wear

occasional use, make it an unaffordable luxury. This is particularly true since individual micrometers are limited to measurements in 25 mm (1-inch) increments and you would need a set of two or three micrometers to be completely prepared for any measuring job. The basic outside micrometer consists of a U-shaped metal frame covering a 25 mm (1-inch) size range. At one end is a precision ground stop, called the anvil, while at the other end is an adjustable stop called the spindle (see illustration). The spindle is moved in-or-out of the frame on a very precise, fine thread by a calibrated thimble, usually incorporating a ratchet to prevent damage to the threads. In use, the spindle is turned very carefully until the object to be measured is gripped very lightly between the anvil and spindle. A calibrated line on the fixed sleeve below the spindle indicates the rough size (base figure), while a more accurate measurement (down to 0.025 mm or 1/1000-inch) is calculated by adding an additional number indicated on the thimble scale to the base figure.

Micrometers are available in a wide range of sizes, starting with 0-25 mm (0-1 inch) (for small engine repair, anything over 50-75 mm or 2-3 inch is useless). There are also versions called inside micrometers, designed for making internal measurements such as cylinder bore sizes. Small hole gauges and telescoping gauges can be used along with outside micrometers to avoid the need for them (see illustrations).

All micrometers are precision instruments and easily damaged if misused or stored with other tools. They also require regular checks and calibration to maintain their accuracy. Given the fragile nature and high cost of these tools, as a general rule you should make do without them until you know for sure there's a definite need for them.

Basic maintenance and repair techniques

General repair hints

Although it was mentioned in the Environmental safety section, it's worth repeating here – sometimes waste oil, drained from the engine during normal maintenance or repairs, presents a disposal problem. To avoid pouring oil on the ground or into the sewage system, pour it into large containers, seal them with caps and take them to an authorised disposal site or garage.

Keep a supply of old newspapers and clean rags available. Old towels are excellent for mopping up spills. Many mechanics use paper towels for most work because they're readily available and disposable. To help keep the area under the engine or equipment clean, a large cardboard box can be cut open and flattened to protect the garage or workshop floor.

Always clean an engine before attempting to fix or service it. You can remove most of the dirt and grime from an

Note: It is antisocial and illegal to dump oil down the drain. To find the location of your local oil recycling bank, call this number free.

When used in conjunction with a small hole gauge . . .

. . . or a telescoping gauge, a micrometer can also make internal measurements – valve guide and cylinder bore checks are two typical examples

Chapter 2

Degreasers, which are normally sprayed on and rinsed off with water or solvent, are widely available at motor factors/car accessory shops and will make any maintenance or repair job easier and less frustrating

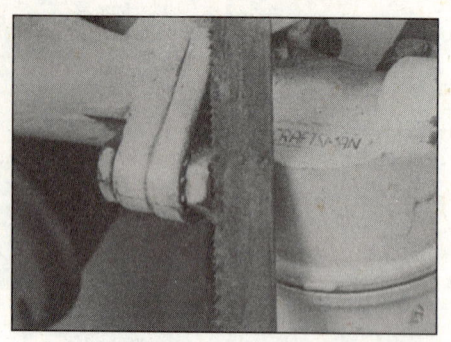

To remove a seized or rounded-off nut, use a hacksaw to saw off one side, then open the nut with a chisel or turn it with self-locking pliers

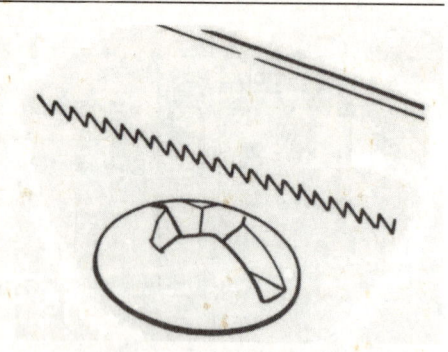

A hacksaw can be used to make a slot in a damaged Phillips screw head so it can be removed with a standard screwdriver

engine with an aerosol degreaser *(see illustration)* before removing many parts. This makes the repair job much easier and more pleasant and will reduce the possibility of getting abrasive dirt particles inside the engine.

Lay parts out in the order of disassembly and keep them in order during the cleaning and inspection procedures. This will help ensure correct reassembly. Another good practice is to draw a sketch of an assembly before or while you take it apart. Then if the parts get mixed up, you'll have a guide to follow when putting them together again.

When working on an engine, look for conditions that may cause future trouble. Check for unusual wear and damage. You may be able to prevent future problems by making an adjustment or repairing a part before it fails.

Fasteners

Fasteners, basically, are nuts, bolts and screws used to hold two or more parts together. There are a few things to keep in mind when working with fasteners. Many of them require a locking device of some type (either a lock washer, locknut, locking tab or thread locking fluid). All fasteners should be clean and straight with undamaged threads and sharp corners on the hex-head where the spanner fits. Develop the habit of replacing damaged nuts and bolts with new ones.

Rusted nuts or bolts should be treated with penetrating oil to make removal easier and help prevent breaking off the fastener. After applying the penetrating oil, let it soak in for a few minutes before trying to loosen the nut or bolt. Badly rusted fasteners may have to be chiselled off, sawn off with a hacksaw, or removed using a special nut splitter, available from a tool suppliers or hardware store *(see illustration)*. If you mess up the recess in a Phillips/Posi-drive screw head, make a slot in it with a hacksaw blade so a standard screwdriver can be used to remove it *(see illustration)*. The same holds true for slotted screws – if you deform the slot, use a hacksaw to enlarge or deepen it and try again. It was mentioned in the tool section, but it's worth repeating here – when using a Phillips screwdriver, if the screw is extremely tight and the tip tends to back out of the recess rather than turn the screw, apply a small amount of valve lapping compound to the screwdriver tip so it'll grip better.

Flat washers and lock washers, when removed from an assembly, should always be replaced in their original locations. Discard damaged washers and replace them with new ones. Always use a flat washer between a lock washer and any soft metal surface (such as aluminium), thin sheet metal or plastic. Special locknuts can only be used once or twice before they lose their locking ability and must be replaced.

If a bolt or stud breaks off in an assembly, it can be drilled out and removed with a special tool called a screw extractor. Broken fastener removal and thread repairs are covered later in this chapter. If you don't have the tools or don't want to do it yourself, most small engine dealers and repair shops – as well as automotive machine shops – can perform these tasks.

Tightening sequences and procedures

When threaded fasteners are tightened, they're often tightened to a specific torque value (torque is basically a twisting force). Over-tightening the fastener can weaken it and cause it to break, while under-tightening can cause it to eventually come loose from engine vibration. Important fasteners, depending on the material they're made of, the diameter of the thread and, in the case of bolts, the material they're threaded into, have specific torque values, which are noted in the Specifications at the beginning of each chapter or in the text. Be sure to follow the torque recommendations closely. For fasteners not requiring a specific torque, use common sense when tightening them.

Fasteners laid out in a pattern (such as cylinder head bolts) must be loosened and tightened in a sequence to avoid warping the component. Initially, the bolts should go in finger-tight only. Next, they should be tightened 1/2-turn each, in a criss-cross or diagonal pattern. After each one has been tightened 1/2-turn, return to the first one and tighten each of them 1/4-turn at a time until each fastener has been tightened to the proper torque. To loosen the fasteners the procedure can be reversed.

Workshop practice

Disassembly sequence

Engine disassembly should be done slowly and deliberately to make sure the parts go back together properly during reassembly. Always keep track of the sequence parts are removed in. Note special characteristics or marks on parts that can be installed more than one way. It's good idea to lay the disassembled parts out on a clean surface in the order they were removed. As mentioned before, it may also be helpful to make sketches or take instant photos of components before removal.

When removing fasteners from a component, keep track of their locations. Sometimes threading a bolt back in a part, or putting the washers and nut back on a stud, can prevent mix-ups later. If nuts and bolts can't be returned to their original locations, they should be kept in a compartmented box or a series of small boxes. A cupcake or muffin tin is ideal for this purpose, since each cavity can hold the bolts and nuts from a particular area or sub-assembly. A pan of this type is especially helpful when working on components with very small parts (such as the carburetor and valve train). The cavities can be marked with a felt-tip pen or tape to identify the contents.

Gasket sealing surfaces

Gaskets are used to seal the mating surfaces between components and keep lubricants, fuel, vacuum or pressure contained in an assembly.

Gaskets are often coated with a liquid or paste-type gasket sealant before assembly. Age, heat and pressure can sometimes cause the two parts to stick together so tightly they're very difficult to separate. In most cases, the part can be loosened by striking it with a soft-face hammer near the joint. A regular hammer can be used if a block of wood is placed between the hammer and part.

> **Caution:** *Do not hammer on cast parts or parts that could be easily damaged.*

With any particularly stubborn part, always recheck to make sure all fasteners have been removed.

Avoid using a screwdriver or bar to prise components apart, as they can easily damage the gasket sealing surfaces of the parts (which must remain smooth). If prising is absolutely necessary, use a piece of wood, but keep in mind that extra clean-up will be necessary if the wood splinters.

After the parts are separated, the old gasket must be carefully scraped off and the engine surfaces cleaned. Stubborn gasket material can be soaked with gasket removal solvent (available in aerosol cans) to soften it so it can be easily removed. Gasket scrapers are widely available – just be careful not to gouge the seating surfaces if you use one. Some gaskets can be removed with a wire brush, but regardless of the method used, the mating surfaces must be left clean and smooth. If the gasket surface is scratched or gouged, then a gasket sealant thick enough to fill scratches should be used during reassembly of the components. For most applications, non-drying (or semi-drying) gasket sealant is best.

How to remove broken bolts and repair stripped threads

Removing broken-off bolts

If a bolt breaks off in the hole, a drill, drill bit and screw extractor will be required to remove it. First select the screw extractor needed for the job (based on the bolt size).

Before attempting to remove a broken-off bolt, apply penetrating oil and let it soak in for a while

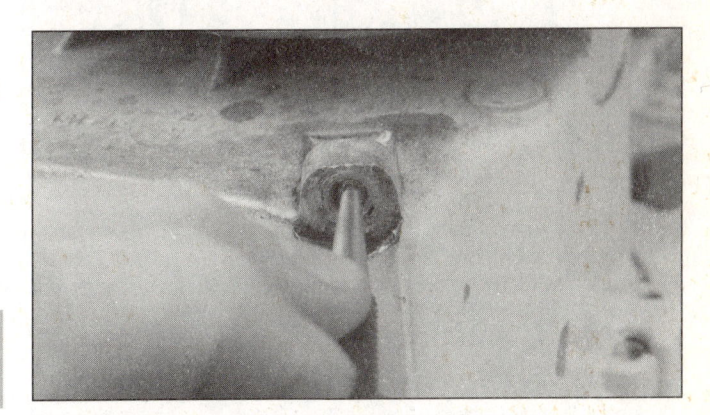

Use a centre punch to make an indentation as close to the centre of the bolt as you can

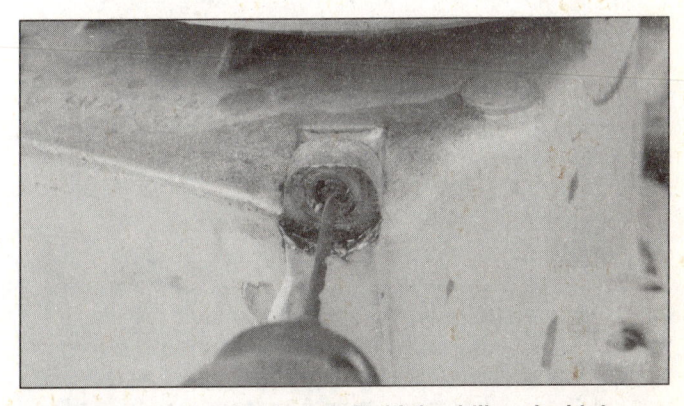

Carefully drill a hole in the bolt (hold the drill so the bit is parallel to the bolt) – the bit should be about two-thirds the diameter of the bolt and the hole should be as deep as possible without going through the bolt

2•25

Chapter 2

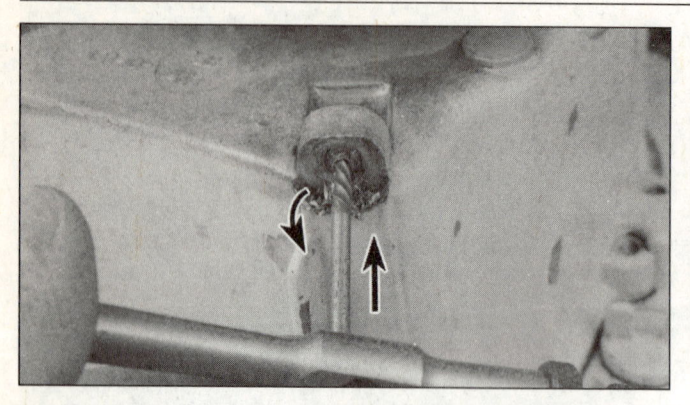

Tap the screw extractor into the hole and turn it with a die stock or adjustable spanner – keep pressure on the extractor so it doesn't turn in the hole instead of moving the bolt

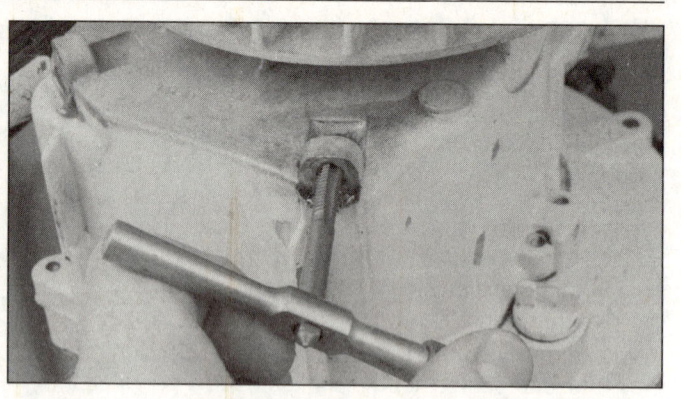

If you have one of the right size, run a tap into the hole after the bolt is out to clean up the threads and remove any rust or corrosion

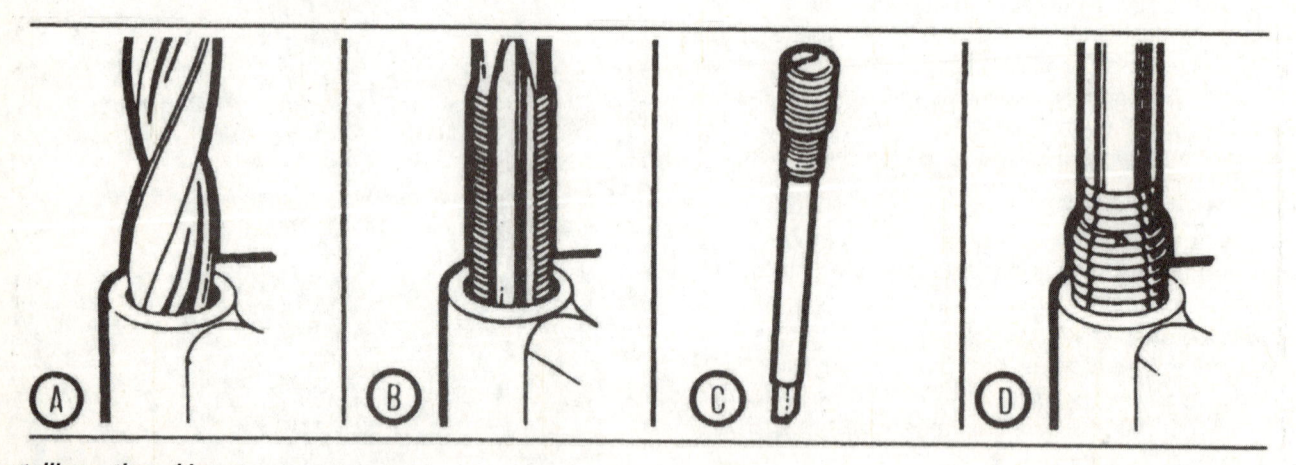

Installing a thread insert
A Drill out the hole to remove the old threads (this isn't required with all insert brands)
B Use a tap to cut new threads in the hole (the tap is included with some thread repair kits)
C Attach the insert to the installation tool (included with the kit)
D Screw the insert into the newly-threaded hole (when it's flush with the top of the hole, break off the drive tang and remove the tool)

Repairing stripped threads

If the thread isn't totally ruined, a tap or die can be used to clean it up so the fastener can be re-used. If the nut or bolt is a standard size, or an extremely important fastener like a head bolt or flywheel nut, don't worry about salvaging it – buy and install a new one. Remember, if a bolt is stripped, the threads in the bolt hole may also be damaged. **Note:** *Always use thread locking fluid on the threads of a restored nut or bolt when it's reinstalled and tighten it carefully to avoid further damage.*

If the thread in a bolt hole is completely stripped or seriously damaged, retapping may not work. In such cases a thread insert will be needed. The most commonly available inserts require drilling out the hole and cutting an oversize thread with a special tap. The resulting new thread is then reduced to the original size by installing a stainless steel wire insert in the threaded hole *(see illustration)*. This allows the original bolts or stud to be reinstalled *(see illustration)*. Heli-Coil thread inserts are the most common and sets with the required tap, several inserts, an installation tool (mandrel) for common thread sizes and comprehensive instructions are available.

Thread inserts look like springs prior to installation and have a small drive tang at the lower end. The thread insert is attached to a special mandrel and the tang engages in a slot in the end of the tool. The insert is screwed into the hole until the upper end is flush with or slightly below the

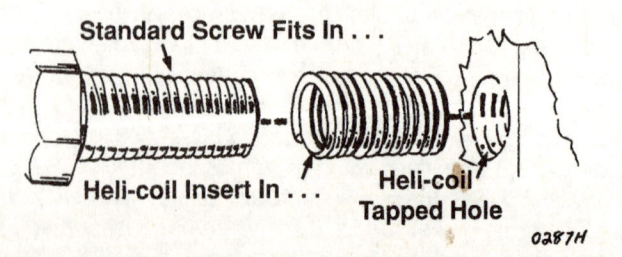

The thread insert allows the original fastener to be used in the repaired hole

Workshop practice

surface. Once in position, the drive tang is broken off, leaving the insert locked in place. If the drive tang doesn't break off when backing out the mandrel, use a pin punch or needle-nose pliers to snap it off.

This type of repair is a good way to reclaim badly worn or stripped threads in aluminum parts (very common in small engines). The new thread formed by the stainless steel insert is permanent and more durable than the original. In some cases, the original hole doesn't have to be enlarged prior to retapping, making the repair quick and simple to carry out. The only drawback for the home workshop is the high cost of purchasing a range of taps and inserts. The taps needed for thread inserts are not standard sizes – they're made specially for use with each insert size. The inserts aren't expensive individually, but stocking up on them in each size that could be required on a small engine is probably too expensive for most home workshops.

Small engine lubricants and chemicals

A number of lubricants and chemicals are required for small engine maintenance and repair. They include a wide variety of products ranging from cleaning solvents and degreasers to lubricants and penetrating oil.

> **Caution:** Always follow the directions and heed the precautions and warnings printed on the containers of lubricants and chemicals.

Carburettor cleaner is a strong solvent used for cleaning carburettors, and it may leave a slight oily residue. It isn't normally needed for small engine carburettors, but if deposits are heavy it will work faster and more effectively than an ordinary solvent.

Silicone-based lubricants are used to protect rubber parts such as hoses and grommets.

Multi-purpose grease *(see illustration)* is an all purpose lubricant used wherever grease is more practical than a liquid lubricant such as oil. Some multi-purpose grease is coloured white and specially formulated to be more resistant to water than ordinary grease.

Motor oil, of course, is the lubricant specially formulated for use in an engine. It normally contains a wide variety of additives to prevent corrosion and reduce foaming and wear. Motor oil comes in various weights (viscosity ratings) from 5 to 80. The recommended weight of the oil depends on the seasonal temperature and the demands on the engine. Light oil is used in cold climates and under light load conditions; heavy oil is used in hot climates and where high loads are encountered. Multi-viscosity oils are designed to have characteristics of both light and heavy oils and are available in a number of weights from 5W-20 to 20W-50. Be sure to follow the engine manufacturer's recommendations.

Multi-purpose grease

Petrol additives perform several functions, depending on their chemical make-up. They usually contain solvents that help dissolve gum and varnish that build up on carburetor and intake parts. They also serve to break down carbon deposits that form on the inside surfaces of the combustion chambers. Some types contain upper cylinder lubricants for valves and piston rings. For small engine use, a useful additive (if available) is a petrol stabiliser, used when equipment is stored for long periods.

Degreasers are heavy duty solvents used to remove grease and grime that may accumulate on engine and machinery. They can be sprayed or brushed on and, depending on the type, are rinsed off with either water or solvent.

Solvents are used alone or in combination with degreasers to clean parts during repairs and overhauls. The home mechanic should use only solvents that are non-flammable and that don't produce irritating fumes.

Gasket sealants *(see illustration)* may be used in conjunction with gaskets, to improve their sealing capabilities, or alone, to seal metal-to-metal joints. Many

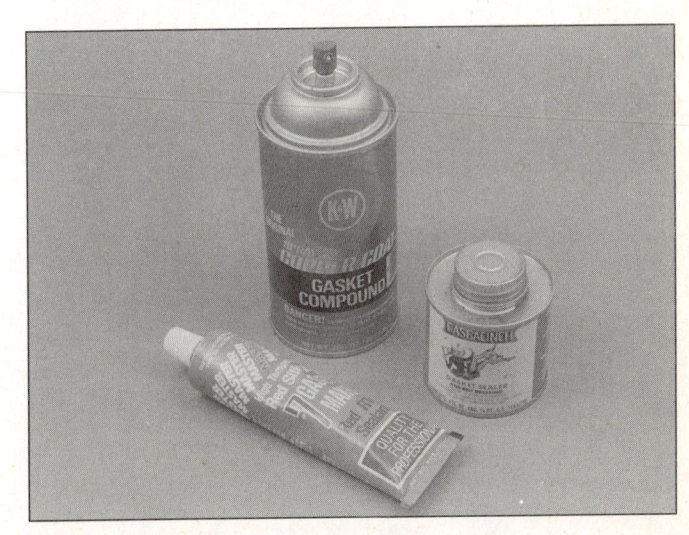

Sealants needed for small engine repair work

2•27

Chapter 2

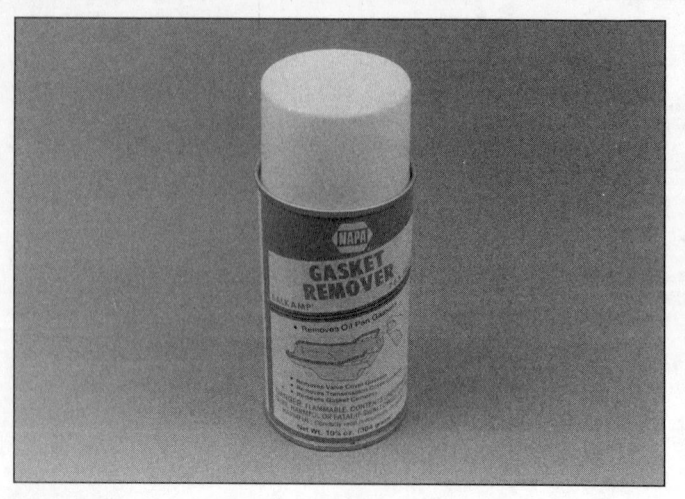

Aerosol gasket remover

Thread locking fluid

gasket sealants can withstand extreme heat, some are impervious to petrol and lubricants, while others are capable of filling and sealing cavities. Depending on the intended use, gasket sealants either dry hard or stay relatively soft and pliable. They're usually applied by hand, with a brush, or are sprayed on the gasket sealing surfaces.

Gasket/sealant removal solvents *(see illustration)* are available at motor factors, and are helpful when removing gaskets that are baked on, or stuck to, engine components. They're usually powerful chemicals, and should be used with care.

Thread locking fluid *(see illustration)* is an adhesive compound that prevents threaded fasteners from loosening because of vibration. It's available in a variety of types for different applications.

Moisture dispersants *(see illustration)* are usually sprays that can be used to dry out ignition system components and wire connections. Some types are also very good solvents and lubricants for cables and other components.

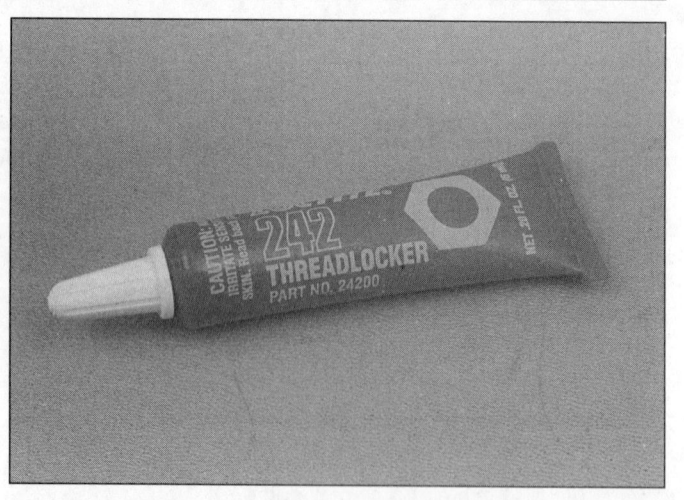

WD-40 is a good moisture dispersant, solvent and lubricant

Troubleshooting 3

How an engine works
Introduction to troubleshooting

Troubleshooting a four-stroke engine
Troubleshooting a two-stroke engine

How an engine works

All small, air-cooled, petrol engines are internal-combustion engines much like the ones used in cars, trucks and motorcycles. The term 'internal-combustion' is used because energy for turning the crankshaft is developed inside the engine.

This happens when the fuel/air mixture is burned inside a confined space called a combustion chamber (or cylinder). Because of the heat produced, the mixture expands, which then forces the piston to move. The piston is connected to the crankshaft, which changes linear motion into rotary motion. The crankshaft may be oriented vertically or horizontally, depending on the engine application. The crankshaft is situated at a right angle to the cylinder bore.

To supply power – motion – to the crankshaft, a series of events must occur. This series of events is called a combustion cycle. The events in the cycle are.

1 Intake of the fuel/air mixture into the cylinder
2 Compression of the fuel/air mixture
3 Ignition/expansion of the fuel/air mixture
4 Expulsion of the burned gases

The movement of the piston in one direction, either toward the crankshaft or away from it, is called a stroke. Some small engines complete a cycle during one revolution of the crankshaft (two strokes of the piston). Other types require two revolutions of the crankshaft (four strokes of the piston). In this manual, the shortened terms 'two-stroke' and 'four- stroke' are used in place of the technically correct terms 'two-stroke cycle' and 'four-stroke cycle.' The major differences between four-stroke and two-stroke engines are:

The number of power strokes per crankshaft revolution
The method of getting the fuel/air mixture into the combustion chamber and the burned gases out
The number of moving parts in the engine
The method used to lubricate the internal engine components

Four-stroke engines

As mentioned above, a four-stroke engine completes one combustion cycle during two revolutions of the crankshaft, or four strokes of the piston. This is due to the design of the engine and the way the fuel/air mixture is introduced into the cylinder. A camshaft, which is driven off the crankshaft, opens valves that allow the fuel/air mixture in and exhaust gases out of the engine. The valves are closed by spring pressure. The four strokes of the piston have been labelled to describe what happens during each one *(see illustration overleaf)*:

INTAKE STROKE – During the intake stroke, the piston moves down in the cylinder with the intake valve open. The fuel/air mixture is forced into the cylinder through the open intake valve. Near the end of the piston's movement, the intake valve closes, sealing off the combustion chamber.

COMPRESSION STROKE – The piston changes direction at the end of the intake stroke and begins to move up in the cylinder, which compresses and heats the fuel/air mixture.

POWER STROKE – As the piston reaches the end of the compression stroke, the ignition system fires the spark plug, which ignites the compressed fuel/air mixture in the combustion chamber. The piston changes direction again and moves down in the cylinder with great force produced by the burning/expanding gases. The connecting rod transfers the movement of the piston to the crankshaft, which changes the linear motion to rotary (turning) motion, which can be used to do work.

EXHAUST STROKE – When the piston reaches the end of the power stroke, it changes direction again and the exhaust valve opens. As the piston moves up in the cylinder, the exhaust gases are pushed out through the exhaust valve. When the piston reaches the end of the exhaust stroke, the cycle starts all over again.

Chapter 3

The four-stroke engine combustion cycle

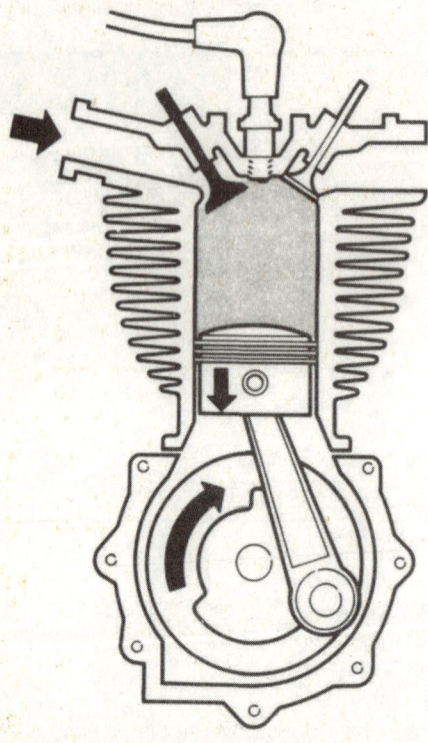

Induction: As the piston descends the inlet valve opens, allowing the fuel/air mixture to be drawn directly into the combustion chamber

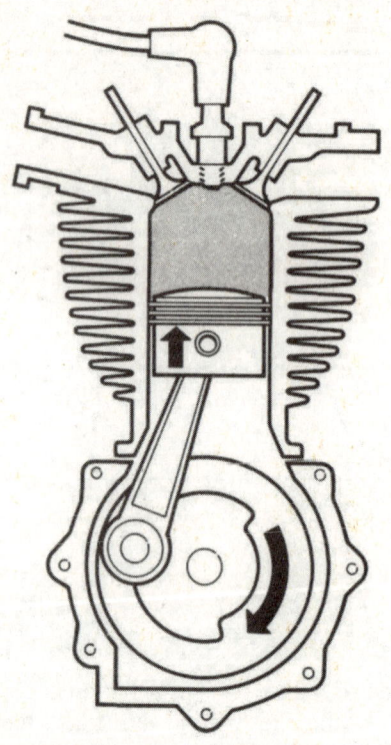

Compression: The piston starts to ascend with both valves closed. The mixture is compressed

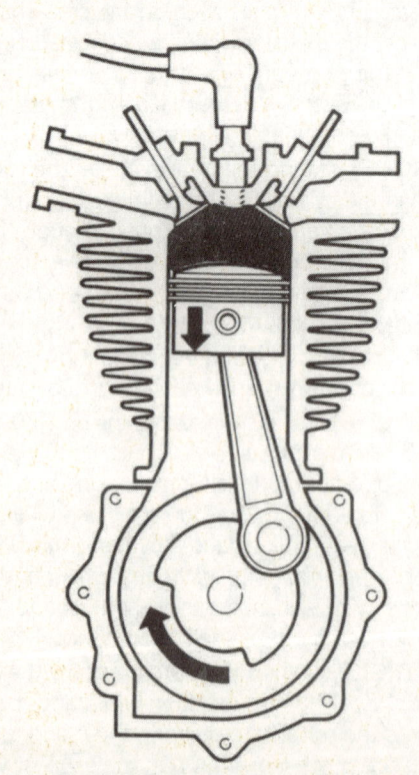

Ignition: The spark plug ignites the compressed mixture, forcing the piston down the bore

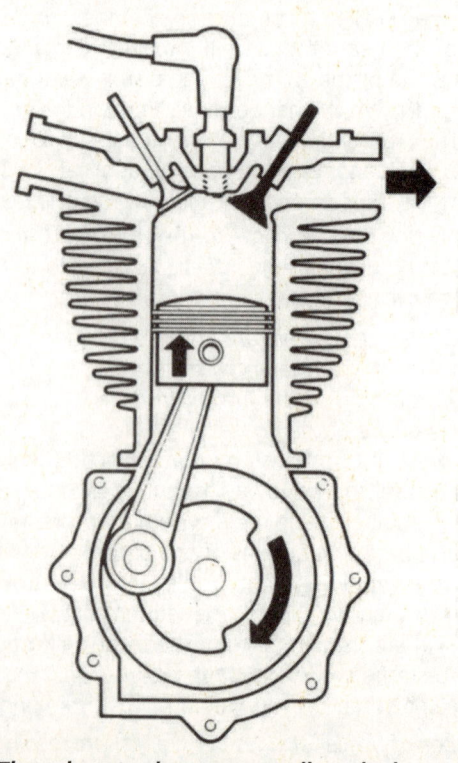

Exhaust: The exhaust valve opens to allow the burnt gases to be expelled through the exhaust port

Troubleshooting

Two-stroke engines

Two stroke engines have a slightly different design that doesn't require valves. Instead, openings called ports are used to route the fuel/air mixture to the cylinder. Also, the crankcase is used as a temporary storage area as the fuel mixture is on its way to the cylinder, so it must be leakproof. The piston serves to open and close off the ports to seal off the combustion chamber.

A two-stroke engine is designed to complete the same cycle described for a four-stroke engine, but it does it during one revolution of the crankshaft. The INTAKE and COMPRESSION strokes actually occur simultaneously, during one stroke of the piston, and so do the POWER and EXHAUST STROKES *(see illustration)*.

As the piston moves down in the cylinder, pushed by the burning/expanding gases, the fresh fuel/air charge in the crankcase is being pressurized slightly. Once the piston uncovers the exhaust port, the spent gases begin to exit the cylinder. Next, the piston uncovers the transfer ports and the fresh fuel/air charge begins to flow out of the crankcase, through the transfer ports and into the cylinder, helping to push out the exhaust gases. At the bottom of the stroke, the piston changes direction and begins to move up in the cylinder, sealing off the transfer and exhaust ports and compressing the fuel/air mixture in the cylinder. At the same time, the intake port (which may be sealed off by a one-way valve called a reed valve, disc valve or by the piston skirt) opens and more fuel/air mixture is forced into the crankcase;

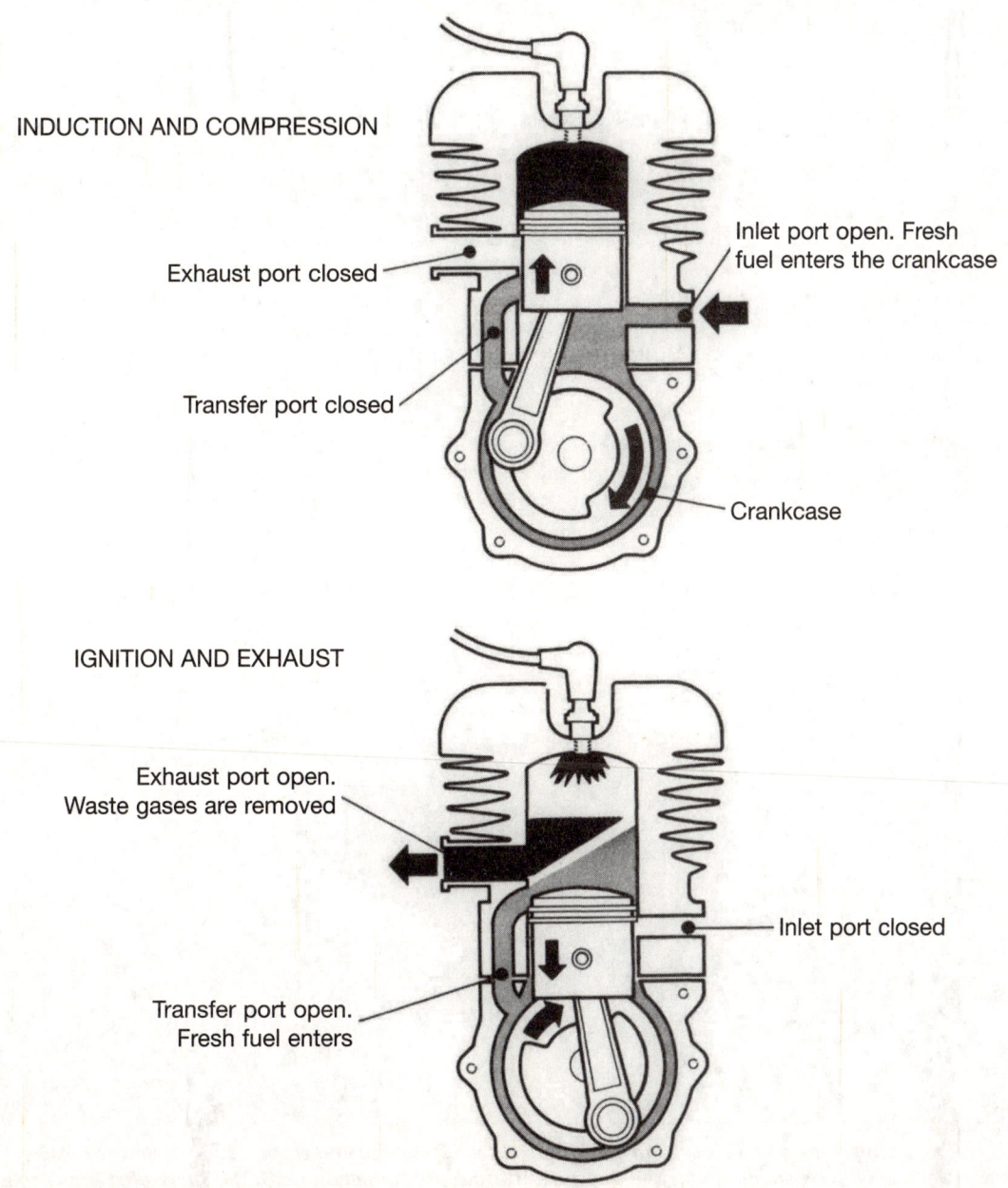

The two-stroke engine combustion cycle

Chapter 3

this is because a slight vacuum is created as the piston moves up in the cylinder. At the top of the piston's stroke, the spark plug fires, which ignites the compressed fuel/air mixture in the combustion chamber. The piston changes direction again and moves down in the cylinder with great force produced by the burning/expanding gases. This overlapping cycle is repeated continuously as the engine runs.

Since a two-stroke engine uses the crankcase for storing a reserve charge of fuel/air mixture, the crankcase can't be used as an oil reservoir for lubricating the engine. Instead, lubrication is supplied by a specific quantity of oil that's mixed with the petrol and circulated through the engine as it runs. Never put petrol in a two-stroke engine without mixing oil with it – the engine will overheat because of improper lubrication. It won't run very long before the piston and bearings will overheat, score and seize!

The three things an engine needs to run

Any engine, whether it's a two or four-stroke, must have three essential elements to run:

1 *Fuel and air mixed together in the correct proportions*
2 *Compression of the fuel/air mixture*
3 *Ignition at the right time*

If any one of these three elements is missing, the engine simply will not run. Troubleshooting is the process of determining which one is missing and why. Once you figure this out, repairs are done to restore the missing element.

Introduction to trouble-shooting

Possible causes for various engine problems and recommendations for correcting them are covered in detail in separate sections for two and four-stroke engines in this chapter. **Note:** *What appears to be an engine malfunction may be a problem in the power equipment rather than the engine.*

You won't find any absolutely foolproof troubleshooting procedures for small engines that won't start and run properly. Some symptoms can be so obscure that it takes a professional mechanic to spot the problem. However, in general, malfunctioning engines have symptoms that are relatively easy to identify. By thoroughly checking the problem in an orderly manner, as outlined in this chapter, you usually will be able to find the problem and save a trip to the repair workshop.

Where to start

When the cause of a malfunction isn't obvious, check the compression, ignition and carburettor, in that order, first (remember the three elements required for an engine to run?). This check, which must be done in a systematic manner, will only take a few minutes. It's the quickest and surest way to find out what the problem is. It will also reveal possible causes of future problems, which can be corrected at the same time. The procedure is basically the same for all engines.

To check the compression . . .

Remove the spark plug and earth the plug wire on the engine, then seal off the plug hole with your thumb (*see illustration*). Operate the starter – if the compression pressure blows your thumb off the hole, the compression is adequate for the engine to run; be careful not to touch the plug wire as this is done – you'll get quite a jolt if you do! Another way to check the compression with the spark plug in place is to remove the cooling shroud/recoil starter mechanism and spin the flywheel in reverse (anti-clockwise) (*see illustration*). The flywheel should rebound (change directions) sharply; if it does, the compression is adequate for the engine to run.

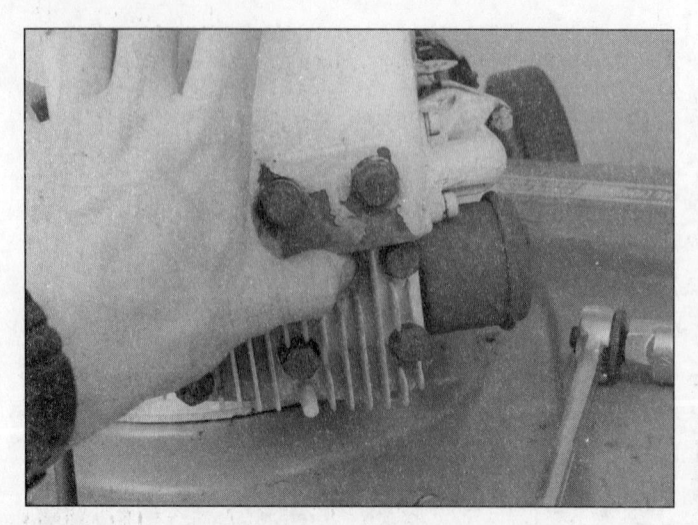

As a general rule, if the engine's compression will blow your thumb off the spark plug hole, it should be adequate for the engine to run

If the recoil starter/cooling shroud is off, spin the flywheel in an anti-clockwise direction (with the spark plug in place) and see if it rebounds back in response to engine compression

Troubleshooting

If the compression is low, it may be due to:
1. *Loose spark plug*
2. *Loose cylinder head bolts*
3. *Blown head gasket*
4. *Damaged valves/valve seats (four-stroke engine only)*
5. *Insufficient valve tappet clearance (four-stroke engine only)*
6. *Warped cylinder head*
7. *Bent valve stem(s) (four- stroke engine only)*
8. *Worn cylinder bore and/or piston rings*
9. *Broken connecting rod or piston*

To check the ignition system

Remove the spark plug, reconnect the HT lead, and earth the threaded end on the engine (see illustration), then operate the starter. If bright blue, well-defined sparks occur at the plug electrodes, the ignition system is functioning properly. **Note:** *Sparks produced by electronic (CDI) ignition systems may not last very long, so be sure to pull vigorously on the recoil starter handle. It may also help to work in the shade so the sparks are easier to see.* If sparks aren't produced, or if they're intermittent, attach a spark tester to the plug wire (see illustration) and earth the tester on the engine, then operate the starter so the engine turns over rapidly. If bright blue, well-defined sparks are produced at the tester gap (4.0 mm or 3/16-inch wide), you can assume the ignition system is functioning properly – try a new spark plug and see if the engine will start and run.

If sparks do not occur, it may be due to:
1. *A sheared flywheel key*
2. *Incorrect contact breaker point gap**
3. *Dirty or burned contact breaker points**
4. *Coil failure/electronic ignition failure*
5. *Incorrect armature air gap*
6. *Worn bearings and/or crankshaft on flywheel side only*
7. *Contact breaker point plunger stuck or worn***
8. *Shorted ground wire (if equipped)*
9. *Shorted stop switch (if equipped)*
10. *Condenser failure**
11. *Malfunctioning starter interlock system*
12. *Defective spark plug wire*

* *Engines with ignition points only*
***Briggs & Stratton engines with ignition points only*

If the engine runs but misses during operation, a quick check to determine if the ignition system is or is not at fault can be made by attaching a spark tester between the plug wire and the spark plug. An ignition system misfire will be apparent when watching the tester (it should spark continually). **Note:** *When conducting this test on Magnamatic equipped Briggs & Stratton engines, use a new spark plug with the gap set to 1.5 mm (0.060-inch) in place of the old plug.*

To check the carburettor . . .

Before proceeding, be sure the fuel tank is refilled with fresh, clean petrol (or petrol/oil mixed as required), the fuel shut-off valve is open (if equipped) and fuel flows freely through the fuel line. Check/adjust the mixture adjusting screw (if equipped) and make sure it's open and make sure the choke closes completely (see illustration). If the engine won't start,

To check for spark, remove the plug and earth it on the engine with the wire attached, then operate the starter – if sparks occur at the plug, the ignition system is okay; if no sparks occur, the plug may be worn, so don't automatically condemn the ignition system

A spark tester with the gap set at about 4.0 mm (3/16-inch) is the best tool to use for checking the ignition system – if it will produce a spark strong enough to jump the tester gap, it's adequate for the engine to run

The choke must be closed when starting the engine cold – if it isn't closing, free it up so it will (typical engine shown)

Chapter 3

remove and check the spark plug – if it's wet, it may be due to:
1 Stuck choke
2 Overly-rich fuel mixture
3 Water in fuel
4 Inlet needle valve stuck open (not all carburettors)
5 Clogged silencer
6 Plugged crankcase breather
7 Too much oil in crankcase
8 Worn piston rings

If the spark plug is dry, check for:
1 Leaking carburettor mounting gaskets
2 Gummy or dirty carburettor internal parts
3 Inlet needle valve stuck shut (not all carburettors)
4 Damaged or deteriorated rubber diaphragms in carburettor (not all carburettors)
5 Plugged fuel line or filter (not all engines)

If the engine has good compression and spark, try priming it by carefully pouring petrol directly into the plug hole with a small funnel – if the engine starts, you have a fuel delivery problem to find and fix

Make sure the control cable (if used) is securely clamped to the engine so it doesn't slip when the control lever is moved (if the clamp is loose, tighten it and check the cable to see if it needs lubrication)

A simple check to determine if fuel is getting to the combustion chamber through the carburettor is to remove the spark plug and pour a small amount of petrol (about one teaspoonful) into the engine through the spark plug hole (this is called 'priming' the engine) *(see illustration)*. Reinstall the plug. If the engine fires a few times and then stops, look for the same conditions described under If the spark plug is dry.

Trouble-shooting a four-stroke engine

Most four-stroke engine problems will fall into one or more of the following categories:
1 Won't start
2 Hard to start/kicks back when starting
3 Stops suddenly
4 Lack of power/erratic operation
5 Excessive vibration
6 Noise
7 Engine smokes
8 Overheating
9 Excessive oil use

1 Won't start

Note: *When an engine won't start, it's usually because the controls are improperly set, the safety interlock devices are interrupting the ignition system or the ignition system is malfunctioning, although carburettor problems and low compression can also prevent an engine from starting (see the information under the heading 'Where to start' to rule out lack of compression as a cause).*

1 Make sure the controls are positioned properly.

Follow the control cable from the lever to the carburettor. The throttle should be all the way open and the choke should operate when the lever is set on START. As you move the control lever from START to FAST to STOP, the cable should be clamped so the throttle operates properly *(see illustration)*. The cable may be slipping in the clamp just enough to cause the throttle to malfunction and you might not see the slight movement.

Move the throttle to the open or START position with your fingers. You may have to move the control lever with your other hand to open the throttle.

If the engine now starts, let it run for several minutes, then pull the control lever back to STOP. If the engine slows down but doesn't stop, loosen the cable clamp with a screwdriver and pull the cable toward the control lever very slightly until the engine stops, then retighten the clamp. Start the engine again and run through the control positions. The engine should start, run slowly, run fast and stop when the lever is positioned next to the appropriate label on the control.

2 Make sure the tank is at least half full of fresh fuel and that fuel is reaching the carburettor (the line between the

Troubleshooting

tank and carburettor could be blocked, kinked or detached or the filter – if used – could be blocked).

3 Check the plug wire to make sure it's securely attached to the spark plug.

The terminal on the end of the spark plug wire can come loose and get corroded. Crimp the loop with a pair of pliers *(see illustration)* and remove corrosion with sandpaper, a wire brush or a round file. If necessary replace the sparkplug cap.

4 Check the spark plug to make sure it's tight.

5 Check the spark plug earth strap to make sure it's not malfunctioning.

Some engines have a metal strap that's used to short out the spark plug to stop the engine. If the engine has one, make sure it's not touching the plug.

6 If the engine has a fuel priming device, make sure it's working properly.

It should be pushed four or five times when the engine is cold to fill the carburettor. If the engine is hot, don't operate the primer – it may flood the carburettor. Instead, pull the starter handle several times with the control lever in the STOP position. This will help clear excess fuel out of the engine. Put the control lever on START and start the engine normally.

7 Make sure the grass catcher is properly installed.

Some lawnmowers have a safety switch for the grass catcher where it attaches to the mower housing. This device prevents the engine from starting until the grass catcher is properly installed. If the grass catcher isn't being used, make sure the chute is properly attached to the mower deck.

8 See if the petrol tank cap vent is clogged.

If the petrol tank vent is clogged, a vacuum will eventually form in the tank and prevent fuel from reaching the carburettor (the engine will act like it's out of petrol).

Remove the cap and check the gasket in it. Sometimes the space between the gasket and cap gets clogged with debris, shutting off the air supply to the tank. Check the hole(s) in the cap to make sure it's open *(see illustration)*. If you're not sure if the vent is open or not, leave the cap off and try to start the engine. If the engine runs, the cap vent is the problem. Either open the vent or install a new cap. DO NOT run the engine without a cap on the petrol tank.

9 Check the air filter to see if it's clean and make sure the gasket between the filter and carburettor is in good shape *(see illustration)*.

10 Check to see if the plug is firing (see *To check the ignition system.* in the section headed *Where to start*).

You can clean spark plugs, but a new one should be installed – they're not expensive and you can usually be sure the new plug is sound.

Every once in a while, a new plug will turn out to be faulty. If you install a new plug and the engine won't fire even though everything else seems to be okay, try another new plug or a spark tester.

Spark plug wires are always coming loose – crimp the terminal with a pair of pliers so it fits snugly on the plug tip

If the petrol tank cap vent is blocked, the engine will be starved of fuel until you remove the cap to see if there's petrol in the tank. Removing the cap will relieve the vacuum, and the engine will then start and run for a while before stalling again. Clear the tank cap vent, or install a new cap

If the air filter is dirty or clogged with debris, remove and clean it or install a new one – foam types and pleated paper types are the most common

Chapter 3

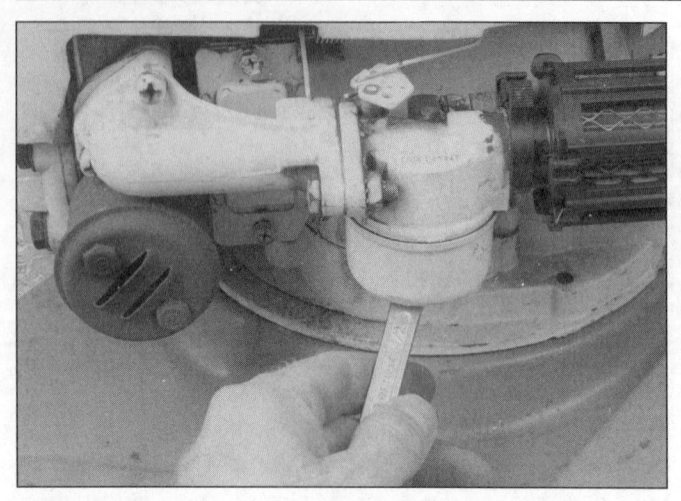

One way to check to make sure petrol is getting to the carburettor is to remove the float bowl (if used) – it's usually held in place with a nut on the bottom, which is hard to get at and easily damaged

Engines with an 'Auto-prime' carburettor often won't run because this fuel inlet gets clogged with dirt or sludge – clean it with a fine piece of wire and the engine should run fine

11 Make sure the plug wire is in good condition.
 Bend the wire by hand and look for cracks in the insulation. Also look for burned or melted insulation. If damage is noted, you may have to replace the ignition coil, since the wire usually is permanently attached to it.
12 See if the blade is loose – it must be tight on the shaft or adaptor.
13 If the equipment has a chain, drivebelt or belts, check to see if it's loose. A loose chain or belt, like a loose blade, can cause a backlash effect, which will work against engine cranking effort.
14 You may be trying to start the engine when it's under load.
 See if the equipment is disengaged when the engine is started, or, if engaged, doesn't create an unusual starting load.
15 Remove the float bowl (if fitted), and see if the carburettor is dirty or gummed up *(see illustration)*.

> **Caution:** *Shut off the fuel valve, or remove the tank, before detaching the float bowl – if you don't, petrol will leak out until the tank is empty!*

If there's dirt or sludge in the float bowl, the carburettor passages may be blocked. Remove the carburettor and clean it thoroughly. Some carburettors have a small spring-loaded valve on the bottom of the float bowl that's used to drain out sediment and water. Push up on it with a small screwdriver and let petrol run out until it looks clean (you'll see little droplets if water comes out)
Note: *Many Tecumseh engines are equipped with an 'Auto-prime' float carburettor. The fuel inlet on this type gets clogged easily by fuel residue, particularly if the engine isn't run for a long time. Suspect this in lawn mowers that are stored all winter without draining the petrol from the tank.*

Drain the fuel out of the tank or detach the tank from the engine and set it aside. Remove the float bowl and clean it out, then clear the fuel inlet with a very fine wire *(see illustration)*. Reinstall the float bowl and tank, add petrol and try to start the engine.

2 Hard to start/kicks back when starting

These problems are quite common and are usually caused by belts or chains that aren't disengaged when the engine is cranked or by a loose blade.

1 See if the blade is loose – it must be tight on the shaft or adaptor.
2 If the equipment has a chain, drive belt or belts, check to see if it's loose. A loose chain or belt, like a loose blade, can cause a backlash effect which will work against engine cranking effort.
3 You may be trying to start the engine when it's under load. See if the equipment is disengaged when the engine is started, or, if engaged, doesn't create a heavy starting load.
4 The recoil starter may not be operating properly.
5 The ignition timing may be incorrect.

3 Stops suddenly

1 Check the fuel tank to make sure it hasn't run dry.
2 Check the flywheel key to see if it has sheared off and check the condenser to see if it has shorted out.
 Sometimes when everything is running perfectly, the engine will stop suddenly and you won't be able to get it started again. If the problem isn't a empty fuel tank, this problem can usually be traced to one of two things:
A sheared-off flywheel key
A defective condenser (engines with contact breaker points only)

Troubleshooting

The flywheel key will shear if the equipment blade strikes an immovable object (this is to protect the crankshaft and other expensive engine components). It can happen without any indication to the equipment operator. The flywheel key is important for proper ignition timing – if it's damaged, the engine won't run.

The condenser (located under the flywheel) can stop working at any time without warning. Even brand new condensers can be faulty, so don't be fooled into thinking the problem is something else if the engine has new, or nearly new, ignition parts. Instructions for getting to the condenser are included in Chapter 4 (under contact breaker point renewal).

You can also check the flywheel key at the same time you check the condenser. It's a rectangular piece of soft metal that fits into a slot in the flywheel and crankshaft taper to index the flywheel to the crankshaft *(see illustration)*. As mentioned above, the metal is soft for a reason – when the blade strikes something hard, the key shears and releases the force on the crankshaft. This prevents damage to the crankshaft piston, valves, gears and other major (expensive) parts of the engine.

Replacement of the key is covered in each engine chapter (flywheel removal and installation).

3 Check the oil in the crankcase.

When you remove the oil check/fill cap, the engine may appear to be full but still need oil. Add more oil with a funnel until it runs out of the hole *(see illustration)*. If the engine has a dipstick, the safe level will be clearly indicated.

Start the engine. If it's noisy, the lack of lubrication has probably damaged the engine. It may have to be overhauled or replaced.

4 Check the fuel lines and filter (if used) to make sure they're clear.

5 See if the silencer/exhaust pipe is clogged.

A blocked exhaust system can stop the engine and damage it. So can a defective silencer. Remove the silencer and see if the engine will start and run.

6 Check the plug wire to make sure it's securely attached to the spark plug.

The terminal on the end of the spark plug wire can come loose and get corroded. Crimp the loop with a pair of pliers *(see illustration on page 3•7)* and remove corrosion with sandpaper, a wire brush or a round file.

7 Check the cable and linkage between the handle controls, throttle and governor to see if they're binding or if anything has come loose. Lubricate the cable with WD-40 if necessary *(see illustration)*.

4 Lack of power/erratic operation

These symptoms are usually caused by problems in the ignition system (especially on engines with contact breaker points), or by problems with the carburettor (particularly the idle adjustment).

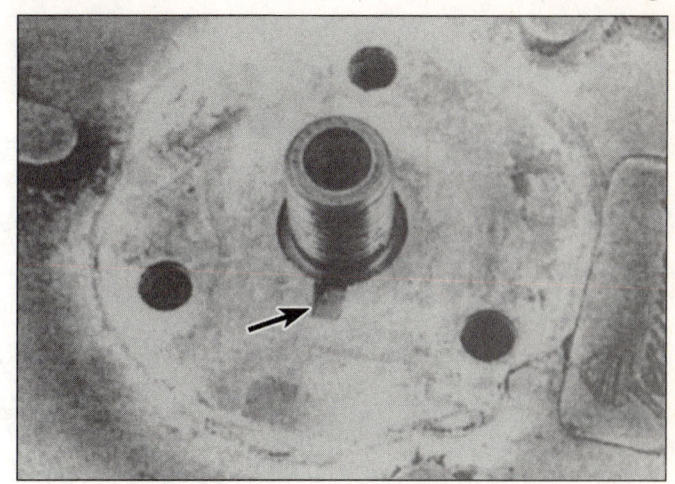

If the flywheel key (arrowed) is sheared, the ignition timing will be out and the engine won't run

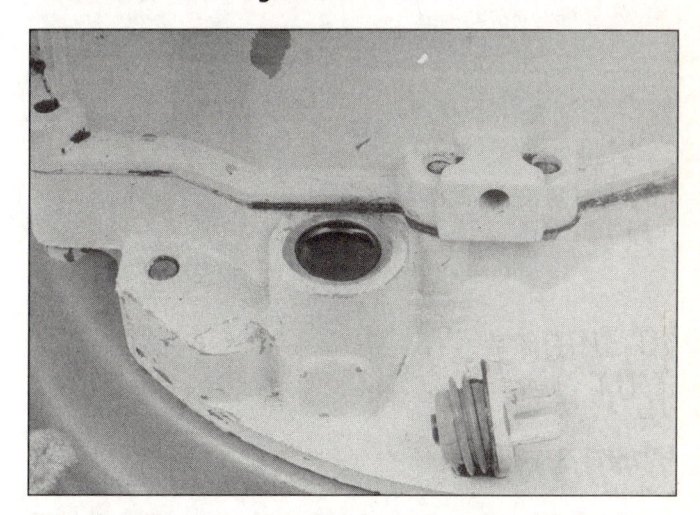

Even though you can see oil in the engine after the plug is removed, it must be at the very top of the hole or the crankcase will be dangerously low! – some engines have a dipstick with the safe level clearly marked on it

If the controls stick, lubricate the cable – from the top down – with WD-40 or a similar solvent/lubricant

Chapter 3

If the plug is covered with deposits, clean it with a wire brush, then file the electrode tips until they have sharp edges (this makes it easier for the ignition system to fire the plug when the engine is running)

Some carburettors have one or two adjusting screws for changing the fuel/air mixture – this one is typical of the types used on small engines

If the mixture screw tip is bent or worn, the correct adjustment will be difficult to maintain

1 Check the petrol in the tank to make sure it's fresh and doesn't have any water in it. Drain the tank and refill it with fresh petrol.
2 Check the flywheel key (see the section headed *Stops suddenly*).
3 Check the engine compression (see the section headed *Where to start*).
4 Check the plug wire to make sure it's securely attached to the spark plug.
   The terminal on the end of the spark plug wire can come loose and get corroded. Crimp the loop with a pair of pliers (see top illustration on page 3•7) and remove corrosion with sandpaper, a wire brush or a round file. If necessary, replace the spark plug cap.
5 Make sure the control lever is free and working properly (not stuck on any of the settings).
6 Make sure the air filter is clean *(see bottom illustration on page 3•7)*.
7 Remove the spark plug and check the gap and the base of the plug for dirt. Clean the electrodes with a wire brush and use a fine file to square the side electrode tip so any worn edges are sharp *(see illustration)*. **Note:** *As a general rule, the spark plug gap can be set at 0.6 mm (0.024 in).*
8 Check the carburettor mixture screw to see if it's out of adjustment. **Note:** *Some carburettors don't have any mixture screws, while others have one for either high-speed adjustments or low speed adjustments, but not both. Still others have one screw to adjust the fuel/air mixture at high speeds and another screw that controls the mixture at low speeds – if two screws are used, they must be adjusted separately.*
   The mixture screw is used to control the flow of fuel through the carburettor *(see illustration)*. If the screw is damaged or incorrectly adjusted, loss of power and erratic engine operation will result.
   Remove the mixture screw and check the tip – if it looks bent or a groove has been worn in the tapered portion, install a new one *(see illustration)*. Do not attempt to straighten it. If the O-ring on the screw is damaged or deteriorated, replace it before attempting to adjust the mixture
   If the screw isn't bent or worn, reinstall it and turn it in until it stops – tighten it with your fingers only, don't force it. Back it out about 1 ½ turns (anti-clockwise) *(see illustration)*. **Note:** *The actual factory-recommended number of turns out is different for each carburettor type, but the figure given here is an average for most engines.*

When turning the mixture screw, make small changes only and wait to see the effect on the engine (don't confuse the mixture screw with the idle speed screw, which acts on the throttle linkage in some manner)

Troubleshooting

Start the engine and turn the screw clockwise until the engine starts to slow down. This means the fuel mixture is too lean (not enough fuel). Slowly turn the screw out (anti-clockwise) until the engine begins to run smoothly. Keep going very slowly until the engine just begins to run rough again. Finally, turn the screw in again (clockwise) to a point about half-way between rough operation and smooth operation. This is the perfect setting.

If an idle (low-speed) mixture screw is used, adjust it in the same manner with the engine idling. After the low-speed mixture has been set, recheck the high-speed adjustment (if applicable) – it may be affected by the idle adjustment.

Some carburettors also have an idle speed adjusting screw that's used to open or close the throttle valve slightly to change the idle speed only, not the fuel/air mixture. Turning it will cause the engine to speed up or slow down.

9 Check to see if the engine is flooded.

Running equipment on hills and slopes can cause flooding. Flooding can also occur when the engine is cranked with the spark plug wire disconnected and when the mixture is too rich (when the carburettor mixture screw is out of adjustment).

Set the control lever to the STOP position. Pull the starter rope or crank the engine over several times. The closed throttle produces a high vacuum and opens the choke, which cleans excess fuel out of the engine. Start the engine.

If the engine continues to flood, adjust the mixture screws as outlined above. If this doesn't work, there is another alternative, but you must be very careful when doing it (there is a possibility of fuel igniting in the carburettor).

Remove the air filter and hold the choke/throttle valves open with a small screwdriver *(see illustration)*. Keep your face and hands away from the carburettor and crank the engine several times. The engine should start. When it starts, remove the screwdriver and reinstall the air filter.

When the engine is running, adjust the mixture screw as described above.

5 Excessive vibration

Engine vibration can be caused by a bent crankshaft, which results from hitting something with the blade.

Many small engine repair workshops can straighten a crankshaft without disassembling the engine. If the power take-off end of the crankshaft wobbles as it's turned by hand, remove the engine from the equipment and take it to a repair workshop for crankshaft straightening.

1 Look for an out-of-balance blade. Mower blades can get twisted or badly nicked and may have poor lift. Sometimes sharpening the blade unevenly can throw it off. Resharpen the blade or install a new one.

2 Check to see if the blade is tight. Tighten the blade mounting bolt or bolts. Turn them anti-clockwise.

3 Check the engine mounting bolts to see if they're tight. These bolts hold the engine to the equipment *(see illustration)*. You may have to hold the bolts on top while you tighten the nuts under the deck.

If the engine is flooded (the spark plug is wet with petrol), hold the choke and throttle valves – if possible – wide open with a screwdriver while cranking the engine to clear out the excess fuel

4 Check the deck for damage. If it's broken, cracked or badly rusted, the engine may get out of alignment and vibrate. If the deck is damaged, it must be repaired or replaced. Repairs usually involve welding (a job for a professional). If the deck must be replaced, get several estimates; a new mower may be cheaper.

5 Check the carburettor adjustment (see section 4 above.) A rough-running engine can cause vibration.

6 Noise

Excessive or unusual noise is almost always the result of a silencer that's holed (by rust), deformed, or even missing completely! A new silencer will remedy the problem.

1 Check the condition of the silencer. A deteriorated silencer must be renewed (see Chapter 5).

2 If the noise isn't caused by the exhaust system, but is in the engine itself, check the oil level immediately!

3 If you notice that the engine is suddenly running quieter, check the silencer and exhaust system for matted grass clippings, dirt and other debris.

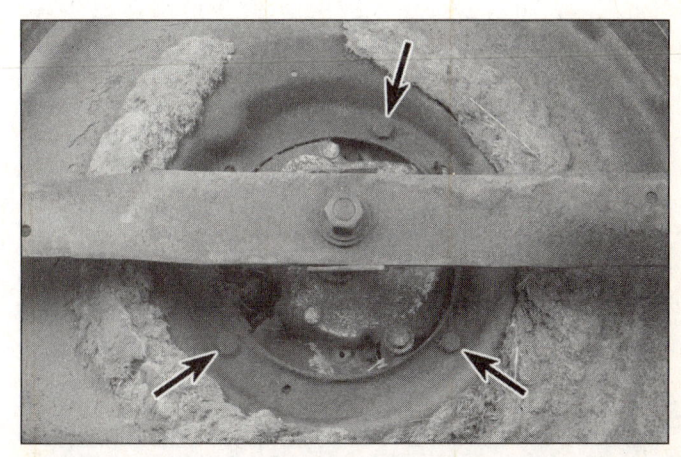

If the mounting bolts (arrowed) are loose, the engine will vibrate and damage will result

Chapter 3

7 Engine smokes

This may be caused by a broken piston or ring or a damaged cylinder, although other causes are more likely.

1 Check the carburettor to see if it's adjusted properly (see Section 4 above).

Start the engine and allow it to idle (if possible), then open it up. If black smoke comes out of the exhaust, the mixture is probably too rich. Adjust the fuel mixture (if possible) (follow the procedure in Section 4).

2 If the smoke is blue and smells like burned oil, the trouble is probably with the rings, piston or cylinder bore (more than likely all three). The blue smoke may be accompanied by excessive internal engine noises – the engine may make a dull, knocking sound. It will have to be overhauled.

8 Overheating

This is usually a minor problem, but don't ignore it. Prolonged overheating can cause serious engine damage.

1 Check the oil level immediately. Add clean, fresh oil as needed. Make sure the oil used is the proper viscosity – if it's too thin or contaminated with fuel (from flooding the engine), lubrication will be inadequate.

2 Make sure the cooling fins aren't clogged with debris. Clean them with a putty knife and paint brush.

3 Make sure all shrouds and blower housings are correctly installed. If they aren't, air can't circulate properly through the cooling fins.

4 Check the carburettor to see if it's adjusted properly (see section 4 above).

5 See if the silencer is obstructed by dirt or debris.

6 Make sure the engine isn't overloaded. You may be running it too fast for too long (has the governor been tampered with?). Also, the engine may be overburdened with too much equipment. Stop the engine, let it cool and disengage the extra equipment.

7 Check the cylinder head for excessive carbon build-up (see Chapter 4 for instructions to remove the head and clean it).

8 Check the valve tappet clearances to see if they're too tight (see Chapter 4).

9 Make sure the correct spark plug is installed.

9 Excessive oil use

This problem can have several causes.

1 Check the oil level – if the engine is overfilled, excess oil will be blown out through the crankcase breather and get all over the engine.

2 Check the governor. The engine may be operating at speeds that are too high.

3 See if the oil level check/fill plug gasket is missing. The oil may be leaking out around the plug (it'll run down the engine if it is).

4 Check the crankcase breather assembly *(see illustration)*. Clean or renew it as required.

Make sure the oil drain back hole is open.

The crankcase breather assembly is used to vent the crankcase and keep oil from being expelled in the process

5 The rings or cylinder bore may be worn or damaged. To check this you'll have to disassemble the engine.

Trouble-shooting a two-stroke engine

Most two-stroke engine problems will fall into one or more of the following categories:
1 *Won't start/hard to start*
2 *Won't turn over*
3 *Stalls*
4 *Erratic operation*
5 *Lack of power*
6 *Excessive vibration*
7 *Overheating*
8 *Excessive smoke*

1 Won't start/hard to start

Note: *When an engine won't start, it's usually because the controls are improperly set, the safety interlock devices are interrupting the ignition system or the ignition system is malfunctioning, although fuel problems and lack of compression can also prevent a two-stroke engine from starting (see the information under the heading 'Where to start' to rule out lack of compression as a cause).*

As mentioned in the section headed How an engine works, a two-stroke engine crankcase must be air-tight. If air leaks develop at seals or gaskets (or because of a porous casting), the engine may not want to start. Air leaks of this type are exasperating to locate, so if you eliminate all other possible reasons why the engine won't start or is very difficult to start, take it to a dealer with the special pressure-checking equipment required to isolate crankcase air leaks.

1 Make sure the controls are positioned properly.

Follow the control cable from the lever to the carburettor.

Troubleshooting

The throttle should be all the way open and the choke should operate when the lever is set on START. As you move the control lever from START to FAST to STOP, the cable should be clamped so the throttle operates properly. The cable may be slipping in the clamp just enough to cause the throttle to malfunction and you might not see the slight movement.

Move the throttle to the open or START position with your fingers. You may have to move the control lever with your other hand to open the throttle.

If the engine now starts, let it run for several minutes, then pull the control lever back to STOP. If the engine slows down but doesn't stop, loosen the cable clamp with a screwdriver and pull the cable toward the control lever very slightly until the engine stops, then retighten the clamp. Start the engine again and run through the control positions. The engine should start, run slowly, run fast and stop when the lever is positioned next to the appropriate label on the control.

2 Make sure the fuel tank is at least half-full of fresh petrol/oil mix (and that the ratio of petrol to oil is correct). Also ensure that fuel is reaching the carburettor (the line from the tank to the carburettor could be blocked, kinked or detached).

3 Check the plug wire to make sure it's securely attached to the spark plug.

The terminal on the end of the spark plug wire can come loose and get corroded. Crimp the loop with a pair of pliers *(see top illustration on page 3•7)* and remove corrosion with sandpaper, a wire brush or a round file.

4 Check the spark plug earth strap to make sure it's not malfunctioning. Some engines have a metal strap that's used to short out the spark plug to stop the engine. If the engine has one, make sure it's not touching the plug *(see illustration)*.

5 Make sure the grass catcher is properly installed.

Some lawn mowers have a safety switch for the grass catcher where it attaches to the mower housing. This device prevents the engine from starting until the grass catcher is properly installed. If the grass catcher isn't being used, make sure the chute is properly attached to the mower deck.

6 If the engine has a fuel priming device, make sure it's working properly.

It should be pushed four or five times when the engine is cold to fill the carburettor. If the engine is hot, don't operate the primer - it may flood the engine. Instead, pull the starter handle several times with the control lever in the STOP position. This will help clear excess fuel out of the engine. Put the control lever on START and start the engine normally.

7 See if the fuel tank cap vent is clogged.

If the fuel tank vent is clogged, a vacuum will eventually form in the tank and prevent fuel from reaching the carburettor (the engine will act like it's out of fuel).

Remove the cap and check the gasket in it. Sometimes the space between the gasket and cap gets clogged with debris, shutting off the air supply to the tank. Check the hole(s) in the cap to make sure it's open *(see centre illustration on page 3•7)*. If you're not sure if the vent is open or not, leave the cap off and try to start the engine. If the engine runs, the cap vent is the problem. Either open the vent or install a new cap. DO NOT run the engine without a cap on the fuel tank.

8 Check the air filter to see if it's clean and make sure the gasket between the filter and carburettor is in good shape.

9 Remove the spark plug and check the gap and the base of the plug for dirt. Clean the electrodes with a wire brush and use a fine file to square the side electrode tip so any worn edges are sharp *(see illustration on page 3•10)*. As a general rule, the spark plug gap can be set at 0.60 mm (0.025-inch).

10 Check to see if the plug is firing (see *To check the ignition system.* in the section headed *Where to start*).

If it's fouled, you can clean it, as mentioned above, but a new one should be installed – they're not expensive and you can usually be sure the new plug is sound.

Every once in a while, a new plug will turn out to be faulty. If you install a new plug and the engine won't fire even though everything else seems to be okay, try another new plug or use a spark tester.

11 Make sure the plug wire is in good condition.

Bend the wire by hand and look for cracks in the insulation. Also look for burned or melted insulation. If damage is noted, you may have to replace the ignition coil, since the wire usually is permanently attached to it.

12 Check the choke to make sure it's operating properly – if it doesn't close all the way, the engine may not start. If it doesn't open after the engine starts, flooding may occur.

13 See if the blade is loose - it must be tight on the shaft or adaptor.

2 Won't turn over

1 Check to see if something is blocking the blade.

2 See if the starter is jammed (removal is covered in Chapter 5).

3 Make sure dirt isn't jamming the flywheel and see if the key is sheared off. Refer to the information in Section 3 under the heading *Troubleshooting a four-stroke engine*.

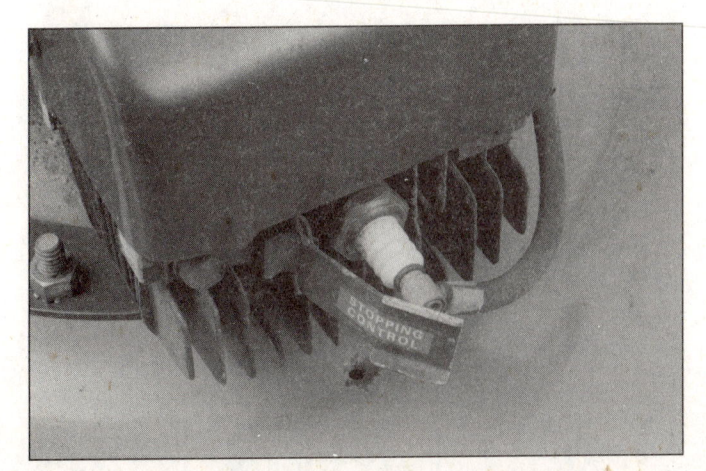

Make sure the earth strap used to stop the engine isn't touching the spark plug when trying to start the engine

Chapter 3

4 The piston ring(s) may be broken and jammed in one of the ports. The engine will have to be disassembled to check it.
5 The connecting rod may be broken or seized. This will also require engine disassembly to know for sure.

3 Stalls

1 Make sure that the fuel tank is at least half-full of fresh petrol/oil mixture (and that the ratio of petrol to oil is correct). Also ensure that fuel is reaching the carburettor (the line from the tank to the carburettor could be blocked, kinked or detached).
2 Check the air filter to make sure it isn't clogged.
3 See if the fuel tank cap vent is clogged.

If the fuel tank vent is clogged, a vacuum will eventually form in the tank and prevent fuel from reaching the carburettor (the engine will act like it's out of fuel).

Remove the cap and check the gasket in it. Sometimes the space between the gasket and cap gets clogged with debris, shutting off the air supply to the tank. Check the hole(s) in the cap to make sure it's open *(see centre illustration on page 3•7)*. If you're not sure if the vent is open or not, leave the cap off and try to start the engine. If the engine runs, the cap vent is the problem. Either open the vent or install a new cap. DO NOT run the engine without a cap on the fuel tank.
4 See if the carburettor is adjusted correctly. Turn the mixture screw out for a richer fuel mixture (follow the procedure in Section 4 under the heading *Troubleshooting a four-stroke engine*).
5 If the engine is equipped with contact breaker points, check them; they could be dirty, burned or out-of-adjustment (see Chapter 4).

4 Erratic operation

1 Make sure the fuel tank is at least half-full of fresh petrol/oil mixture (and that the ratio of petrol to oil is correct). Also ensure that fuel is reaching the carburettor (the line from the tank to the carburettor could be blocked, kinked or detached).
2 Check the carburettor to make sure it's adjusted properly. Refer to the information in Section 4 under the heading *Troubleshooting a four-stroke engine*.
3 Remove the spark plug and check the gap and the base of the plug for dirt. Clean the electrodes with a wire brush and use a fine file to square the side electrode tip so any worn edges are sharp *(see illustration on page 3•10)*. As a general rule, the spark plug gap can be set at 0.6 mm (0.024 in).
4 Check to see if the plug is firing (see *To check the ignition system.* in the section headed *Where to start*).

If the plug is fouled, you can clean it, as mentioned above, but a new one should be installed – they're not expensive and you can usually be sure the new plug is sound.

Every once in a while, a new plug will turn out to be faulty. If you install a new plug and the engine won't fire even though everything else seems to be okay, try another new plug or use a spark tester.

5 If the engine is equipped with contact breaker points, check them; they could be dirty, burned or out-of-adjustment (see Chapter 4).
6 Check the crankcase reed valve (mounted where the carburettor is attached to the crankcase) to see if it's stuck or clogged (not used on all engines).
7 If the crankcase isn't air-tight, the engine may run erratically (see the Note at the beginning of this section).
8 Check the wires for the engine stop switch. Loose connections in the wires can cause the engine to cut out when the machine is being used.

5 Lack of power

1 Make sure the fuel tank is at least half-full of fresh petrol/oil mixture (and that the ratio of petrol to oil is correct). Also ensure that fuel is reaching the carburettor (the line from the tank to the carburettor could be blocked, kinked or detached).
2 Check the air filter to see if it's clogged.
3 Remove the spark plug and check the gap and the base of the plug for dirt. Clean the electrodes with a wire brush and use a fine file to square the side electrode tip so any worn edges are sharp *(see illustration on page 3•10)*. As a general rule, the spark plug gap can be set at 0.6 mm (0.024 in).
4 Check to see if the plug is firing (see *To check the ignition system.* in the section headed *Where to start*).

If the plug is fouled, you can clean it, as mentioned above, but a new one should be installed – they're not expensive and you can usually be sure the new plug is sound.

Every once in a while, a new plug will turn out to be faulty. If you install a new plug and the engine won't fire even though everything else seems to be okay, try another new plug or use a spark tester.

5 Check for carbon build-up in the exhaust port and silencer. You'll have to remove the silencer for this check (Chapter 5).
6 Check the carburettor to make sure it's adjusted properly. Refer to the information in Section 4 under the heading *Troubleshooting a four-stroke engine*.
7 Check the choke and throttle controls to make sure they aren't allowing the valves to move during engine operation.
8 Check the crankcase reed valve (mounted where the carburettor is attached to the crankcase) to see if it's stuck or clogged (not used on all engines).
9 If the crankcase isn't air-tight, the engine may lack power (see the Note at the beginning of this section).
10 If the piston rings are worn or the cylinder is damaged, power output can be reduced.

6 Excessive vibration

1 Check the blade to see if it's tight and in balance.
2 See if the engine mounting bolts are loose *(see illustration on page 3•11)*.
3 Other causes may include damaged crankshaft ball bearings, crankshaft or connecting rod.

Troubleshooting

If the cooling fins are clogged with grass and other debris, clean them with a paint brush or compressed air

The exhaust ports on a two-stroke engine can get clogged with carbon – use a hardwood stick to knock the carbon out to avoid damage to the piston and rings

7 Overheating

1 Make sure the petrol/oil mixture ratio is correct – too little oil will result in poor lubrication and heat; too much oil can actually lean out the mixture.
2 Check the air filter to see if it's dirty.
3 Make sure the correct spark plug is installed.
4 Check the cooling fins to see if they're clogged *(see illustration)*. Remove debris from the fins with a brush or compressed air.
5 Check the exhaust ports to see if they're clogged with carbon *(see illustration)*. The silencer will have to be removed to get at the ports. If carbon is built-up, remove it with a hardwood stick.
6 See if the carburettor is dirty or out-of-adjustment. The mixture screw may be set too lean (turned in too far).
7 Check the nuts, bolts or screws holding the carburettor in place to see if they're tight *(see illustration)*.
8 See if the flywheel nut is loose.
9 If the crankcase isn't air-tight, the engine may overheat (see the Note at the beginning of this section).
10 Don't overload the engine or run it too fast for too long.

8 Excessive smoke

1 Make sure the choke is off.
2 Make sure the petrol/oil mixture ratio is correct – too much oil will result in excessive smoke.

3 See if the carburettor mixture screw is set too rich (too far out).
4 Check the exhaust ports to see if they're clogged with carbon *(see illustration)*. The silencer will have to be removed to get at the ports. If carbon is built-up, remove it with a hardwood stick.

Two-stroke engines are especially sensitive to air leaks, so make sure the carburettor mounting nuts, bolts or screws are tightened evenly

3•15

Chapter 3

Tune-up and routine maintenance 4

Introduction

Tune-up and maintenance checklist

Preparing an engine for storage

Introduction

This chapter covers the checks and procedures necessary for the tune-up and routine maintenance of typical small petrol engines. It includes a checklist of service procedures designed to keep the engine in proper running condition and prevent possible problems. Separate sections contain detailed instructions for doing the jobs on the checklist, as well as additional maintenance information designed to increase the engine's reliability.

The sections detailing the maintenance and inspection procedures are written as step-by-step comprehensive guides to the actual performance of the work. References to additional information in other chapters is also included and shouldn't be overlooked.

The first step in this or any maintenance plan is to prepare yourself before the actual work begins. Read through the appropriate sections covering the procedures to be done before you begin. Gather up all necessary parts and tools. If it appears that you could have a problem during a particular job, don't hesitate to seek advice from a dealer, repair workshop or experienced do-it-yourselfer.

Before attacking the engine with spanners and screwdrivers, clean it with a degreaser to ensure that dirt doesn't contaminate the internal parts. This will also allow you to detect wear and damage that could otherwise easily go unnoticed.

Tune-up and maintenance checklist

Every time the engine is refuelled
Check the oil level (four-stroke engines only)
Check control operation

Yearly maintenance
Note: *The following procedures should be done at least once a year under normal circumstances (approximately 25 hours of engine use per year) and more often if the engine is used extensively.*
Service the air cleaner
Clean the petrol tank and line
Clean the carburettor float bowl
Change the oil (four-stroke engines only)
Check the starter
Clean the cooling fins and shroud
Check the compression
Check the governor and linkage
Replace or clean/adjust the contact breaker points (if fitted)
Check the coil and ignition wires
Decarbonise the cylinder head
Check the silencer
Check the valve tappet clearances (four-stroke engines only)
Install a new spark plug
Check/adjust the controls
Adjust the carburettor
Check the engine mount bolts/nuts

Chapter 4

The engine oil check/fill plug should be clearly marked – clean it off before removing it

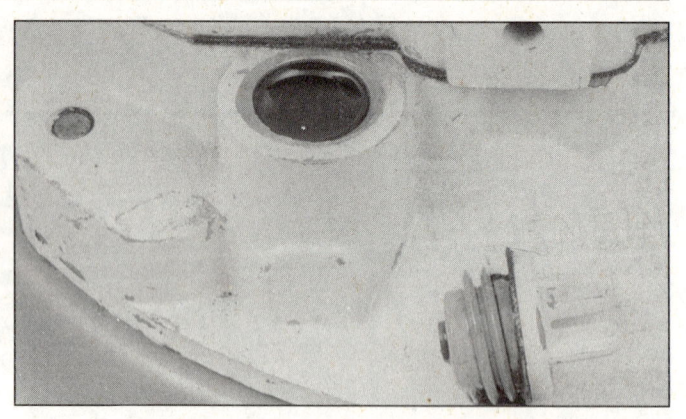

The oil level on engines that don't have a dipstick should be level with the top of the check/fill plug opening as shown here

1 Check the oil level (four-stroke engines only)

Each time you refill the petrol tank, or every two or three hours of engine operation, check the crankcase oil level and add more oil as needed. Some manufacturers may recommend more or less frequent oil checks – follow the instructions in your owner's manual if they differ from the information here.

1 Locate the cap used to check the oil level and add oil to the engine – it may be a threaded or friction fit cap or plug. The cap may be marked 'Engine oil' or 'Oil fill' *(see illustration)*.

2 Clean the plug and the area around it to prevent dirt from falling into the engine when the plug is removed.

3 Make sure the engine is level, then remove the oil check/fill cap or plug.

4 If the cap or plug doesn't have a dipstick attached to it, the oil level should be at the top of the opening *(see illustration)* or level with a mark or the top of a slot that indicates the FULL level.

5 If the cap or plug has a dipstick, wipe the oil off, then reinsert it into the engine and pull it out again. Follow the instructions on the dipstick – sometimes the plug must be threaded back in to get an accurate reading.

6 Note the oil level on the dipstick. It should be between the marks on the dipstick (usually ADD and FULL), not above the upper mark or below the lower mark.

7 Add oil to bring it up to the correct level. If it's time to change the oil, don't add any now – change the oil instead (see Section 5).

2 Service the air cleaner

Most small engine air cleaners are either foam or pleated-paper types that should be checked/cleaned frequently to ensure proper engine operation. Some engines have a pleated-paper filter that's covered with a foam type filter. If the filter isn't serviced regularly, dirt will get into the engine or it'll build up on the filter and cause an excessively rich fuel mixture – either condition will shorten the engine's life.

1 Remove the filter from the engine. Some filters simply snap into place, while others are under a cover attached with screw(s) or wing nut(s) *(see illustrations)*.

2 If the filter is made of pleated-paper, tap it on a workbench to dislodge the dirt or blow it out from the inside with LOW PRESSURE compressed air. If it's torn, bent, crushed, wet or damaged in any other way, install a new

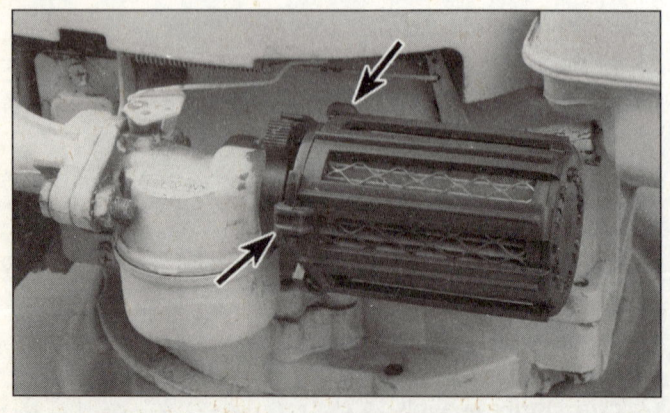

A typical pleated-paper air cleaner – this one is held in place with three plastic clips (arrowed) that must be released to remove the element

This typical foam air cleaner is mounted in a housing – the cover is attached with one screw

Tune-up and routine maintenance

Most foam filters can be washed in soapy water and re-used, although some of them are disposable and should be replaced with a new one

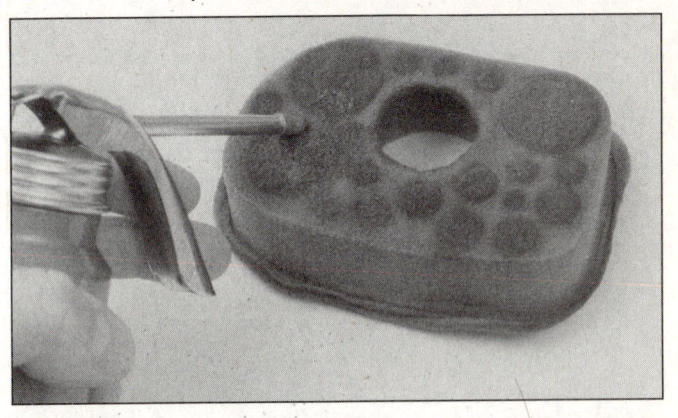

Work about two or three teaspoons of oil into the foam filter before reinstalling it in the housing

one. DO NOT wash a pleated-paper filter to clean it!

3 If the filter is foam, wash it in hot soapy water *(see illustration)* and wring it out, then let it dry thoroughly. Add about two teaspoons of engine oil to the filter and squeeze it several times to distribute the oil evenly *(see illustration)*. This is very important – the oil is what catches the dirt in the filter. If the filter is torn or falling apart, install a new one.

4 Remove any dirt from the air cleaner housing and check the gasket between it and the carburettor. If the gasket is deteriorated or missing, dirt will get past the filter into the engine.

5 Reinstall the filter.

3 Clean the fuel tank and fuel line

> **Warning:** *Petrol is extremely flammable and highly explosive under certain conditions – safety precautions must be followed when working on any part of the fuel system! Don't smoke or allow open flames or unshielded light bulbs in or near the work area. Don't do this procedure in a garage with a natural gas appliance (such as a water heater or clothes dryer).*

During its life, the fuel tank will collect dust, grass clippings, dirt, water and other debris. It must be cleaned out on a regular basis to prevent these contaminants from reaching the carburettor, or from blocking the fuel line. The tank may be mounted separately, or attached directly to the carburettor. **Note:** *If the tank is attached to the carburettor, removing the screws may free it, but there's usually not enough room to manoeuvre it out of position unless the carburettor is removed first.*

1 Remove any covers or shrouds mounted over the fuel tank, then remove the tank mounting screws (if fitted).

2 If a fuel shut-off valve is fitted, turn it off.

3 Detach the fuel line from the tank and plug the fitting with your finger to prevent fuel loss (this is not necessary if a shut-off valve is fitted).

4 Lift the tank off the engine.

5 Drain the fuel out of the tank into a petrol can, then rinse the tank with solvent and dry it out with compressed air (if available) or let it sit out in the sun for several minutes. If it has a strainer at the outlet fitting, make sure it's clean.

6 Loosen the hose clamps, if used, and detach the fuel line from the carburettor fitting.

7 Make sure the line is clean and unobstructed. If it's cracked or otherwise deteriorated, install a new line and new clamps.
Note: *If a filter is installed in the line at the tank outlet fitting, clean it and install a new one.*

8 Proceed to section 4 and clean the float bowl (if equipped), then reinstall the tank.

4 Clean the carburettor float bowl

Some carburettors have a float bowl (a reservoir for fuel) that collects sediment and water which will clog the jets and cause the engine to run poorly or not at all. The float bowl should be drained/cleaned frequently.

1 Some carburettors have a drain plug or small spring-loaded valve on the bottom of the float bowl that's used to drain out sediment and water *(see illustration)*. Lay a rag under the carburettor, then push up on the valve with a small

Some carburettors have a spring-loaded drain valve on the bottom of the float bowl (arrowed) to get rid of sediment and water in the carburettor

4•3

Chapter 4

The float bowl is usually attached to the carburettor with a bolt or other fitting at the bottom (and it's usually hard to get at)

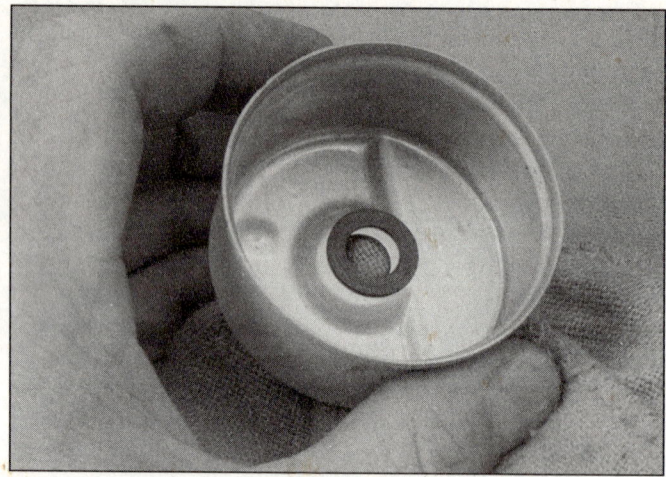

Wipe out the float bowl and check the gasket before reinstalling it

screwdriver and let fuel run out until it looks clean (you'll see little droplets if water comes out).

2 On engines that don't have a drain valve, DO NOT remove the float bowl until the fuel tank is drained, the fuel line is pinched off or the tank is removed, otherwise fuel will run all over when the float bowl is detached.

3 You'll have to remove a bolt or fitting to detach the float bowl *(see illustration)*. Use a well-fitting spanner to avoid rounding off the bolt. On some engines you may have to remove the carburettor to get the bolt out so the float bowl will come off.

4 Pour the fuel out of the float bowl and clean it with a rag *(see illustration)*.

5 Check the condition of the gasket – if it's deteriorated or deformed, install a new one.

6 Reinstall the float bowl and tighten the bolt securely. Make sure the fibre washer is in place on the bolt (if used).

7 Reinstall the tank, remove the fuel line clamp or add fuel to the tank, then start the engine and make sure it runs okay.

5 Change the oil (four-stroke engines only)

Oil is the lifeblood of an engine; check and change it often to ensure maximum performance and the longest engine life possible. If the equipment is operated in dusty conditions, change the oil more frequently than you normally would.

Note: *Most small engine manufacturers recommend 30-weight oil (viscosity SAE 30W) – check your owner's manual for exact recommendations.*

1 Start the engine and allow it to warm up (warm oil will drain easier and more contaminants will be removed with it).

2 Stop the engine – never attempt to drain the oil with the engine running!

3 Disconnect the spark plug wire from the spark plug and position it out of the way.

4 Locate the drain plug. Some are located on the outside edge of the bottom of the engine *(see illustration)*, while others (particularly on engines used on rotary mowers) are on the bottom of the engine *(see illustration)*. **Note:** *Some engines don't have a drain plug – the oil is drained out through the filler hole by tilting the engine.*

On some engines, the oil drain plug is on the side of the crankcase . . .

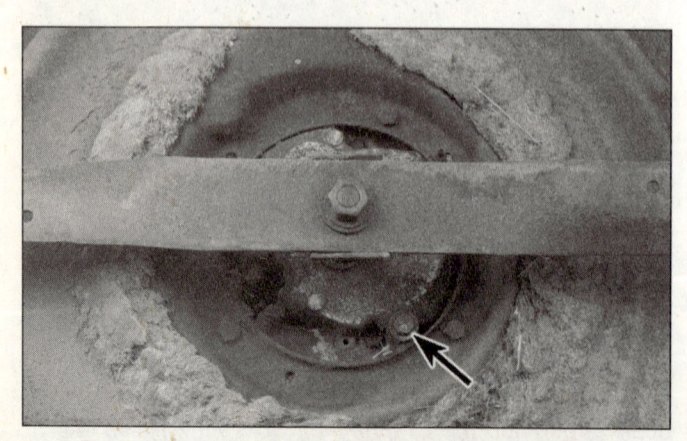

. . . while on others it's at the bottom – don't work under a mower deck unless the spark plug wire is disconnected!

Tune-up and routine maintenance

5 Clean the plug and the area around it, then remove it from the engine and allow the oil to drain into a container. Don't rush this part of the procedure – let the oil drain until the engine is completely empty. Tip the engine so oil runs toward the opening if necessary.

6 Remove the oil check/fill plug also.

7 Clean the drain plug and reinstall it in the engine. If a gasket is used, be sure it's in place and undamaged. Tighten the plug securely.

8 Refill the crankcase with new, clean oil. Use a funnel to avoid spills, but be sure to wipe it out before pouring oil into it. Add oil until the level is at the top of the opening, then clean the plug and reinstall it. Wipe up any spilled oil.

9 Reconnect the spark plug wire and start the engine, then check for leaks and shut it off.

10 Recheck the oil level and add more oil if necessary, but don't overfill it.

11 Dispose of oily rags and the old oil properly.

6 Check the recoil starter (where fitted)

This is a simple check that can be done without removing anything from the engine.

Note: *Disconnect the wire from the spark plug to prevent the engine from starting.*

1 Pull the starter rope out slowly.

2 If the starter is noisy, binding or rough, the return spring, pulley or rope may be jammed.

3 If the crankshaft doesn't turn as the rope is pulled out, the ratcheting drive mechanism isn't engaging.

4 After the rope is all the way out, check it for wear along its entire length.

5 Allow the rope to rewind, but don't release the handle so the rope flies back.

6 If the rope won't rewind, the pulley may be binding, the return spring may be broken, disengaged or insufficiently tensioned or the starter may be assembled incorrectly.

7 Clean the cooling fins and shroud

The shroud air intake and the engine cooling fins must be clean so air can circulate properly to prevent overheating and prolong the engine's life.

1 Refer to Chapter 5 and remove the shroud from the engine.

2 Use a brush or compressed air to clean the shroud screen *(see illustration)*.

3 Do the same for the fins on the cylinder and head *(see illustration)*.

4 Proceed to Section 8.

The compression should be routinely checked once a year or every 50 hours of engine operation (more often if the engine is hard to start or power loss is evident). If the engine is run with low compression, fuel and oil consumption will increase and engine wear will be accelerated.

Honda is the only manufacturer of engines covered in this manual that recommends a gauge to check the compression – the other manufacturers don't publish compression pressure specifications, so a gauge can't be used to draw any conclusions about engine condition.

8 Check the compression

Among other things, poor engine performance may be caused by leaking valves, incorrect valve tappet clearances, a leaking head gasket or worn piston, rings and/or cylinder. A compression check will help pinpoint these conditions.

1 Remove the spark plug, position the plug wire well away from the engine/mower, then seal off the plug hole with your thumb *(see illustration on page 3•4)*.

2 Operate the starter – if the compression pressure blows your thumb off the hole, the compression is adequate for the engine to run; be careful not to touch the plug wire as this is done – you'll get quite a jolt if you do!

3 Another way to check the compression with the spark plug in place is to remove the cooling shroud/starter mechanism

The shroud air intake is usually protected by a screen, which should be cleaned regularly

Use a paint brush or compressed air (if available) to remove grass, dirt and other debris from the engine cooling fins

Chapter 4

and spin the flywheel in reverse (anti-clockwise) *(see illustration on page 3•4 in Chapter 3)*. It should return sharply; if it does, the compression is adequate for the engine to run.

4 To further confirm your findings, add about 10 cc (1/2-ounce) of engine oil to the cylinder by inserting the nozzle of a squirt-type oil can through the spark plug hole *(see illustration)*. The oil will tend to seal the piston rings if they're leaking. Repeat the test.

5 If the compression increases significantly after the addition of oil, the piston rings and/or cylinder are definitely worn. If the compression doesn't increase, the pressure is leaking past the valves or the head gasket. Leakage past the valves may be caused by burned or cracked valve seats or faces, warped or bent valves or insufficient valve clearances.

6 To summarize, if the compression is low, it may be due to:
Loose spark plug
Loose cylinder head bolts
Blown head gasket
Damaged valves/valve seats (four-stroke engine only)
Insufficient valve tappet clearance (four-stroke engine only)
Warped cylinder head
Bent valve stem(s) (four- stroke engine only)
Worn cylinder bore and/or piston rings
Broken connecting rod or piston

9 Check the governor and linkage

Two types of governors are in common use on small engines: the air-vane type and the mechanical (centrifugal) type. Routine checks of an air-vane governor require removal of the shroud (see Chapter 5). The mechanical governor is usually mounted inside the engine, but the linkage connected to the carburettor is visible on the outside of the engine. **Note:** *If the governor isn't hooked up or seems to be malfunctioning, it should be repaired and the engine operating speed adjusted by a dealer or repair workshop with the necessary special tools.*

1 Clean grass clippings and other debris out of the governor linkage *(see illustration)*.
2 See if the linkage moves freely.
3 The throttle valve on the carburettor should be wide-open with the engine stopped. If it isn't, the linkage may be binding or connected incorrectly.
4 Look for worn links and holes and disconnected springs.
5 If the engine has an air-vane governor, the vane should move freely and operate the linkage *(see illustration)*. If the vane is bent or distorted, the governor may not operate correctly.
6 If the engine has a mechanical governor, make sure the lever is securely attached to the shaft where it exits the crankcase.

10 Service the contact breaker points

The contact breaker points should be checked at least once a year, and replaced if necessary. On all engines covered in this manual that are fitted with points, they are mounted under the flywheel, so it must come off first (see the appropriate engine chapter).

> **Warning:** *Be sure to remove the spark plug from the engine before working on the ignition system.*

Separate step-by-step procedures for Briggs & Stratton and Tecumseh engines are included here – follow the

A compression gauge can be used on Honda engines because the manufacturer provides compression specifications

If the compression increases significantly after oil is squirted into the cylinder, the piston rings are worn, and the engine should be disassembled for additional checks

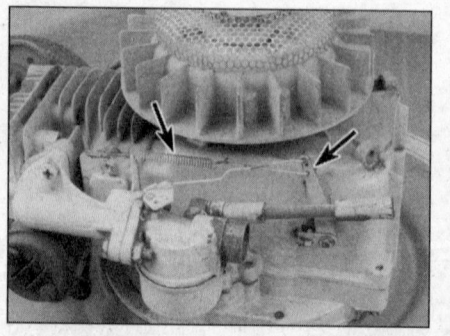

Typical governor linkage and springs – make sure nothing is disconnected and check for free movement

The air vane should be undamaged and move freely to operate the linkage correctly

Tune-up and routine maintenance

appropriate photo sequence and be sure to read the caption accompanying each illustration. **Note:** *Some Honda GV150 engines were also equipped with contact breaker points. The procedure is very similar to the one for Tecumseh engines, but the factory specifies a special ignition timing check after new points have been fitted. This is done by first attaching an ohmmeter or test light to the points wire and a good earth. Turn the flywheel, and watch the ohmmeter or test light to see if the points open when the 'F' mark on the flywheel is aligned with the index mark on the engine* block (the ohmmeter will deflect or the light will go off when the points open). *If adjustment is needed, remove the flywheel and open or close the point gap until the timing is correct.*

Since the flywheel is off to get at the points, be sure to check for oil leakage past the crankshaft seal under the flywheel. If the seal is leaking, oil more than likely will eventually foul the points and you'll have to remove the flywheel for additional repairs. Seal replacement is covered in Chapter 5.

BRIGGS & STRATTON IGNITION POINT CHECK AND REPLACEMENT

Note: *If oil is leaking past the plunger and fouling the points, the plunger bore is probably worn. Take the engine to a dealer and have the bore checked (a special gauge is available for this purpose). If it's worn, the dealer will ream it out and install a bushing to restore the bore.*

Check the flywheel key (arrowed) – if it's sheared off install a new one; look for oil leaking past the crankshaft seal

Remove the screws and lift off the points cover – check the points to see if they are burned, pitted, worn down or covered with oil; if they're in good condition, they can be dressed with a point file, cleaned and readjusted (steps 9 to 11), but once you've gone to the trouble of removing the flywheel, new points should be installed (they don't cost much)

Remove the screw and detach the condenser, then depress the small spring and release the primary wire from the terminal on the end of the condenser

Remove the screw and lift out the movable point, return spring and post

4•7

Chapter 4

5 Pull out the plunger and check it for wear – if it's worn to less than 22 mm (0.87 in) in length or damaged in any way, install a new one (take the old one with you to the dealer)

6 Clean the points recess, using a mild solvent if wished and wipe it out with a rag. If a solvent is available, use it to ensure that the new points faces are clean before fitting

7 Reinstall the plunger (with the grooved end out, against the movable point), the movable point, the return spring and the post – make sure the slot in the post engages the nub in the recess, the movable point arm is seated in the slot in the post and the earth wire is under the screw

8 Attach the wire to the new condenser (the new points should have a little plastic tool designed to compress the spring that holds the wire on the condenser) and carefully clamp the condenser to the engine – leave the screw loose enough to move the condenser back-and-forth

9 Slowly turn the crankshaft until the plunger/movable point is open as far as possible – you may have to try this several times until you get it just right

10 Insert a clean feeler gauge – 0.5 mm (0.020 in) thick – between the contact points and move the condenser very carefully with a screwdriver until the gap between the points is the same thickness as the feeler gauge (be careful not to change the position of the movable point as this is done)

11 Fully tighten the condenser clamp screw. Turn the crankshaft and make sure the movable arm opens and closes

12 Reinstall the cover and tighten the screws – if the cover is distorted, replace it with a new one or oil and moisture will foul the points

13 Use RTV sealant to seal off the wires to prevent oil and moisture from getting to the points

Tune-up and routine maintenance

TECUMSEH IGNITION POINT CHECK AND REPLACEMENT

1 Check the flywheel key (arrowed) – if it's sheared off, install a new one – check the contact points to see if they're burned, pitted, worn down or covered with oil; if they're in good condition, they can be dressed with a point file, cleaned and readjusted (steps 10 to 12), but once you've gone to the trouble of removing the flywheel, new points should be installed (they don't cost much)

2 Release the retainer clip and lift off the points cover and gasket; look for oil leaking past the crankshaft seal

3 Remove the nut and detach the primary wires from the points terminal – when installing a new condenser, you'll have to cut the original wire at the terminal (the new one will have a terminal that fits over the post)

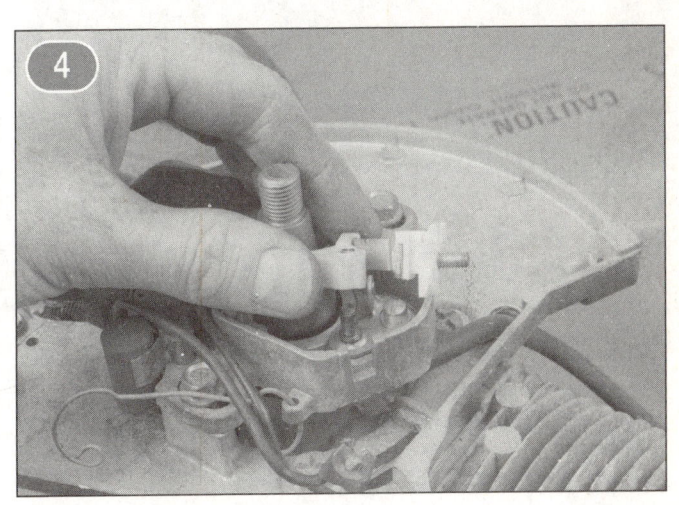

4 Slide the movable point up, off the post, and remove the spring and the terminal and insulator

5 Remove the screw and lift out the fixed point

6 Remove the mounting screw and detach the condenser, then install the new one in its place and route the wire over to the point terminal

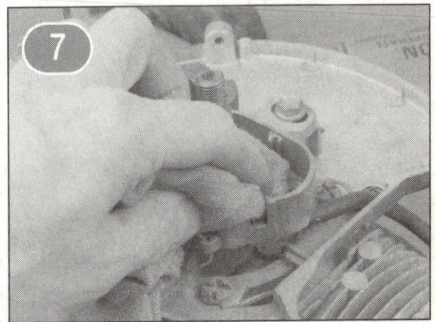

7 Clean the points recess, using a mild solvent if wished, and wipe it out with a rag. If a solvent is available, use it to ensure that the new points faces are clean before fitting

4•9

Chapter 4

8 Install the new fixed point – leave the screw loose enough to allow movement of the plate

9 Slip the new movable point over the post and position the insulator in the cutout – slip the primary and condenser wires onto the terminal and install the nut

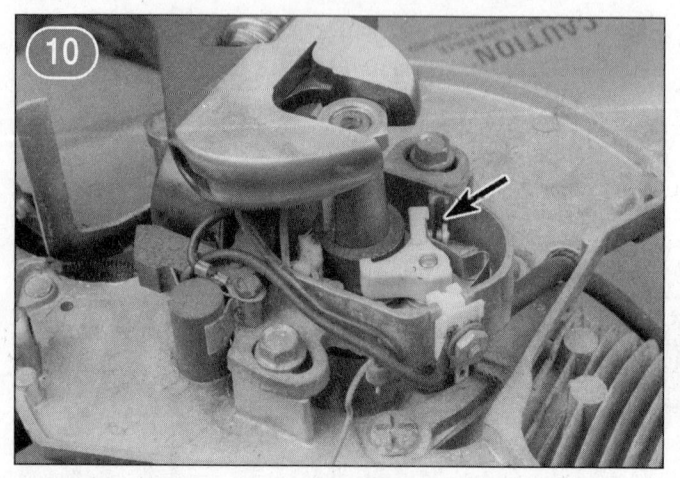

10 Turn the crankshaft very slowly until the cam opens the movable point as far as possible – if the cam was removed to replace the oil seal, make sure it's installed with the correct side out

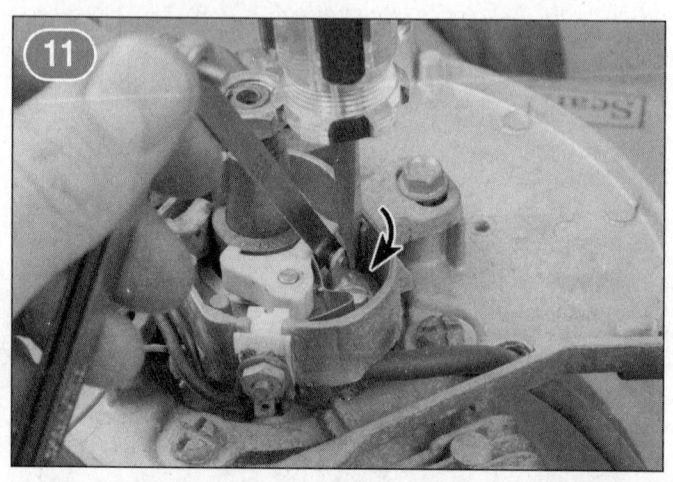

11 Insert a clean feeler gauge – 0.5 mm (0.020-inch) thick – between the contact points and move the fixed point very carefully with a screwdriver until the gap between the points is the same thickness as the feeler gauge (be careful not to change the position of the movable point as this is done)

12 Fully tighten the fixed point securing screw. Turn the crankshaft and make sure the movable arm opens and closes

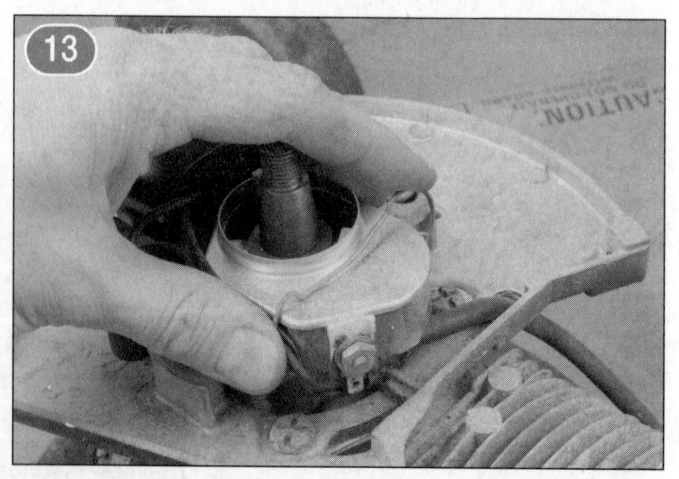

13 Install the gasket and points cover and snap the retainer clip into place

Tune-up and routine maintenance

Check the spark plug wire for cracked and melted insulation and make sure it's securely attached at the coil

This simple engine stop switch earths the ignition system when the control lever is moved to STOP – if the arm doesn't contact the switch, adjust the cable until it does

11 Check the coil and ignition wires

The ignition coil is usually mounted next to the flywheel, so the shroud will have to be removed to check the wires.

1 Check the spark plug wire for cracked and melted insulation and make sure it's securely attached to the ignition coil *(see illustration)*.

2 Make sure the terminal fits snugly on the spark plug end. Crimp it with a pair of pliers if necessary.

3 Check the primary (small) wires as well. Look for loose and corroded connections and abraded or melted insulation. Now is also a good time to check the engine stop switch. Make sure the switch is actuated when the control lever is moved to STOP. If it isn't, adjust the cable *(see illustration)*.

12 Decarbonise the cylinder head

With modern fuels, carbon build-up in the cylinder head is not the problem it used to be. However, it's still a good idea to remove the head during a Spring tune-up to scrape out the carbon and other deposits. Before beginning this procedure, buy a new head gasket for your engine. **Note:** *This procedure does not apply to OHV (overhead valve) or OHC (overhead camshaft) engines.*

1 Begin by disconnecting the wire from the spark plug.

2 Next, remove the shroud and any covers that prevent direct access to the cylinder head and bolts. **Note:** *On many engines, some of the head bolts are also used to attach the shroud or carburettor mounting bracket to the engine* (see illustration). If you're working on one, loosen all of the head bolts in 1/4-turn increments, following a criss-cross pattern, until the shroud mounting bolts can be removed by hand.

3 Using the new head gasket, outline the head bolt pattern on a piece of cardboard *(see illustration)*. Punch holes at the bolt locations.

4 If not already done, loosen the cylinder head bolts in 1/4-turn increments until they can be removed by hand. Follow a criss-cross pattern to avoid warping the head.

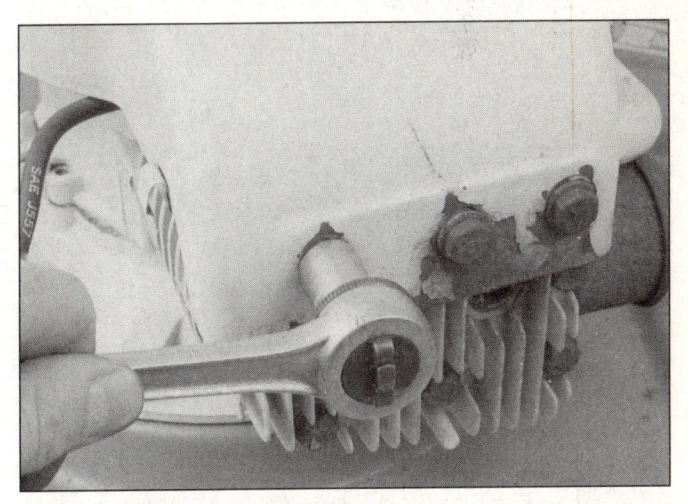

On some engines, cylinder head bolts are used to attach the shroud or mounting brackets as well

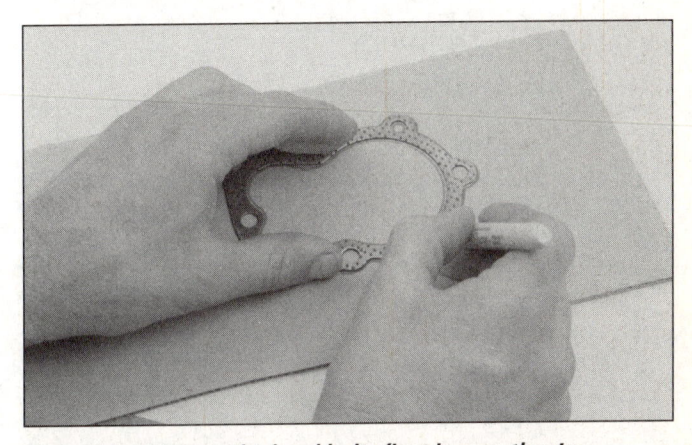

To avoid mixing up the head bolts (just in case they're different lengths), use the new gasket to transfer the hole pattern to a piece of cardboard, punch holes to accept the bolts and push each bolt through the matching hole in the cardboard as it's removed

4•11

Chapter 4

5 Store the bolts in the cardboard holder as they're removed – this will guarantee that they're reinstalled in their original locations, which is essential (different length bolts are used on some engines).

6 Detach the head from the engine. If it's stuck, tap it with a soft-face hammer to break the gasket seal – DO NOT prise it off with a screwdriver!

7 Remove and discard the gasket – use the new one when the cylinder head is reinstalled.

8 Turn the crankshaft until the piston is at the top of the cylinder, then use a scraper or putty knife and wire brush to remove all deposits from the top of the piston and the area around the valves (see illustration). Be careful not to nick the gasket mating surface.

9 Turn the crankshaft to open each valve and check them for burned and cracked faces and seats (see illustration). If the valves are cracked, pitted or bent and the seats are in bad shape, major engine repairs are required.

10 Remove the deposits from the combustion chamber in the head (see illustration).

11 The mating surfaces of the head and block must be perfectly clean when the head is reinstalled.

12 Use a gasket scraper or putty knife to remove all traces of carbon and old gasket material, then clean the mating surfaces with solvent. If there's oil on the mating surfaces when the head is installed, the gasket may not seal correctly and leaks could develop.

13 Check the block and head mating surfaces for nicks, deep scratches and other damage. If damage is slight, it can be removed with a file (see illustration).

14 Use a tap of the correct size – if you have one – to chase the threads in the head bolt holes (see illustration), then clean the holes with compressed air (if available) – make sure that nothing remains in the holes.

> **Warning:** Wear eye protection when using compressed air!

15 If you have the correct size die, mount each bolt in a vice and run the die down the threads to remove corrosion and restore the threads (see illustration). Dirt, corrosion, sealant and damaged threads will affect torque readings.

16 Reinstall the head using the new gasket. Do not use sealant on the gasket.

17 Once the head bolts are finger-tight, if you have a torque

Use a putty knife to remove the deposits from the piston and valves – don't nick or gouge the block or piston (if the deposits are oily, the rings may be worn)

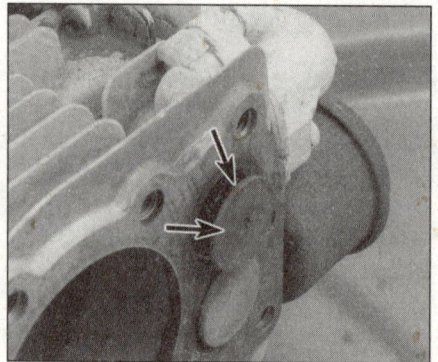

Turn the crankshaft to open each valve and check the seats and faces (arrowed) for cracks and other damage

Scrape the deposits out of the head, then use a wire brush and solvent to finish cleaning it

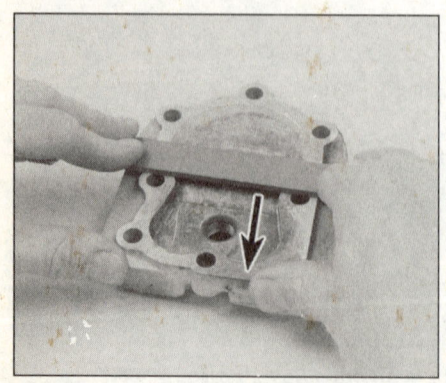

Use a single-cut file to flatten and restore the block and head mating surface – move the file sideways (arrowed) and don't apply excessive pressure

If you have one of the correct size, use a tap to clean and restore the head bolt holes in the block

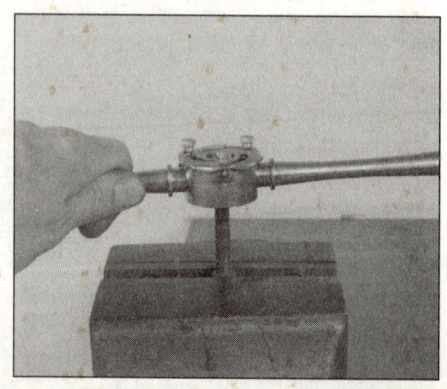

Mount each head bolt in a vice and restore the threads with a die of the correct size

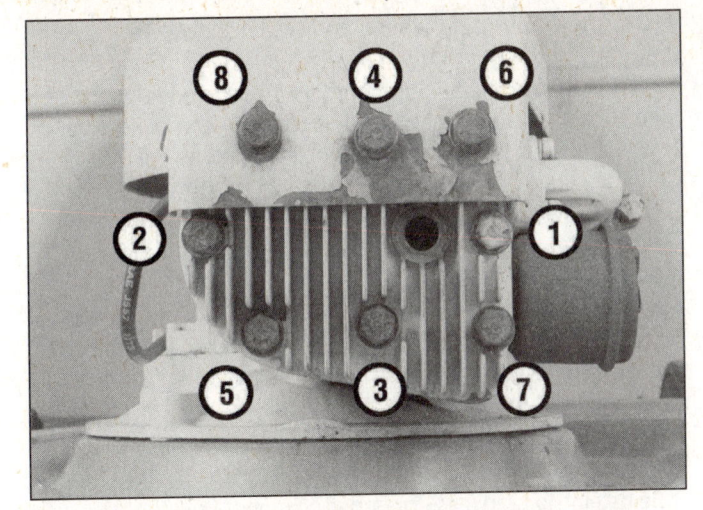

Tune-up and routine maintenance

When tightening the head bolts, follow a criss-cross pattern – never tighten them in order around the edge of the head

wrench, tighten them in 1/4 turn increments to the torque listed in the specifications in the relevant engine specific Chapter. When tightening the bolts, follow a criss-cross pattern to avoid warping the head *(see illustration)*. **Note:** *Don't forget to install the shroud first if some of the bolts are used to hold it in place!*

18 If you don't have a torque wrench, tighten the bolts securely with a socket and ratchet or swivel-drive handle.

13 Check the silencer

1 Make sure the silencer isn't restricted (if it's bent, dented, rusted or falling apart, install a new one).
2 Check the mounting bolts to ensure they're tight. A loose silencer can damage the engine.
3 If the silencer screws directly into the engine, make sure it's tight.
4 If the engine is a two-stroke, remove the silencer and check for carbon build-up in the exhaust ports *(see illustration)*. Scrape the carbon out of the ports and reinstall the silencer.

14 Check the valve tappet clearance (four-stroke engines only)

Correct valve tappet clearance is essential for efficient fuel use, easy starting, maximum power output, prevention of overheating and smooth engine operation. It also ensures the valves will last as long as possible

When the valve is closed, clearance should exist between the end of the stem and the tappet/rocker arm. The clearance is very small, but it's very important. The recommended clearances are listed in the Technical Data in the relevant engine specific Chapter. Note that intake and exhaust valves often require different clearances.
Note: *The engine must be cold when the clearances are checked.*

A feeler gauge with a blade thickness equal to the valve clearance(s) will be needed for this procedure.

On most side-valve (L-Head) engines, if the clearances are too small, the valves will have to be removed and the stem ends ground down carefully and lapped to provide more clearance (this is a major job, covered in the overhaul and repair procedures in the appropriate engine chapter). If the clearances are too great, new valves will have to be installed (again, a major repair procedure). **Note:** *OHV/OHC engines have adjustable rocker arms for changing the valve clearances.*

1 Disconnect the wire from the spark plug and position it clear of the engine/mower.

All except OHV/OHC engines

2 Remove the bolts and detach the tappet cover plate or the crankcase breather assembly *(see illustration)*.
Note: *On some engines the crankcase breather is behind the carburettor, so the carburettor will have to be removed first (see illustration).*

The exhaust ports on a two-stroke engine can get clogged with carbon, which should be removed with a hardwood stick

Remove the bolts and detach the tappet cover or crankcase breather from the engine

On some engines, the carburettor must be removed to get at the tappet chamber

4•13

Chapter 4

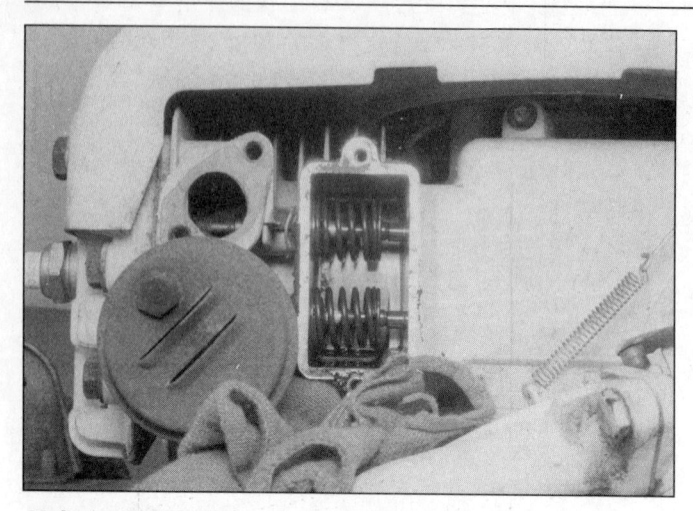

Make sure the valves are completely closed when checking the clearances

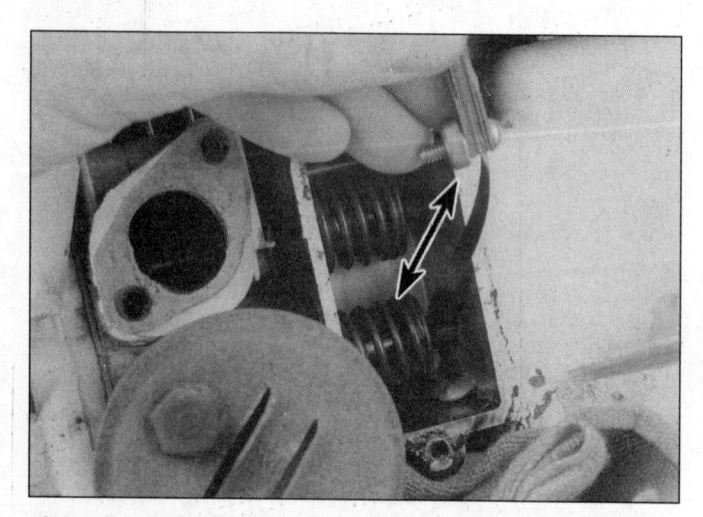

If the clearance is correct, the feeler gauge will fit between the valve stem and tappet with a slight drag

On OHV/OHC engines, the valve clearance is checked between the valve stem and rocker arm

3 Turn the crankshaft by hand and watch the valves to see if they stick in the guide(s).

4 Turn the crankshaft until the intake valve is wide open, then turn it an additional 360-degrees (one complete turn). This will ensure the valves are completely closed for the clearance check *(see illustration)*.

5 Select a feeler gauge thickness equal to the specified valve clearance and slip it between the valve stem end and the tappet *(see illustration)*.

6 If the feeler gauge can be moved back-and-forth with a slight drag, the clearance is correct. If it's loose, the clearance is excessive; if it's tight (watch the valve to see if it's forced open slightly), the clearance is inadequate.

7 If the clearance is incorrect, refer to the appropriate chapter for valve service procedures.

8 Reinstall the crankcase breather or tappet cover plate.

OHV/OHC engines

9 Remove the bolts and detach the cylinder head cover from the engine. **Note:** *On some engines the shroud will have to be removed first to get the cylinder head cover off.*

10 Remove the spark plug and place your thumb over the plug hole, then slowly turn the crankshaft with the starter or blade until you feel pressure building up in the cylinder. Use a torch to look into the spark plug hole and see if the piston is at the top of its stroke. Continue to turn the crankshaft until it is.

11 Select a feeler gauge thickness equal to the specified valve clearance and slip it between the valve stem end and the rocker arm *(see illustration)*.

12 If the feeler gauge can be moved back-and-forth with a slight drag, the clearance is correct. If it's loose, the clearance is excessive; if it's tight (watch the valve to see if it's forced open slightly), the clearance is inadequate.

13 To adjust the clearance on OHV engines, loosen the rocker arm locknut and turn the pivot in or out as required (turn it out to increase the clearance; turn it in to decrease the clearance). On OHC engines, slacken the lock nut and turn the tappet adjusting screw until the correct clearance is obtained.

14 Hold the pivot/tappet screw with a spanner and tighten the locknut securely, then recheck the clearance.

15 Install a new spark plug

A defective spark plug will increase fuel consumption, lead to formation of deposits in the cylinder head, cause hard starting, contribute to engine oil dilution (from contamination with petrol) and cause the engine to misfire. The spark plug in a two-stroke engine is particularly prone to fouling and should be checked and cleaned frequently.

1 Detach the wire from the spark plug.

Tune-up and routine maintenance

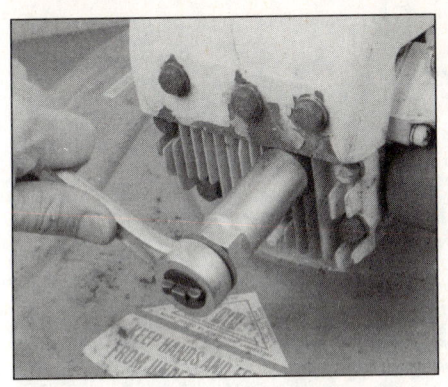

Use a spark plug socket to remove and install the plug

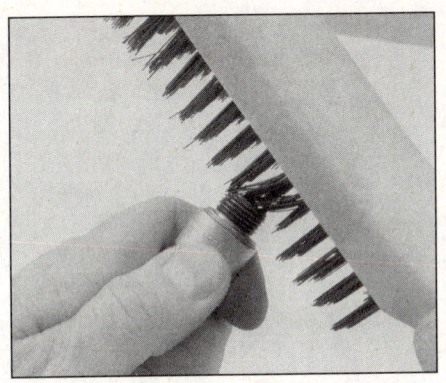

Use a wire brush to remove deposits from the plug tip

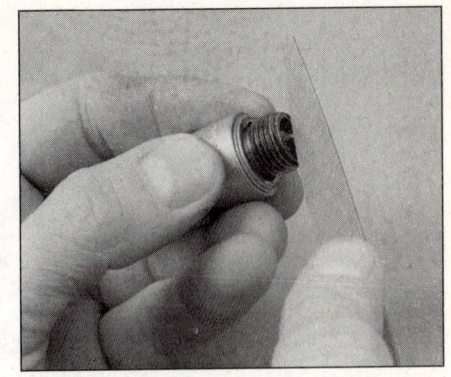

The spark plug electrodes should be square and sharp – use a fine file to dress them

2 Remove the spark plug from the engine (see illustration).
3 If the plug is coated with deposits, it can be cleaned with a wire brush (see illustration).
4 If the deposits are thick or hard, use a knife to remove them, then resort to the wire brush.
5 If the electrodes are slightly rounded off, use a small file to square them up (see illustration). The sharp edges will make it easier for the spark to occur.
6 If the electrodes are worn smooth or the porcelain insulator is cracked, install a new spark plug – the cost is minimal. Make sure the new plug has the same length threads and tip as the original.
7 Check the gap with a wire-type gauge (see illustration). The correct gap is listed in the Technical Data in the relevant engine specific Chapter.
8 If adjustment is required, bend the side electrode only with the special notched adjuster on the gap gauge (see illustration).
9 Check the threaded hole in the cylinder head. If the threads are damaged or stripped out, a special insert can be installed to salvage the head (see Chapter 2).
10 Install the plug in the engine and tighten it finger-tight. A torque wrench should be used for final tightening of the spark plug to a specified torque value, but the torque figure isn't always readily available (it'll vary depending on the size of the plug, the type of seat and the material the head is made of). As a general rule, the plug should be tightened 1/2-to-3/4 turn after the gasket contacts the cylinder head.
11 Reconnect the spark plug wire. If it's loose on the plug, crimp the wire terminal loop with a pair of pliers (see illustration).

16 Check/adjust the controls

The engine controls normally consist of a single lever that operates a cable connected to the governor linkage and/or choke valve on the carburettor. Some types of power equipment also have safety-related controls that shut down the engine if the operator releases his grip on the equipment.

There are so many different control configurations in use on small engines that it would be impossible to cover the correct connection and adjustment of all of them, so the following information is general in nature.

Spark plug manufacturers recommend using a wire-type gauge when checking the gap – if the wire doesn't slide between the electrodes with a slight drag, adjustment is required

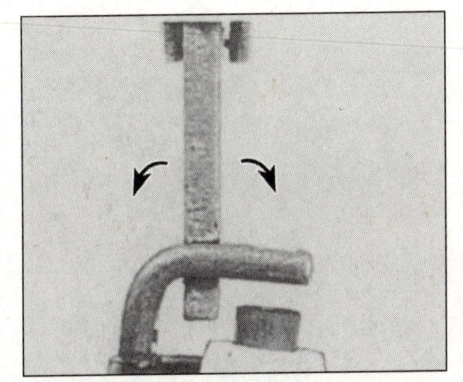

To change the gap, bend the side electrode only, as indicated by the arrows, and be very careful not to crack or chip the porcelain insulator surrounding the centre electrode

Use a pair of pliers to crimp the plug wire terminal so it fits snugly on the plug

Chapter 4

Lubricate the cable with WD-40 (apply the lubricant at the upper end of the cable)

The cable must be securely attached at the engine or the controls won't work properly

1 Check the lever to make sure it operates smoothly and moves the cable. Lubricate the lever pivot and cable if necessary *(see illustration)*.
2 The cable must be clamped in a stationary position at the engine. Tighten the clamp if necessary *(see illustration)*.
3 When the lever is moved to the STOP position, the switch on the carburettor must operate and short out (earth) the ignition system *(see illustration on page 4•11)*.

17 Adjust the carburettor

Carburettor adjustments are done by turning the high and/or low speed mixture screws. Some carburettors don't have any mixture screws, while others have one for either high-speed adjustments or low speed adjustments, but not both. Still others have one screw to adjust the fuel/air mixture at high speeds and another screw that controls the mixture at low speeds – the low speed screw is usually the one closest to the engine end of the carburettor. If two screws are used, they must be adjusted separately.

The mixture screws control the flow of fuel through the carburettor circuit(s) *(see illustration)*. If the tip is damaged or the screw is incorrectly adjusted, loss of power and erratic engine operation will result.

1 Remove the mixture screw and check the tip – if it looks bent or a groove has been worn in the tapered portion, install a new one *(see illustration)*. Do not attempt to straighten it. If the o-ring on the screw is damaged or deteriorated, replace it before attempting to adjust the mixture.
2 If the screw isn't bent or worn, reinstall it and turn it in until it stops – tighten it with your fingers only, don't force it.
3 Back it out about 1-1/4 turns (anti-clockwise) *(see illustration)*. **Note:** *The actual recommended number of turns out is different for each carburettor type, but the figure given here is an average for most engines.*

Typical mixture adjusting screws

Check the mixture screw tip to make sure it isn't damaged

Turn the mixture screw in small increments and wait for the engine to respond before continuing

4•16

Tune-up and routine maintenance

4 Start the engine and turn the screw clockwise until the engine starts to slow down. This means the fuel mixture is too lean (not enough fuel).

5 Slowly turn the screw out (anti-clockwise) until the engine begins to run smoothly. Keep going very slowly until the engine just begins to run rough again. Also watch for black smoke from the exhaust.

6 Finally, turn the screw in again (clockwise) to a point about half-way between rough operation and smooth operation. This is the right setting.

7 If an idle (low-speed) mixture screw is used, adjust it in the same manner with the engine idling. **Note:** *Honda engines are equipped with a pilot air screw, rather than a low-speed mixture screw. Turning the pilot screw has the same effect (it changes the fuel/air mixture), but it's reversed. When the pilot screw is turned in, it causes a richer mixture; conversely, when it's backed out, the mixture becomes leaner.* After the low-speed mixture has been set, recheck the high-speed adjustment – it may be affected by the idle adjustment.

8 Some carburettors also have an idle speed adjusting screw that's used to open or close the throttle valve slightly to change the idle speed only, not the fuel/air mixture. Turning it will cause the engine to speed up or slow down. You can tell the idle speed screw from the mixture screw(s) because it acts on the throttle linkage and doesn't screw into the carburettor body.

18 Check the engine mounting bolts/nuts

If the engine mounting bolts/nuts are loose, the engine will vibrate excessively and damage the equipment it's mounted on.

1 Disconnect the spark plug wire from the plug and earth it on the engine.

2 Use spanners and sockets to tighten the mounting fasteners securely.

3 If the nuts/bolts are stripped, install new ones.

4 Reconnect the spark plug wire.

Preparing an engine for storage

Since power equipment is often designed for use only during certain times of the year (like lawn mowers for example), small engines usually end up being stored for months at a time. As a result, needed repairs are neglected, corrosion takes place, fuel left in the tank and carburettor gums up, moisture collects in ignition and fuel system components and the equipment is subjected to physical damage as it's moved to get at something stored behind it.

After a long dormant period, the equipment is hauled out, fuel is added to the tank, the oil is checked (not always!) and the engine is fired up – but it won't start or it won't run very well. To avoid problems caused by seasonal storage, run down the following checklist of things to do and make sure the engine is properly prepared to survive a long period of non-use so it'll start and run well when you need it.

- Operate the engine until it runs out of fuel, then drain the float bowl (if equipped)
- An alternative to running the engine out of fuel is to add a petrol stabilizing additive to the fuel. These additives (although not yet widely available in this country) will 'preserve' the fuel left in the tank during storage, making restarting the engine easier.
- Wipe off all dust and remove debris from engine parts
- Service the air cleaner (see section 2 in this chapter)
- Remove the spark plug and squirt some clean engine oil into the spark plug hole, then operate the starter to distribute the oil in the cylinder
- Clean and regap the spark plug, then reinstall it (see section 15 in this chapter)
- Store the equipment in a dry place and cover the engine with plastic – don't seal the plastic around the base of the engine or condensation may occur

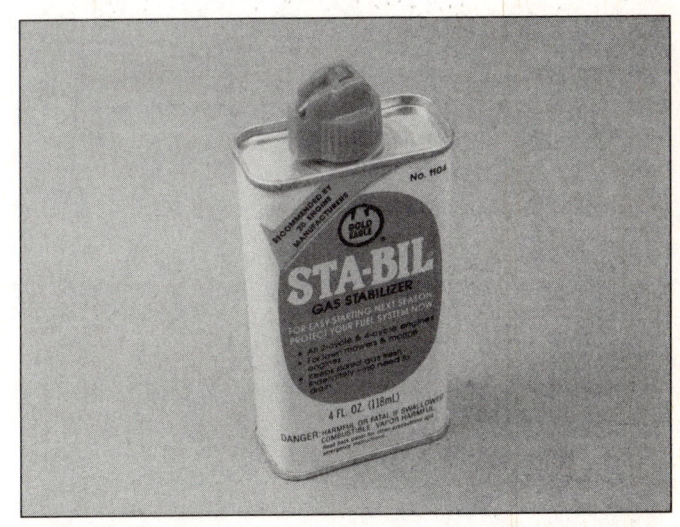

When preparing an engine for storage, either drain the fuel system, run the engine out of fuel, or add a petrol stabilising additive (if available)

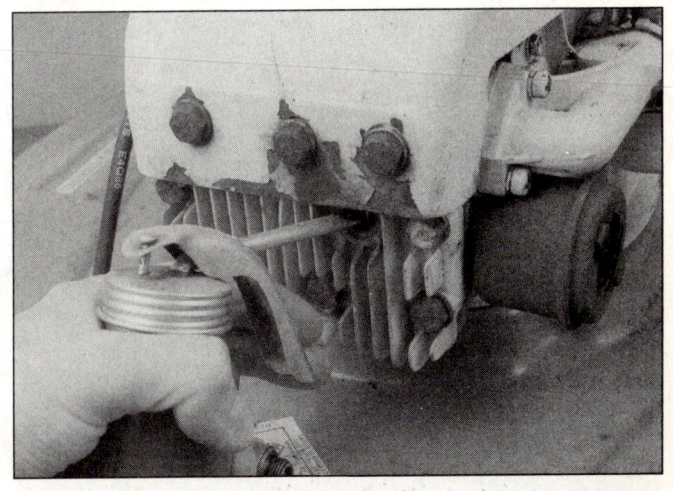

Squirt oil into the spark plug hole to coat the piston, rings and cylinder and prevent rust

Chapter 4

Repair procedures common to all engines 5

Engine removal and installation
Silencer removal and installation
Shroud/recoil starter removal and installation
Oil seal replacement
Carburettor removal
Carburettor overhaul
Engine block cleaning

Engine block inspection
Cylinder honing
Crankshaft and bearing inspection
Camshaft and bearing inspection
Piston/connecting rod inspection
Piston ring installation
Valve/tappet inspection and servicing

Engine removal and installation

Engine removal is usually done only if major repairs or an overhaul are required (or, obviously, if a new engine is being installed on the equipment). In most cases, minor repairs can be accomplished without removing the engine.

1 Detach the spark plug wire and position it clear of the engine.

2 Disconnect the control cables from the engine. **Note:** *On many newer pieces of equipment, a flywheel brake cable and wire harness may have to be detached as well as the throttle cable.*

3 Drain and/or remove the fuel tank, so fuel doesn't run all over if the equipment must be tipped to get at the blade or engine mount bolts.

4 Remove the blade and hub or drivebelt(s)/chain from the power take-off end of the crankshaft.

The bolt(s) holding a lawn mower blade in place are usually very tight and often corroded. Apply penetrating oil and let it soak in for several minutes, then use a six-point socket and swivel-drive handle for added leverage. Wear a leather glove so the blade doesn't cut your hand, or wedge a block of wood between the mower deck and blade so it doesn't turn. If all else fails, take the mower to a dealer or garage and have the bolt(s) removed with an air impact wrench.

5 Remove the mounting nuts/bolts and detach the engine from the equipment.

6 If major repairs are planned, use a degreaser to clean the engine before disassembling it.

7 Installation is the reverse of removal.

Silencer removal and installation

Some silencers screw into the engine, while others are attached with bolts. Some are located above the mower deck; some (particularly on two-stroke engines) are located below it. **Note:** *If the silencer is in good condition, it can be cleaned by tapping it with a soft-face hammer and dumping out the carbon that's dislodged.*

Screw-in silencers

1 To remove a screw-in type, first apply penetrating oil to the threads and let it sit for several minutes. You may have to tip the equipment to do this.

Chapter 5

Screw-in silencers can be removed/installed with a pipe wrench. If the silencer has a built-in hex for an open-end spanner, it makes sense to use it. Only use a pipe wrench on the pipe which screws into the engine, not on the silencer body

2 Try to remove the silencer with a pipe wrench by turning it anti-clockwise *(see illustration)*. Some silencers have a locking ring that must be loosened with a hammer and punch before the pipe will turn. Others have a built-in hex to accept an open-end spanner (usually there's not enough room to use a pipe wrench with this type).

3 If it breaks off, try to remove the part left in the engine (if there's enough left to grasp with the wrench). If it won't come out, use a large screw extractor or cold chisel to remove it. The silencer material is fairly soft, so don't damage the threads in the engine.

4 Screw in the new silencer, but don't over tighten it. If a lock ring is used, tighten it with a hammer and punch.

Bolt-on silencers

5 Apply penetrating oil to the bolt(s) and let it soak in for several minutes.

6 Remove the bolts and detach the silencer (some silencers also have a gasket).

7 If a bolt breaks off in the engine block (which they often do), you may be able to remove it with a screw extractor (read Chapter 2 before deciding to tackle this job). If it protrudes far enough, you may be able to grip it with self-locking pliers and unscrew it. Apply more penetrating oil before attempting this.

8 Install the new silencer (with a new gasket, if used) and tighten the bolt(s) securely.

Shroud/recoil starter removal and installation

The recoil starter on most engines is an integral part of the shroud that's used to direct the cooling air around the cylinder and head. On some engines, the starter is attached to the shroud or engine with nuts or bolts and can be removed separately for repairs or replacement *(see illustrations)*.

1 Detach any control cables/wire harnesses clamped to the shroud.

2 If the fuel tank is mounted on the shroud, remove it, or detach the fuel line from the carburettor, and plug it to prevent fuel loss. **Note:** *Some engines are equipped with a shut-off valve on the tank – if your engine has one, turn it off before detaching the fuel line from the carburettor.*

3 Remove the nuts/bolts and lift the shroud off the engine *(see illustration)*.

4 Before installing the shroud, clean it to remove grass clippings and other debris. Also, make sure the bolt threads in the engine are clean and in good condition.

Oil seal replacement

Two seals are used to keep oil inside the crankcase (four-stroke engines) or the petrol/oil mixture inside the crankcase and air out (two-stroke engines) – one on the flywheel side

Some recoil starters are attached to the shroud with screws . . .

. . .while others are bolted to the engine and can be removed separately from the shroud

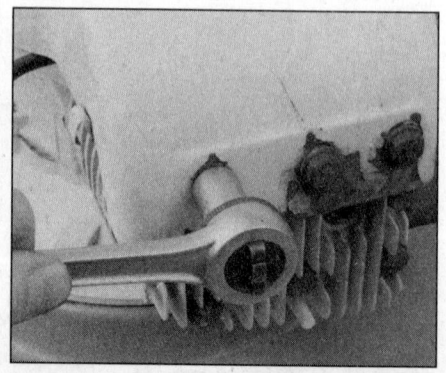

Three or four bolts are usually used to hold the shroud to the engine – cylinder head bolts are often used to attach it at one end

Repair procedures common to all engines

and one on the drive or power take-off side of the crankshaft.

If an oil seal fails, oil will leak out all over the engine, and performance will suffer. This is particularly so on engines with contact breaker points, as the points get fouled by the oil. Two-stroke engines can suffer from difficult starting and erratic operation, and could even sustain damage due to a lean fuel/air mixture, caused by extra air entering the crankcase through the leaking seal(s).

Seals can often be replaced without removing the crankshaft. If the seal on the power take-off end of the crankshaft is leaking, the blade or drive pulley/sprocket will have to be removed first. The flywheel will have to be removed first if the seal under it is leaking (refer to the appropriate engine chapter for the flywheel removal procedure).

Once the seal is exposed, proceed as follows:

1 Note how the seal is installed (what the side that faces out looks like and how far it's recessed into the bore), then remove it. On most engines, the seal can be prised out with a screwdriver *(see illustration)*. Be careful not to nick or otherwise damage the seal bore if this is done.

Some seals consist of three separate pieces – a lock ring, a retainer and the seal. **Note:** *Experience has shown that this type of seal is difficult to replace with the crankshaft installed. There's usually very little room to work, which makes the job very exasperating, and increases the chance the new seal may not be airtight, which defeats the whole purpose of doing the job. Additionally, the magneto will probably have to be removed to make room, so it may be easier in the long run to go ahead and disassemble the engine (remove the crankshaft) to replace the seal.*

Prise the lock ring out with a sharp tool like a bradawl, scribe or ice pick, then turn the engine upside-down and tap the end of the crankshaft to dislodge the retainer. Remove the seal with a sharp tool. If it won't come out, you may have to remove the crankshaft (which requires engine disassembly).

2 Clean the seal bore and the crankshaft. Remove any burrs that could damage the new seal from the crankshaft with a file or whetstone.

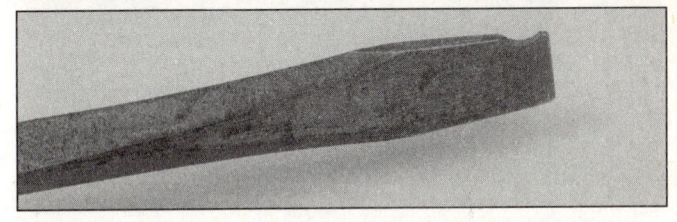

Carefully prise out the oil seal with a screwdriver (above); grind a small groove in the side of the screwdriver tip so it'll grip the seal better (below)

3 If necessary, wrap electrician's tape around the crankshaft to protect the new seal as it's installed. The keyway in the crankshaft is particularly apt to cut or otherwise damage the seal as it's slipped over it.

4 Apply a thin layer of multi-purpose grease to the outer edge of the new seal and lubricate the seal lip(s) with plenty of grease *(see illustration)*.

5 Place the seal squarely in the bore with the open side facing into the engine.

6 Carefully tap the seal into place with a large socket or section of pipe and a hammer until it's seated in the bore *(see illustration)*. The outer diameter of the socket or pipe should be the same size as the seal outer diameter.

7 If the seal consists of several pieces, install the retainer and lock ring and make sure the lock ring is seated in the groove.

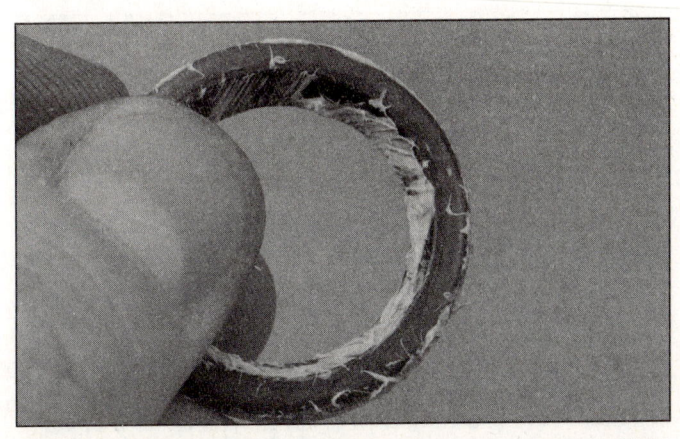

Apply multi-purpose grease to the outer edge and the lip(s) of the new seal before installing it

A socket or a piece of pipe makes a handy seal installation tool

5•3

Chapter 5

Governor linkages are unique and somewhat complex, so make a sketch of how all the parts fit together before disconnecting anything

A governor link (arrowed) typically must be detached from the carburettor during removal

Carburettor removal

1 If equipped, turn the fuel valve off.
2 Remove the air cleaner assembly.

> **Warning:** Petrol is extremely flammable, and highly explosive under certain conditions – safety precautions must be followed when working on the carburettor or fuel tank! Don't smoke or allow open flames or unshielded light bulbs in or near the work area. Don't do this procedure in a garage with a natural gas appliance (such as a water heater or clothes dryer) and have a fire extinguisher handy.

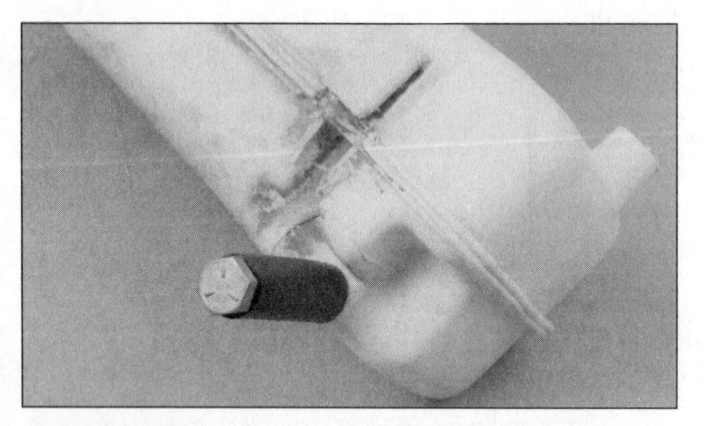

Plug the fuel line with a snug-fitting bolt or steel rod to prevent fuel loss

3 Disconnect the governor spring(s) *(see illustration)*.

This is very important – most governor linkages have several holes for connecting things up and it can get very confusing. Don't rely on your memory or you may not be able to get everything connected up correctly. Make a simple sketch to refer to later.

Sometimes it's easier to disconnect the governor linkage after the carburettor is detached from the engine.

4 Disconnect the throttle cable and kill switch wire (if equipped) from the carburettor. This isn't necessary on all engines – try to determine if the cable/wire will interfere with the actual carburettor removal before disconnecting them (sometimes they're attached to the governor linkage and don't have to be removed). Note that after the mounting bolts are removed, the governor link *(see illustration)* will have to be manipulated out of the throttle lever as the carburettor is detached.

5 Detach the fuel line from the carburettor or fuel tank fitting and plug it (if a shut-off valve isn't used) *(see illustration)*. Now is a good time to inspect the fuel line and install a new one if it's damaged or deteriorated. **Note:** *Some carburettors are mounted directly on the fuel tank and no fuel line is used.*

6 Remove the nuts/bolts and detach the carburettor (or fuel tank/carburettor assembly) from the engine, then disconnect any control linkage still attached to it. Watch for spacers on engines with the carburettor mounted on the tank – make sure they're returned to their original location(s) when the bolts are installed. The carburettor may be attached directly to the engine or to an intake manifold *(see illustration)*. If an intake manifold

Most carburettors are attached to a manifold, which is bolted to the engine – don't try to separate the carburettor from the manifold until after they're detached from the engine

5•4

Repair procedures common to all engines

is used, it's usually easier to detach the manifold from the engine and separate the carburettor afterwards.

7 Remove the gasket and discard it – use a new one when the carburettor is reinstalled. Some engines also have an insulator and/or heat shield (and a second gasket) between the carburettor and engine. **Note:** *On Honda engines, the insulator must be reinstalled with the grooved side against the carburettor.*

8 Due to the many differences from manufacturer to manufacturer, carburettor disassembly and reassembly is covered in each engine chapter.

9 Reverse the removal procedure when installing the carburettor.

Carburettor overhaul

> *Warning: Petrol is extremely flammable and highly explosive under certain conditions – safety precautions must be followed when working on the carburettor! Don't smoke or allow open flames or unshielded light bulbs in or near the work area. Don't do this procedure in a garage with a natural gas appliance (such as a water heater or clothes dryer), and have a fire extinguisher handy.*

Poor engine performance, hesitation, black smoke and little or no engine response to fuel/air mixture adjustments are all signs that major carburettor maintenance is required.

Keep in mind that many so-called carburettor problems are really not carburettor problems at all, but mechanical problems in the engine or ignition system faults. Establish for certain the carburettor needs servicing before assuming an overhaul is necessary. For example, fuel starvation is often mistaken for a carburettor problem. Make sure the fuel filter (if used), the fuel line and the fuel tank cap vent hole aren't blocked before blaming the carburettor for this relatively common malfunction.

Most carburettor problems are caused by dirt particles, varnish and other deposits which build up in and block the fuel and air passages. Also, in time, gaskets and O-rings shrink and cause fuel and air leaks which lead to poor performance.

When the carburettor is overhauled, it's generally disassembled completely – disassembly is covered in the appropriate engine chapter – and the metal components are soaked in carburettor cleaner (which dissolves fuel deposits, varnish, dirt and sludge). The parts are then rinsed thoroughly with degreaser and dried with compressed air. The fuel and air passages are also blown out with compressed air to force out any dirt that may have been loosened but not removed by the carburettor cleaner. Once the cleaning process is complete, the carburettor is reassembled using new gaskets, O-rings, diaphragms and, generally, a new inlet needle and seat (not used in all carburettors).

Before taking the carburettor apart, make sure you have a rebuild kit (which will include all necessary gaskets and other parts), some carburettor cleaner, solvent, a supply of rags, some means of blowing out the carburettor passages and a clean place to work.

Some of the carburettor settings, such as the sizes of the jets and the internal passageways are predetermined by the manufacturer. Under normal circumstances, they won't have to be changed or modified and they should never be enlarged. Before disassembling the carburettor, clean the outside with degreaser and lay it on a clean sheet of paper.

After it's been completely disassembled, submerge the metal components in carburettor cleaner and allow them to soak for approximately 30 minutes.

> *Caution: Do not soak plastic or rubber parts in carburettor cleaner – they'll be damaged or dissolved. Also, don't allow excessive amounts of carburettor cleaner to get on your skin.*

After the carburettor has soaked long enough for the cleaner to loosen and dissolve the varnish and other deposits, rinse it thoroughly with degreaser and blow it dry with compressed air. Also, blow out all the fuel and air passages in the carburettor body. **Note:** *Never clean the jets or passages with a piece of wire or drill bit – they could be enlarged, causing the fuel and air metering rates to be upset.*

Reassembly and carburettor adjustment is covered in the appropriate engine chapter.

Engine block cleaning

After the engine has been completely disassembled, clean the block as described here before conducting a thorough inspection to determine if it's re-usable.

1 Using a gasket scraper, remove all traces of gasket material and old sealant from the block *(see illustration)*. Be very careful not to nick or gouge the gasket sealing surfaces.

Use a scraper or putty knife to remove old gaskets from the engine components – if the gasket is stubborn, use a gasket removal solvent on it

Chapter 5

2 Clean the block with solvent to remove dirt, sludge and oil, then dry it with compressed air (if available). Take your time and do a thorough job.

3 The threaded holes in the block must be clean to ensure accurate torque readings, and to prevent damaged threads during reassembly. Run the proper size tap into each of the holes to remove rust, corrosion, thread locking fluid or dirt and restore damaged threads. If possible, use compressed air to clear the holes of debris produced by this operation. Now is a good time to clean the threads on the head bolts and the connecting rod cap bolts as well.

Engine block inspection

1 Before the block is inspected, it should be cleaned as described above. Double-check to make sure the carbon or wear ridge at the top of the cylinder has been completely removed.

2 Visually check the block for cracks, rust and corrosion. Look for stripped threads in the threaded holes. It's also a good idea to have the block checked for hidden cracks by an automotive engineering workshop that has the special equipment to do this type of work. If defects are found, have the block repaired, if possible, or replaced.

3 Check the cylinder bore for scuffing and score marks.

4 Measure the diameter of the cylinder bore.

This should be done at the top (just under the ridge area), centre and bottom of the cylinder bore, parallel to the crankshaft (see illustrations).

Next, measure the cylinder diameter at the same three locations across the crankshaft. Note the results and consult your local small engine specialist as to whether the block is usable.

If the cylinder is badly scuffed or scored, or if it's out-of-round or tapered beyond the limits given in the specifications, have the engine block rebored and honed at a small engine dealer or an automotive engineering workshop. If a rebore is done, an oversize piston and rings will be required.

5 If the cylinder is in reasonably good condition and not worn to the outside of the limits, and if the piston-to-cylinder clearance can be maintained properly, then it doesn't have to be resized. Honing is all that's necessary (see the next section).

Cylinder honing

Prior to engine reassembly, the cylinder bore should be honed so the new piston rings will seat correctly and provide the best possible combustion chamber seal. **Note:** *This procedure applies to engines with an iron bore only – aluminium cylinder bores do not require honing for the rings*

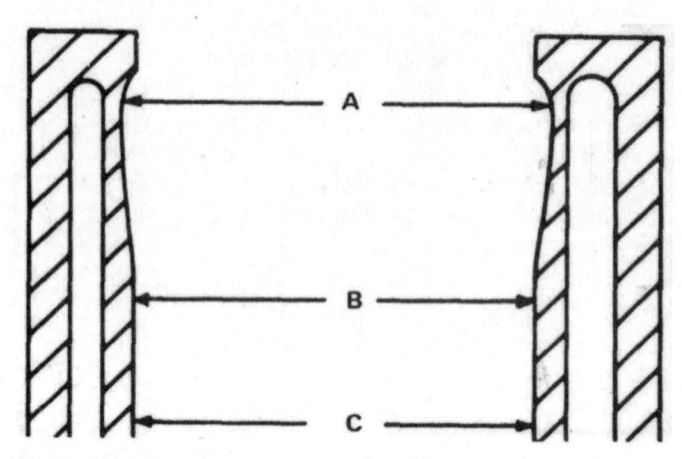

Measure the diameter of each cylinder just under the wear ridge (A), at the centre (B) and at the bottom (C)

to seat. Also, most small engine manufacturers provide chrome ring sets (for both aluminium and iron-bore engines) that don't require cylinder honing before installation. If you don't have the tools or don't want to tackle the honing operation, most automotive engineering workshops and small engine dealers will do it for a reasonable fee.

Two types of cylinder hones are commonly available – the flex hone or 'bottle brush' type and the more traditional surfacing hone with spring-loaded stones. Both will do the job, but for the less experienced mechanic the 'bottle brush' hone will probably be easier to use.

You'll also need plenty of light oil or honing oil, some rags and an electric drill motor. Proceed as follows:

1 Mount the hone in the drill, compress the stones and slip

The ability to 'feel' when the telescoping gauge is at the correct point will be developed over time, so work slowly and repeat the check until you're satisfied the bore measurement is accurate – the telescoping gauge is measured with a micrometer to determine the actual bore size

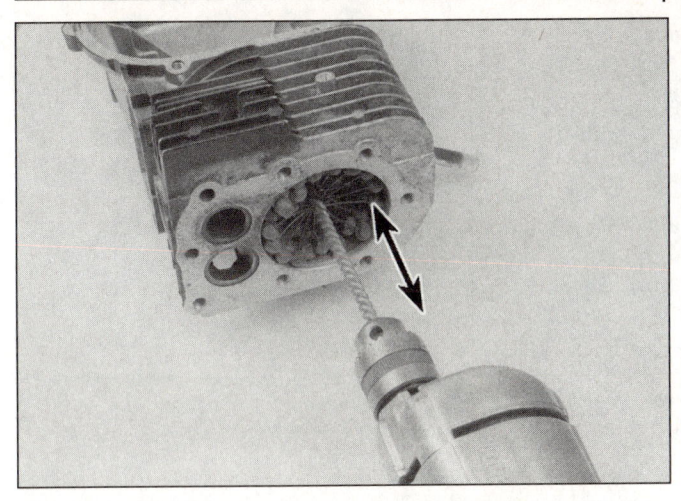

Repair procedures common to all engines

If this is the first time you've ever honed cylinders, you'll get better results with a 'bottle brush' hone that you will with a traditional spring-loaded hone

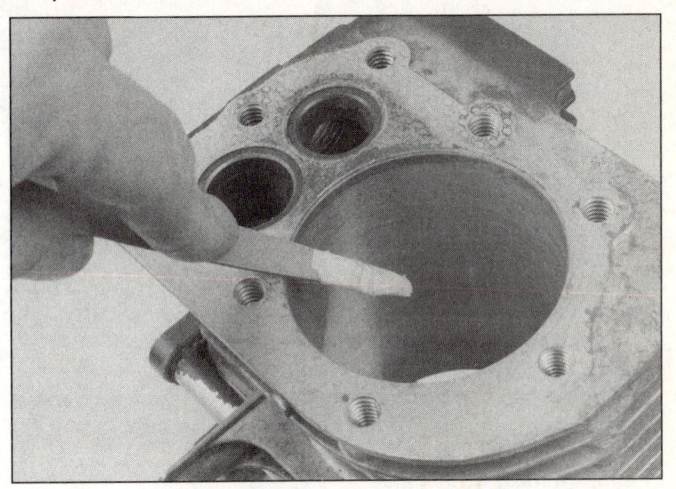

After honing the cylinder, run a file around the top edge of the bore to knock off the sharp edge so the rings don't catch when the piston is reinstalled – note the tape on the end of the file to prevent nicks in the cylinder wall

it into the cylinder *(see illustration)*. Be sure to wear safety goggles or a face shield!

2 Lubricate the cylinder with plenty of oil, turn on the drill and move the hone up-and-down at a pace that'll produce a fine crosshatch pattern on the cylinder walls.

Ideally, the crosshatch lines should intersect at approximately a 60-degree angle *(see illustration below)*. Be sure to use plenty of lubricant and don't take off any more material than absolutely necessary to produce the desired finish. **Note:** *Piston ring manufacturers may specify a smaller crosshatch angle than the traditional 60-dgrees – read and follow any instructions included with the new rings.*

3 Don't withdraw the hone from the cylinder while it's running. Instead, shut off the drill and continue moving the hone up-and-down in the cylinder until it comes to a complete stop, then compress the stones and withdraw the hone. If you're using a 'bottle brush' type hone, stop the drill, then turn the chuck in the normal direction of rotation while withdrawing the hone from the cylinder.

4 Wipe the oil out of the cylinder.

5 After the honing job is complete, chamfer the top edge of the cylinder bore with a small file so the rings won't catch when the piston

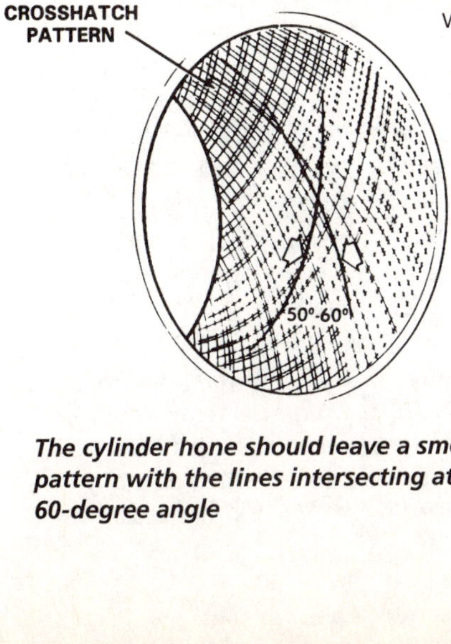

The cylinder hone should leave a smooth, crosshatch pattern with the lines intersecting at approximately a 60-degree angle

is installed *(see illustration)*. Be very careful not to nick the cylinder wall with the end of the file.

6 The engine block must be washed again very thoroughly with warm, soapy water to remove all traces of abrasive grit produced during the honing operation. **Note:** *The bore can be considered clean when a white cloth – dampened with clean engine oil – used to wipe it down doesn't pick up any more honing residue, which will show up as grey areas on the cloth.*

7 After rinsing, dry the block and apply a coat of light oil to the cylinder to prevent the formation of rust. If the engine isn't going to be reassembled right away, store the block in a plastic bag to keep it clean and set it aside until reassembly.

Crankshaft and bearing inspection

Crankshaft

After the crankshaft has been removed from the engine, it should be cleaned thoroughly with solvent and dried with compressed air (if available). If the crankshaft has oil passages drilled in it, clean them out with a wire or stiff plastic bristle brush, then flush them with degreaser.

Caution: Wear eye protection when using compressed air!

1 Check the connecting rod journal for uneven wear, score marks, pits, cracks and flat spots. If the rod journal is damaged or worn, check the connecting rod bearing surface as well. If the crankshaft rides in plain bearings, check the main bearing journals and the thrust faces in the same manner (the thrust faces contact the bearings to restrict the end play of the crankshaft).

Chapter 5

Rubbing a penny lengthwise on the connecting rod journal will give you a quick idea of its condition – if copper rubs off the penny and adheres to the crankshaft, it's too rough and a new crankshaft must be installed

Check the gear teeth for wear and damage . . .

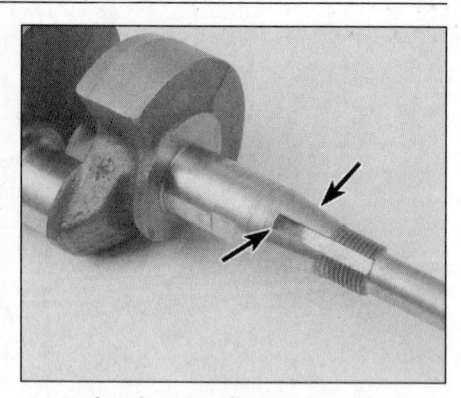

. . . and make sure the taper and keyway are in good shape

2 Rub a penny across each journal several times (if it rides in a plain bearing) *(see illustration)*. If a journal picks up copper from the penny, it's too rough.

3 Check the gear teeth for cracks, chips and excessive wear *(see illustration)*.

4 Check the threads on each end of the crankshaft – if they're worn or damaged, they may be salvageable with a die or thread file. Check the power take-off end to make sure it's not bent.

5 Check the crankshaft taper for rust and damage *(see illustration)*. If damage is noted, check the matching taper in the flywheel.

6 Inspect each keyway for deformation – if the one in the taper is worn or spread open, the ignition timing will be inaccurate. A new crankshaft will be needed.

7 Check the rest of the crankshaft for cracks and other damage.

8 Using a micrometer, measure the diameter of the main and connecting rod journals *(see illustration)*.

9 Note the results and consult your local small engine specialist as to whether or not the crankshaft is usable.

The connecting rod and main bearing journal diameters (if applicable) can be measured with a micrometer

By measuring the diameter at a number of points around each journal's circumference, you'll be able to determine whether or not the journal is out-of-round.

Take the measurement at each end of the rod journal, near the crank throws, to determine if the journal is tapered.

If the crankshaft journals are damaged, tapered, out-of-round or worn beyond the limits given in the specifications, a new crankshaft will be required.

10 Check the oil seal journals at each end of the crankshaft for wear and damage. If the seal has worn a groove in the journal, or if the journal is nicked or scratched, the new seal may leak when the engine is reassembled.

Bearings

The bearings shouldn't be removed from the crankcase unless they're defective or they have to come out with the crankshaft.

11 Clean the bearings with degreaser and allow them to air dry.

> **Caution:** *Do not use compressed air to spin ball bearings – spinning a dry bearing will cause rapid wear and damage.*

12 Check ball or roller bearings for wear, damage and play in the bore. **Note:** *If the engine is a two-stroke, check the connecting rod big end needle bearings and steel liners (if used) for wear, damage and distortion. Look for cracks, pits, flaked areas and flat spots on the needles.*

Rotate them by hand and feel for smooth operation with no axial or radial play. If the bearing is in the engine, make sure the outer race is securely fastened in the bore. If it's loose, the block may have to be peened to grip the bearing tighter or a liquid bearing mount (similar to thread locking fluid) may have to be used.

13 Check plain bearings for wear, score marks and grooves or deep scratches. Be sure to check the thrust faces (they keep the crankshaft from moving end-to-end too much) as

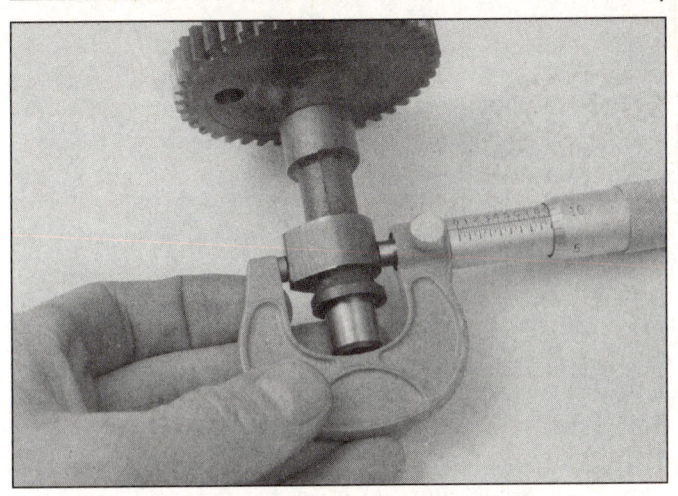

Repair procedures common to all engines

If the cam lobe height is less than specified, engine performance will suffer – install a new camshaft

The camshaft bearing journal diameters can be measured with a micrometer to determine if excessive wear has occurred

well. The bearing face should be smooth and satiny, not brightly polished.

If new plain bearings are needed, have them installed by a dealer so they can be reamed to size as well. **Note:** *On many engines, the crankshaft rides directly in the aluminium material used for the engine block. If the bearing surfaces are worn or damaged, a dealer can ream out the holes and install bushings.*

Camshaft and bearing inspection

After the camshaft has been removed from the engine, it should be cleaned thoroughly with degreaser and dried with compressed air (if available).

Caution: Wear eye protection when using compressed air!

1 Visually inspect the camshaft for wear and/or damage to the gear teeth, lobe surfaces and bearing journals. If the cam lobes are worn or damaged, check the matching tappets as well.

2 Measure the camshaft lobe heights *(see illustration)*, not the results and consult your local small engine specialist as to whether the camshaft is usable.

3 Measure the camshaft bearing journal diameters *(see illustration)*.

4 If the journals or lobes are worn beyond the specified limits, replace the camshaft.

5 If an automatic spark advance mechanism is installed, check the weight for free movement and make sure the spring pulls it back. If it doesn't, and the weight isn't binding, install a new spring (if available separately).

6 If an automatic compression release mechanism is attached to the camshaft, check the components for binding and wear.

Piston/connecting rod inspection

If the cylinder must be rebored, there's no reason to check the piston, since a new (larger) one will have to be installed anyway.

Before the inspection can be carried out, the piston/connecting rod assembly must be cleaned with degreaser and the original piston rings removed from the piston. **Note:** *Always use new piston rings when the engine is reassembled – check with a dealer to ensure the correct ones are purchased and installed.*

1 Using a piston ring installation tool, if available, or your fingers, remove the rings from the piston *(see illustration)*. Be careful not to nick or gouge the piston in the process.

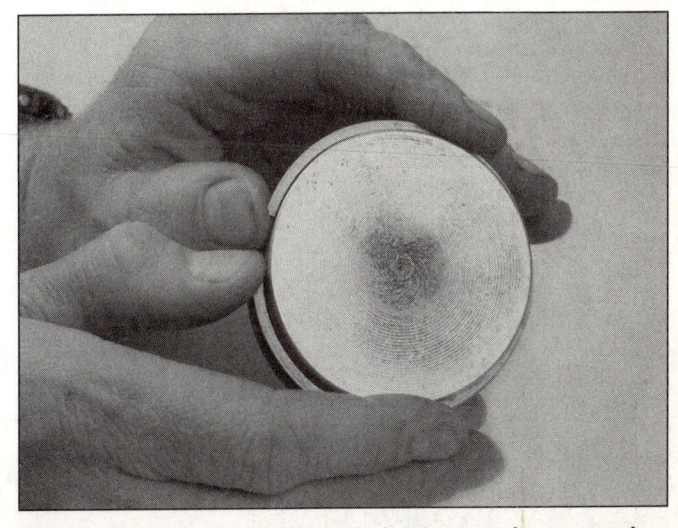

If you don't have the special tool, the rings can be removed from the piston with your fingers, but be careful not to break them (unless new ones are being installed)

5•9

Chapter 5

Remove the carbon from the top of the piston with a scraper or wire brush, then use fine emery cloth or steel wool and solvent to finish the job

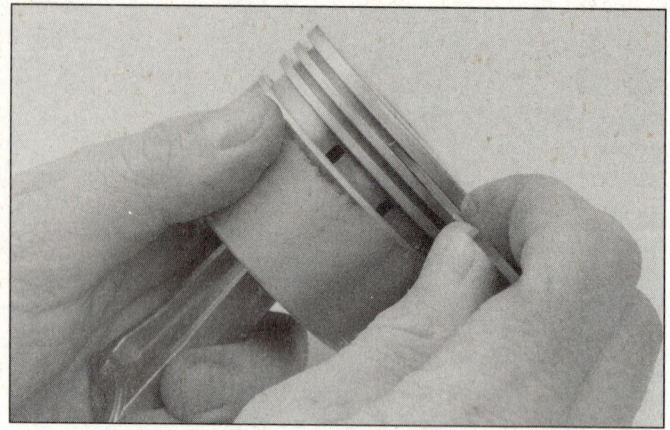

The piston ring grooves can be cleaned with a piece of broken piston ring. Protect your fingers – piston rings are sharp!

2 Scrape all traces of carbon off the top of the piston *(see illustration)*.

A hand-held wire brush or a piece of fine emery cloth can be used once the majority of deposits have been scraped away. Do not, under any circumstances, use a wire brush mounted in an electric drill to remove deposits from the piston – the piston material is soft and will be eroded by the wire brush.

3 Use a piece of broken piston ring to remove carbon deposits from the ring grooves *(see illustration)*. Special tools are also available for this job.

Be very careful to remove only the carbon deposits. Don't remove any metal and don't nick or scratch the sides of the ring grooves.

4 Once the deposits have been removed, clean the piston and connecting rod with degreaser and dry them with compressed air (if available). Make sure the oil return holes in the back side of the oil ring groove and the oil hole in the lower end of the rod are clear *(see illustration)*.

5 If the piston and cylinder aren't damaged or worn excessively, and if the engine block isn't rebored or replaced, a new piston won't be necessary. New piston rings, as mentioned above, should normally be installed when an engine is rebuilt.

6 Carefully inspect the piston for cracks around the skirt, at the pin bosses and at the ring lands. **Note:** *If the piston is from a two-stroke engine, make sure the pins used to restrict rotation of the piston rings are secure*

7 Look for scoring and scuffing on the thrust faces of the skirt, holes in the piston crown and burned areas at the edge of the crown.

8 Measure the piston ring side clearance by laying a new piston ring in each ring groove and slipping a feeler gauge in beside it *(see illustration)*. Check the clearance at three or four locations around each groove. Be sure to use the correct ring for each groove; they are different. If the side clearance appears excessive (more than 0.12 mm – 0.005 inch), a new piston will be required.

9 Check the piston-to-bore clearance by measuring the bore (see *Engine block inspection*) and the piston diameter.

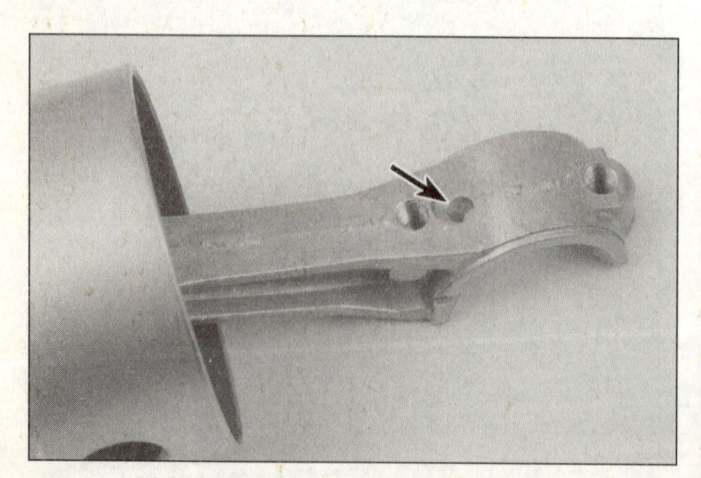

Make sure the oil hole in the connecting rod is clear

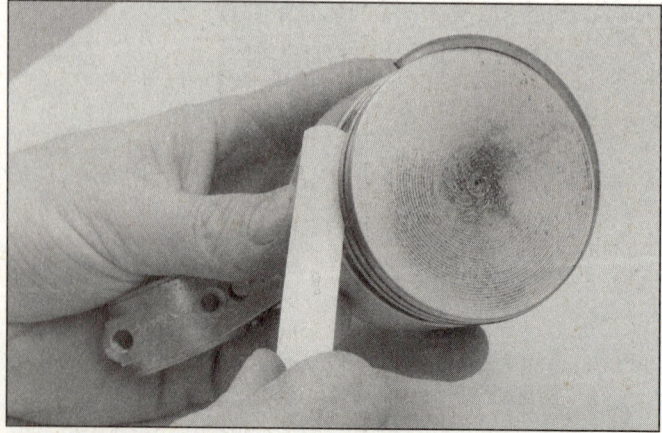

Check the ring side clearance with a feeler gauge at several points around the groove

Repair procedures common to all engines

Measure the piston across the skirt, at a 90-degree angle to the piston pin near the lower edge. Subtract the piston diameter from the bore diameter to obtain the clearance (if applicable – not all manufacturers provide specifications). If it's greater than specified, the cylinder will have to be rebored and a new piston and rings installed.

10 Check the piston-to-rod clearance by twisting the piston and rod in opposite directions. Any noticeable play indicates excessive wear, which must be corrected by installing a new piston, connecting rod or piston pin (or all three – see your dealer).

11 Check the connecting rod for cracks and other damage. Clean and inspect the bearing surface for score marks, gouges and deep scratches.

Piston ring installation

1 Before installing the new piston rings, the ring end gaps must be checked. It's assumed the piston ring side clearance has been checked and verified correct (see *Piston/connecting rod inspection* above).

2 Insert the top (upper compression) ring into the cylinder and square it up with the cylinder wall by pushing it in with the top of the piston *(see illustration)*. The ring should be near the bottom of the cylinder, at the lower limit of ring travel.

3 Measure the end gap.

To do this, slip feeler gauges between the ends of the ring until a gauge equal to the gap width is found *(see illustration)*. The feeler gauge should slide between the ring ends with a slight amount of drag.

Compare the measurement to the Technical Data in the engine specific Chapters of the book. If the gap is larger or smaller than specified, double-check to make sure you have the correct rings before proceeding.

If the gap is too small, it must be enlarged or the ring ends may come in contact with each other during engine operation, which can cause serious damage. The gap can be increased by filing the ring ends very carefully with a fine file. Mount the file in a vice operation, file only from the outside in.

4 Excess end gap isn't critical unless it's greater than 1.0 mm (0.039 in). Again, double-check to make sure you have the correct rings for the engine.

5 Repeat the procedure for each ring.

6 Once the ring end gaps have been checked/corrected, the equipped with soft jaws, slip the ring over the file with the ends contacting the file face and slowly move the ring to remove material from the ends. When performing this rings can be installed on the piston. **Note:** *Follow the instructions with the new piston rings if they differ from the information here.*

7 Install the piston rings.

The oil control ring (lowest one on the piston – four-stroke engines only) is installed first. On most engines it's composed of three separate components. Slip the spacer/expander into the groove first. If an anti-rotation tang is used, make sure it's inserted into the drilled hole in the ring groove.

Next, install the lower side rail. Don't use a piston ring installation tool on the oil ring side rails – they may be damaged. Instead, place one end of the side rail into the groove between the spacer/expander and the ring land, hold it firmly in place and slide a finger around the piston while pushing the rail into the groove. Next, install the upper side rail in the same manner.

After the three oil ring components have been installed, check to make sure both the upper and lower side rails can be turned smoothly in the ring groove.

8 The lower compression ring is installed next (two-stroke engines only have compression rings).

When checking piston ring end gap, the ring must be square in the cylinder bore – this is done by pushing it down with the top of a piston

Once the ring is at the lower limit of travel and square in the cylinder, measure the end gap with a feeler gauge

5•11

Chapter 5

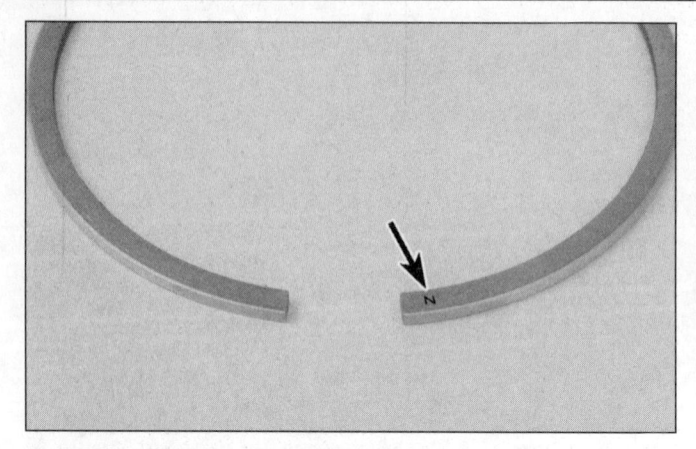

Piston rings are normally marked (arrowed) to indicate the side that faces up, toward the top of the piston

It usually will be stamped with a mark which must face up, toward the top of the piston *(see illustration)*. **Note:** *Always follow the instructions printed on the ring package or box – different manufacturers may require different approaches. Don't mix up the upper and lower compression rings, as they have different cross sections.*

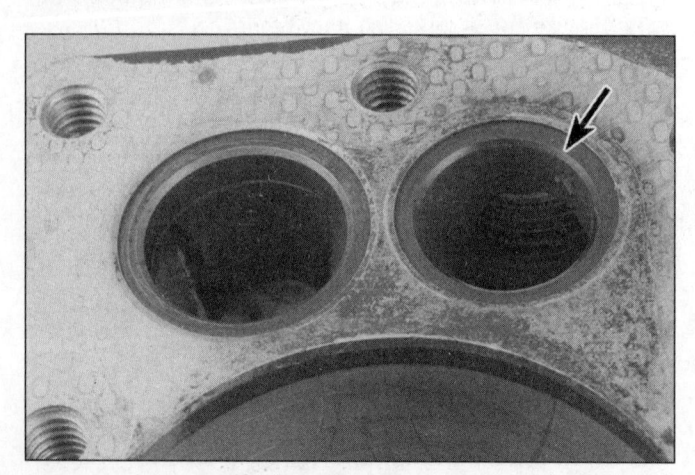

Check the valve seats (arrowed) in the engine block or head – look for pits, cracks and burned areas

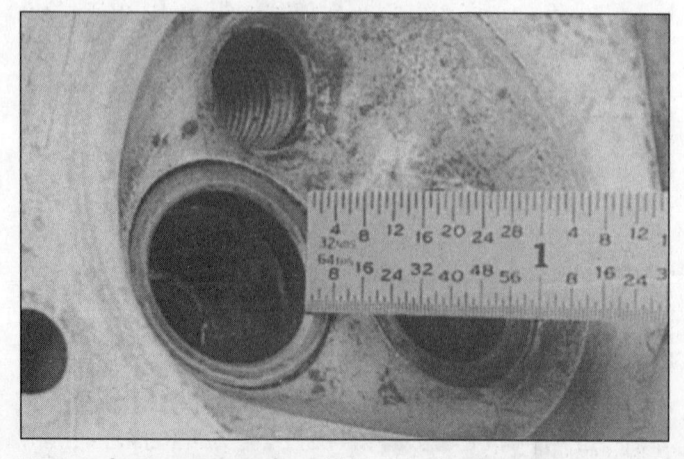

Use a ruler to measure the width of each valve seat

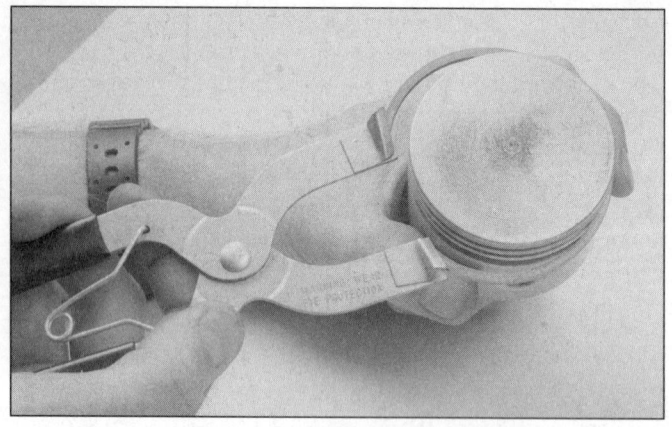

Install the compression rings with a ring expander – remember, the mark must face up!

Use a piston ring installation tool and make sure the identification mark is facing the top of the piston, then slip the ring into the middle groove (lower one on a two-stroke engine) on the piston *(see illustration)*. Don't expand the ring any more than necessary to slide it over the piston.

9 Install the upper (top) compression ring in the same manner. Make sure the mark is facing up. Be careful not to confuse the upper and lower compression rings. **Note:** *On Honda engines, the top ring is usually chrome faced.*

10 Make sure the rings turn freely in the grooves (unless they're pinned in place).

11 Turn the rings so the gaps are staggered about 120-degrees (not lined up).

Valve/tappet inspection and servicing

Inspection

1 If you're working on an OHV/OHC engine, inspect the head very carefully for cracks and other damage. If cracks are found a new head is needed. Use a precision straightedge and feeler gauge(s) to check the head gasket surface for warpage. Lay the straightedge diagonally (corner-to-corner), intersecting the head bolt holes, and try to slip a 0.10 mm (0.004 in) thick feeler gauge under it near each hole. Repeat the check with the straightedge positioned between each pair of holes along the sides of the head. If the feeler gauge will slip between the head surface and the straightedge, the head is warped. See your dealer about the possibility of resurfacing it.

2 Examine the valve seats *(see illustration)*.

If they're pitted, cracked or burned, valve service that's beyond the scope of the home mechanic is required – take the engine or head to a dealer and have new valves and seats installed.

Measure each valve seat width *(see illustration)*. If it's more than 1.5 mm (0.060 inch), or if it varies around its circumference, valve seat service is required.

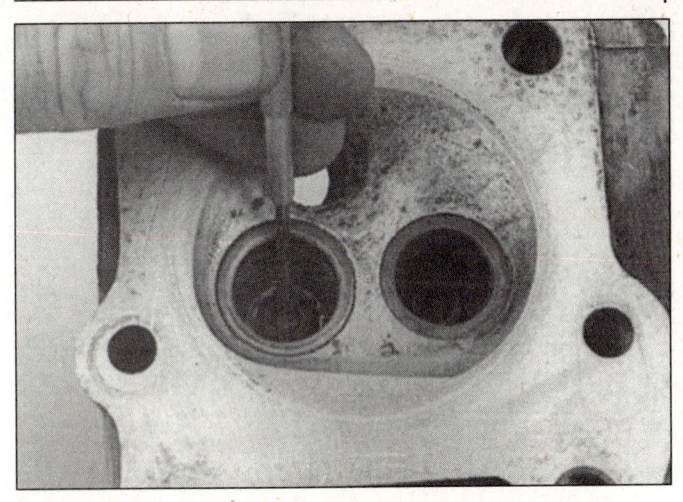

Repair procedures common to all engines

A small hole gauge can be used to determine the inside diameter of the valve guide

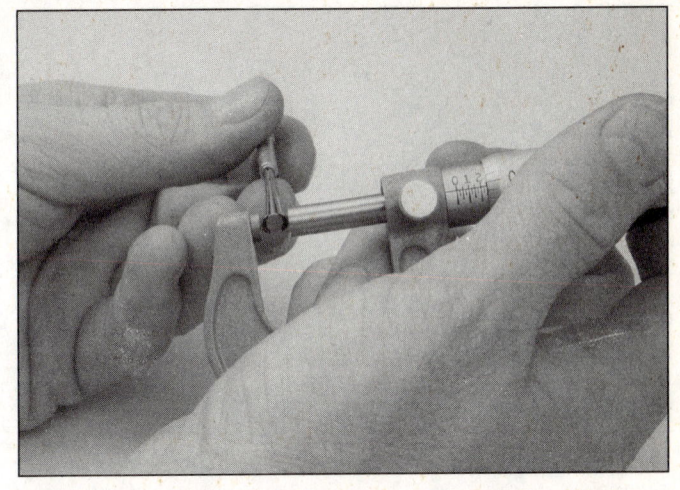

Measure the small hole gauge with a micrometer to obtain the actual size of the guide

3 Clean the valve guides to remove any carbon buildup, then measure the inside diameters of the guides (at both ends and the centre of the guide).

This is done with a small hole gauge and a 0 – 25 mm (0 – 1 inch) micrometer *(see illustrations)*. Record the measurements for future reference. These measurements, along with the valve stem diameter measurements, will enable you to compute the valve-to-guide clearance. This clearance, when compared to the specifications, will be one factor that will determine the extent of valve service work required. The guides are measured at the ends and at the centre to determine if they're worn in a bell-mouth pattern (more wear at the ends). If they are, guide replacement or reconditioning is an absolute must.

Some manufacturers don't publish valve-to-guide clearance specifications. Instead, they distribute special plug gauges that are inserted into the guides to determine how much wear has occurred in the guide. If no specifications are listed for your particular engine, have the guides checked and serviced by a dealer.

4 Carefully inspect each valve.

Check the face (the area that mates with the seat) for cracks, pits and burned spots *(see illustration)*. Check the valve stem and the keeper groove or hole for cracks *(see illustration)*.

Rotate the valve and check for any obvious indication that it's bent. Check the end of the stem for pitting and excessive wear.

The presence of any of the above conditions indicates the need for valve replacement.

5 Measure the valve stem diameter *(see illustration)*.

By subtracting the stem diameter from the valve guide diameter, the valve-to-guide clearance is obtained. If the valve-to-guide clearance is greater than specified, the guides will have to be replaced and new valves may have to be installed, depending on the condition of the old ones.

6 Check the end of each valve spring for wear and pitting.

Measure the free length and compare it to the

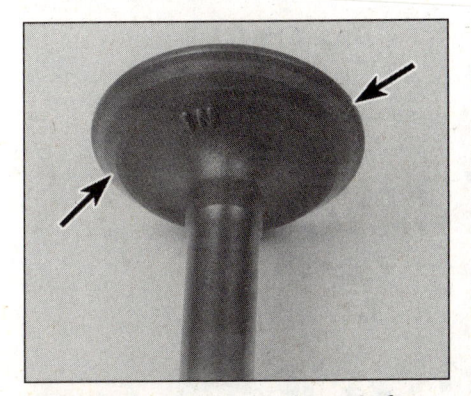

Check each valve face and margin for wear and cracks

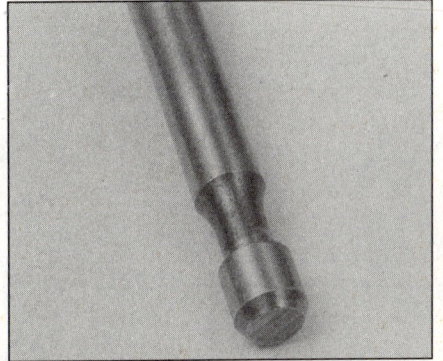

Look for wear on the very end of the valve stem and make sure the keeper groove or pin hole isn't distorted in any way

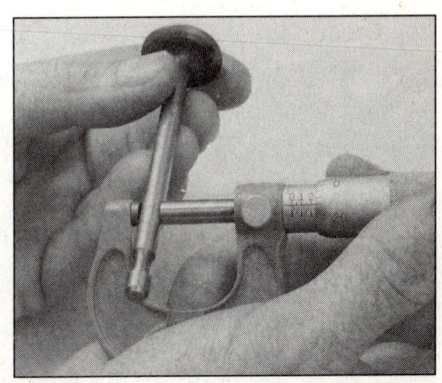

Measure the valve stem diameter with a micrometer

5•13

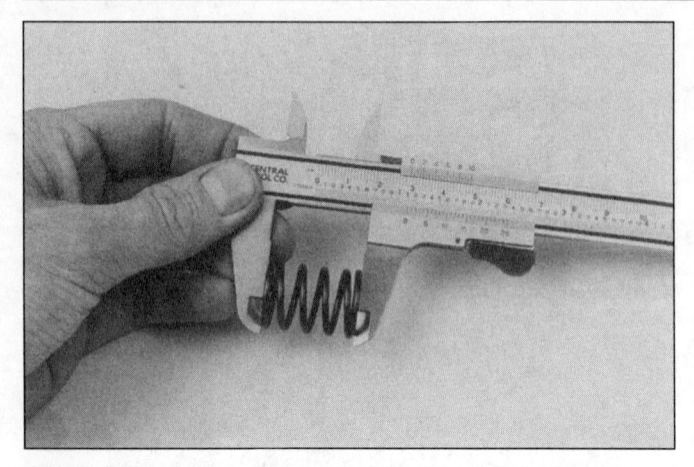

Chapter 5

Measure the valve spring free length with a dial or vernier caliper

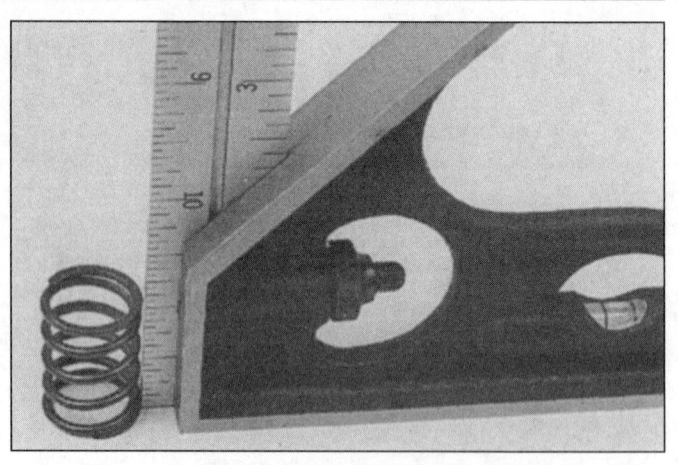

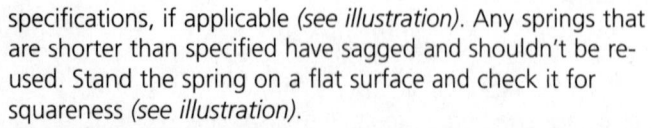

Check each valve spring for distortion with a square

specifications, if applicable *(see illustration)*. Any springs that are shorter than specified have sagged and shouldn't be re-used. Stand the spring on a flat surface and check it for squareness *(see illustration)*.

7 Check the spring retainers and/or keepers or pin for obvious wear and cracks. Questionable parts should not be re-used – extensive damage will occur in the event of failure during engine operation.

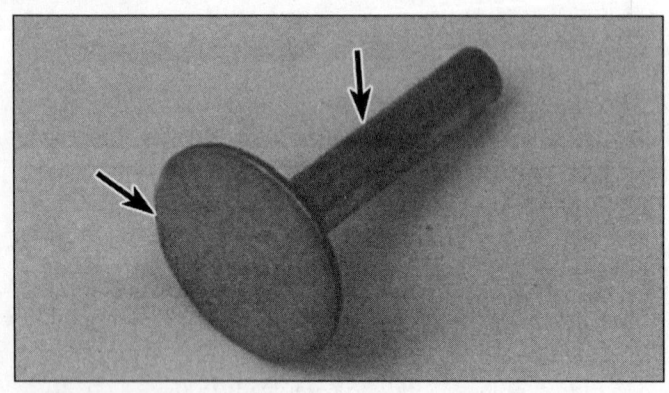

8 Check the tappets for wear, score marks and scuffing *(see illustration)*. Make sure they fit snugly in the holes and move freely without binding or catching.

Valve lapping

If the inspection indicates that no service work is required, the valve components can be reinstalled in the engine block or head (see the appropriate engine chapter).

Before reinstalling the valves, they should be lapped to ensure a positive seal between the faces and seats. This procedure requires fine valve lapping compound (available at a motor factors) and a valve lapping tool (see Chapter 1).

9 Apply a small amount of fine lapping compound to the valve face *(see illustration)*, then slip the valve into the guide. **Note:** *Make sure the valve is installed in the correct guide and be careful not to get any lapping compound on the valve stem.*

10 Attach the lapping tool to the valve and rotate the tool between the palms of your hands. Use a back-and-forth motion rather than a circular motion *(see illustration)*. Lift the

Check the tappet stems and ends (arrowed) for wear and damage

Apply the lapping compound very sparingly, in small dabs, to the valve face only

Rotate the lapping tool back-and-forth between the palms of your hands

Repair procedures common to all engines

valve off the seat at regular intervals to distribute the lapping compound evenly *(see illustration)*.

11 Continue the lapping procedure until the valve face and seat contact area is uniform in width and unbroken around the entire circumference of the valve face and seat *(see illustrations)*.

12 Carefully remove the valve from the guide and wipe off all traces of lapping compound. Use degreaser to clean the valve and wipe the seat area thoroughly with a degreaser-soaked cloth. Repeat the procedure for the remaining valve.

13 Once both valves have been lapped, check for proper valve sealing by pouring a small amount of degreaser into each of the ports with the valves in place and held tightly against the seats. If the degreaser leaks past the valve(s) into the combustion chamber area, repeat the lapping procedure, then reinstall the valve(s) and repeat the check. Repeat the procedure until a satisfactory seal is obtained.

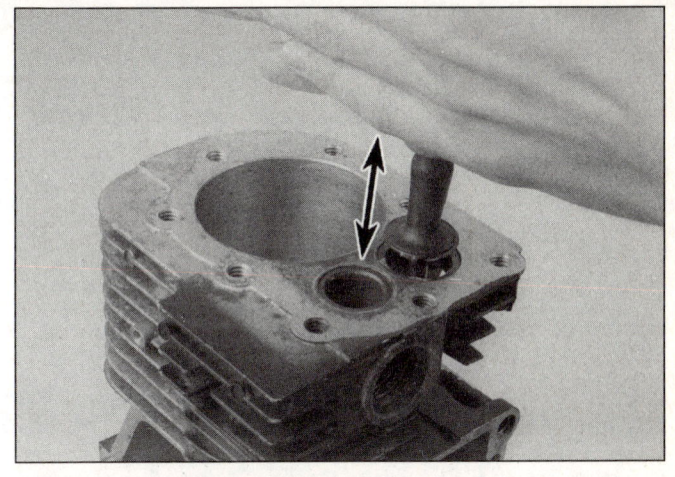

Lift the tool and valve periodically to redistribute the lapping compound on the valve face and seat

After lapping, the valve face should have a uniform, unbroken contact pattern (arrowed) . . .

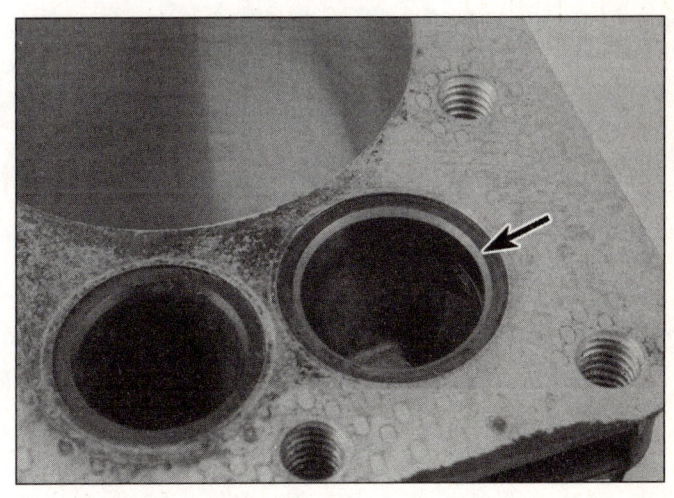

. . . and the seat should be the specified width (arrowed), with a smooth, unbroken appearance

5•15

Chapter 5

Briggs and Stratton MAX 4hp 4-stroke engine

6

Technical data
Dismantling
Reassembly

Electric starter dismantling and reassembly
Recoil starter repair

Technical data

Spark plug gap	0.75 mm (0.030 in)
Armature air gap	0.25 to 0.36 mm (0.010 to 0.014 in)
Valve clearance:	
Inlet	0.13 to 0.18 mm (0.005 to 0.007 in)
Exhaust	0.23 to 0.28 mm (0.009 to 0.011 in)
Breather disc valve clearance	1.10 mm (0.043 in)
Wire gauge must not enter space between valve and body	
Ring gap not to exceed:	
Compression rings	0.80 mm (0.032 in)
Oil ring	1.14 mm (0.045 in)
Cylinder wear:	
Rebore if oversize is greater than	0.08 mm (0.003 in)
Or ovality greater than	0.06 mm (0.002 in)
Oil	SAE 30 or SAE 10W-30

6•1

Chapter 6

Dismantling

Read Chapter 5 for hints and tips on dismantling and reassembly before starting to dismantle. The information given there will assist an orderly and methodical approach to engine overhaul. **Note:** *The following procedure description assumes the engine has been removed from whatever it was fitted to. For general guidelines on engine removal, refer to Chapter 5.*

- [ ] Remove the starter cover.
- [ ] Remove the fuel tank assembly, held by three small bolts and one larger one, disconnect fuel pipe from tap.
- [ ] Remove the engine cowl and dipstick tube.
- [ ] Remove the battery charging coils, note the small spacer under the coil on the back bolt.
- [ ] Take off the air filter housing, disconnect engine breather pipe from rear.
- [ ] Unhook the stop wire from throttle control plate.
- [ ] Unbolt and remove the electric starter unit.
- [ ] Remove the carburettor and throttle control plate, carefully noting positions and order of governor links and spring.
- [ ] Remove the ignition coil.
- [ ] Remove the mesh screen from starter clutch.
- [ ] Unscrew and remove the starter clutch, flywheel may be jammed with screwdriver in starter teeth against rear post. Turn the starter with large Stilsons/Pipe wrench or special removing tool. Remove washer.
- [ ] Remove the flywheel.
- [ ] Remove the exhaust screen then bend back locking tabs and remove two exhaust mounting bolts.
- [ ] Remove the engine breather from valve chest, note steel plate attached to top bolt.
- [ ] Slacken and remove the remaining cylinder head bolts, remove cylinder head and gasket.
- [ ] Turn the engine over and remove the power drive cover and gasket.
- [ ] Remove the shaft retainer from slot then shaft may be slid inwards to give access to sump bolt inside sump.
- [ ] Clean any rust or debris from the crankshaft with emery cloth to avoid damaging the seal when you take the sump off.
- [ ] Remove the six sump bolts, remove the sump.
- [ ] Remove the camshaft with governor and oil slinger, make notes of any shims that may be on the end of the camshaft.
- [ ] Remove the cam followers.
- [ ] Remove the big end cap.
- [ ] Remove any carbon from top of cylinder bore and push the piston out through the top, taking care not to damage the bore. Remove the crankshaft. Remove the valve springs using special valve tool or spanner head, push plate up valve stem and pull towards notch to release. **Note:** *exhaust valve spring is longer than inlet spring.*
- [ ] Finally, remove the valves.

Reassembly

Clean all parts in paraffin or engine degreaser, remove all traces of old gaskets from the mating faces of sump, engine block and cylinder head. Do this very carefully so as not to damage the aluminium castings. Clean any carbon from the valves, exhaust port and piston crown, and lap in the valves as explained in Chapter 5 but do not refit the springs yet as the valve clearances will have to be checked later.

Check the condition of all bearings in the engine (pictures show bearing locations) and check the crankshaft for wear on big end and main bearing journals as described in Chapter 5.

Check condition of cylinder bore for deep scratches. Check the castings for cracks and also check condition of crankshaft seals and PTO shaft seal.

Briggs and Stratton MAX 4hp 4-stroke engine

3 Refit the gear on the power take-off shaft. The roll pin goes through the gear and hole in the shaft, locking the two together.

4 Carefully remove piston rings noting which way up they were and the position in the grooves. Slide them one by one about 25 mm (1 in) down cylinder bore and check that the gap between the ends of the rings does not exceed the limits in the specifications, replace the rings if the ring gap is excessive.

Check small end bearing for wear by holding the piston in one hand and twisting the connecting rod in the other. The piston should slide freely on the pin but not rock. If worn, the connecting rod and gudgeon pin must be replaced.

5 Lubricate the main bearing in the crankcase and the tapered end of the crankshaft with engine oil. Fit crankshaft into the crankcase.

6 Lubricate piston and cylinder bore and refit piston. A piston ring clamp will have to be fitted to compress the piston rings before sliding the piston into bore. The open end of the big end cap should face the valves as shown in this picture. Lower the piston carefully into the bore taking care not to scratch it. Push the piston out of clamp with hammer handle. This should happen reasonably easily, if any obstruction is felt stop to investigate the cause.

7 Oil the big end bearing and refit the big end cap.

8 Be sure to tighten securely as there are no locking tabs. Rotate the crankshaft to check for free movement.

6•3

Chapter 6

9 Lubricate and refit the cam followers making sure they are replaced in their original holes.

10 Rotate the crankshaft so the timing dimple in the gear is facing towards the camshaft bearing hole.

11 Fit the camshaft so that the timing marks in the crankshaft and camshaft align – remembering any shims that were on the camshaft when dismantled.
  Note the position of the oil slinger/governor. Fit a new sump gasket, and lubricate the main bearing with engine oil.

12 Slide the sump gently down the crankshaft. Make sure the oil slinger and camshaft are in their correct positions and the locating dowels line up with their holes.

13 Fit the sump bolts, the short one goes into the hole beside the power takeoff gear. Tighten the bolts evenly to avoid cracking or distorting the sump.

14 Slide the power take-off shaft carefully and twist it to engage gear.

Briggs and Stratton MAX 4hp 4-stroke engine

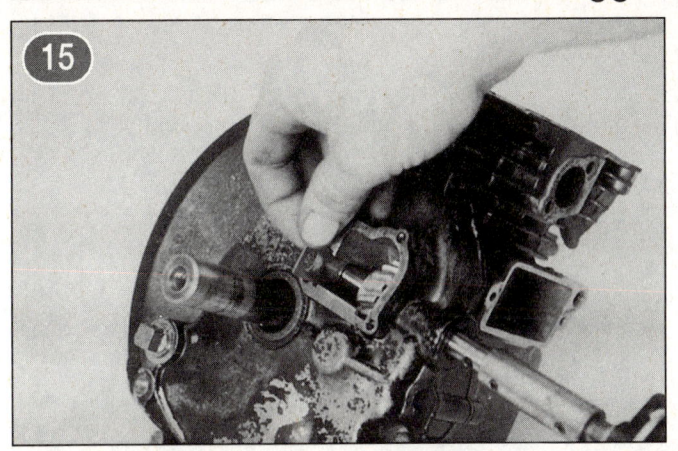

15 The shaft locating plate may now be placed in its slot to lock the shaft in position.

16 Fit a new gasket and secure the power take-off cover with the four small bolts.

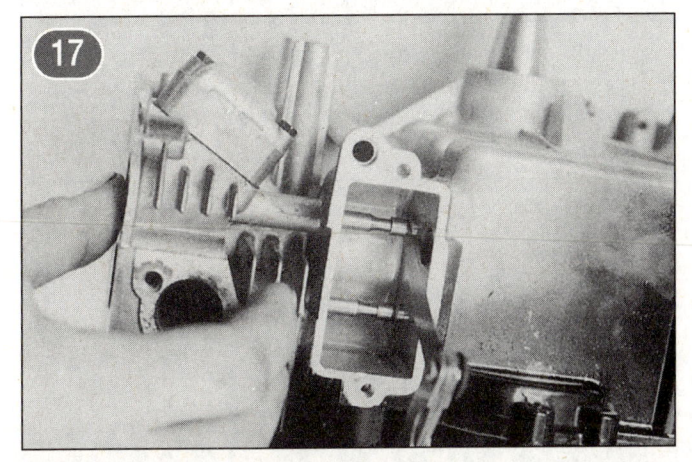

17 Check the valve clearances. The valve must be held down firmly in its seat with the piston at top dead centre on the firing stroke (with both valves closed). The feeler gauge should slide between valve stem and cam followers without moving the valve. Clearances are given in the specifications at the beginning of this chapter. If the clearance is too small, the end of the valve stem must be filed off slightly to give the correct gap (as described in Chapter 4).

18 Refit the valve springs.

19 Remove all the carbon from the cylinder head using a soft scraper or wire brush to avoid scratching the aluminium. Place a new gasket on the cylinder. Fit the cylinder head but leave out the bolts as shown, these will be used to secure the carburettor later.

20 Remove the carburettor from throttle control plate – 2 bolts – check condition of 'O' ring between the plate and carburettor. Check condition of the needle valve, mixture screw and float. Clean all parts in petrol and blow through jets. Do not use wire to clear jets as this will change the size of the holes.

Chapter 6

21 Refit the needle valve and float, slide in the pivot pin to secure. Screw in the mixture adjusting needle gently to avoid damage to seat. Turn out 1-½ turns for initial setting of mixture.

22 Refit the float bowl with the large rubber ring seal on the carburettor body and fibre washer and bolt. Fit the carburettor throttle control plate remembering to put the 'O' ring back between the carburettor and plate.

23 The correct position of governor links and spring are shown.

24 Refit the carburettor to the engine. Wipe the inlet pipe end with oil to help it to enter the carburettor. Hook the governor link back to plastic lever and slide carburettor on to manifold. Fit remaining cylinder head bolts and tighten in diagonal sequence.

25 Inspect the flywheel key for signs of shear or other damage, if necessary replace the key with the correct replacement. Do not use a steel key. Place the key in the slot in the crankshaft.

26 Fit the flywheel onto the crankshaft taper, making sure that the keyway lines up with the key in the crankshaft.

Briggs and Stratton MAX 4hp 4-stroke engine

27 Fit the washer to the crankshaft. If it is a domed washer, fit the dome upwards.

28 Screw on the recoil starter clutch. It will be necessary to jam the flywheel with a large screwdriver placed in the teeth of the flywheel and rested against one of the lugs on the back of the engine. Tighten the starter securely.

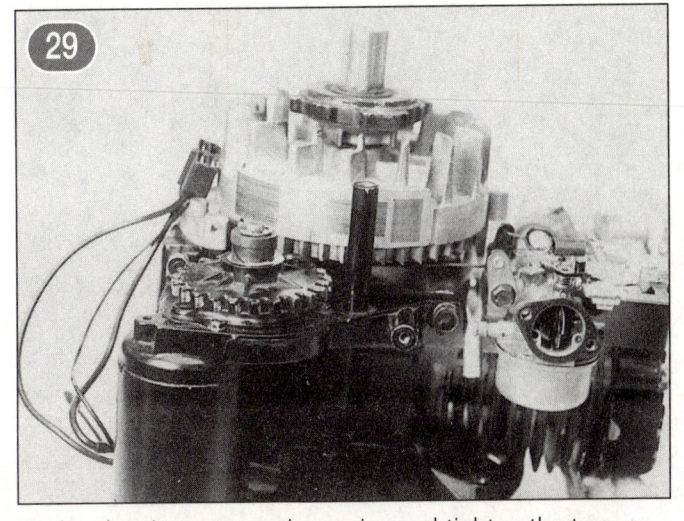

29 Fit the electric starter to the engine and tighten the two bolts that secure the starter.

30 Fit the mesh screen to the starter clutch and secure with the two bolts.
Fit the ignition coil and charging coils, remembering the small spacer on the charging coil. Do not tighten the bolts yet.

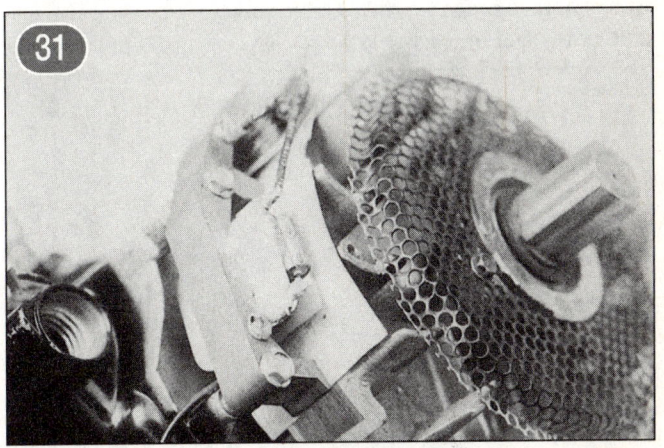

31 Set the air gap on the ignition coil and charging coil. Place a piece of plastic or card of the correct thickness, as given in Technical Data, between the coil and the flywheel magnets. The magnets will attract the coil and hold it against the card. Tighten the bolts and then rotate the flywheel to slide out the card. This process is repeated for the charging coils.

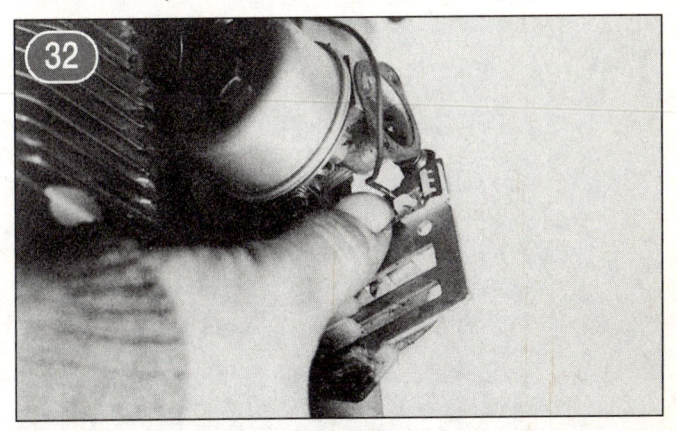

32 Fit the stop wire to throttle control plate. The spring contact should be pushed up towards the plate and the wire is then put through the hole. When the contact is released the wire is held in position.

Chapter 6

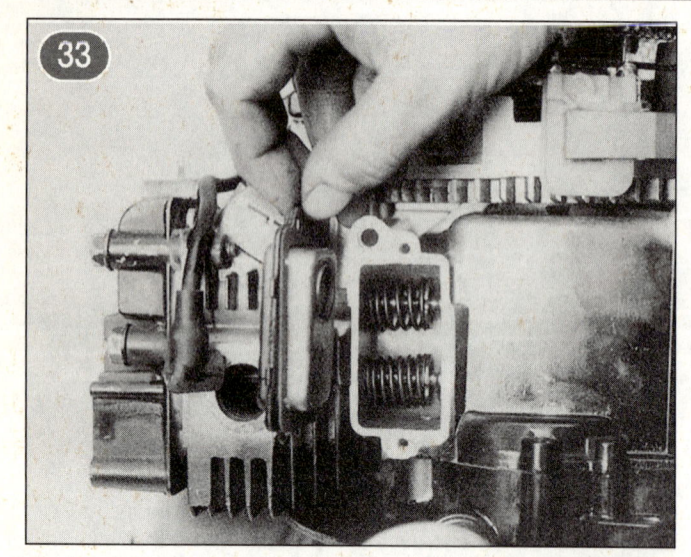

33 Fit the engine breather with a new gasket. Remember to place the plate under the top bolt.

34 Fit the exhaust silencer. Place the locking strip on the silencer then tighten the bolts and bend over the locking tabs to secure.

35 Fit the exhaust cover with three small screws.

36 Fit the starter cover after checking operation of recoil start, (see the end of this section for full information on renewing the spring or rope). Be careful not to trap spark plug lead or charging lead under the cover. Reconnect charging lead.

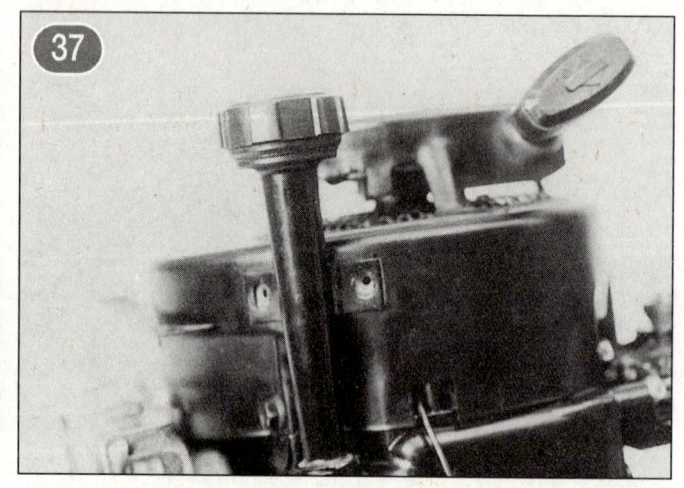

37 Check the 'O' ring seal at the base of the dipstick tube for cracks, or other damage and replace where necessary. Fit the dip stick tube to the engine cowl with two bolts.

38 Fit the air filter housing, re-connecting the breather pipe at the back when it is in position with the carburettor. Secure with the two bolts.

Briggs and Stratton MAX 4hp 4-stroke engine

39

Reconnect the fuel pipe to the fuel tap and fit the fuel tank securing with three small screws and one larger one.

Fit the plastic cover over the recoil starter.

40

Check the condition of the air filter and if it is dirty or contaminated with oil replace it. Place the air filter in its cover and fit to the engine.

Refit engine to its application, then fill the sump with new engine oil to the correct level. Replace the spark plug and reconnect the spark plug cap. Put fresh petrol in the fuel tank.

Electric starter

Dismantling

- [ ] Mark the position of end plate to the motor body, and the motor body to the gear housing as an aid to reassembly
- [ ] Remove the circlip securing main gear.
- [ ] Pull off the gear and engaging spiral, check the gear for wear or broken teeth.
- [ ] Undo three bolts to remove the gearbox cover.
- [ ] Slide off the large and small gears noting which way up they are.
- [ ] Undo the two screws securing the motor back plate and slide the motor away from housing. Note there are two washers on each end of the armature, one plastic on the outside then one steel. On the drive end, the steel one is a dished washer.
- [ ] Remove the brush plate carefully and slide out the cable insulator.
- [ ] Remove the armature and check the copper commutator for burning and wear.
- [ ] Check the brushes for free movement and wear. If they are badly worn or burnt they should be replaced.

Chapter 6

Reassembling

1 Put a drop of oil on bronze bush in brush plate.

2 Spread the brushes and insert the armature into the bearing. Fit the motor body to the armature – carefully, as the magnets will pull the armature in. Align the brush plate with the locating notch and slide in the insulated wire outlet.

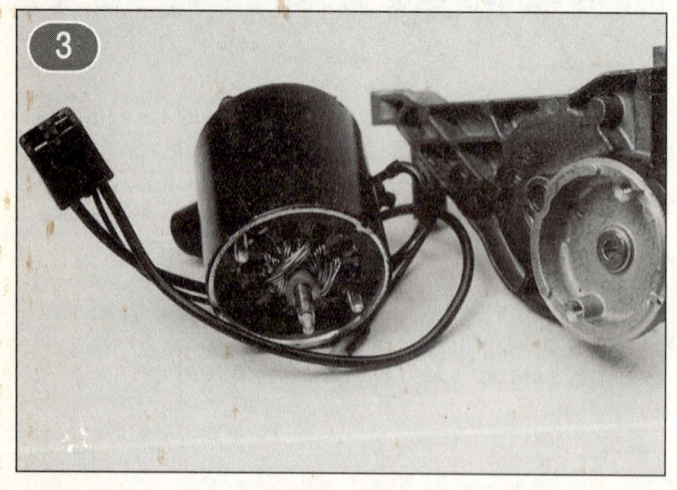

3 Assembled armature and motor body.

Fit the washers to end of the motor shaft, lubricate the shaft with oil and refit it to the gear housing. Make sure the locating notches are aligned.

4 Reassembled motor and greased gears ready for refitting.

5 Refit the gears in the housing, making sure the small one is located correctly on the motor shaft.

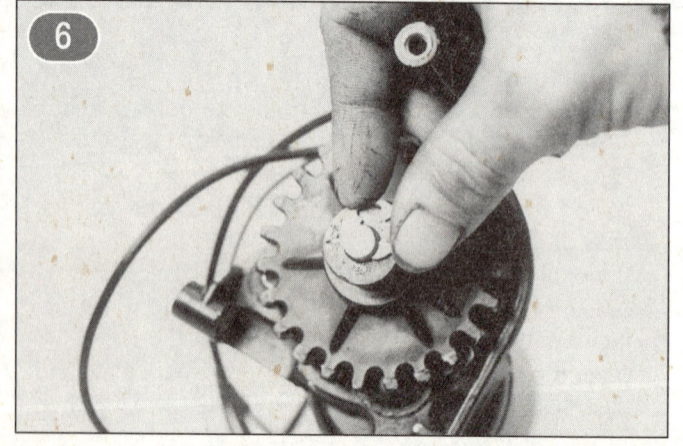

6 Fit the cover and gasket and tighten the three screws. Refit the starter gear and spiral, this engages in the large gear under the cover. It is fully home when the circlip groove on the shaft is visible.

Fit the circlip to secure the starter gear to the shaft.

Briggs and Stratton MAX 4hp 4-stroke engine

Recoil starter repair

If the recoil starter cord fails to wind back into the rewind housing after being pulled, the most likely cause is a broken recoil spring. The spring is situated on top of the rope pulley. To renew the spring, proceed as follows:

1 Pull the rope fully out and clamp the pulley to hold the spring tension. Keep the knot aligned with the rope outlet hole. Cut off the knot and remove rope.

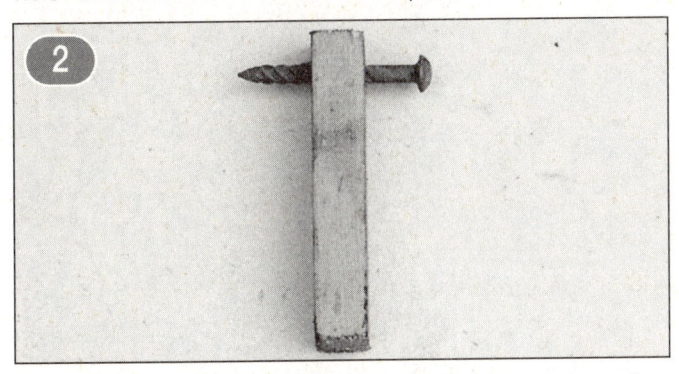

2 Slacken the spring, releasing it slowly with a square piece of wood as follows. Take a 15 cm (6 in) length of batten, 15 mm (3/4 in) square. Drive a 10 cm (4 in) nail through one end (to enable controlled turning) and insert the other end into the centre of the pulley. Bend the tangs up and remove pulley.

3 To fit a new spring, pass the end of the replacement spring through the hole in the side of the starter and engage it in the pulley.

4 Bend down the tangs to secure the pulley. Wind the pulley anti-clockwise to pull the spring in.

5 When fully wound in, the end of the spring will engage in the narrower section in the hole in the cover.

6 Wind the spring up until tight, then back one turn or until the hole lines up with the rope outlet. Lock with self-locking pliers or a clamp and thread rope through.

Fit handle to the other end of the rope. Hold the cord and release the self-locking pliers or clamp. Allow the rope to draw back the starter.

Chapter 6

Briggs and Stratton Intek/Europa OHV engines

7

Technical data
Dismantling
Reassembly

Recoil starter repair
'Sloper' Intek engine
Electric starter

Technical Data

Spark plug gap	0.75 mm (0.030 in)
Spark plug type	NGK B2LM
Cylinder bore ovality limit	0.038 mm (0.0015 in)
Piston ring gap limit	0.8 mm (0.032 in)
Valve clearances:	
Inlet (cold)	0.13 to 0.18 mm (0.005 to 0.007 in)
Exhaust (cold)	0.18 to 0.23 mm (0.007 to 0.009 in)
Armature air gap	0.25 mm (0.010 in)
Oil grade	SAE 30
Oil capacity	0.6 litres

Chapter 7

Dismantling

Before starting to dismantle, read Chapter 5. The procedures outlined apply to all engines and if adopted, will ensure an orderly and methodical approach that will make both dismantling and reassembly much easier.

Remove the engine from the mower, and proceed as follows:

- [ ] Unscrew the two bolts and remove the air filter cover.
- [ ] Remove the fuel filler cap and the two bolts securing the plastic engine cover. Lift off the cover. Replace the fuel filler cap. 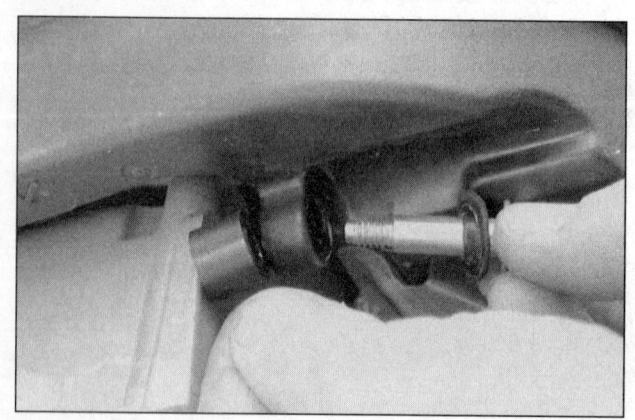
- [ ] Release the clip and pull the supply pipe from the fuel tank. Be prepared for fuel spillage. Unscrew the four bolts securing the fuel tank. Note the position of the spacer fitted to the lower mounting bolt.
- [ ] Using a 3/8" square drive tool, undo the sump plug and drain the engine oil into a suitable container.
- [ ] Unscrew the three bolts and remove the exhaust shield.
- [ ] In order to remove the engine cowling, the oil filler neck must first be removed. Unscrew the one retaining bolt and lift the filler neck away. Note the O-ring at the base of the neck. Unscrew the four bolts and remove the cowling.
- [ ] Unscrew the four retaining bolts, and remove the exhaust system.
- [ ] Disconnect the engine breather pipe from the air filter housing. Unscrew the two retaining bolts and remove the housing.
- [ ] Remove the two carburettor mounting bolts, and unhook the governor linkage as the carburettor is withdrawn.
- [ ] Unscrew the float bowl nut and remove the float bowl. Be prepared for fuel spillage.
- [ ] Push out the float pivot pin, and carefully lift out the float with the needle valve.
- [ ] Check the condition of the needle valve and seat for any damage or wear (*refer to Chapter 5*). Examine the float bowl O-ring for any for cracks, etc. The float bowl nut incorporates the main jet. Check that the holes are clear. If necessary, clear the holes by blowing or by the use of a thin nylon bristle. Never use a needle or wire to clean a jet. Check the float for damage or leaks. 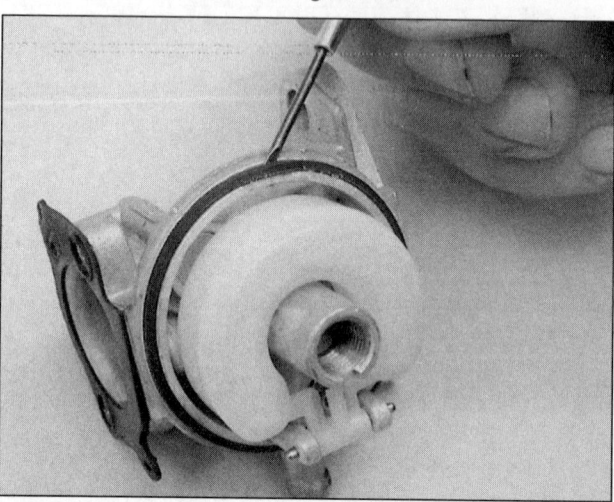
- [ ] Disconnect the engine stop wire from the ignition magneto, and unscrew the carburettor mounting/linkage plate retaining bolt. Lift the plate away.
- [ ] Remove the engine cowling panel by unscrewing the one retaining bolt, and unhooking the governor linkage.
- [ ] Carefully pull the HT cap from the spark plug. Unscrew the two bolts and remove the ignition magneto.
- [ ] In order to remove the flywheel retaining nut, it is necessary to prevent the flywheel from turning. In the absence of the manufacturer's special tool, this can be done by using a strap wrench around the circumference of the flywheel. Do not be tempted to lever a screwdriver against the flywheel fins; being made of aluminium, they are easily damaged.
- [ ] Remove the plastic cooling fin disc from the flywheel. Note the two locating dowels.
- [ ] With reference to Chapter 5, pull the flywheel from the crankshaft. If you are using the manufacturer's puller, it

Briggs and Stratton Intek/Europa OHV engines

may be necessary to cut the threads in the flywheel. The puller holes are clearly labelled in the flywheel, and the puller bolts are specially formed to cut the threads. Recover the key from the crankshaft.

- [ ] Unscrew the four bolts and remove the breather chamber cover.
- [ ] Unscrew the two bolts, and remove the breather cover/valve.
- [ ] Undo the four bolts and remove the rocker cover.
- [ ] Remove the rocker arm mounting nuts and hemispherical washers. Carefully remove the rocker arms, pushrods and valve cap pads. Note or label which components are for the inlet and exhaust valves; it is important that, if re-used, they should be refitted to their original location.
- [ ] Unscrew the four bolts and remove the cylinder head. It may be necessary to gently tap the cylinder head away from the engine block, but avoid levering between the block and cylinder head cooling fins. Note the cylinder head locating dowels.
- [ ] In order to remove a valve, depress the valve collar and push it towards the notch in the rim of the collar. Although a special valve spring compressor is available, due to the size of the spring it is quite possible to compress them sufficiently by hand. The valve collars have two adjoining holes, one of which is larger than the other. This allows the valve stem to slide through the collar. Remove the spring and slide the valve from the cylinder head. It is important to label or arrange the components so that, if re-used, they are refitted to their original locations. Note the seal/spring seat fitted to the inlet valve.
- [ ] Undo the two bolts, and remove the rocker mounting plate. Inspect the valve guides for scoring and excessive wear. Examine the valve seats and renovate as necessary (*refer to Chapter 5*).
- [ ] Undo the retaining bolt and remove the remaining engine block cowling.
- [ ] Slide the belt drive pulley from the crankshaft, and recover the Woodruff (half moon) key.
- [ ] Remove any dirt or rust from the crankshaft, unscrew the seven retaining bolts and remove the sump. It may be necessary to gently tap the sump with a soft hammer, or piece of wood. Note the two locating dowels.
- [ ] Slide the governor/oil slinger assembly from the end of the camshaft, and lift the camshaft from the crankcase.
- [ ] Remove the cam followers. Note or label each follower as exhaust or inlet, as appropriate.
- [ ] Slide the camshaft drive gear from the crankshaft. If the Woodruff (half moon) key is loose – remove it.
- [ ] Unscrew the retaining bolts and remove the big-end cap.
- [ ] Remove any carbon build-up at the lip of the cylinder bore using a soft tool, and gently push the connecting rod and piston assembly up and out of the cylinder. Take care not to mark the bore with the connecting rod.
- [ ] If required, remove the piston rings from the piston by carefully expanding the rings at their ends and sliding them from the piston. Note the orientation of the rings for reassembly.
- [ ] Remove the circlip and push the gudgeon pin from the piston.
- [ ] Carefully withdraw the crankshaft from the crankcase.

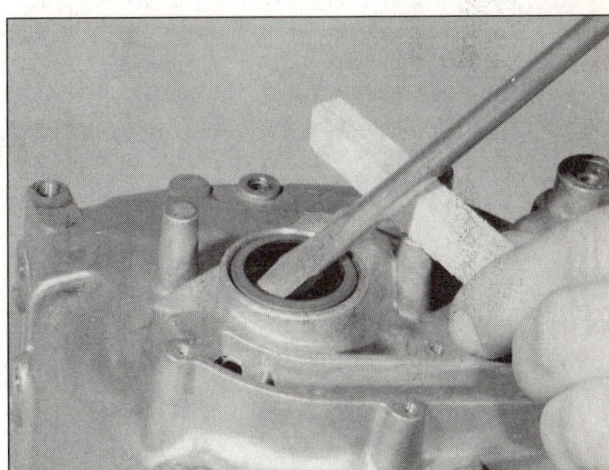

- [ ] The crankshaft oil seals can now be prised out from the crankcase and sump. Note which way round they fit.
- [ ] Prior to removing the governor arm and lever, mark the position of the lever on the shaft. It is essential that the lever be refitted in the original position. Remove the lever pinch-bolt, and pull the lever from the shaft. Prise off the steel 'push-on' clip, and remove the governor arm/shaft from the crankcase.
- [ ] Check the condition of the crankshaft bearing, camshaft bearing and cylinder bore for wear, scores or cracks. If the bore is damaged, worn oval or oversized, then professional skills and special equipment will be necessary to restore it. The same applies to worn or damaged bearings. These can be reamed out to accept bushes obtainable from spares stockists, but special reaming equipment and knowledge are essential. Check all threaded holes for damaged threads, and repair if necessary by fitting a thread insert of the correct size (*refer to Chapter 5*).

Chapter 7

Reassembly

Fit new oil seals into the crankcase and sump by carefully pushing them into place using an appropriate-sized socket. The seals should be fitted with the sharp rubber edge of the seal towards the inside of the engine.

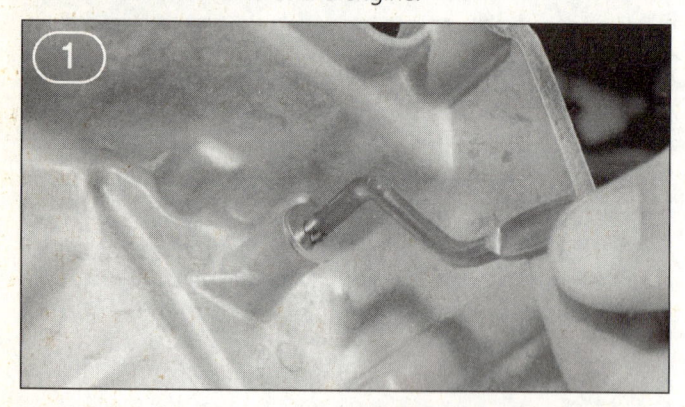

1

Fit the governor arm into the crankcase. Note the washer fitted between the arm and the crankcase on the inside.

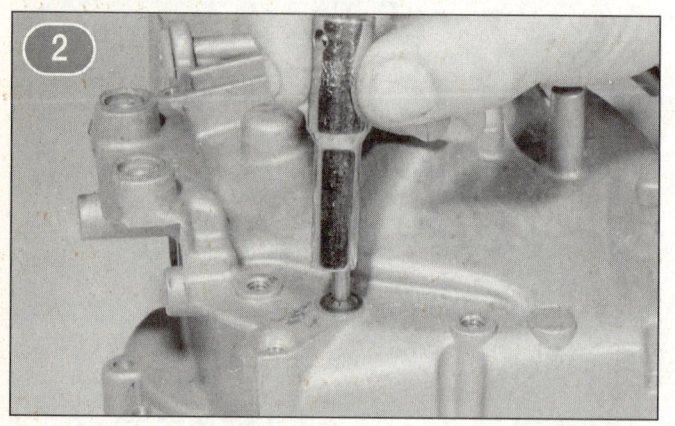

2

Fit a new 'push-on' clip on the arm on the outside of the case.

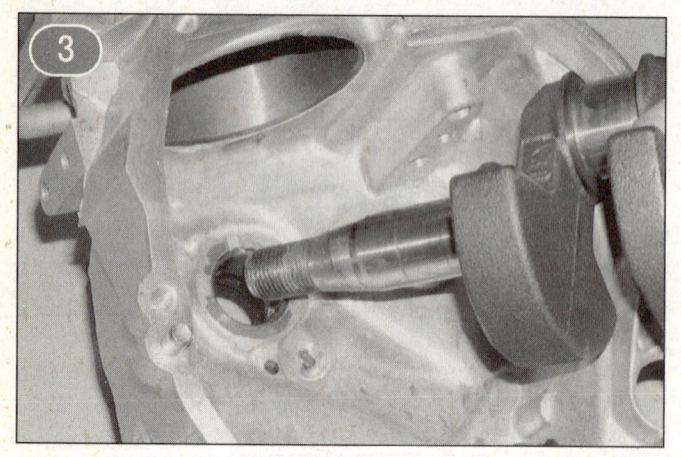

3

Smear the crankcase bearing journal and lip of the oil seal with new engine oil, and fit the crankshaft into the crankcase, tapered end first.

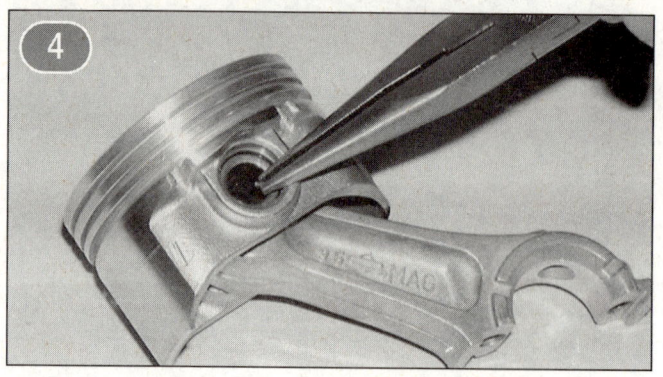

4

If previously removed, fit the gudgeon pin into the piston/connecting rod assembly. The piston is fitted with the arrow on its crown towards the tapered end of the crankshaft, and the 'open' side of the connecting rod towards the camshaft bearing. Always fit a new piston circlip. If the gudgeon pin is reluctant to move, immerse the piston in hot water for a few minutes. This causes the aluminium to expand, and the gudgeon pin to slide easily.

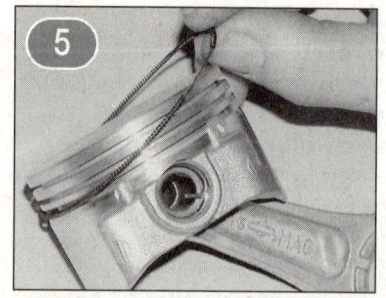

5

Fit the piston rings onto the piston. The oil control (lowest) ring should be fitted first, by carefully expanding the coiled element just enough to slide down over the piston and into its groove.

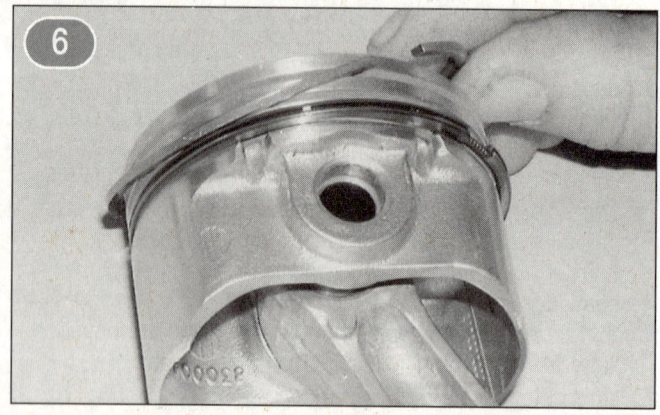

6

Next fit the second element of the oil control ring in the same manner, positioning it so that the coiled element is inside the second element. Next fit the compression ring into the middle groove. This ring must be fitted with the internal chamfer facing down. Finally fit the top compression ring with the internal chamfer facing up. Beware: *Piston rings are very brittle. If the are expanded too much, they will break.* Arrange the three ring-end gaps so that they are spaced out around the circumference of the piston at 120° intervals.

Briggs and Stratton Intek/Europa OHV engines

7 Smear the piston rings and cylinder bore with oil.

8 Using a piston ring clamp, fit the piston into the cylinder from the top by feeding the connecting rod through first. Make sure that the arrow on the top of the piston points towards the tapered end of the crankshaft, and that the connecting rod does not scratch the cylinder walls. Press the piston firmly into the cylinder, sliding it out of the clamp as the rings enter the bore. If necessary, use a piece of wood or hammer handle and gently tap the piston out of the clamp and into the cylinder; stop and investigate any undue resistance.

9 Smear some oil on the crankshaft journal and engage the big-end onto the journal.

10 Fit the big-end cap, arrow mark pointing towards the piston (arrowed), and secure it with the two bolts. Tighten the bolts securely, as there are no locking devices, but do not over-tighten. Rotate the crankshaft to ensure freedom of movement.

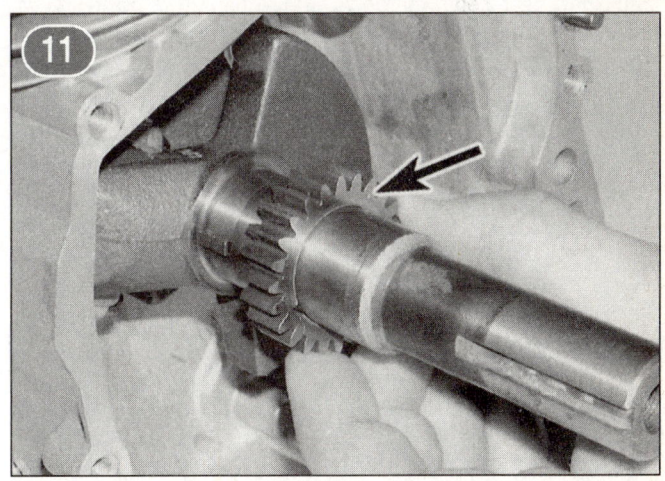

11 If previously removed, fit the Woodruff (half moon) key to the crankshaft, and fit the camshaft drive gear to the crankshaft with the timing mark facing outwards (arrowed).

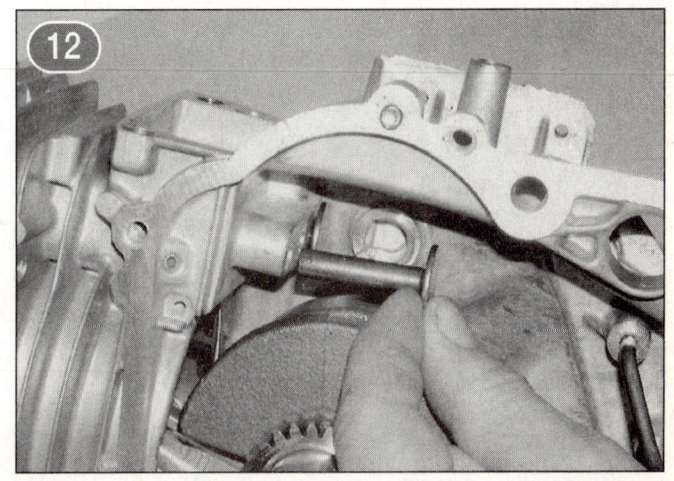

12 Put a drop of oil onto the cam followers, and insert each follower into the same hole from which it was removed.

Chapter 7

13 Turn the crankshaft until the timing mark on the gear is pointing at the middle of the camshaft bearing hole in the crankcase (arrowed). Smear some oil on the camshaft bearing journal, and install the camshaft. The timing dimple drilled in the camshaft gear must aligned exactly with the mark on the crankshaft gear when the gears are meshed. Rotate the crankshaft two revolutions to ensure correct movement.

14 Fit the governor/oil slinger assembly onto the camshaft. Align the head of the bob-weight assembly with the governor arm.

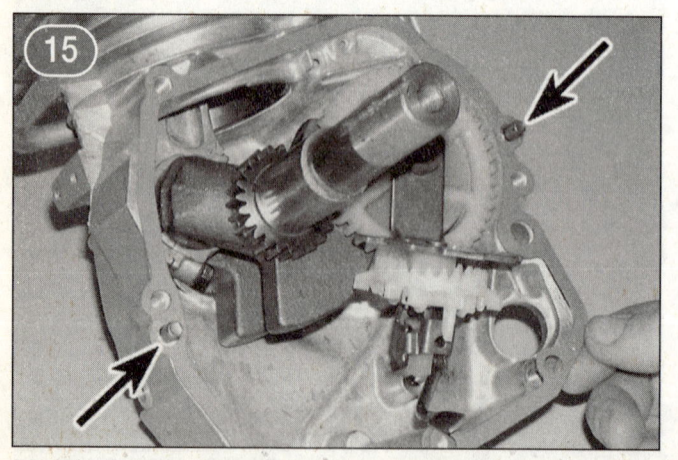

15 Fit a new sump gasket to the crankcase noting the locating dowels.

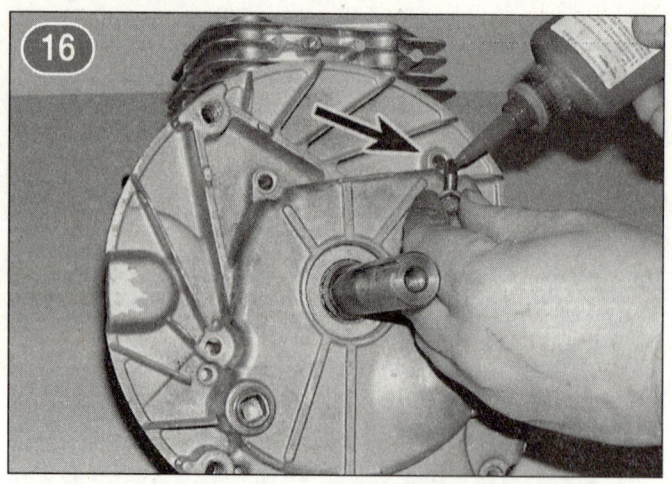

16 Smear some oil onto the crankshaft and camshaft journal. Carefully fit the sump, ensuring that the locating holes engage with the crankcase dowels, and the oil seal lip is not damaged during the process. Tighten the seven bolts securely, using thread locking compound on the bolt that screws into the engine breather chamber (arrowed).

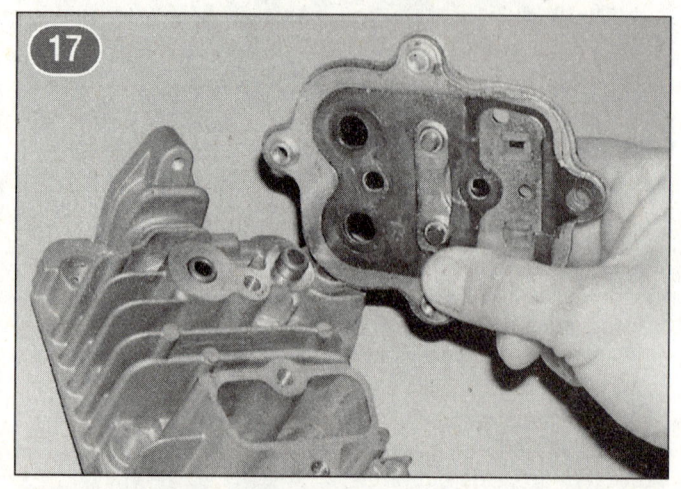

17 With a new gasket in place, fit the rocker mounting plate to the cylinder head.

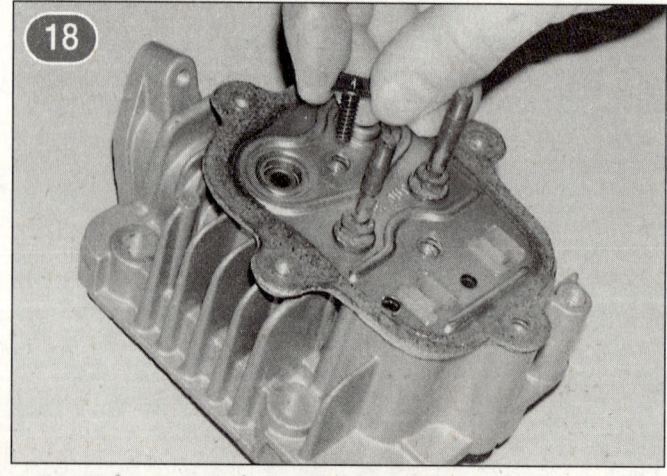

18 Secure the rocker mounting plate with the two bolts.

Briggs and Stratton Intek/Europa OHV engines

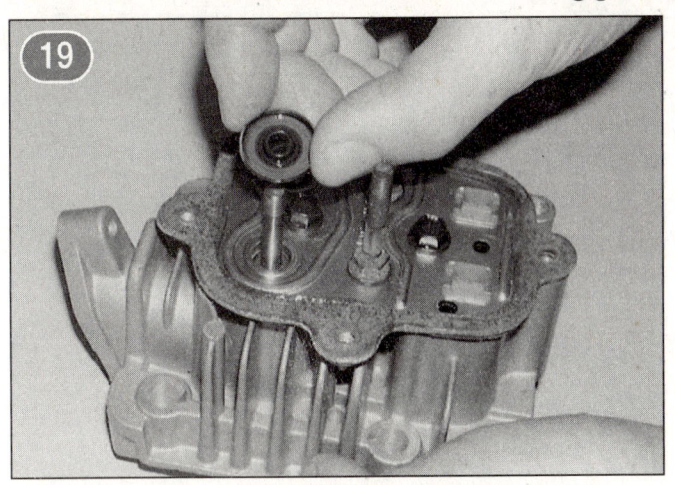

19 Refit the valves into the cylinder head, and a new valve seat/seal to the inlet valve.

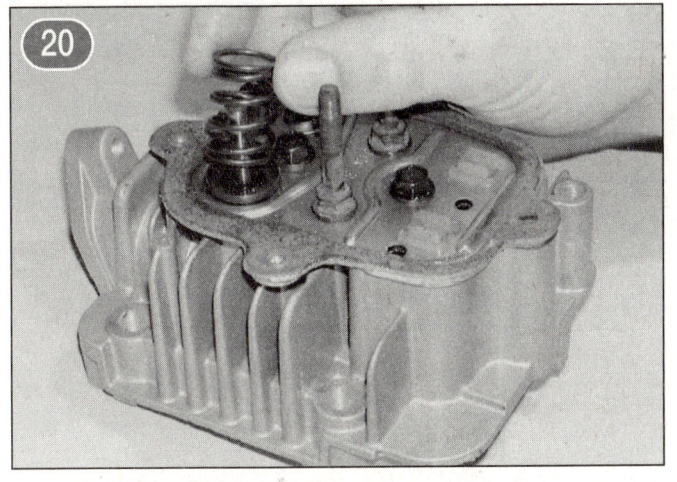

20 Fit and compress the springs to their respective valves.

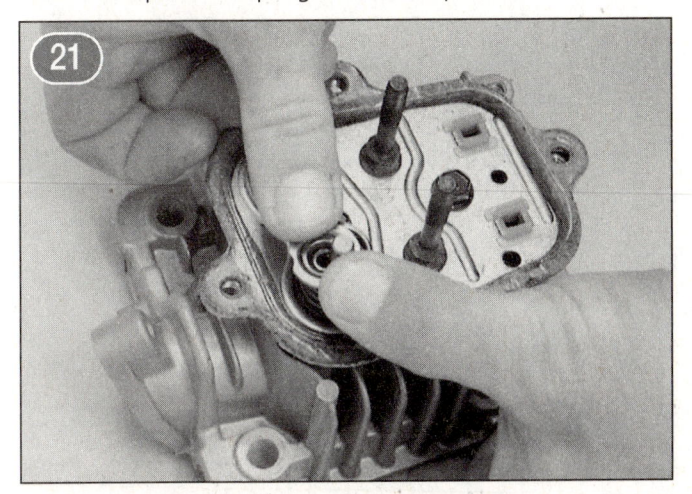

21 Locate the valve collars over the valve stems. Move the collars away from the notch on the rims and slowly release the springs. Ensure that the valve stems have located correctly in their collars.

22 With a new gasket, fit the cylinder head onto the cylinder block. The gasket is not symmetrical, and therefore will only fit one way correctly. Do not use any jointing compound. Ensure that the locating dowels on the underside of the cylinder head engage the gasket and block correctly.

23 Refit the four cylinder head bolts, and tighten securely in a diagonal pattern.

24 Insert the pushrods through the holes in the rocker mounting plate, making sure they locate in the ends of the cam followers. Providing that they are inserted close to vertically, the ends of the pushrods should 'self-locate' in the cam followers. Once the pushrods have been correctly fitted, great care should be taken not to dislodge the protruding ends, as there is a danger of them falling through an oil drain hole and into the crankcase.

7•7

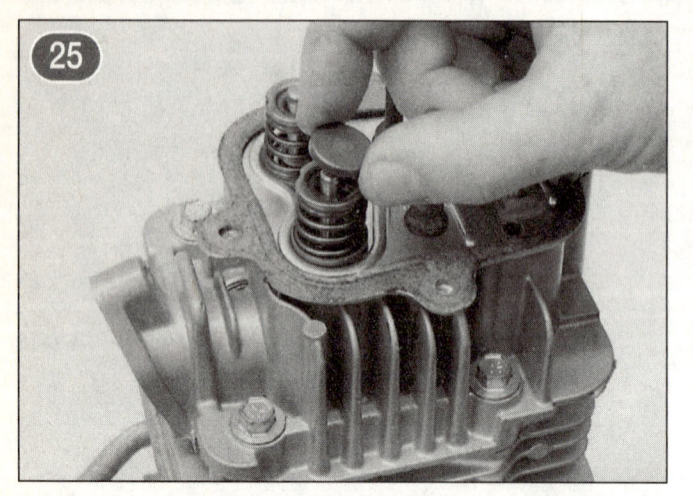

Chapter 7

25 Fit the contact pads to the valve collars. It is essential that the valve pads and pushrods be refitted to their original locations.

26 Refit the rocker arms, hemispherical washers and mounting nuts to their original locations.

27 Adjust the valve clearances. The clearances are adjusted by turning the rocker arm mounting nut. The exhaust valve clearance should be adjusted when the inlet valve is fully open, and the inlet valve clearance adjusted when the exhaust valve is fully open. Turn the crankshaft to open and close the valves. The clearance dimensions are given in the Technical data.

28 With a new gasket, refit the rocker cover. Tighten the four bolts securely.

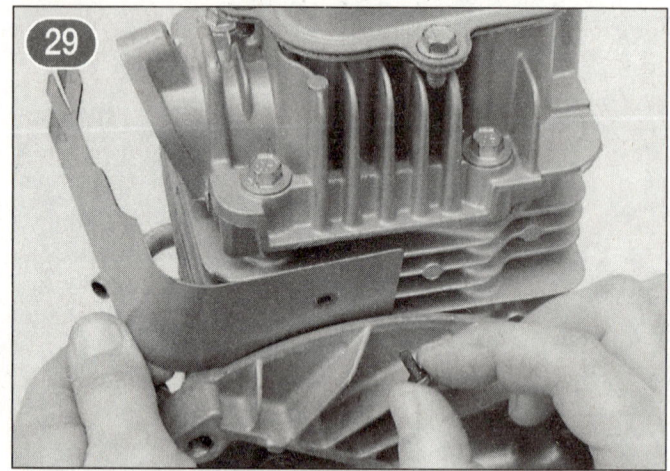

29 Refit the cylinder block cowling. Tighten the bolt securely.

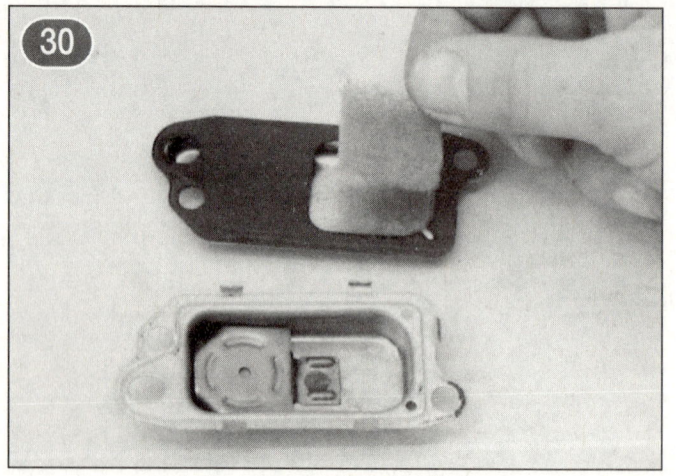

30 Check the fibre disc valve in the engine breather for distortion or cracks. The gap between the disc valve and the body should not exceed 1.1 mm (0.043 in). The valve is held in place by an internal bracket, which will distort if too much pressure is applied to the disc. If the valve is defective, renew the complete breather assembly.

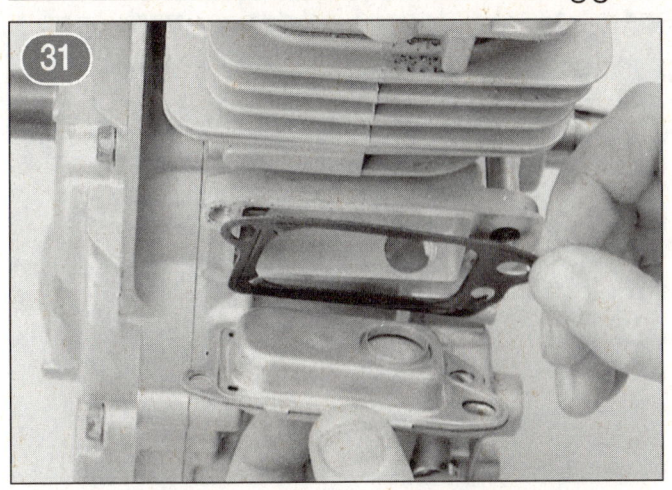

Briggs and Stratton Intek/Europa OHV engines

31 Renew the gasket and refit the valve/cover using the two bolts. Tighten securely.

32 With a new gasket, refit the breather chamber cover. Tighten the four bolts securely.

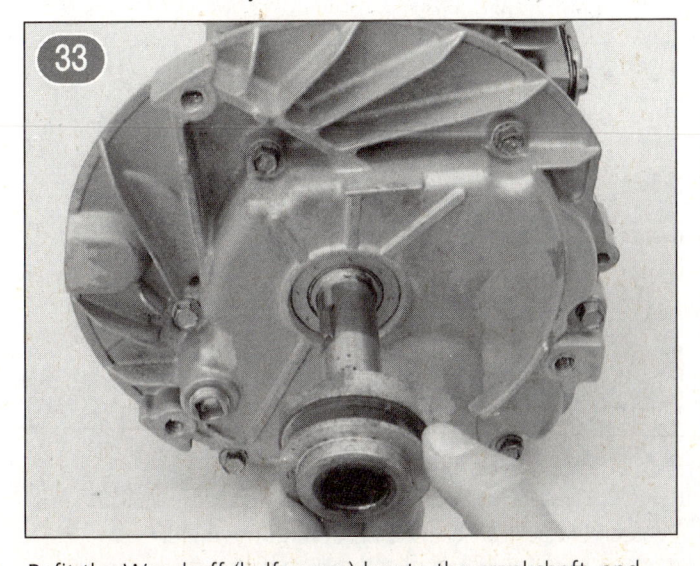

33 Refit the Woodruff (half moon) key to the crankshaft, and slide on the belt drive pulley.

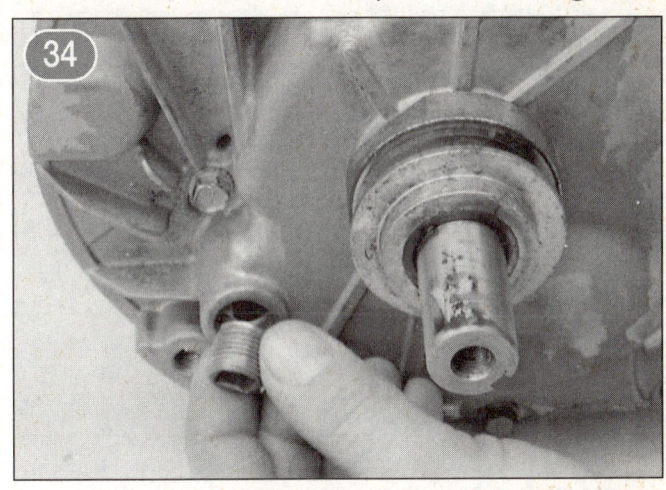

34 Fit and tighten the oil drain plug to the sump, using a 3/8" square drive tool.

35 Refit the governor lever to the arm, aligning the previously made marks. Tighten the pinch-bolt securely. If the aligning marks have been lost, turn the governor shaft until the arm inside the crankshaft comes into contact with the bob-weight assembly. Then push the lever against its stop and tighten the pinch-bolt.

36 Slide the flywheel over the tapered end of the crankshaft and insert the key.

7•9

Chapter 7

37 Fit the plastic cooling fin disc to the flywheel, ensuring that the locating pins have engaged correctly.

38 Fit the starter flange over the end of the crankshaft and fit the retaining nut. Tighten the nut very securely, preventing the flywheel from turning by means of a strap wrench around the circumference of the flywheel.

39 Refit the ignition magneto. The magneto body is marked 'Cylinder side' on one side, and 'This side out' on the other. Before tightening the two mounting bolts, turn the flywheel so that the magnets are on the opposite side to the magneto, and use a feeler gauge to measure the air gap between the two legs of the magneto's armature and the flywheel. The correct air gap is 0.254 mm (0.010 in). The mounting holes in the armature legs are slotted. Move the armature until the correct gap is achieved. Tighten the bolts securely.

40 Connect the governor linkage to the governor lever, and refit the crankcase cowling – secured with a single bolt.

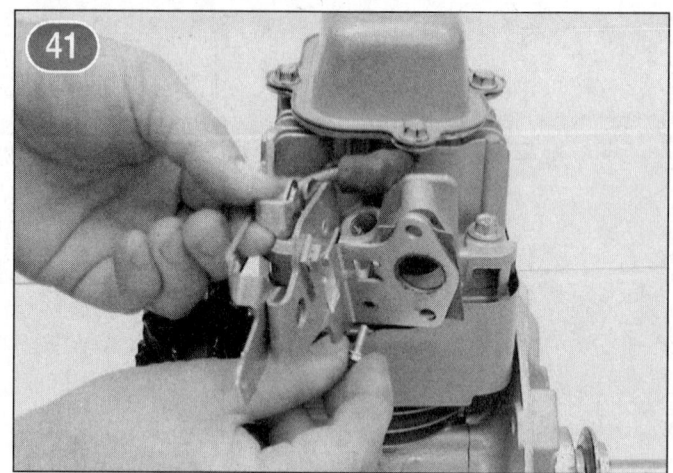

41 Place a new gasket around the inlet port, and refit the carburettor mounting/linkage plate securing the single bolt. Reconnect the magneto earthing wire from the linkage plate to the ignition magneto.

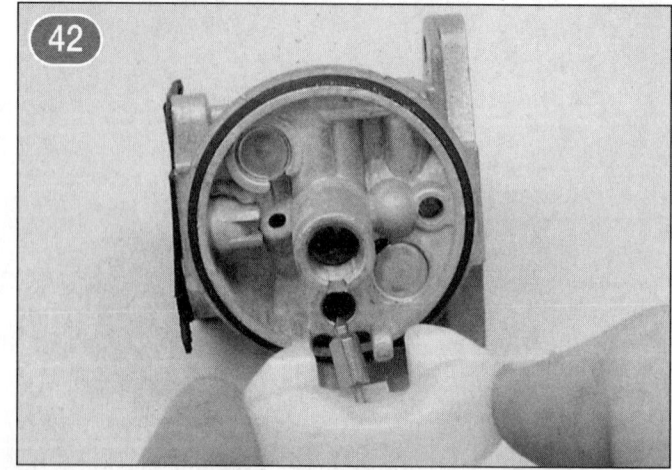

42 Reassemble the carburettor by refitting the needle valve into its holder in the float, and carefully lowering the assembly into place.

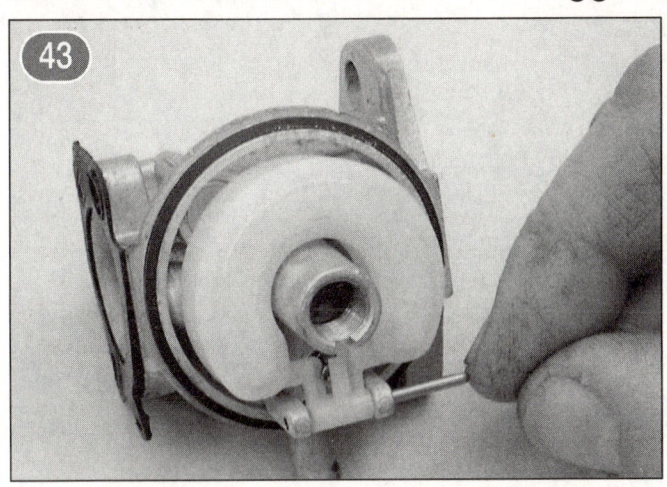

Briggs and Stratton Intek/Europa OHV engines

43 Insert the float pivot pin. There is no provision for adjusting the float height.

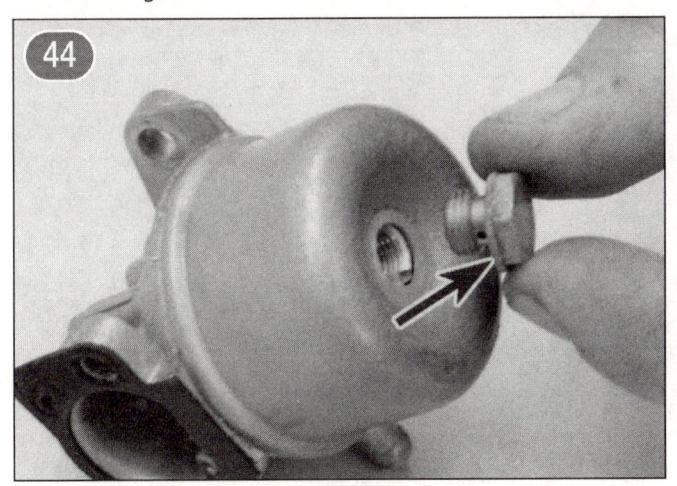

44 Refit the float bowl and secure with the nut. Do not overtighten. Note the fibre washer between the nut and float chamber (arrowed).

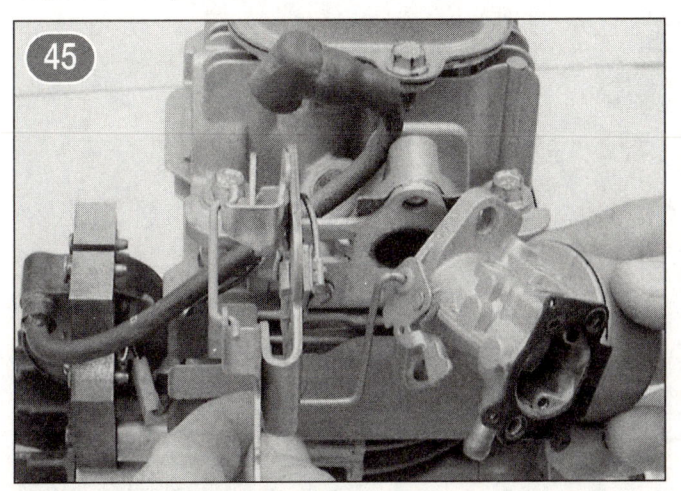

45 Engage the end of the governor linkage with the relevant hole in the carburettor throttle arm.

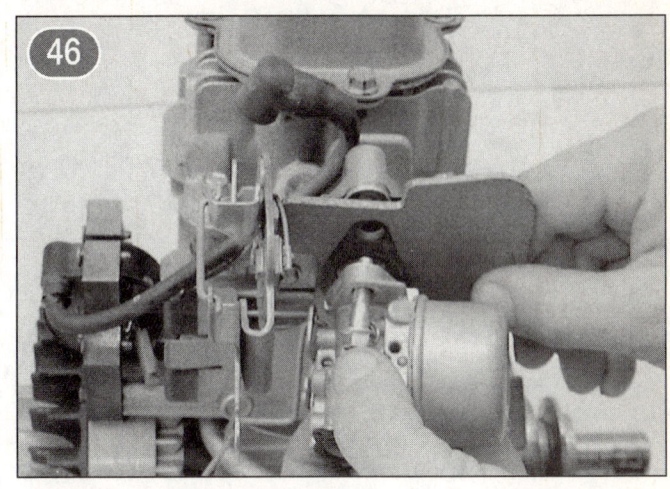

46 Holding the heat shield in place, fit the carburettor using a new gasket. Tighten the two bolts securely.

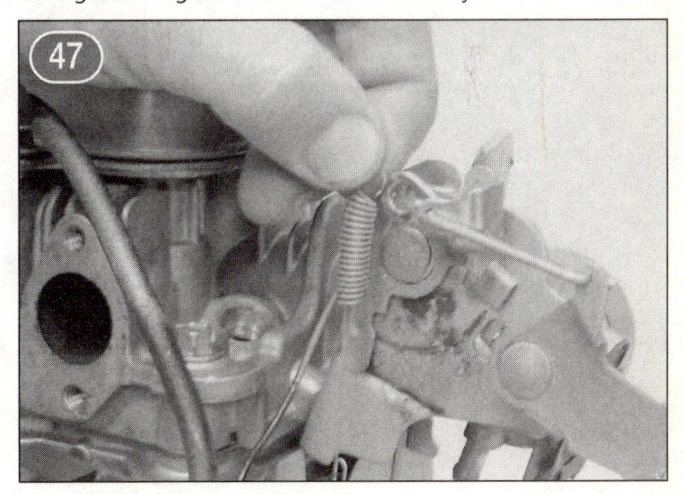

47 Reconnect the end of the governor linkage spring to the relevant hole in the linkage plate.

48 Fit the air filter housing to the carburettor using a new gasket. Note the locating pins on the housing gasket face. Tighten the two bolts.

Chapter 7

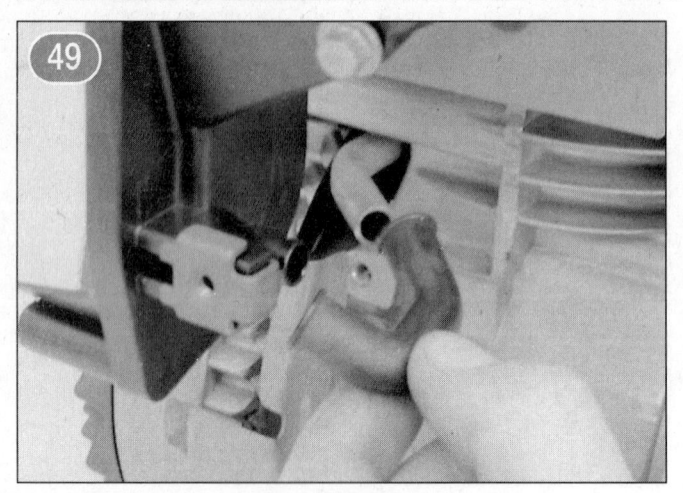

49 Connect the crankcase breather pipe to the air filter housing.

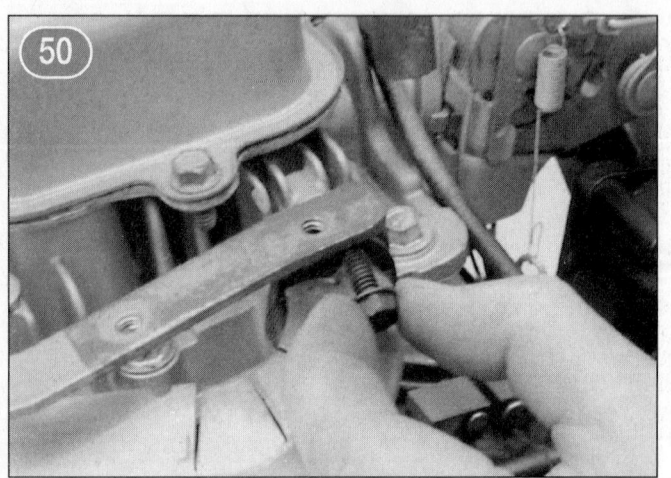

50 Using a new gasket, refit the exhaust system. The two self-tapping bolts fit into the crankcase and the side of the cylinder head, whilst the remaining two bolts secure the system to the exhaust port.

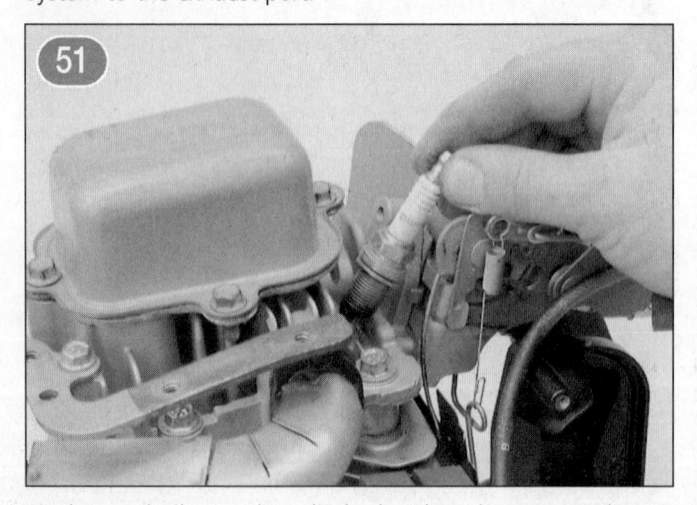

51 Fit the spark plug to the cylinder head, and reconnect the HT lead.

52 Refit the engine cowling, and secure with the four bolts. Ensure that the edge of the cowling interlocks with the crankcase cowling already fitted.

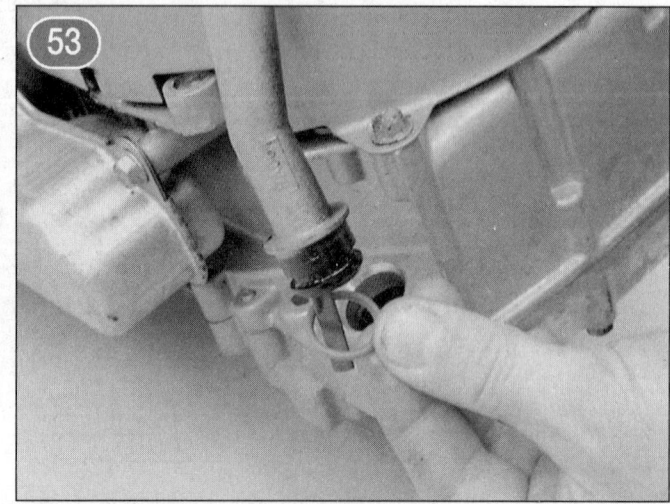

53 Fit a new O-ring to the base of the oil filler spout, and secure the spout in place with the bolt.

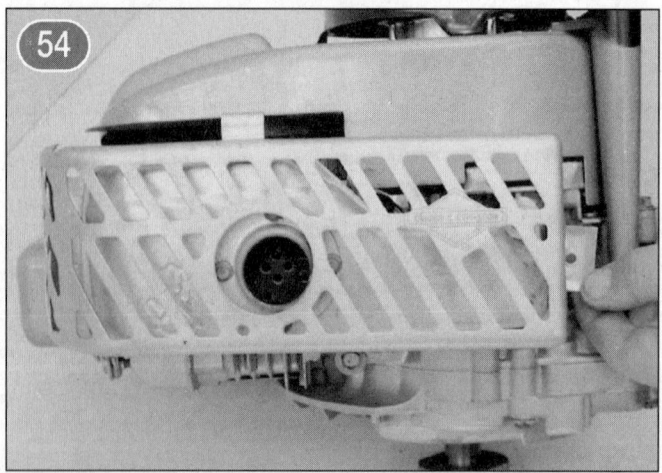

54 Refit the exhaust heat shield. Tighten the three bolts securely.

Briggs and Stratton Intek/Europa OHV engines

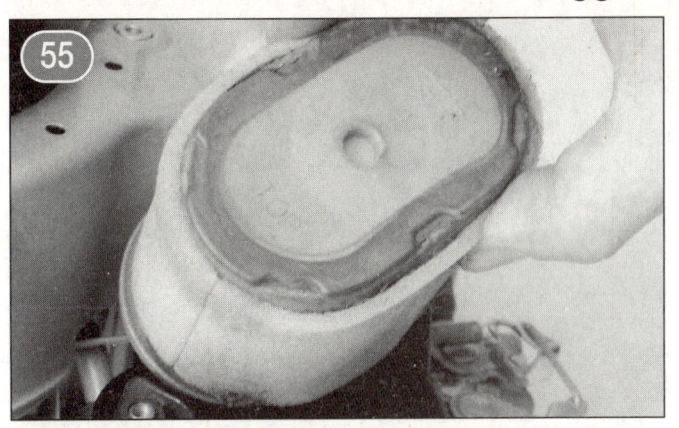

55 Fit the air filter element. One side is marked 'Top'.

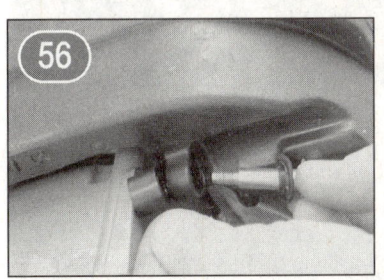

56 The fuel tank is secured by four bolts. Three on the topside, and one longer bolt, one the underside. Note the spacer that locates between the bottom mounting bracket and the crankcase.

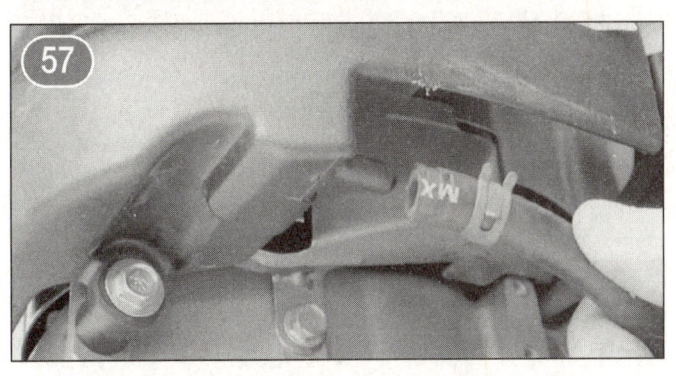

57 Fit the fuel pipe between the fuel tank and the carburettor. Secure the ends of the pipe with the two clips.

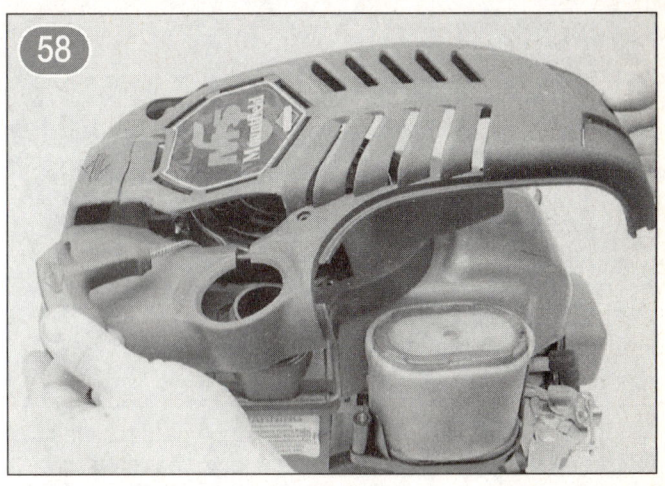

58 Remove the fuel tank cap, and fit the plastic engine cover. Tighten the two bolts, and refit the fuel tank cap.

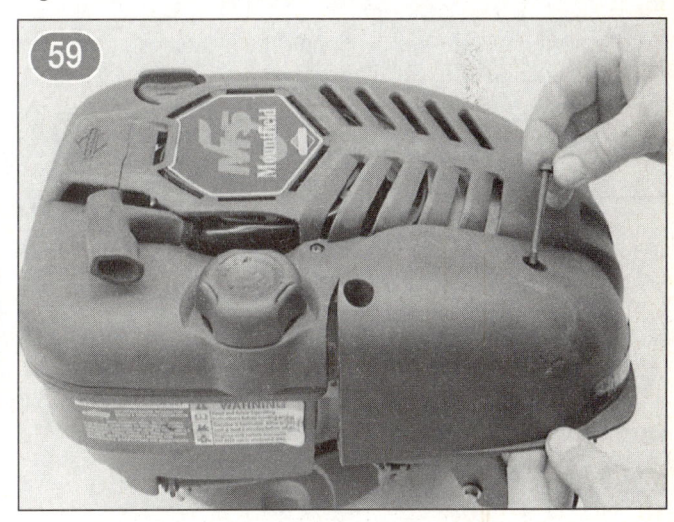

59 Refit the air filter cover, and tighten the two bolts. Remember to fill the engine sump with the correct grade and quantity of oil.

Recoil starter repair

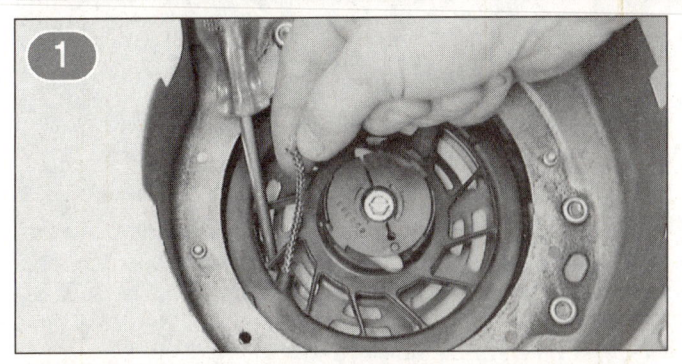

1 With the starter/engine cowling removed, pull the starter rope to its full extension. Lock the rope pulley in this position by inserting a screwdriver (or similar) through the spokes of the pulley and the slots of the engine cowling.

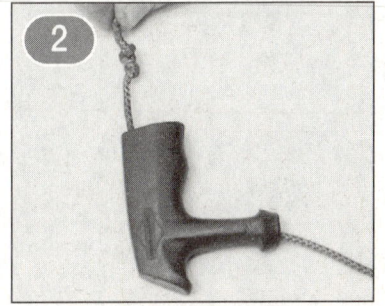

2 To replace the rope: Where the rope goes through the pulley, cut off the knot and pull the rope from the starter. Feed the new rope through the outer hole in the cowling and the hole in the pulley. Tie the knot. Feed the other end of the rope through the hole in the starter handle, again tie the knot. Tension the rope and remove the screwdriver from the pulley spokes. Be prepared for the spring to violently rewind the starter rope. Refit the starter/engine cowling.

Chapter 7

3

To replace the recoil spring: Where the rope goes through the pulley, untie the knot and pull the rope from the starter. Pull the screwdriver from the pulley. Unscrew the central bolt from the pawl mechanism, and lift off the guide plate. Note the position of the pawls, and remove them.

Carefully lift out the pulley, noting the locating slot for the end of the spring. Lift out the spring.

4

Insert the new spring, locating the inner end around the lug on the cowling.

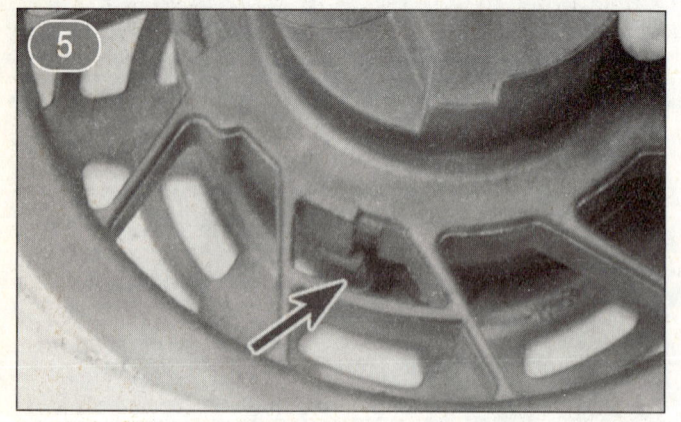

5

Fit the pulley, locating the outer end of the spring in the slot on the pulley (arrowed).

6

Check the starter pawls for damage or excessive wear, and refit them to the pulley. Refit the guide plate onto the pawls, ensuring that the pawl locating pins engage with the slots on the underside of the guide plate. Tighten the central bolt.

Using a screwdriver (or similar), very carefully wind the pulley approximately seven full turns, and align the rope hole in the pulley with the hole in the cowling. The exact number of turns is dependent on the length of rope. Lock the pulley in place by inserting a screwdriver (or similar) through the spokes of the pulley and the slots of the engine cowling. Exercise extreme caution during this procedure. It will take some effort to wind the spring up, and should the screwdriver slip, the pulley will unwind violently.

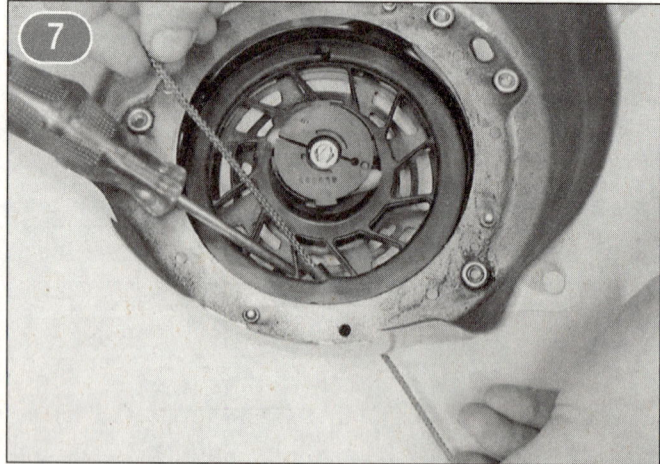

7

Feed the rope through the outer hole in the cowling and the hole in the pulley. Tie a knot in the end of the rope. Tension the rope and remove the screwdriver from the pulley spokes. Be prepared for the spring to violently rewind the starter rope. Refit the starter/engine cowling.

Briggs and Stratton Intek/Europa OHV engines

'Sloper' Intek engine

1 The Briggs and Stratton Intek OHV 'Sloper' engine . . .

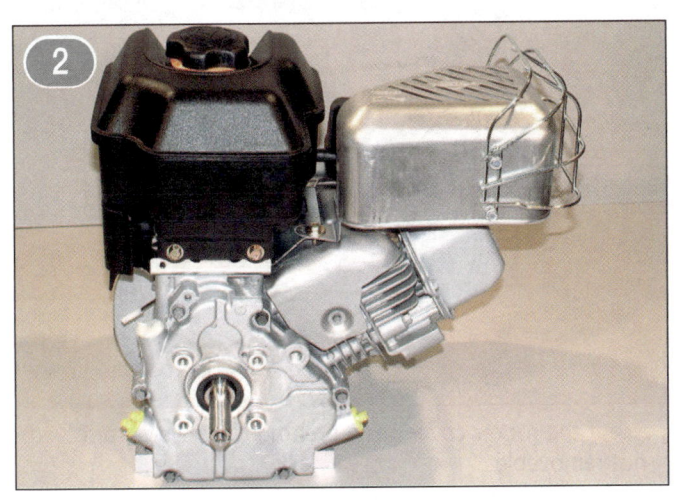

2 . . . is essentially identical to the earlier engine, but the crankshaft is horizontal, and the cylinder is at an angle.

3 Ensure the fuel tap is in the off position . . .

4 . . . then undo the screws (arrowed) and remove the control lever cover.

5 Undo the screw and remove the air filter cover . . .

6 . . . followed by the filter element and pre-filter.

7•15

Chapter 7

7 The filter backplate is secured by two screws.

8 The carburettor is identical to that shown earlier . . .

9 . . . as is the ignition coil . . .

10 . . . and the valve gear . . .

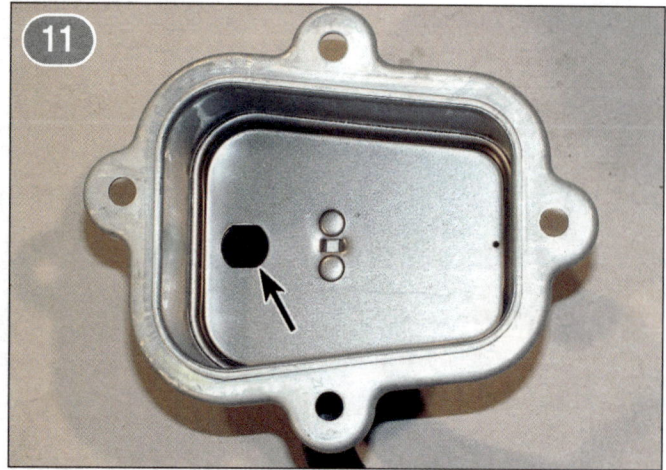

11 . . . but the rocker cover has a breather 'flap' valve (arrowed) – not removable.

12 The crankcase cover is retained by 6 screws (arrowed).

7•16

Briggs and Stratton Intek/Europa OHV engines

13 The crankshaft, connecting rod and piston assembly are identical to the earlier engine . . .

14 . . . but the governor assembly is new. As the crankshaft driven gear rotates, the two arms (A) fling out, and the central rod (B) extends, pushing on the governor lever.

15 When refitting the crankshaft, ensure the sprocket timing marks (arrowed) align.

16 Note the fitted positions of the governor lever and linkages.

17 Ensure the governor spring is refitted into its original position.

18 The intake spacer is fitted with the stub towards the carburettor.

19 Note the small spring (arrowed) wrapped around the carburettor operating lever.

7•17

Chapter 7

Electric starter

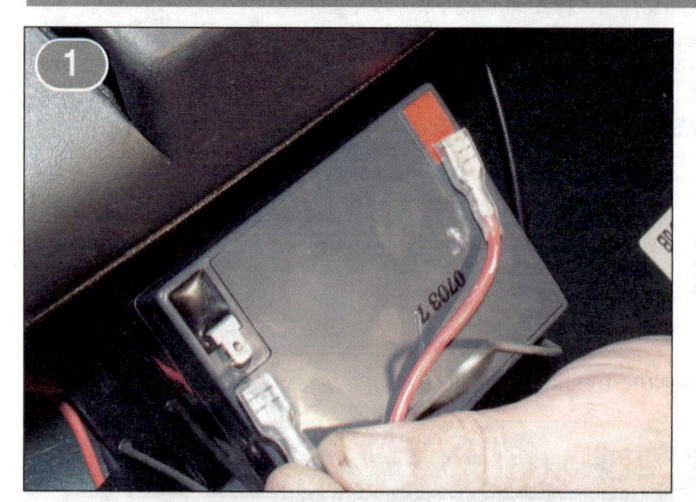

1 Disconnect the battery negative lead.

2 Undo the two bolts and remove the air filter cover . . .

3 . . . followed by the air filter element.

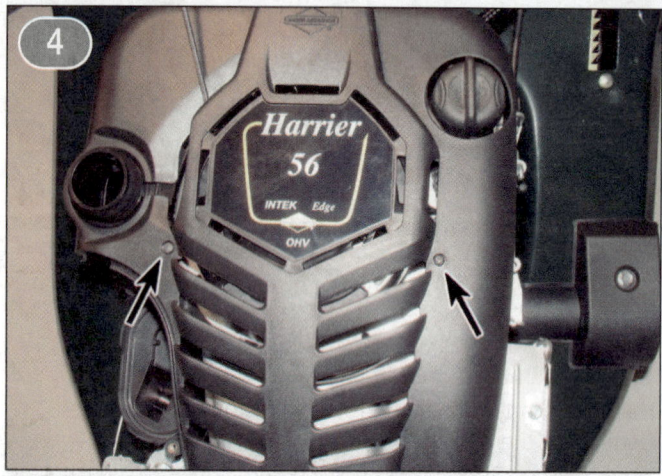

4 Remove the fuel filler cap, undo the two screws (arrowed), and remove the plastic top cover.

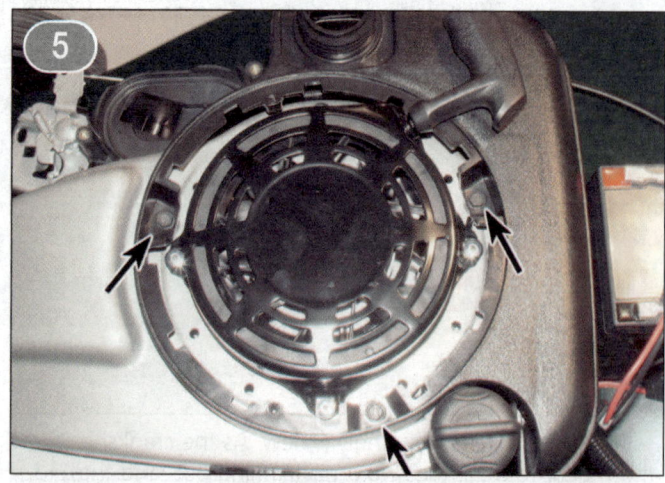

5 Undo the three screws securing the fuel tank at the top (arrowed) . . .

6 . . . and the bolt at the tanks lower edge – don't forget the spacer between the tank and the crankcase.

Briggs and Stratton Intek/Europa OHV engines

7 Release the clip and disconnect the fuel pipe from the tank. Be prepared for fuel spillage and plug or drain the tank as it's removed.

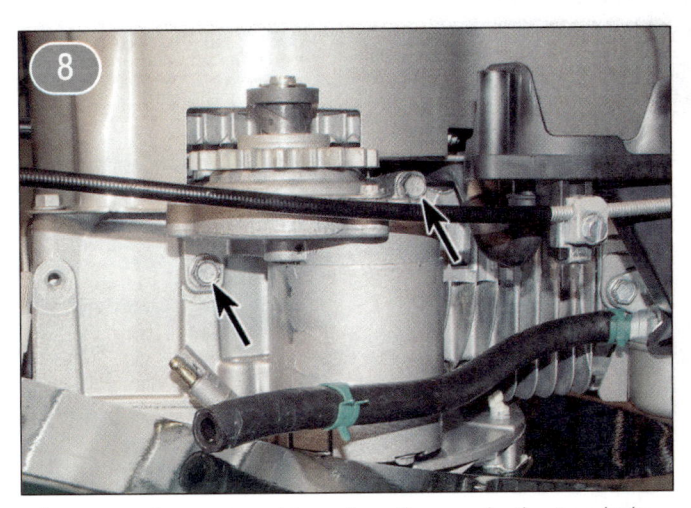

8 Disconnect the starter wiring plug, then undo the two bolts (arrowed) . . .

9 . . . and remove the starter.

10 To dismantle the starter reduction drive, prise away the circlip . . .

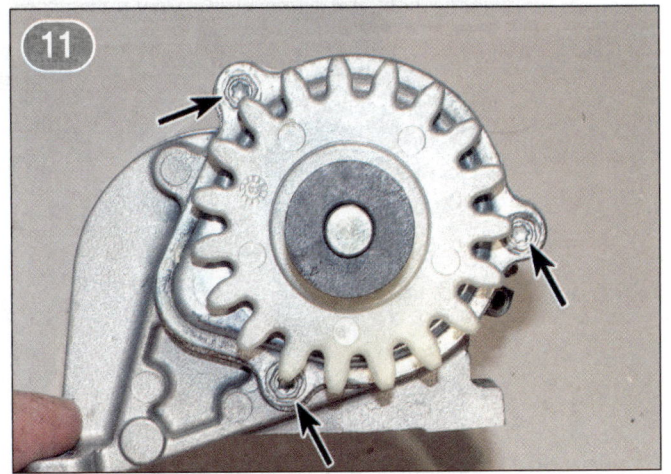

11 . . . undo the three bolts (arrowed) securing the reduction drive cover . . .

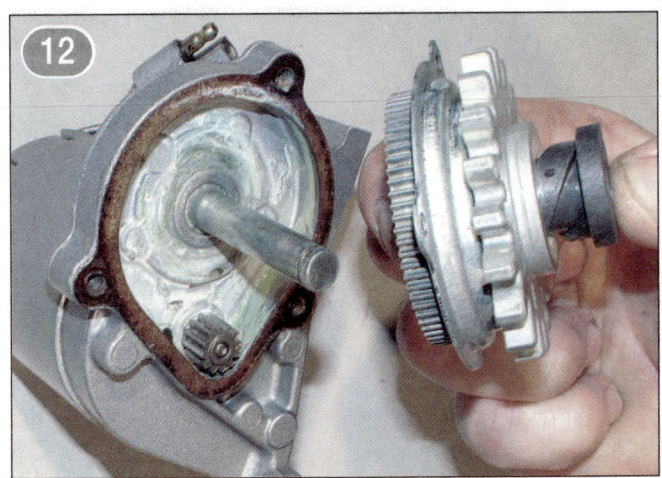

12 . . . and remove the gear, quick-thread drive gear and cover.

7•19

Chapter 7

13 The drive gear is slotted internally to fit over two machined flats in the motor spindle.

14 Fit the felt seal into the recess in the reduction gear.

15 Fit the quick-thread gear through the plastic drive gear . . .

16 . . . then through the cover . . .

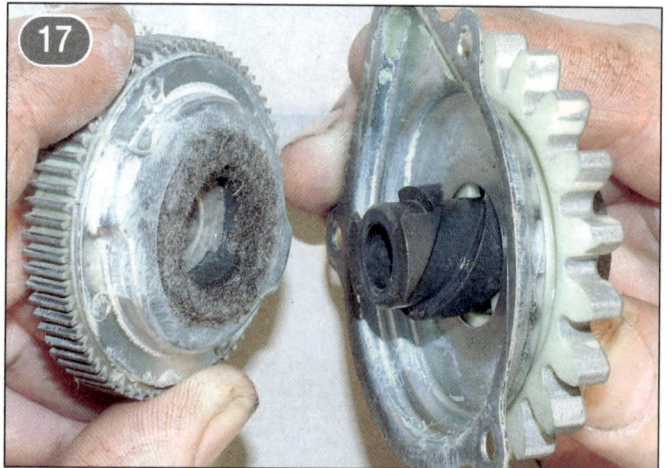

17 . . . and into the centre of the reduction gear, taking care not to trap the felt seal.

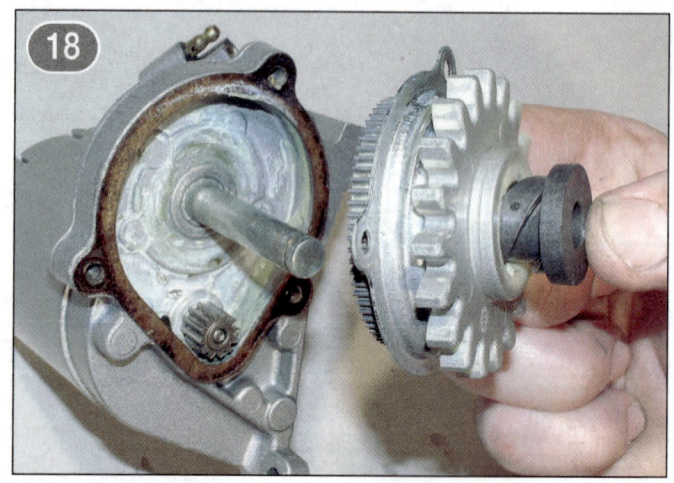

18 Slide the assembly over the shaft, tighten the three cover screws, fit the circlip and refit the starter to the engine.

Briggs and Stratton Quantum 55 'L' Head 4-stroke engine

8

Technical data
Recoil starter repair
Touch-N-Mow starter

Dismantling
Reassembly

Technical Data

Spark plug type	NGK B2LM
Spark plug gap	0.75 mm (0.030 in)
Valve clearances (cold):	
Inlet	0.12 to 0.17 mm (0.005 to 0.007 in)
Exhaust	0.17 to 0.22 mm (0.007 to 0.009 in)
Armature air gap	0.15 to 0.25 mm (0.006 to 0.010 in)
Oil grade	SAE 30
Oil capacity	0.6 litres
Torque wrench settings:	
Flywheel nut	74 Nm
Big-end bolts	11 Nm
Cylinder head	16 Nm

Chapter 8

Recoil starter repair

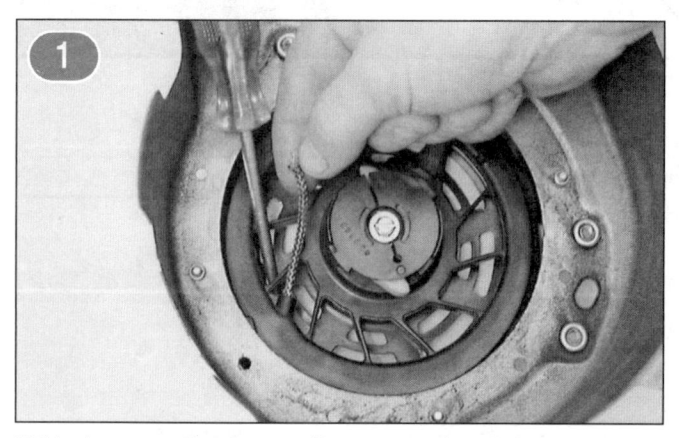

1 With the starter/engine cowling removed, pull the starter rope to its full extension. Lock the rope pulley in this position by inserting a screwdriver (or similar) through the spokes of the pulley and the slots of the engine cowling.

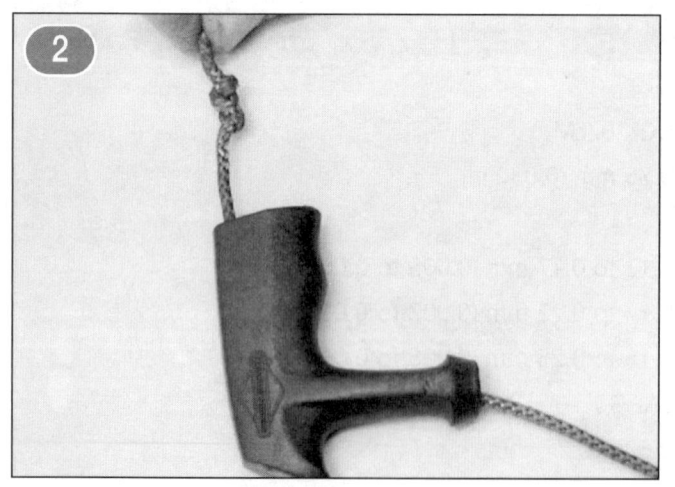

2 To replace the rope: Where the rope goes through the pulley, cut off the knot and pull the rope from the starter. Feed the new rope through the outer hole in the cowling and the inner hole in the pulley. Tie the knot. Then feed the other end of the rope through the hole in the starter handle, again tie the knot. Tension the rope and remove the screwdriver from the pulley spokes. Be prepared for the spring to violently rewind the starter rope. Refit the starter/engine cowling.

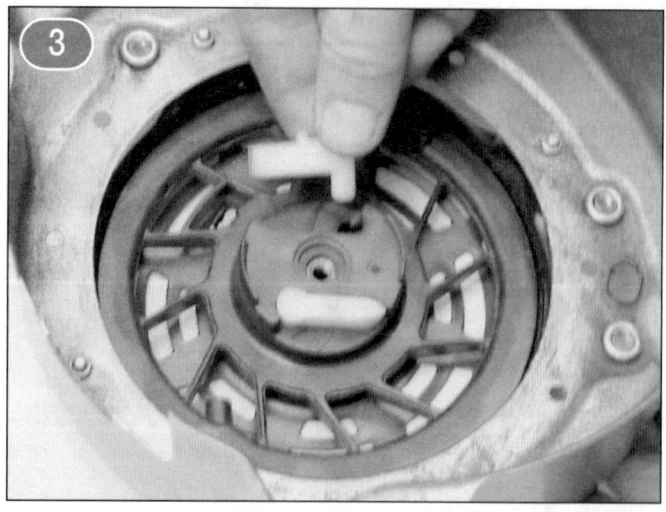

3 To replace the recoil spring: Where the rope goes through the pulley, untie the knot and pull the rope from the starter. Pull the screwdriver from the pulley. Unscrew the central bolt from the pawl mechanism, and lift off the guide plate. Note the position of the pawls, and remove them.

Carefully lift out the pulley, noting the locating slot for the end of the spring. Lift out the spring.

4 Insert the new spring, locating the inner end around the lug on the cowling.

Briggs and Stratton Quantum 55 'L' Head 4-stroke engine

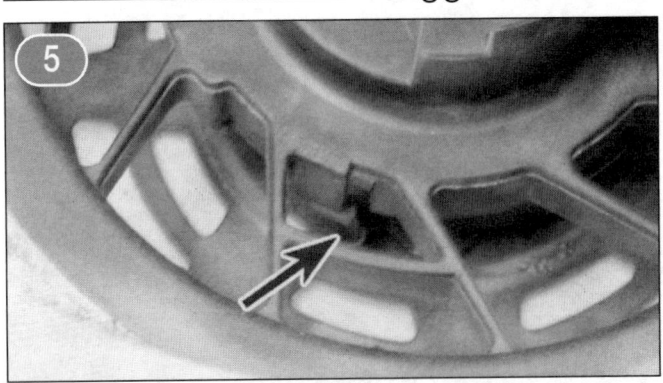

Fit the pulley, locating the outer end of the spring in the slot on the pulley (arrowed).

Check the starter pawls for damage or excessive wear, and refit them to the pulley. Refit the guide plate onto the pawls, ensuring that the pawl locating pins engage with the slots on the underside of the guide plate. Tighten the central bolt.

Using a screwdriver (or similar), very carefully wind the pulley approximately seven full turns, and align the rope hole in the pulley with the hole in the cowling. The exact number of turns is dependent on the length of rope. Lock the pulley in place by inserting a screwdriver (or similar) through the spokes of the pulley and the slots of the engine cowling. Exercise extreme caution during this procedure. It will take some effort to wind the spring up, and should the screwdriver slip, the pulley will unwind violently.

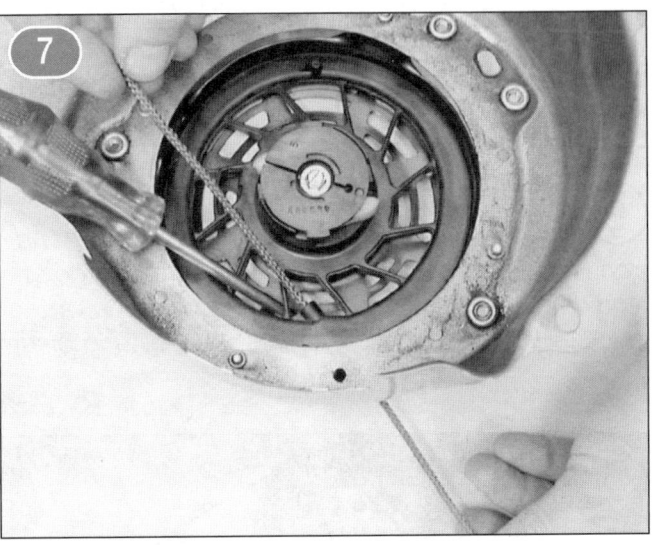

Feed the rope through the outer hole in the cowling and the hole in the pulley. Tie a knot in the end of the rope. Tension the rope and remove the screwdriver from the pulley spokes. Be prepared for the spring to violently rewind the starter rope. Refit the starter/engine cowling.

Chapter 8

Touch-N-Mow™ starter

Touch-N-Mow™ is the Trade Mark of the Briggs & Stratton Corporation

The 'Touch-N-Mow' system uses a coiled spring to store the energy of the last few revolutions of the engine. When it's time to start the engine again, the mechanism uses the spring energy to rotate the flywheel/crankshaft, and start the engine. Before attempting to remove the mechanism, it must be de-energised.

> **Caution!** It is essential to de-energise the 'Touch-N-Mow' mechanism before attempting any repairs on this type of engine. Failure to do so could result in unexpected and rapid rotation of the flywheel/crankshaft and therefore, any cutting blade attached to it!

1 Turn the 'Touch-N-Mow' safety key to the unlocked position . . .

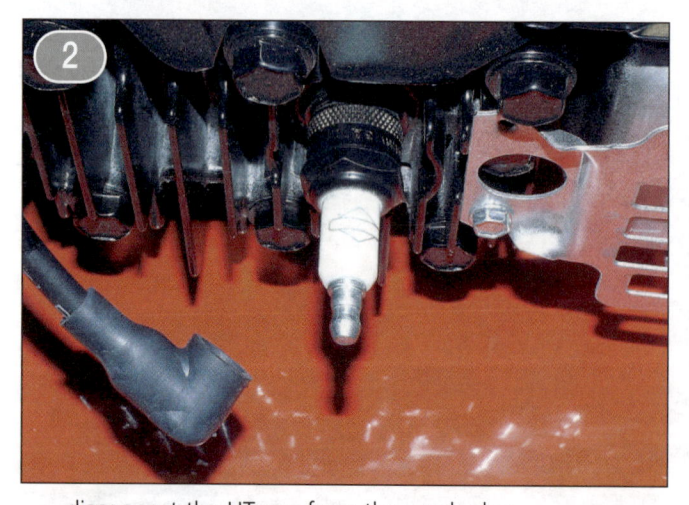

2 . . . disconnect the HT cap from the spark plug . . .

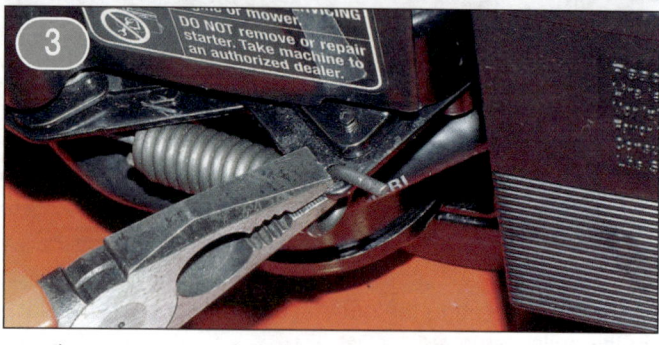

3 . . . then use a pair of pliers to pull the release lever outwards and to the rear.

The system is now de-energised.

> **Caution!** Pulling the lever outwards will cause the 'Touch-N-Mow' starter to operate, rotating the flywheel/crankshaft – ensure all fingers etc. are clear of any cutting blades/flywheel teeth.

4 Release the three retaining clips and remove the plastic cover from the centre of the recoil starter assembly.

5 Remove the orange safety key. Disconnect the pipe and drain the fuel tank, or be prepared for fuel spillage. Undo the three screws (arrowed) at the top, and the one at the lower rear edge (which also helps secure the starter assembly) . . .

8•4

Briggs and Stratton Quantum 55 'L' Head 4-stroke engine

6 ... then remove the fuel tank/top cover, noting how it fits over the safety key shaft (arrowed).

7 Remove the air filter cover ...

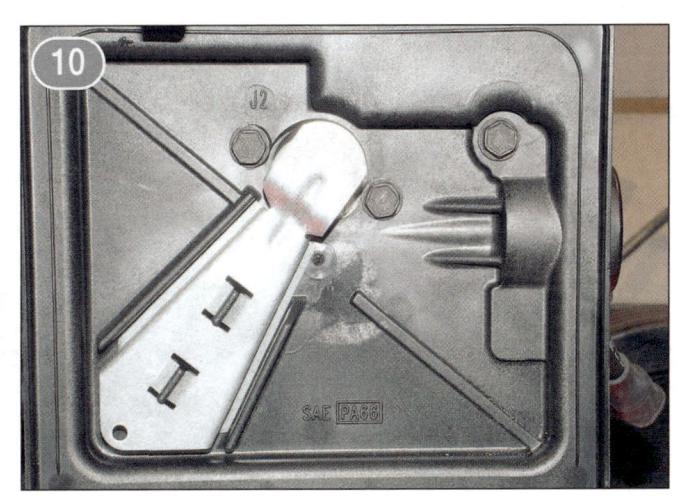

8 ... air filter element ...

9 ... top cover ...

10 ... and back plate.

11 Recover the gasket between the back plate and the carburettor. Note the breather hose which connects to the back plate (arrowed).

8•5

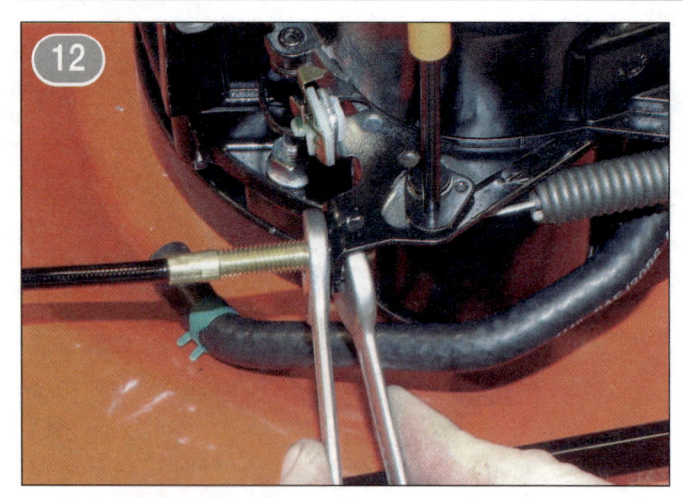

Chapter 8

12 Slacken the starter operating cable lock nuts, and slide the cable from the bracket on the starter.

13 Press the brass contact in, and disconnect the ignition 'kill' wire from the starter housing.

14 Using a T30 Torx driver bit (Briggs & Stratton part no. 19518) undo the remaining starter securing bolt (arrowed), and remove the 'Touch-N-Mow' assembly.

15 There are no user serviceable parts within the starter assembly. Do <u>not</u> attempt any further dismantling, or serious injury could result. If the unit fails, replace it as a whole.

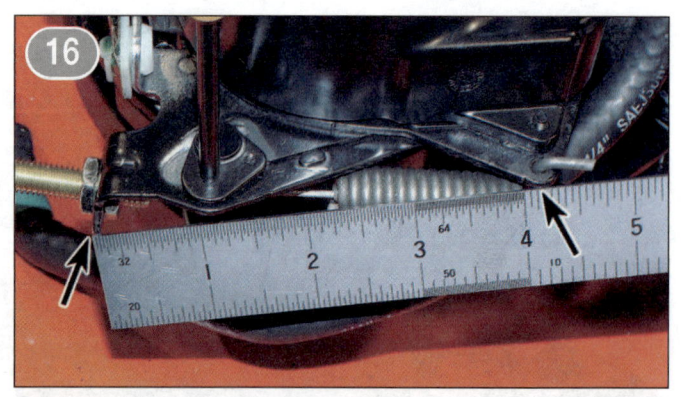

16 Refitting is a reversal of removal, but it's essential that the start operating cable is correctly adjusted. With the cable in the stop position (fully extended), the distance from the rear edge of the cable support bracket to the centre of the spring locating hole must be a minimum of 104.78 mm (4.125 inches) . . .

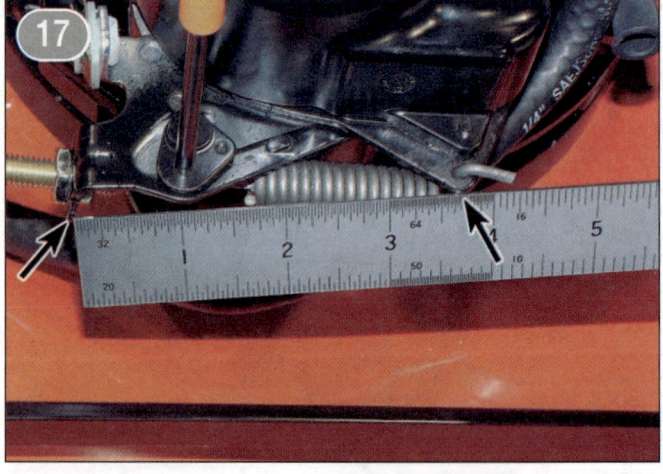

17 . . . and with the cable in the start position, the distance must be between 92.07 and 95.25 mm (3.625 and 3.75 inches).

8•6

Briggs and Stratton Quantum 55 'L' Head 4-stroke engine

Dismantling

Before starting to dismantle the engine, read Chapter 5. The procedures outlined apply to all engines and if adopted, will ensure an orderly and methodical approach that will make both dismantling and reassembly much easier.

Remove the engine from the application, and proceed as follows:

- [ ] Refer to Chapter 2 for dismantling hints and tips.
- [ ] Remove the two bolts and the carburettor shielding.
- [ ] Unscrew the retaining bolt and remove the air filter cover. Withdraw the element.
- [ ] Remove the air filter housing and primer assembly. Note the use of thread locking compound on the three bolts. Disconnect the engine breather tube from the housing.
- [ ] Remove the top plastic mesh from the engine by squeezing at the thumb shaped recess, and lifting the retaining lug clear.
- [ ] Disconnect the fuel pipe from the carburettor to the fuel tank. Be prepared for fuel spillage.
- [ ] In order to remove the fuel tank, unscrew the three retaining bolts at the top, and the bolt under the side securing the tank to the crankcase. Note the position of the spacer and washer.
- [ ] Unscrew the bolt and remove the oil filler tube. Note the O-ring fitted to the base of the tube.
- [ ] Remove the four retaining bolts, and lift the engine cowling/starter away.
- [ ] Unscrew the two retaining bolts, disconnect the magneto earthing wire, and remove the flywheel brake assembly.
- [ ] Remove the two bolts retaining the exhaust heat shield.
- [ ] The two exhaust system mounting bolts are locked using a tab washer. Bend back the washer tabs, unscrew the bolts, and remove the exhaust system.
- [ ] Undo the bolts securing the carburettor. As the carburettor is withdrawn, disengage the linkage rod and spring from the governor arm.
- [ ] Unscrew the float bowl bolt and remove the float bowl. Be prepared for fuel spillage.
- [ ] Push out the float pivot pin, and carefully lift out the float with the needle valve.
- [ ] Check the condition of the needle valve and seat for any damage or wear (refer to Chapter 5). Examine the float bowl O-ring for any for cracks, etc. The float bowl nut incorporates the main jet. Check that the holes are clear. If necessary, clear the holes by blowing or by the use of a thin nylon bristle. Never use a needle or wire to clean a jet. Check the float for damage or leaks.

- [ ] Disconnect the earthing wire from the magneto, unscrew the two bolts, and remove the carburettor mounting/linkage plate. Note the locations of the fibre washers.
- [ ] Remove the cylinder block cowling.
- [ ] Remove the crankcase cowling.
- [ ] Disengage the linkage rod from the governor lever.
- [ ] Pull the HT cap from the spark plug, unscrew the two bolts, and remove the magneto.
- [ ] The nut retaining the flywheel to the crankshaft can be extremely tight. To prevent the flywheel from turning, in the absence of the manufacturer's special tool, use a strap wrench around the circumference of the flywheel, and undo the nut. The help of an assistant to steady the engine may be necessary.

- [ ] Remove the starter flange. With reference to Chapter 5, pull the flywheel from the crankshaft. If you are using the manufacturer's puller, it may be necessary to cut the threads in the flywheel. The puller holes are clearly labelled in the flywheel, and the puller bolts are specially formed to cut the threads. Recover the key from the crankshaft.
- [ ] Remove the inlet manifold.
- [ ] Undo the two retaining bolts, and prise away the engine breather valve/tappet cover.
- [ ] Remove the breather chamber cover – four bolts.
- [ ] Remove the spark plug.
- [ ] Using a 3/8" square drive tool, unscrew the sump plug and drain the engine oil into a suitable container.
- [ ] Unscrew the eight cylinder head bolts, and with the assistance of a light tap from a soft hammer if necessary, lift away the cylinder head.

8•7

Chapter 8

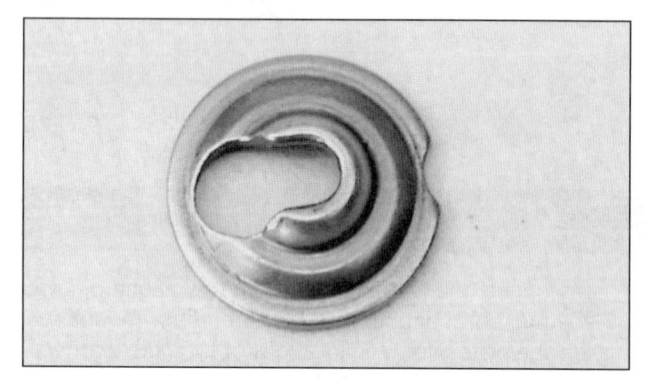

- [ ] Turn the exhaust valve spring collar until the notch in its rim faces out. The valve collars have two adjoining holes, one of which is larger than the other. This allows the valve stem to slide through the collar. Using a pair of thin-nosed pliers (or similar) compress the spring, move the collar away from the cylinder, slide the collar off the end of the valve stem, and remove the valve. Repeat for the inlet valve. It is important to label or arrange the components so that, if re-used, they are refitted to their original locations.
- [ ] Inspect the valve guides for scoring and excessive wear. Examine the valve seats and renovate as necessary (refer to Chapter 5).
- [ ] Unscrew the seven retaining bolts, and remove the sump. A light tap from a soft hammer may be necessary as the sump locates over two dowels in the crankcase gasket face. Note the shim fitted to the end of the camshaft.
- [ ] In order to remove the power take-off (PTO) shaft, undo the Allen screw from the outside of the sump. Using a suitable punch through the hole left by the screw, drive the roll-pin from the gear on the PTO shaft. Remove the retaining screw and lock plate, slide the shaft from the sump.
- [ ] Pull the camshaft and governor assembly from the crankcase. Recover the shims fitted to both ends of the shaft. No further dismantling of this assembly is possible.
- [ ] Slide out the cam followers. It is important to label or arrange the followers so that, if re-used, they are refitted to their original locations.
- [ ] The camshaft drive gear should slide easily from the crankshaft. Note, and if loose recover, the Woodruff (half moon) key.
- [ ] Unscrew the big-end bolts and withdraw the bearing cap.
- [ ] Remove any carbon build-up at the lip of the cylinder bore using a soft tool, and gently push the connecting rod and piston assembly up and out of the cylinder. Take care not to mark the bore with the connecting rod.
- [ ] Carefully withdraw the crankshaft from the crankcase.
- [ ] The crankshaft oil seals can now be prised out from the crankcase and sump. Note which way round they fit.
- [ ] Prior to removing the governor arm and lever, mark the position of the lever on the shaft. It is essential that the lever be refitted in the original position. Remove the lever pinch-bolt, and pull the lever from the shaft. Prise off the steel 'push-on' clip, and remove the governor arm/shaft from the crankcase.
- [ ] Check the condition of the crankshaft bearing, camshaft bearing and cylinder bore for wear, scores or cracks. If the bore is damaged, worn oval or oversized, then professional skills and special equipment will be necessary to restore it. The same applies to worn or damaged bearings. These can be reamed out to accept bushes obtainable from spares stockists, but special reaming equipment and knowledge are essential. Check all threaded holes for damaged threads, and repair if necessary by fitting a thread insert of the correct size (refer to Chapter 2).
- [ ] If required, remove the piston rings from the piston by carefully expanding the rings at their ends and sliding them from the piston. Note the orientation of the rings for reassembly.
- [ ] Remove the circlip and push the gudgeon pin from the piston.

Briggs and Stratton Quantum 55 'L' Head 4-stroke engine

Reassembly

Fit new oil seals into the crankcase and sump by carefully pushing them into place using an appropriate sized socket. The seals should be fitted with the sharp rubber edge of the seal towards the inside of the engine.

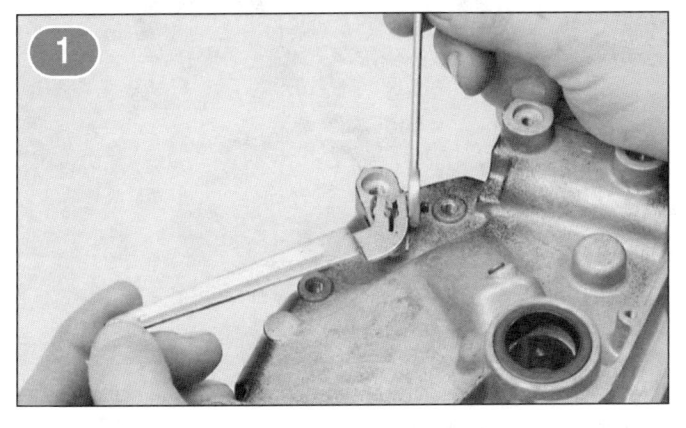

1

Fit the governor arm into the crankcase. Note the washer fitted between the arm and the crankcase on the inside. Fit a new 'push-on' clip on the arm on the outside of the case. Align the previously made mark, and refit the governor lever. Tighten the pinch-bolt.

2

Smear the lip of the crankcase oil seal with new engine oil, and fit the crankshaft into the crankcase, tapered end first.

3

If previously removed, fit the gudgeon pin into the piston/connecting rod assembly. The piston is fitted with the notch on its crown towards the tapered end of the crankshaft, and the 'open' side of the connecting rod towards the camshaft bearing. If the gudgeon pin is reluctant to move, immerse the piston in hot water for a few minutes. This causes the aluminium to expand, and the gudgeon pin to slide easily.

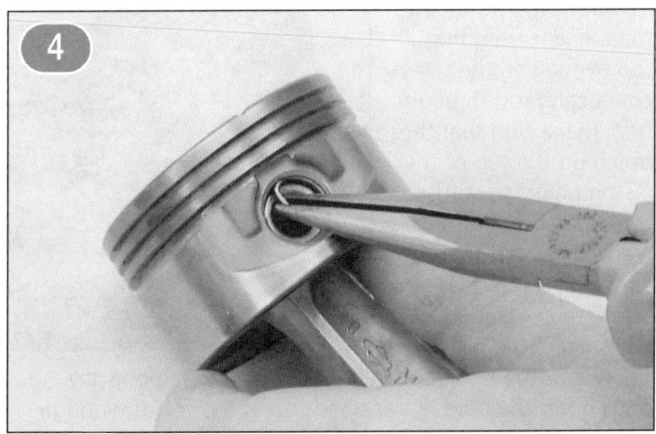

4

Always fit a new piston circlip.

8•9

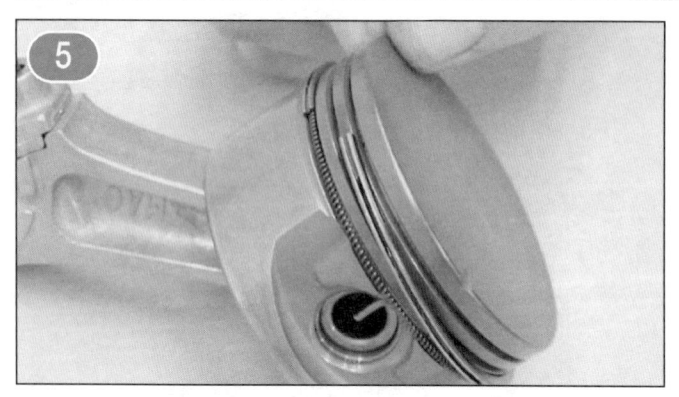

Chapter 8

5 Fit the piston rings onto the piston. The oil control (lowest) ring should be fitted first, by carefully expanding the coiled element just enough to slide down over the piston and into its groove.

6 Fit the second element of the oil control ring in the same manner, positioning it so that the coiled element is inside the second element. Next fit the compression ring into the middle groove. This ring must be fitted with the step in its circumference facing down. The top compression ring is symmetrical in profile. However, if the rings are marked with a dot, fit the ring with the dot facing up.

Beware: *Piston rings are very brittle. If the are expanded too much, they will break.* Arrange the three ring-end gaps so that they are spaced out around the circumference of the piston at 120° intervals.

7 Smear the piston rings and cylinder bore with oil. Using a piston ring clamp, fit the piston into the cylinder from the top by feeding the connecting rod through first. Make sure that the notch on the top of the piston points towards the tapered end of the crankshaft, and that the connecting rod does not scratch the cylinder walls. Press the piston firmly into the cylinder, sliding it out of the clamp as the rings enter the bore. If necessary, using a piece of wood or hammer handle, gently tap the piston out of the clamp and into the cylinder, but stop and investigate any undue resistance.

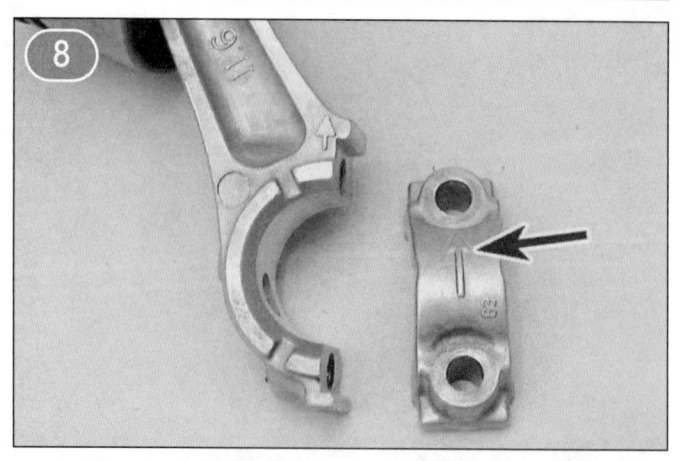

8 Smear some oil on the crankshaft journal and engage the big-end onto the journal. Fit the big-end cap with the arrow pointing towards the piston (arrowed).

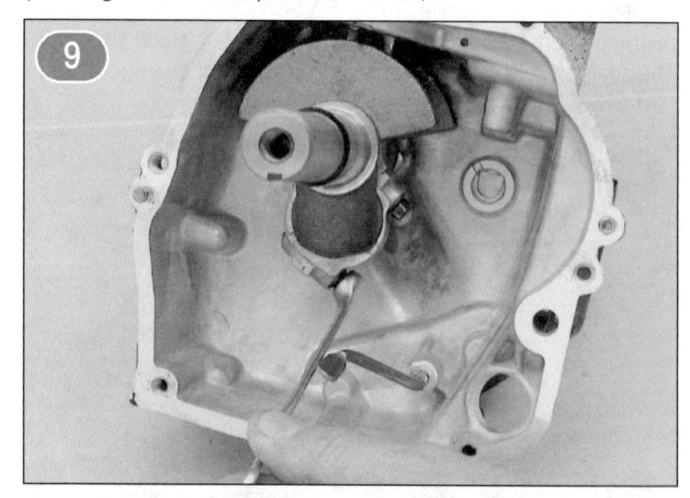

9 If you have a suitable torque wrench, tighten the bolts to the torque given in Technical Data. If not, tighten the bolts securely, but do not over-tighten. Rotate the crankshaft to ensure freedom of movement.

10 If previously removed, fit the Woodruff (half moon) key to the crankshaft, and fit the camshaft drive gear to the crankshaft with the timing mark facing outwards (arrowed).

Briggs and Stratton Quantum 55 'L' Head 4-stroke engine

11 Put a drop of oil onto the cam followers, and insert each follower into the same hole from which it was removed.

12 Turn the crankshaft until the timing mark on the gear is pointing at the middle of the camshaft bearing hole in the crankcase. Smear some oil on the camshaft bearing journal, and install the camshaft with relevant shims fitted to each end. The timing dimple drilled in the camshaft gear must aligned exactly with the mark on the crankshaft gear when the gears are meshed. Rotate the crankshaft two revolutions to ensure correct movement. Align the head of the governor with the arm.

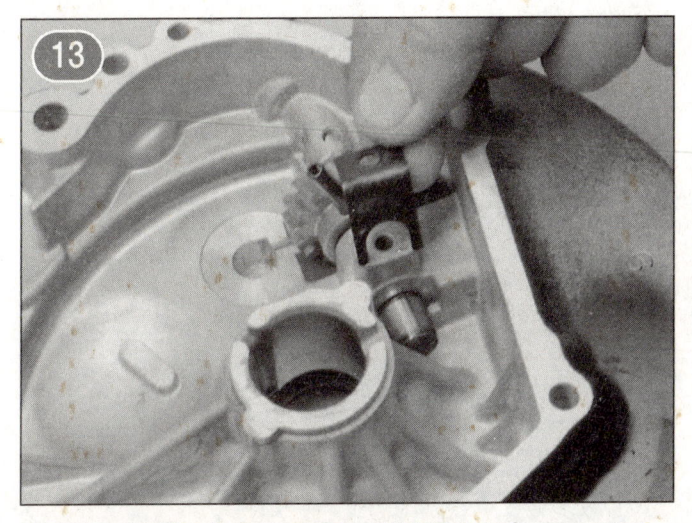

13 If removed, slide the power take off (PTO) shaft gear onto the shaft as it is inserted into the sump. Fit the locking plate and tighten the retaining bolt securely.

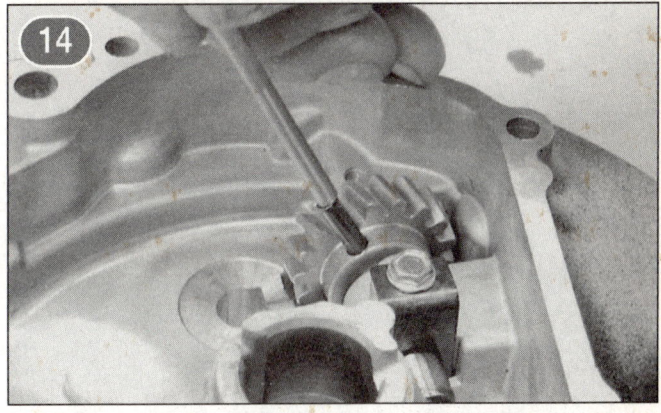

14 Align the holes in the PTO gear and shaft, and drive a new roll-pin into the gear until its end is flush. Fit the Allen screw into the hole in the sump.

15 Fit a new gasket over the locating dowels in to the crankcase gasket face. Refit the sump, and tighten the seven retaining bolts securely. Use thread-locking compound on the bolt that enters the engine breather chamber (arrowed). Refit the sump plug.

16 Prior to fitting the valve springs, turn the crankshaft until the piston is at TDC on the compression stroke. Slowly continue to turn the crankshaft until the piston has moved down the bore approximately 6 mm. Insert the valves into their respective guides and, with reference to Chapter 5, check both valve clearances. The dimensions are given in Technical Data. Once the correct clearances have been achieved, remove the valves.

Chapter 8

17 Fit the exhaust valve spring and collar into place in the tappet chest. Ensure that the notch in the rim of the collar is facing out.

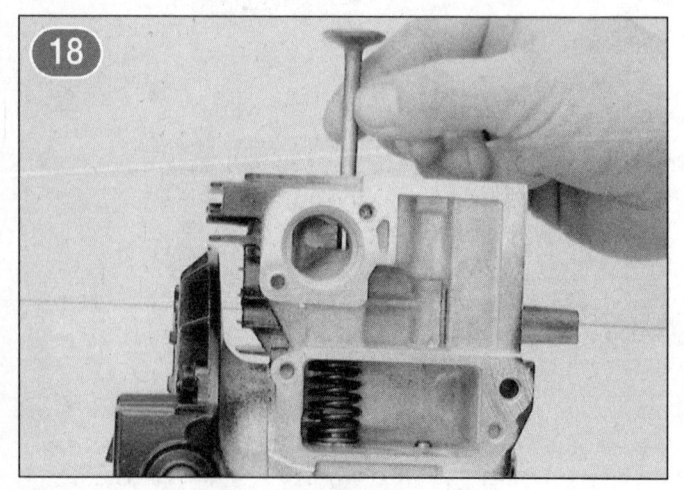

18 Fit the valve.

19 Using a pair of thin-nosed pliers (or similar), compress the valve spring, slide the collar over the end of the valve stem, and move the collar in towards the cylinder. Slowly allow the spring to uncompress, and check that the collar has located correctly on the end of the valve stem. Repeat this procedure for the inlet valve.

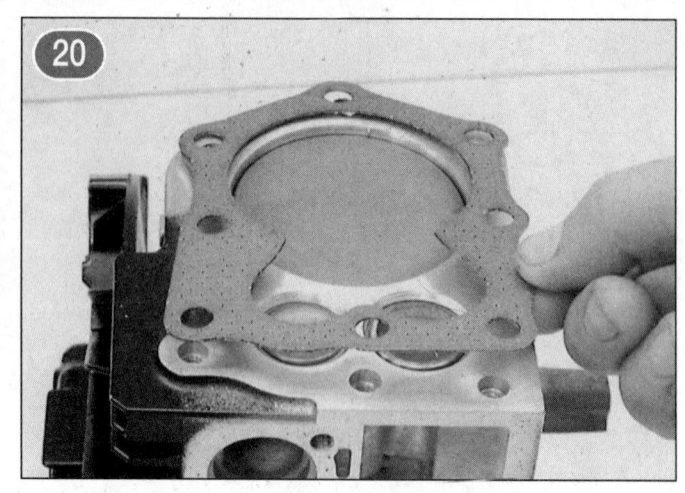

20 Place the new head gasket in the correct position. The gasket will only align with the bolt holes one way round. Do not use any jointing compound.

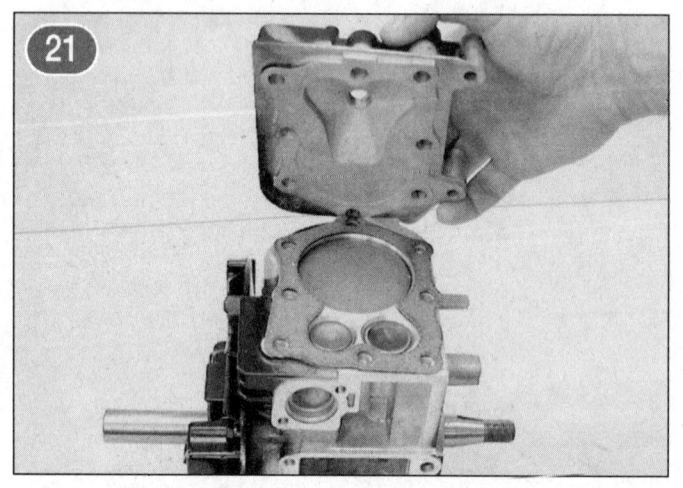

21 Refit the cylinder head, and tighten the eight retaining bolts evenly, in a diagonal sequence, to the torque given in Technical Data.

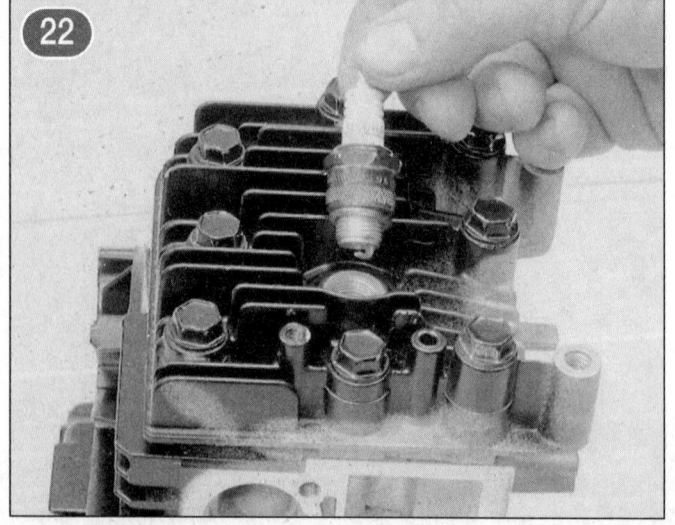

22 Refit the spark plug.

Briggs and Stratton Quantum 55 'L' Head 4-stroke engine

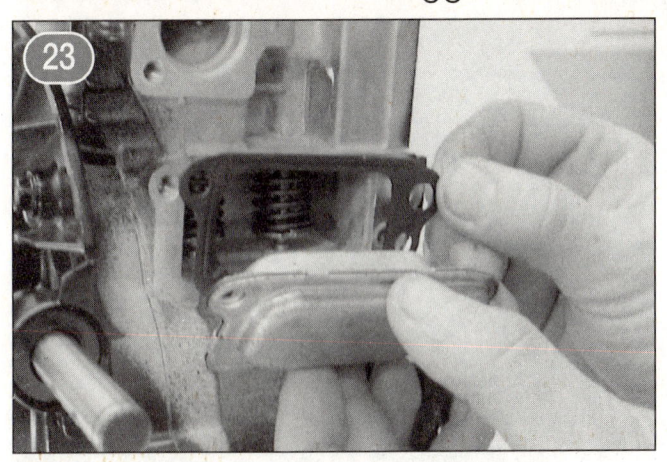

23 Check the fibre disc valve in the engine breather for distortion or cracks. The gap between the disc valve and the body should not exceed 1.1 mm (0.043 in). The valve is held in place by an internal bracket, which will distort if too much pressure is applied to the disc. If the valve is defective, renew the complete breather assembly. Renew the gasket and refit the valve/cover using the two bolts. Tighten securely.

24 With a new gasket, refit the breather chamber cover. Tighten the four bolts securely.

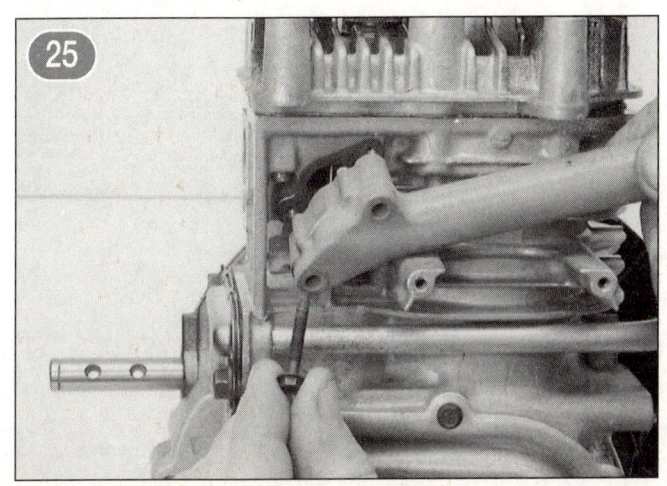

25 Renew the gasket, and refit the inlet manifold.

26 Slide the flywheel over the tapered end of the crankshaft and insert the key.

27 Fit the starter flange over the end of the crankshaft and fit the retaining nut. Tighten the nut to the torque given in Technical Data, preventing the flywheel from turning by means of a strap wrench around the circumference of the flywheel. The help of an assistant may be required to steady the engine.

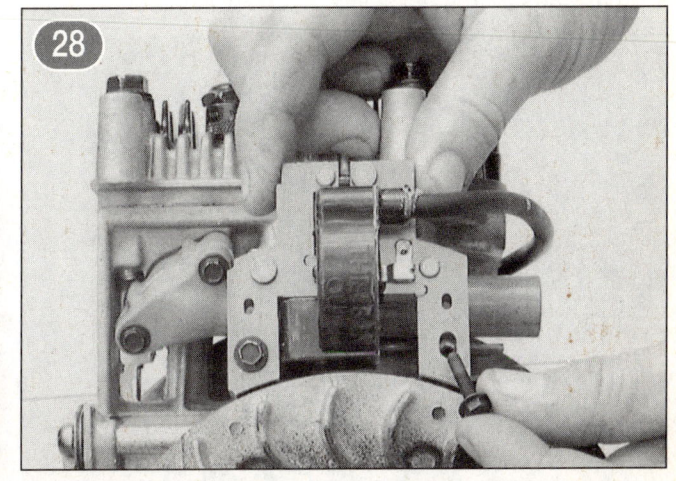

28 Refit the ignition magneto. The magneto body is marked 'Cylinder side' on one side, and 'This side out' on the other.

Chapter 8

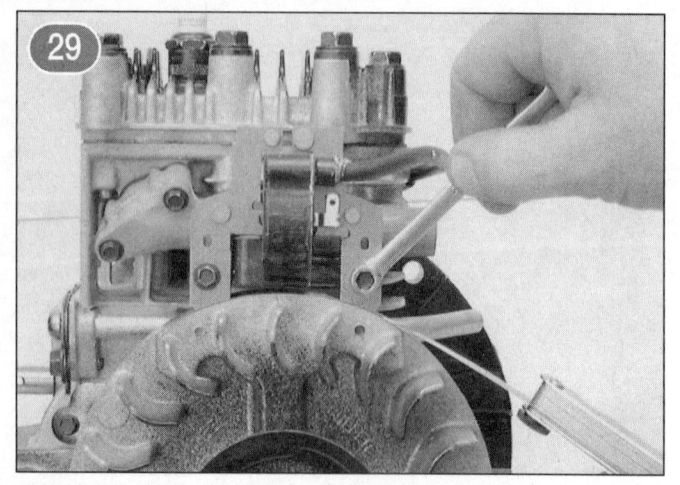

29 Before tightening the two mounting bolts, turn the flywheel so that the magnets are on the opposite side to the magneto, and use a feeler gauge to measure the air gap between the two legs of the magneto's armature and the flywheel. The correct air gap is given in Technical Data. The mounting holes in the armature legs are slotted. Move the armature until the correct gap is achieved. Tighten the bolts securely. Refit the HT cap to the spark plug.

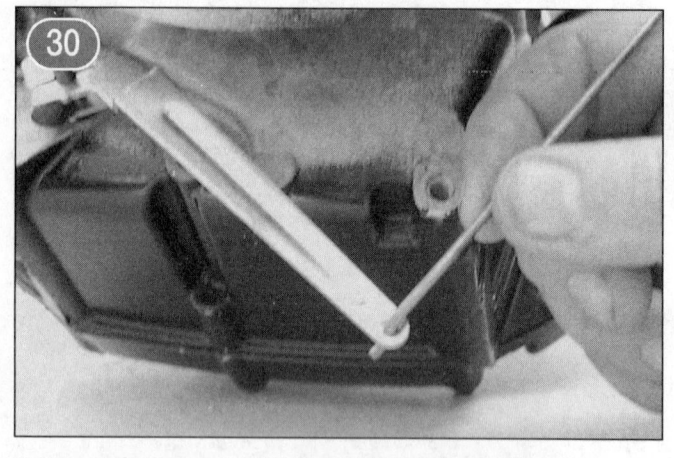

30 Connect the governor linkage to the governor lever.

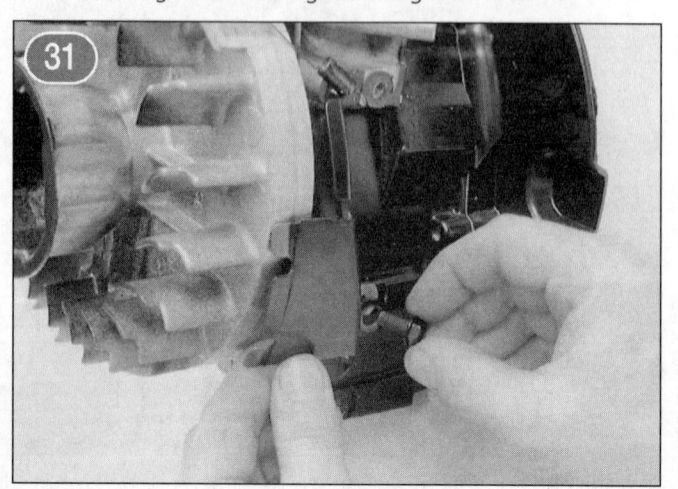

31 Refit the crankcase cowling – secured with a single bolt.

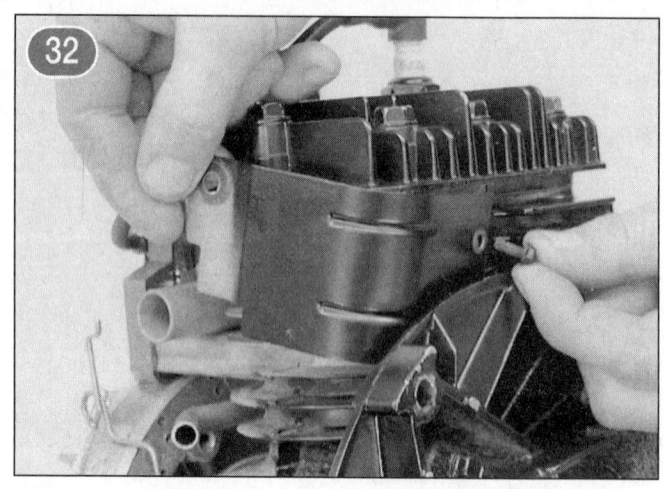

32 Refit the cylinder block cowling – also secured with a single bolt.

33 With the fibre washers in their correct locations, refit the carburettor mounting/linkage plate. Make sure that the HT lead is routed under the plate. Reconnect the earthing wire to the magneto. Feed the other wire behind the magneto, under the breather pipe to the flywheel brake mounting location.

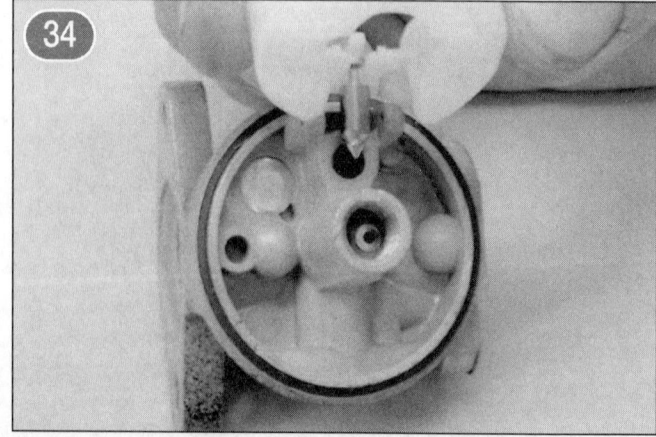

34 Reassemble the carburettor by refitting the needle valve into its holder in the float, and carefully lowering the assembly into place.

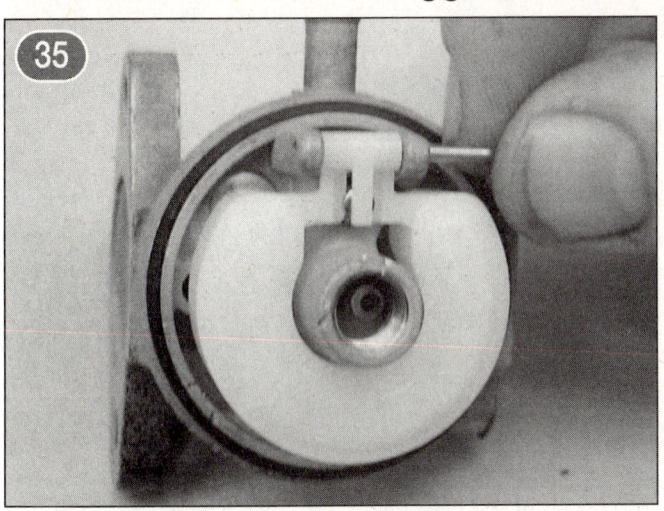

Briggs and Stratton Quantum 55 'L' Head 4-stroke engine

35 Insert the float pivot pin. There is no provision for adjusting the float height.

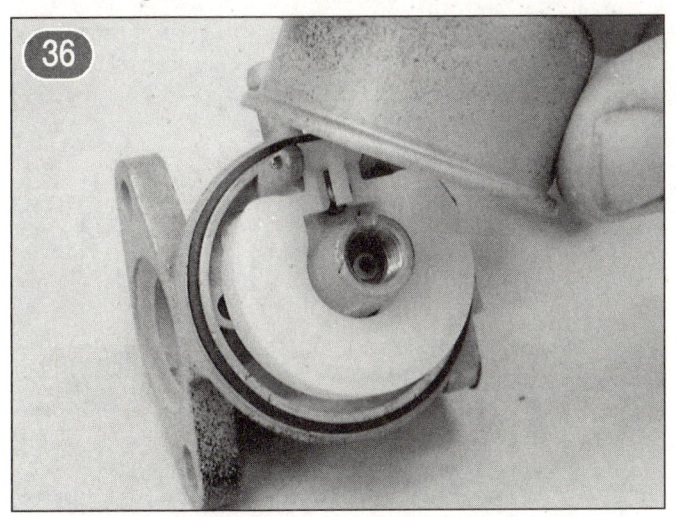

36 Refit the float bowl and secure with the bolt. Do not overtighten.

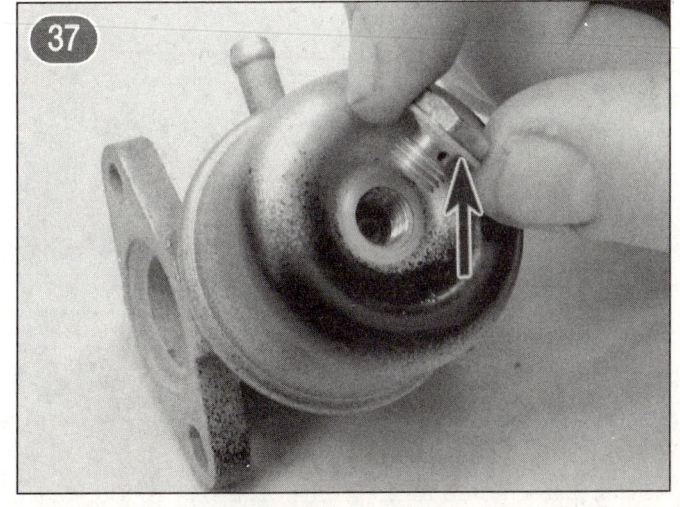

37 Note the fibre washer between the bolt and float chamber (arrowed).

38 Using a new O-ring (arrowed), refit the carburettor. Tighten the two screws securely.

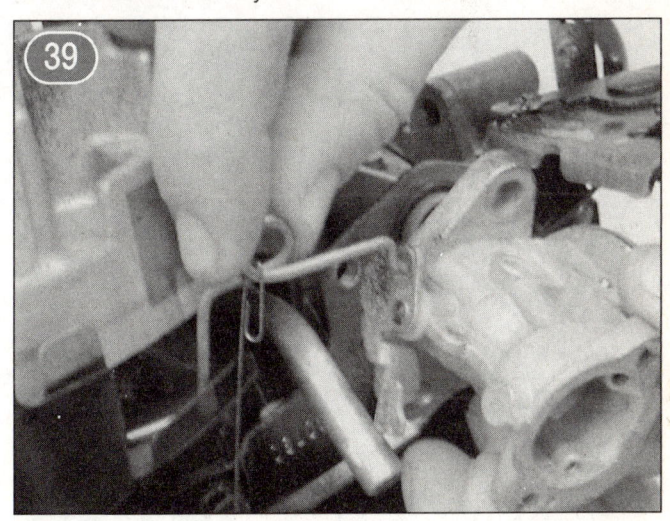

39 Engage the end of the governor linkage with the throttle arm.

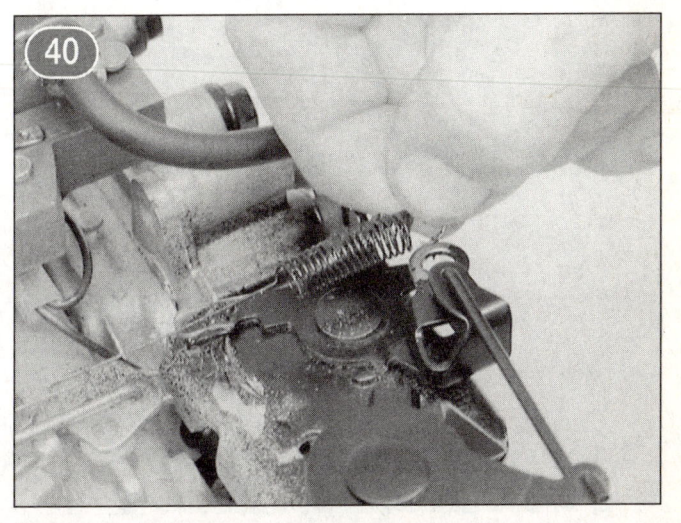

40 Reconnect the governor linkage spring.

8•15

Chapter 8

41 Refit the exhaust system, and tighten the two mounting bolts.

42 Bend the tabs of the locking washer to secure the bolts.

43 Refit the exhaust shield. Tighten the two retaining bolts securely.

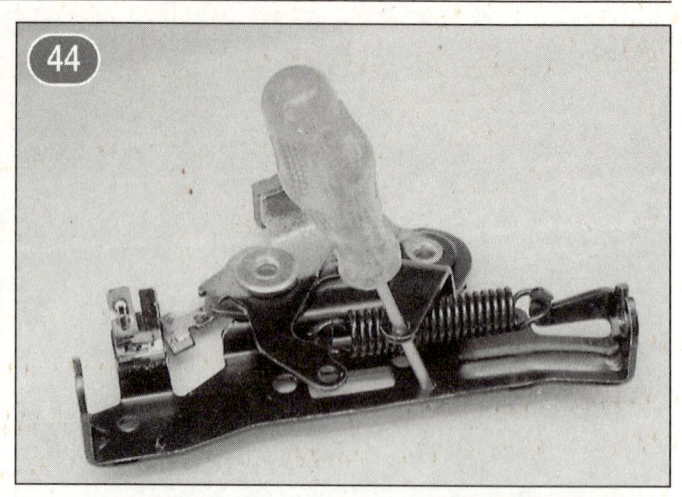

44 In order to fit the flywheel brake, it is necessary to expand the brake spring. Pull the brake levers apart and insert a screwdriver through the brackets.

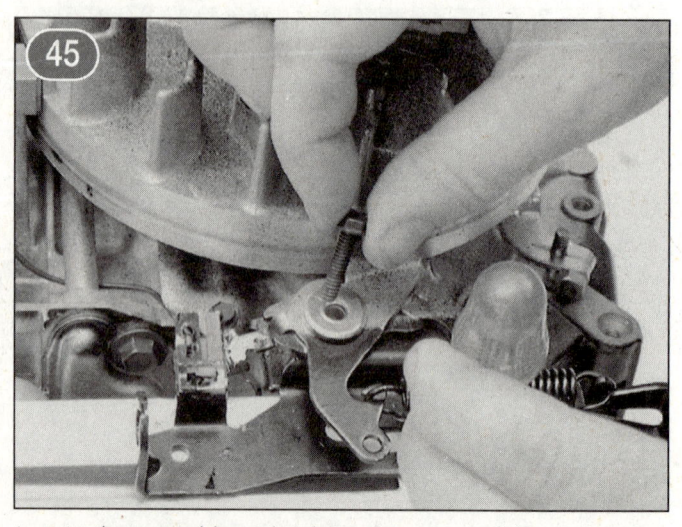

45 Locate the assembly and tighten the two retaining bolts. Remove the screwdriver.

46 Reconnect the magneto earthing wire.

Briggs and Stratton Quantum 55 'L' Head 4-stroke engine

47 Refit the engine cowling/starter. Before tightening the four retaining bolts, ensure that the cowling edge is correctly interlocked with the crankcase cowling already fitted.

48 Refit the oil filler tube. Note the O-ring at its base (arrowed).

49 The fuel tank is secured by four bolts. Three on the topside, and one longer bolt, on the underside.

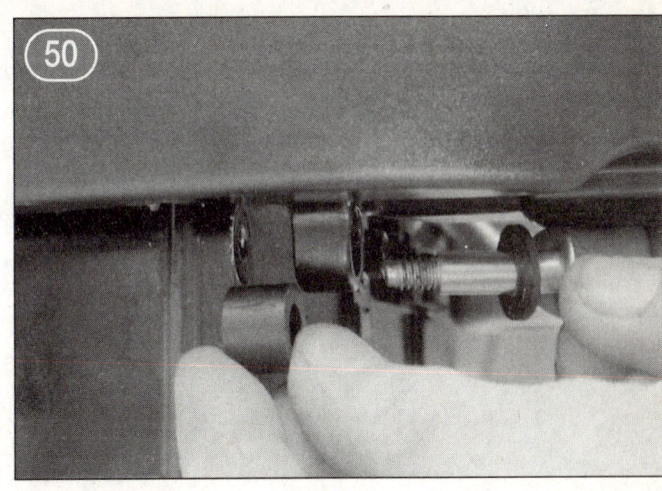

50 Note the spacer that locates between the bottom mounting bracket and the crankcase, and the washer under the head of the bolt.

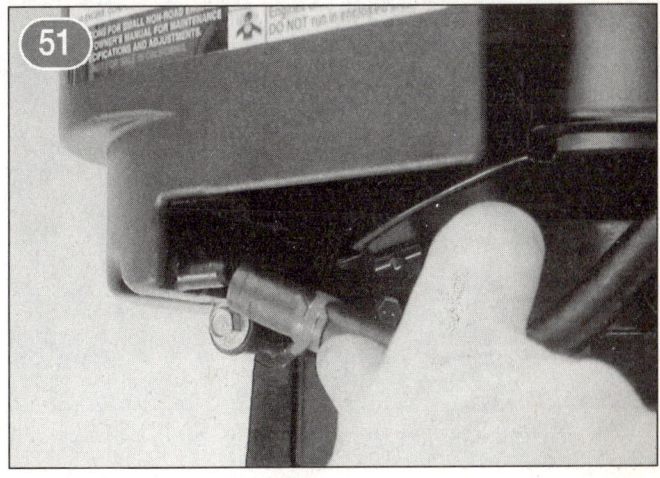

51 Reconnect the fuel pipe between the fuel tank and the carburettor. Secure the ends of the pipe with the two clips.

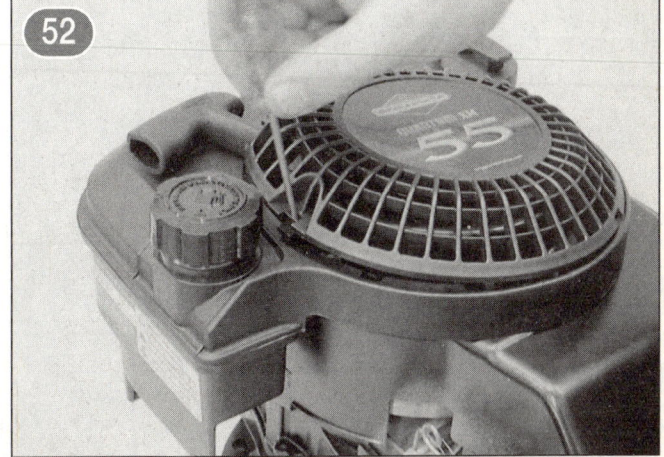

52 Refit the top plastic cover.

8•17

Chapter 8

53 Using a new gasket, and locking compound on the three retaining bolts, refit the housing to the carburettor...

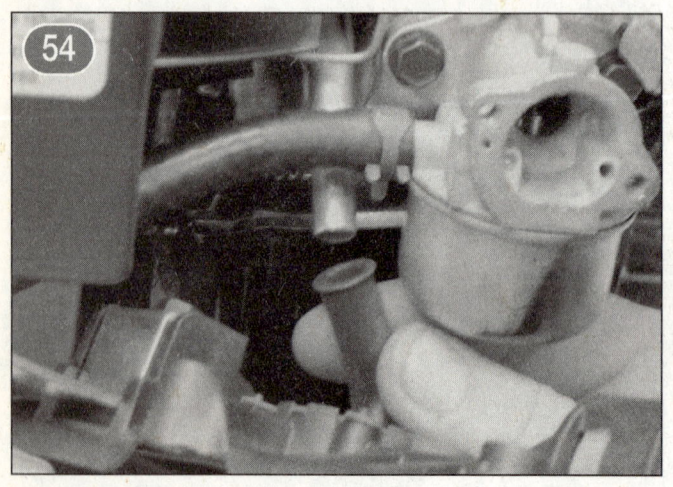

54 ...connecting the air filter housing/primer to the engine breather pipe.

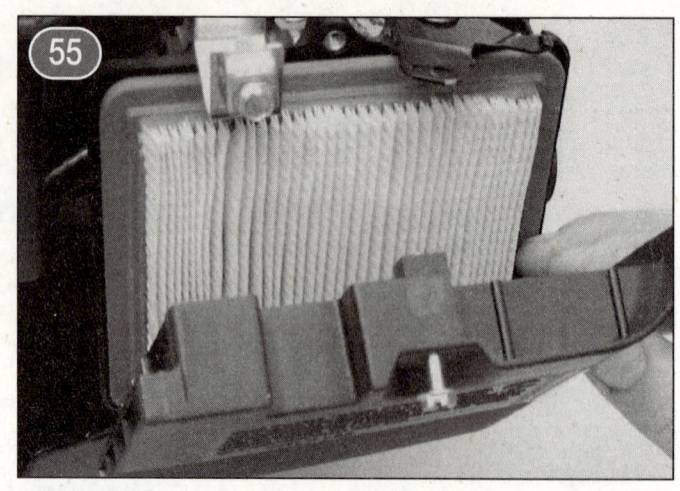

55 Refit the air filter element and cover. Tighten the retaining bolt securely.

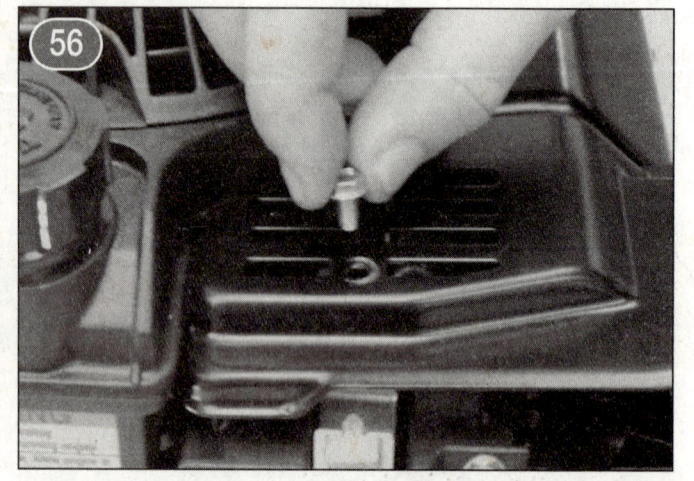

56 Using the two retaining bolts, refit the carburettor shielding. Remember to fill the sump with the correct grade and quantity of oil.

Briggs and Stratton I/C horizontal crank 'L' Head 5 hp engine

9

Technical data
Dismantling

Reassembly
Starter repair

Technical Data

Valve clearances (cold):
    Inlet .... 0.13 to 0.18 mm (0.005 to 0.007 in)
    Exhaust .... 0.23 to 0.28 mm (0.009 to 0.011 in)
Spark plug type .... NGK B2LM
Spark plug gap .... 0.75 mm (0.030 in)
Crankshaft end float .... 0.05 to 0.20 mm (0.002 to 0.008 in)
Magneto armature air gap .... 0.254 to 0.355 mm (0.010 to 0.014 in)
Piston ring gap:
    Compression rings .... 0.80 mm (0.032 in) max
    Oil control ring .... 1.14 mm (0.045 in) max
Oil grade .... SAE 30, SAE 10W–30
Oil capacity .... 0.62 litres
Torque wrench settings:
    Big-end bolts .... 11 Nm
    Cylinder head bolts .... 16 Nm
    Flywheel nut .... 88 Nm
    Crankcase end plate bolts .... 10 Nm

Chapter 9

Dismantling

Before starting to dismantle, read Chapter 5. The procedures outlined apply to all engines and if adopted, will ensure an orderly and methodical approach that will make both dismantling and reassembly much easier.

- [ ] Unscrew the two bolts, and remove the air filter cover. Lift out the filter element.
- [ ] Remove the air filter housing.
- [ ] The engine cowling/starter in secured by four bolts. Two on the top, and one on each side at the crankcase base. Remove the cowling.
- [ ] Bend back the tab washers, and undo the exhaust system mounting bolts. Remove the system.
- [ ] Loosen the Torx screw securing the carburettor to the fuel tank sufficiently to allow the engine breather pipe to be disconnected and removed.
- [ ] Unscrew the two Torx screws, and remove the remote control panel. Disconnect the linkage and the magneto earthing wire as the panel is removed.
- [ ] Disconnect the magneto earthing wire under the fuel tank, by unscrewing the retaining nut.
- [ ] Remove the carburettor and fuel tank together. Two bolts secure the carburettor to the cylinder head, and one, under the fuel tank, secures the tank to the crankcase. As the assembly is withdrawn, recover the heat shield, disconnect the governor arm-to-throttle butterfly linkage, and the spring between the governor arm and pivot plate.
- [ ] To separate the carburettor from the fuel tank, undo the Torx screws, and disengage the throttle linkage. Lift the carburettor from the tank. Be prepared for fuel spillage.
- [ ] Remove the wire gauze over the main jet, and clean if required. To gain access to the pilot jet for cleaning, undo the brass cover screw.
- [ ] Inspect the screen in the base of the fuel pick-up pipe damage and cleanliness. Do not brush or rub the screen, as it is very delicate.
- [ ] The fuel pump is integral with the carburettor. Remove the four Torx screws, withdraw the cover, diaphragm, cup and spring. Check for cleanliness and diaphragm damage.
- [ ] Unscrew the two magneto retaining bolts, disconnect the HT cap from the spark plug, and remove the magneto. Note how the deflector plate slots under the armature post.
- [ ] The nut retaining the flywheel to the crankshaft can be extremely tight. To prevent the flywheel from turning, in the absence of the manufacturer's special tool, use a strap wrench around the circumference of the flywheel, and undo the nut. The help of an assistant to steady the engine may be necessary.
- [ ] Remove the starter flange and mesh.

- [ ] To remove the flywheel, tap the back of the flywheel with a soft hammer, whilst pulling the flywheel away from the crankcase. Do not tap the aluminium element or the magnets of the flywheel. Recover the key from the crankshaft.
- [ ] Unscrew the two retaining bolts, and remove the crankcase cowling.
- [ ] In order to remove the cylinder block cowling, unscrew the three cylinder head bolts, and the bolt on the side of the cylinder block.
- [ ] Remove the remaining five bolts, and lift away the cylinder head. Note that the three bolts around the exhaust valve are slightly longer than the others.
- [ ] Unscrew the two retaining bolts, and prise away the tappet cover/breather valve.
- [ ] Turn the exhaust valve spring collar until the notch in its rim faces out. The valve collars have two adjoining holes, on of which is larger than the other. This allows the valve stem to slide through the collar. Using a pair of thin-nosed pliers (or similar) compress the spring, move the collar away from the cylinder, slide the collar off the end of the valve stem, and remove the valve. Repeat for the inlet valve. It is important to label or arrange the components so that, if re-used, they are refitted to their original locations.
- [ ] Inspect the valve guides for scoring and excessive wear. Examine the valve seats and renovate as necessary (*refer to Chapter 5*).
- [ ] Using a 3/8" square drive tool, undo the sump plug and drain the engine oil into a suitable container.
- [ ] Remove all rust and dirt from the crankshaft. Unscrew the six retaining bolts, and remove the crankcase end plate.
- [ ] If required, the governor cup assembly can be removed from the end plate by pulling.
- [ ] Unscrew the big-end bolts. Recover the oil dipper and the bearing cap.

Briggs and Stratton I/C horizontal crank 'L' Head 5 hp engine

- Remove any carbon build-up at the lip of the cylinder bore using a soft tool, and gently push the connecting rod and piston assembly up and out of the cylinder. Take care not to mark the bore with the connecting rod. If required, remove the piston rings from the piston by carefully expanding the rings at their ends and sliding them from the piston. Note the orientation of the rings for reassembly. Remove the circlip and push the gudgeon pin from the piston.
- Align the timing mark on the crankshaft counterweight with the drilling on the camshaft gear, and withdraw the crankshaft and camshaft together.
- Slide out the cam followers. It is important to label or arrange the followers so that, if re-used, they are refitted to their original locations. 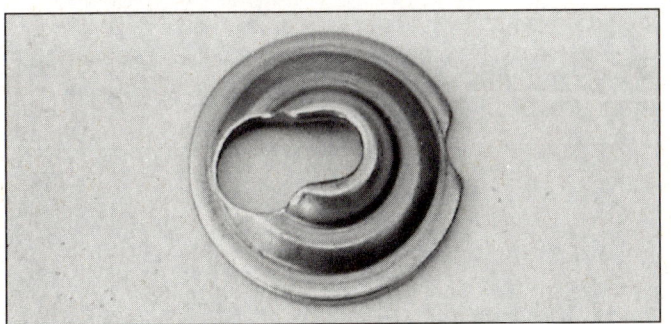
- If it is necessary to remove the governor lever from the shaft, mark the position of the lever on the shaft before undoing the pinch-bolt. Pull out the 'R-clip', and withdraw the governor shaft from the crankcase.
- If required, prise out the crankcase and end plate oil seals. Note which way round they are fitted.

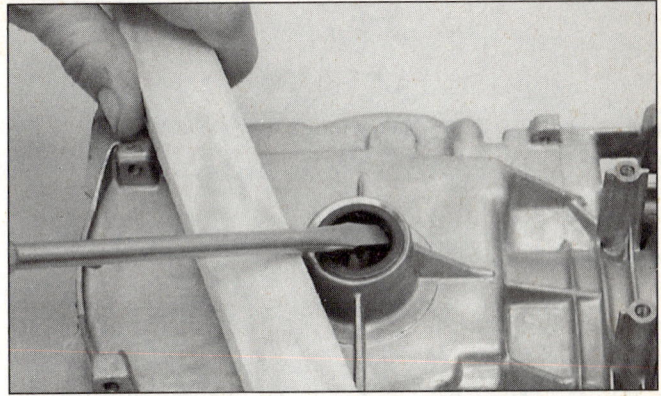

- Check the condition of the crankshaft bearing, camshaft bearing and cylinder bore for wear, scores or cracks. If the bore is damaged, worn oval or oversized, then professional skills and special equipment will be necessary to restore it. The same applies to worn or damaged bearings. It may be possible to have these reamed out to accept bushes obtainable from spares stockists, but special reaming equipment and knowledge are essential. Check all threaded holes for damaged threads, and repair if necessary by fitting a thread insert of the correct size (refer to Chapter 2).
- If the output side crankshaft main ball-bearing requires replacement, a bearing press will be needed, as the bearing is a press fit on the shaft. To install a new bearing, suspend the bearing in hot oil at 120°C. Take all necessary safety measures to protect the skin from hot oil splashes. With the crankshaft clamp in a soft-jawed vice, slide the bearing onto the shaft with the shield side inwards. As the bearing cools, it will tighten on the journal. Do not quench the bearing.

Reassembly

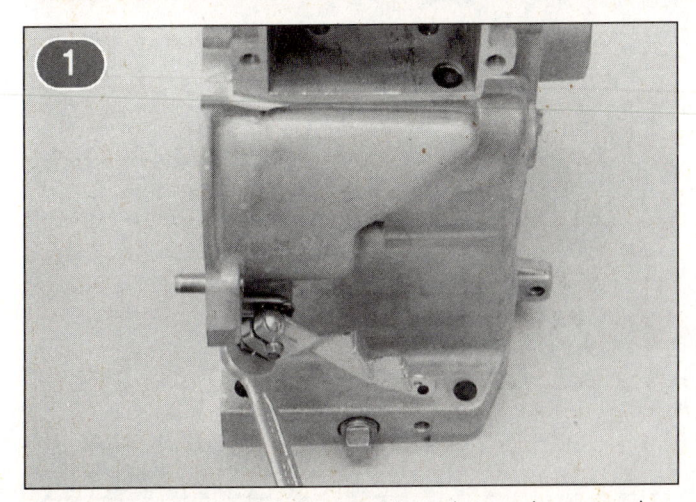

1 If removed, refit the governor arm into the crankcase, and secure with the 'R-clip'. Refit the governor lever to the arm, aligning the previously made marks. Tighten the pinch-bolt.

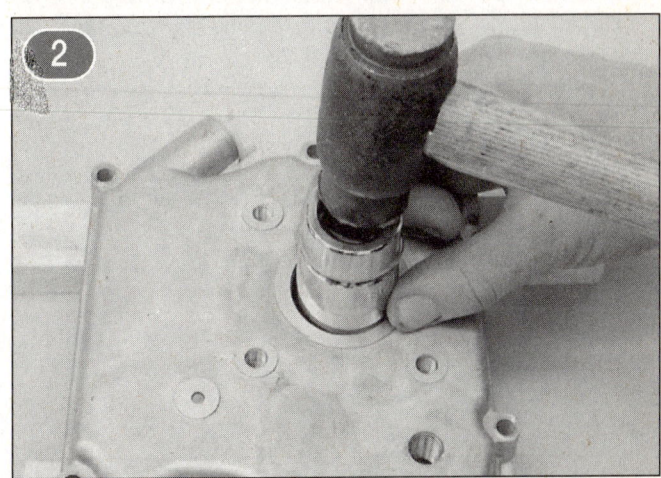

2 Fit new oil seals into the crankcase and sump by carefully pushing them into place using an appropriate sized socket. The seals should be fitted with the sharp rubber edge of the seal towards the inside of the engine.

Chapter 9

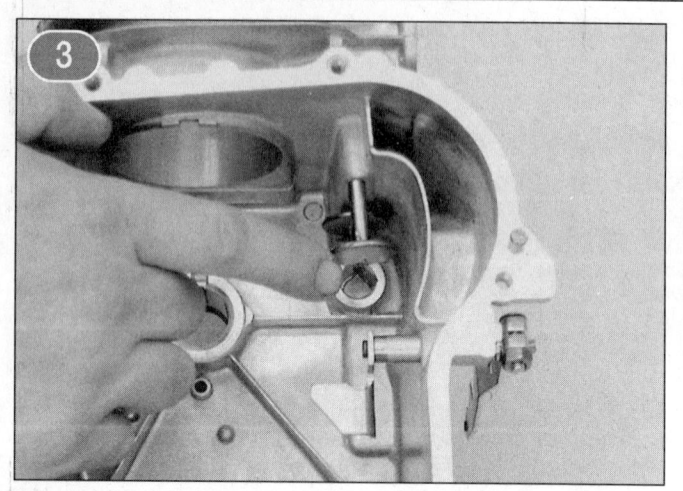

3 Refit the cam followers to their respective holes. A smear of grease can be useful to hold the followers in place.

4 Oil the crankshaft and camshaft bearing journals. The crankshaft and camshaft must be inserted together. Prior to fitting the shafts into the crankcase, mesh the drive gear on the crankshaft with the camshaft gear, and align the timing marks. Fit the shafts into the crankcase.

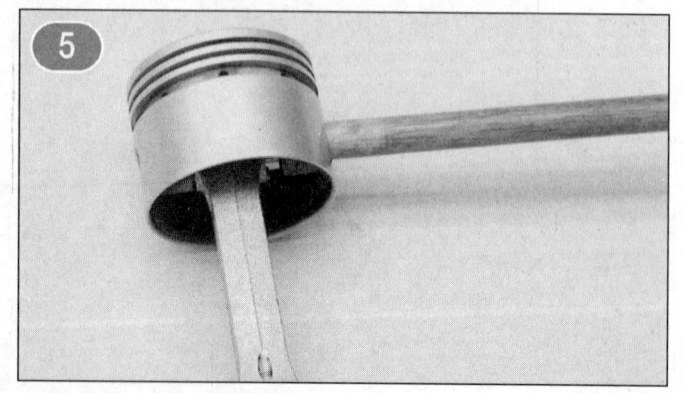

5 If previously removed, fit the gudgeon pin into the piston/connecting rod assembly. If the gudgeon pin is reluctant to move, immerse the piston in hot water for a few minutes. This causes the aluminium to expand, and the gudgeon pin to slide easily.

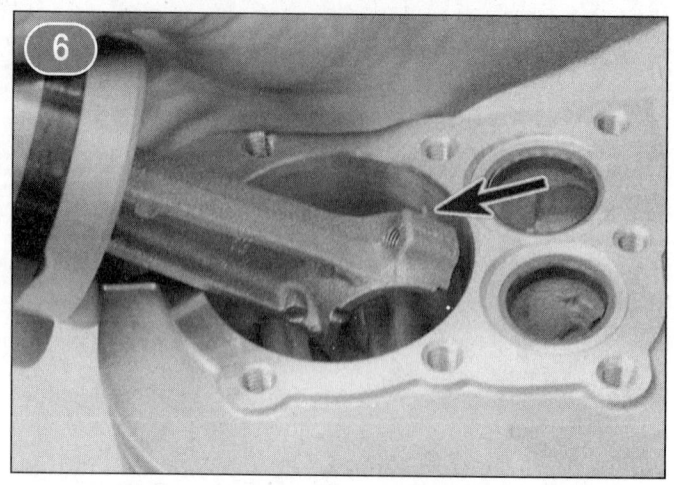

6 The piston is fitted with the circlip groove towards the tapered end of the crankshaft, and the connecting rod with the cast lug (arrowed) at the big-end journal towards the camshaft bearing.

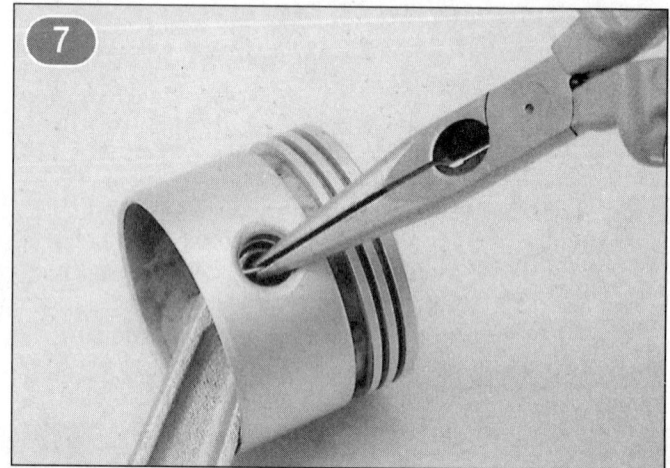

7 Always fit a new piston circlip.

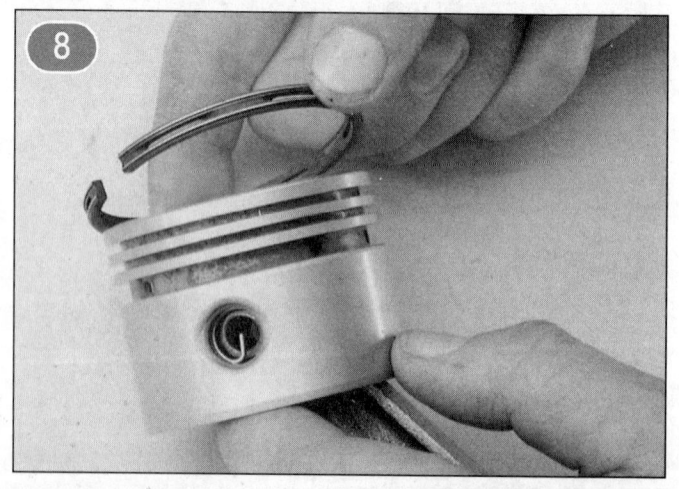

8 Fit the piston rings onto the piston. The oil control (lowest) ring should be fitted first, by carefully expanding the ring just enough to slide down over the piston and into its groove. The oil control ring is symmetrical in profile.

Briggs and Stratton I/C horizontal crank 'L' Head 5 hp engine

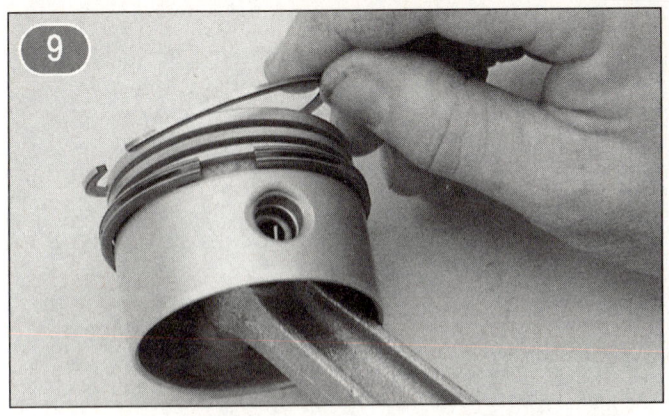

9

Next fit the compression ring into the middle groove. This ring must be fitted with the step in its circumference facing down. The top compression ring is symmetrical in profile. However, if the rings are marked with a dot, fit the ring with the dot facing up. **Beware:** *Piston rings are very brittle. If they are expanded too much, they will break.* Arrange the three ring-end gaps so that they are spaced out around the circumference of the piston at 120° intervals.

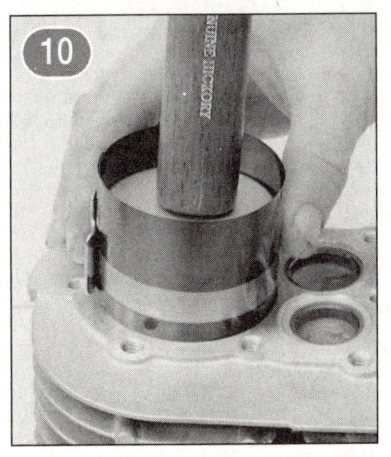

10

Smear the piston rings and cylinder bore with oil. Using a piston ring clamp, fit the piston into the cylinder from the top by feeding the connecting rod through first. Make sure that the connecting rod does not scratch the cylinder walls. Press the piston firmly into the cylinder, sliding it out of the clamp as the rings enter the bore. If necessary, using a piece of wood or hammer handle, gently tap the piston out of the clamp and into the cylinder, but stop and investigate any undue resistance.

11

Smear some oil on the crankshaft journal and engage the big-end onto the journal. Fit the big-end cap with the cast lug (arrowed) towards the camshaft.

12

Fit the oil dipper, and, if you have a suitable torque wrench, tighten the bolts to the torque given in Technical Data. If not, tighten the bolts securely, but do not over-tighten. Rotate the crankshaft to ensure freedom of movement.

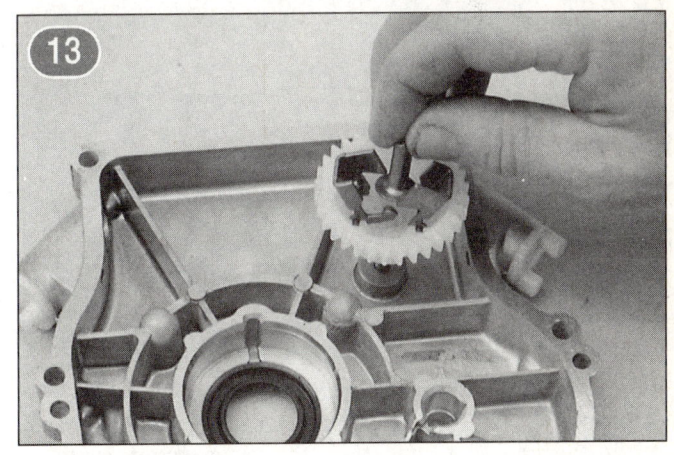

13

If removed, push the washer and governor cup assembly onto its mounting shaft on the inside of the crankcase end plate.

14

Liberally grease the main bearing ball race. Place a new gasket over the locating dowels, and refit the crankcase end plate. As the cover engages on the locating dowels, it may be necessary to rotate the governor cup gear, in order for it to mesh with the camshaft gear.

9•5

Chapter 9

15 Tighten the crankcase end plate bolts, evenly in a diagonal sequence, to the torque given in Technical Data. Check the crankshaft end float is within the limits given in the Specifications. If it is less than the lower limit, an additional paper gasket must be fitted under the crankcase end plate. If it is more than the upper limit, a thrust washer is available, and must be fitted on the crankshaft between the camshaft drive gear and the main bearing.

16 Prior to fitting the valve springs, turn the crankshaft until the piston is at TDC on the compression stroke. Slowly continue to turn the crankshaft until the piston has moved down the bore approximately 6 mm. Insert the valves into their respective guides and, with reference to Chapter 4, check both valve clearances. The dimensions are given in the Technical Data. Once the correct clearances have been achieved, remove the valves.

17 Fit the inlet valve spring and collar into place in the tappet chest. Ensure that the notch in the rim of the collar is facing out.

18 Using a pair of thin-nosed pliers (or similar), compress the valve spring, slide the collar over the end of the valve stem, and move the collar in towards the cylinder. Slowly allow the spring to uncompress, and check that the collar has located correctly on the end of the valve stem. Repeat this procedure for the exhaust valve, noting that a spring seat should be fitted on top of the exhaust spring.

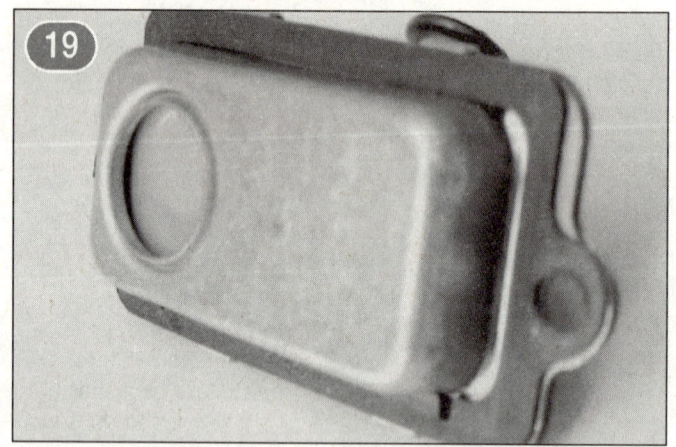

19 Check the fibre disc valve in the engine breather for distortion or cracks. The gap between the disc valve and the body should not exceed 1.1 mm (0.043 in). The valve is held in place by an internal bracket, which will distort if too much pressure is applied to the disc. If the valve is defective, renew the complete breather assembly. Renew the gasket and refit the valve/cover using the two bolts. Tighten securely.

20 Place the new head gasket in the correct position. The gasket will only align with the bolt holes one way round. Do not use any jointing compound.

Briggs and Stratton I/C horizontal crank 'L' Head 5 hp engine

21 Fit the cylinder head and cowling.

22 The three long bolts (arrowed) fit into the holes around the exhaust valve. The bolt with the stud extension is located as shown. Tighten the cylinder head bolts evenly, in a diagonal sequence, to the torque given in Technical Data.

23 Tighten the bolt retaining the cylinder block cowling.

24 Refit the crankcase cowling using the two retaining bolts.

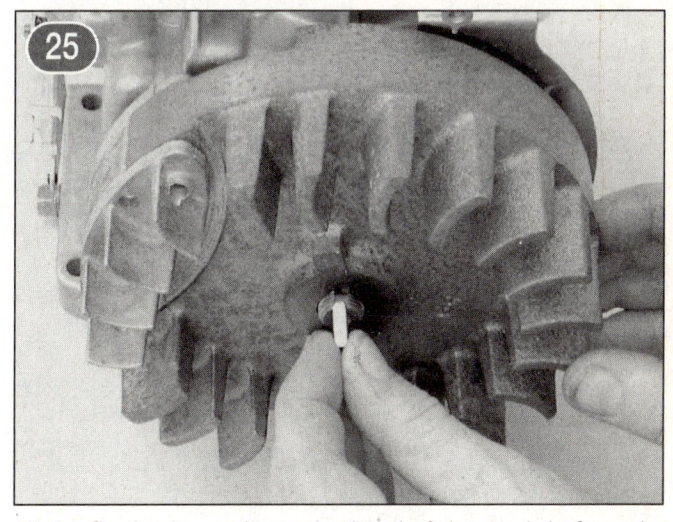

25 Fit the flywheel over the tapered end of the crankshaft, and insert the square section key into the keyway.

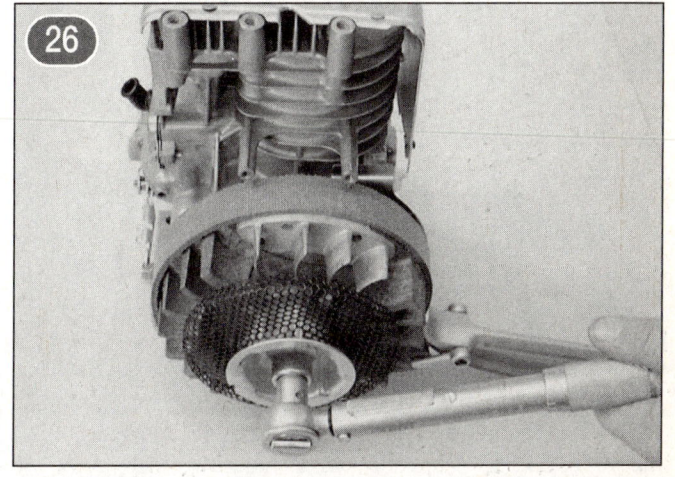

26 After fitting the flywheel mesh and starter flange, tighten the flywheel nut to the torque given in Technical Data. Use a strap wrench around the circumference of the flywheel to prevent it from turning. The help of an assistant will be necessary.

9•7

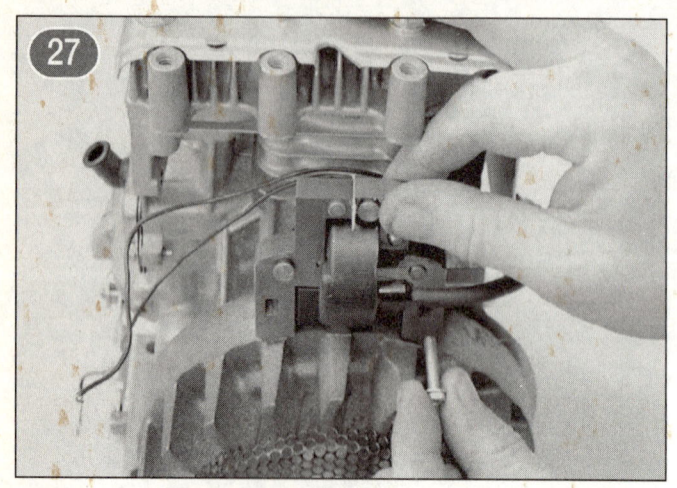

Chapter 9

27 Refit the ignition magneto. The magneto body is marked 'Cylinder side' on one side, and 'This side out' on the other.

28 Fit the deflector plate over its locating post on the armature.

29 Before tightening the two mounting bolts, turn the flywheel so that the magnets are on the opposite side to the magneto, and use a feeler gauge to measure the air gap between the two legs of the magneto's armature and the flywheel. The correct air gap is given in Technical Data. The mounting holes in the armature legs are slotted. Move the armature until the correct gap is achieved. Tighten the bolts securely. Refit the HT cap to the spark plug.

30 Refit the fuel pump spring, cup and diaphragm to the carburettor. Secure the cover with the four Torx screws.

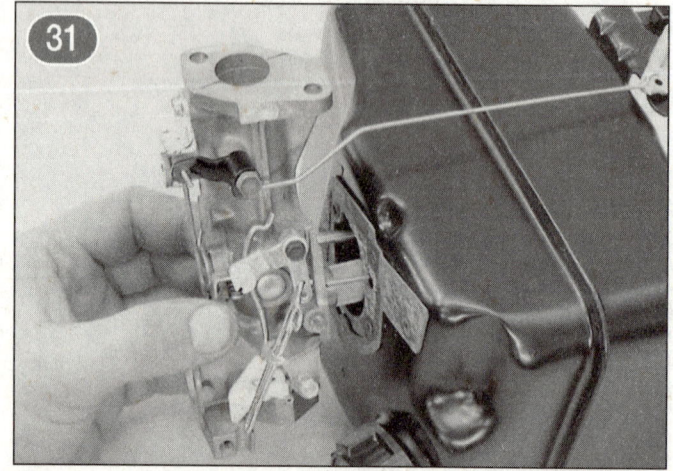

31 Using a new gasket, refit the carburettor to the fuel tank. The carburettor is secured to the tank by two Torx screws – one long one down through the body of the carburettor, and one short Torx screw through the mounting flange.

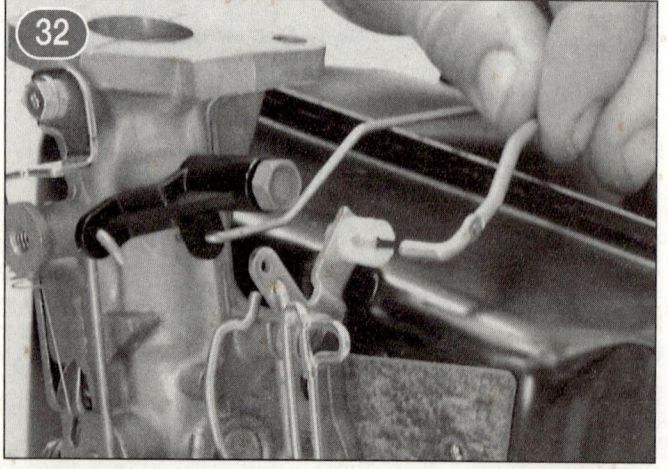

32 Reconnect the throttle linkage.

Briggs and Stratton I/C horizontal crank 'L' Head 5 hp engine

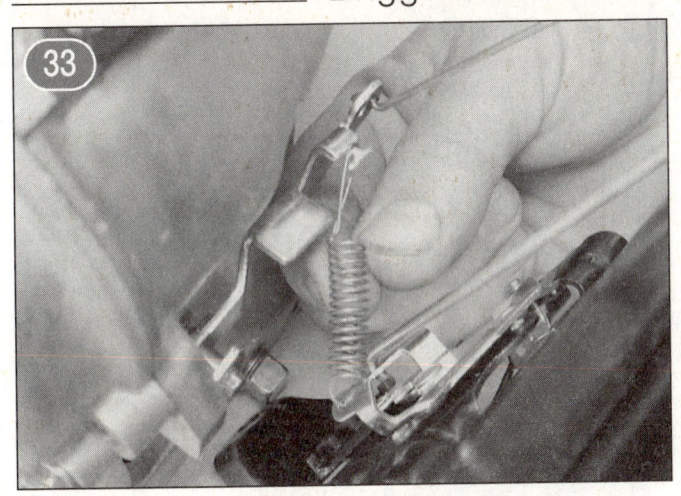

33 Refit the carburettor and fuel tank assembly. As the assembly is fitted, reconnect the governor linkage and spring.

34 Fit the heat shield between the carburettor and cylinder head. Secure with the two retaining bolts. The fuel tank is secured with one bolt to the crankcase base.

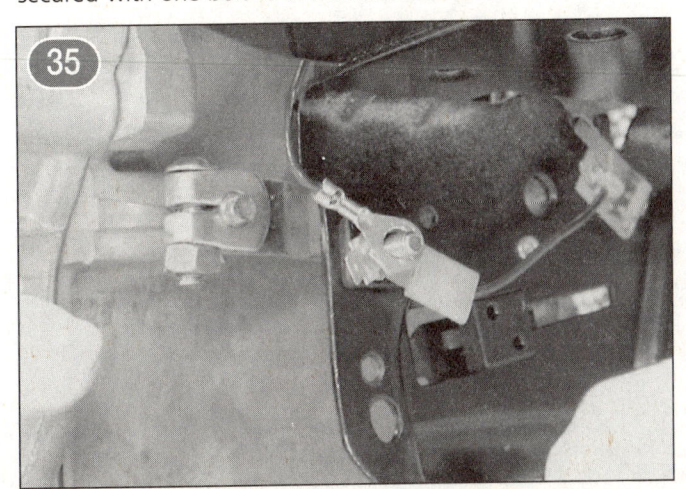

35 Reconnect the magneto earthing wire under the fuel tank.

36 Refit the remote control panel to the carburettor/fuel tank assembly. As the panel, is fitted reconnect the choke linkage, and ensure that the throttle lever pin engages with the sliding linkage. Secure the panel with the two Torx screws.

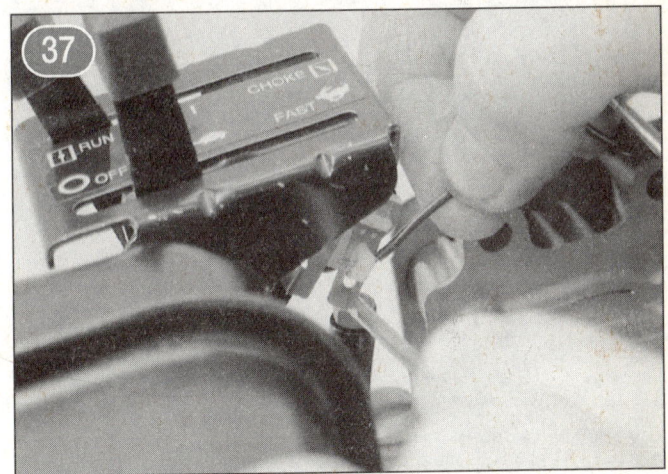

37 Reconnect the magneto earthing wire. Check for correct operation.

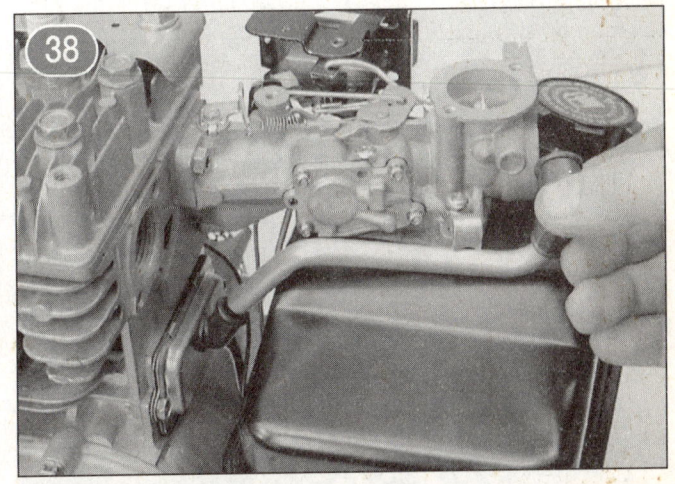

38 Install the engine breather pipe between the breather valve cover and air intake. The pipe is retained by a clamp under a carburettor-to-fuel tank mounting Torx screw.

Chapter 9

39 Fit the exhaust system. Tighten the retaining bolts, and secure them by bending the tabs of the locking washer.

40 The engine cowling/starter is retained by four bolts. Two on the top, and one on each side secures the cowling to the crankcase. Before tightening the bolts, ensure that it interlocks correctly with the cylinder block cowling already fitted, and that the HT lead has not been trapped.

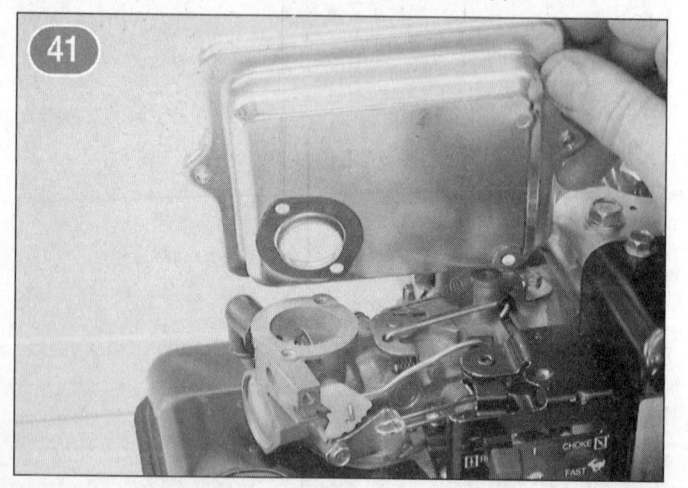

41 Refit the air filter housing using the four bolts with integral shakeproof washers.

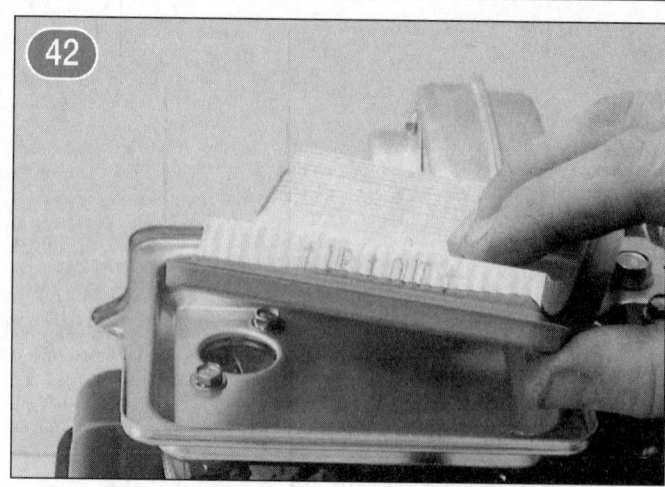

42 Refit the air filter element. One side is marked 'UP'.

43 Secure the air filter cover with two bolts.
Remember to fill the sump with the correct grade and quantity of oil.

Briggs and Stratton I/C horizontal crank 'L' Head 5 hp engine

Starter repair

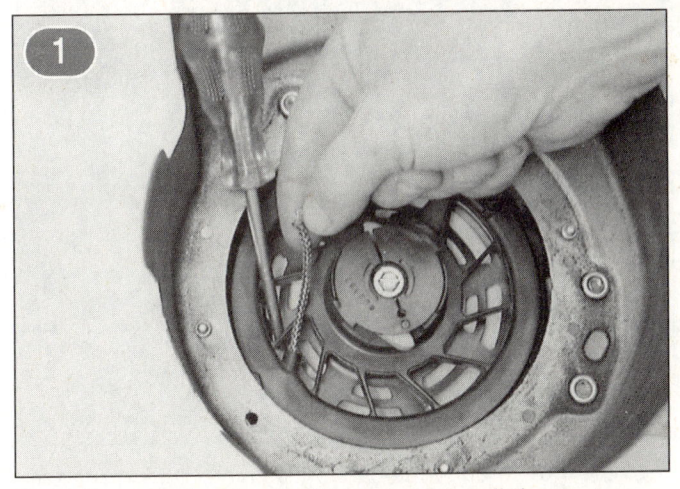

1 With the starter/engine cowling removed, pull the starter rope to its full extension. Lock the rope pulley in this position by inserting a screwdriver (or similar) through the spokes of the pulley and the slots of the engine cowling.

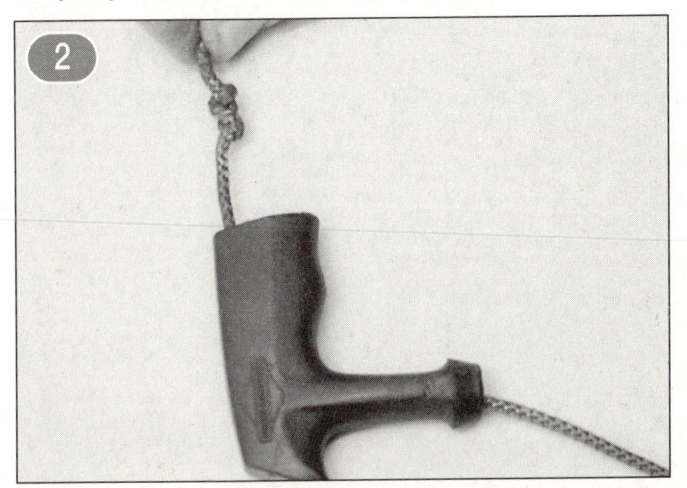

2 To replace the rope: Where the rope goes through the pulley, cut off the knot and pull the rope from the starter. Feed the new rope through the outer hole in the cowling and the inner hole in the pulley. Tie the knot. Then feed the other end of the rope through the hole in the starter handle, again tie the knot. Tension the rope and remove the screwdriver from the pulley spokes. Be prepared for the spring to violently rewind the starter rope. Refit the starter/engine cowling.

3 To replace the recoil spring: Where the rope goes through the pulley, untie the knot and pull the rope from the starter. Pull the screwdriver from the pulley. Unscrew the central bolt from the pawl mechanism, and lift off the guide plate. Note the position of the pawls, and remove them.
Carefully lift out the pulley, noting the locating slot for the end of the spring. Lift out the spring.

4 Insert the new spring, locating the inner end around the lug on the cowling.

Chapter 9

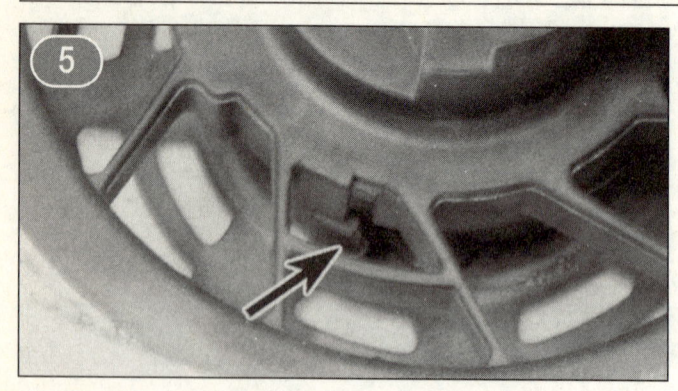

5 Fit the pulley, locating the outer end of the spring in the slot on the pulley (arrowed).

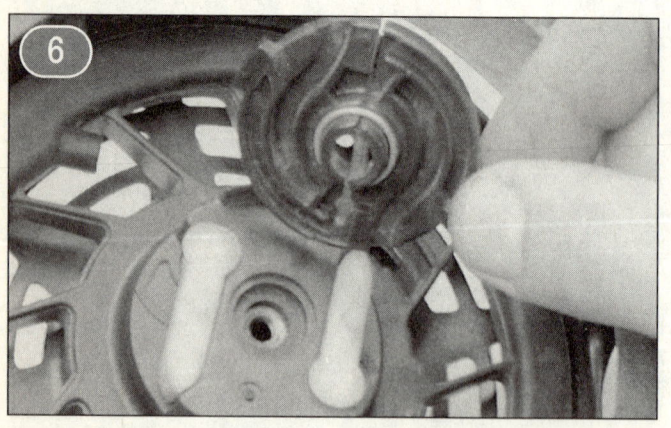

6 Check the starter pawls for damage or excessive wear, and refit them to the pulley. Refit the guide plate onto the pawls, ensuring that the pawl locating pins engage with the slots on the underside of the guide plate. Tighten the central bolt.

Using a screwdriver (or similar), very carefully wind the pulley approximately seven full turns, and align the rope hole in the pulley with the hole in the cowling. The exact number of turns is dependent on the length of rope. Lock the pulley in place by inserting a screwdriver (or similar) through the spokes of the pulley and the slots of the engine cowling. Exercise extreme caution during this procedure. It will take some effort to wind the spring up, and should the screwdriver slip, the pulley will unwind violently.

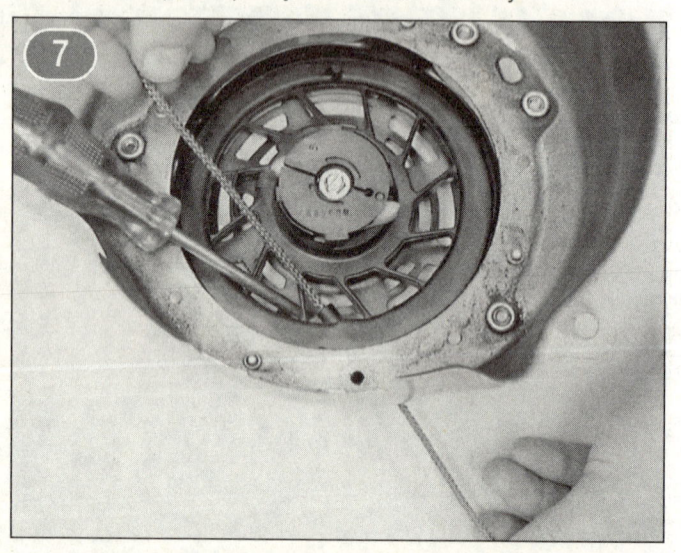

7 Feed the rope through the outer hole in the cowling and the hole in the pulley. Tie a knot in the end of the rope. Tension the rope and remove the screwdriver from the pulley spokes. Be prepared for the spring to violently rewind the starter rope. Refit the starter/engine cowling.

Briggs and Stratton 35 Sprint/Classic 2.6kW 4-stroke engine

10

Technical data

Dismantling

Reassembly

Starter repair

Technical Data

Spark plug gap	0.76 mm (0.030 in)
Spark plug type	NGK B2LM
Valve clearances (cold):	
Inlet	0.13 to 0.18 mm (0.005 to 0.007 in)
Exhaust	0.18 to 0.23 mm (0.007 to 0.009 in)
Armature air gap	0.15 to 0.25 mm (0.006 to 0.010 in)
Oil grade	SAE 30
Oil capacity	0.6 litres
Torque wrench settings:	
Flywheel nut	74 Nm
Big-end bolts	11 Nm
Cylinder head bolts	16 Nm

Chapter 10

Dismantling

Before starting to dismantle, read Chapter 5. The procedures outlined apply to all engines and if adopted, will ensure an orderly and methodical approach that will make both dismantling and reassembly much easier. The following assumes the engine has been removed from its application.

- [ ] Using a 3/8" square drive tool, remove the sump plug and drain the oil into a suitable container.
- [ ] Undo the retaining bolt, and remove the air filter/cover assembly. Recover the sealing washer.
- [ ] Remove the flywheel brake cover.
- [ ] Unscrew the two retaining bolts, and remove the exhaust shield.
- [ ] The engine cowling/starter is secured by two bolts. One into the cylinder head, and the other into the crankcase at the side. Unscrew the bolts and remove the cowling/starter.
- [ ] Note their location, and disconnect the two throttle springs from the throttle linkage.
- [ ] Undo the two mounting bolts and remove the carburettor and fuel tank together. As the assembly is withdrawn, disengage the throttle linkage from the engine governor.
- [ ] To separate the carburettor from the fuel tank, undo the six mounting screws, and very carefully prise the carburettor from the fuel tank. As the carburettor is removed, take care not to lose the spring that fits between the carburettor body and the mounting gasket/diaphragm. Be prepared for fuel spillage.
- [ ] Remove the wire gauze over the main jet, and clean if required. Carefully clean the wire gauze in the end of the fuel pick-up pipe. Clean any obscured jets, or air/fuel passages by blowing only.
- [ ] The carburettor has fixed main and pilot jets, and no further dismantling is possible.
- [ ] Remove the crankcase cowling between the fuel tank and crankcase.
- [ ] Carefully pull the HT cap from the spark plug.
- [ ] Undo the two retaining bolts, and remove the ignition magneto together with the governor arm. As the magneto is removed, disconnect the earthing wire.
- [ ] In order to remove the flywheel brake assembly, use a screwdriver to wedge the brake in the 'OFF' position. Unscrew the two retaining bolts and remove the brake. Disconnect and remove the magneto earthing wire.
- [ ] Bend back the two tab washers, undo the bolts, and remove the exhaust system.
- [ ] The nut retaining the flywheel to the crankshaft can be extremely tight. To prevent the flywheel from turning, in the absence of the manufacturer's special tool, use a strap wrench around the circumference of the flywheel, and undo the nut. The help of an assistant to steady the engine may be necessary.

- [ ] Remove the starter flange. With reference to Chapter 2, pull the flywheel from the crankshaft. If you are using the manufacturer's puller, it may be necessary to cut the threads in the flywheel. The puller holes are clearly labelled in the flywheel, and the puller bolts are specially formed to cut the threads. Recover the key from the crankshaft.
- [ ] Remove the inlet manifold.
- [ ] Undo the two retaining bolts, and prise away the engine breather valve/tappet cover.
- [ ] Remove the spark plug.
- [ ] Unscrew the eight cylinder head bolts, and lift away the head with the cowling.

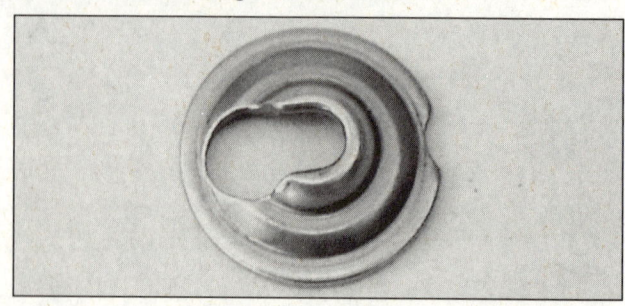

- [ ] Turn the exhaust valve spring collar until the notch in its rim faces out. The valve collars have two adjoining holes, one of which is larger than the other. This allows the valve stem to slide through the collar. Using a pair of thin-nosed pliers (or similar) compress the spring, move the collar away from the cylinder, slide the collar off the end of the valve stem, and remove the valve. Repeat for the inlet valve. It is important to label or arrange the components so that, if re-used, they are refitted to their original locations.

10•2

Briggs and Stratton 35 Sprint/Classic 2.6kW 4-stroke engine

- [ ] Inspect the valve guides for scoring and excessive wear. Examine the valve seats and renovate as necessary (*refer to Chapter 5*).
- [ ] Unscrew the engine breather pipe from the crankcase.
- [ ] Ensure that the crankshaft is free of dirt and rust. Unscrew the 6 retaining bolts, and remove the sump. A light tap from a soft hammer may be necessary as the sump locates over two dowels in the crankcase gasket face.
- [ ] Remove the oil slinger from the end of the camshaft.
- [ ] Align the timing mark on the camshaft gear with the mark on the camshaft drive gear fitted to the crankshaft. Carefully remove the camshaft.
- [ ] Slide out the cam followers. It is important to label or arrange the followers so that, if re-used, they are refitted to their original locations.
- [ ] The camshaft drive gear should slide easily from the crankshaft.
- [ ] Unscrew the big-end bolts and withdraw the bearing cap.
- [ ] Remove any carbon build-up at the lip of the cylinder bore using a soft tool, and gently push the connecting rod and piston assembly up and out of the cylinder. Take care not to mark the bore with the connecting rod.
- [ ] If required, remove the piston rings from the piston by carefully expanding the rings at their ends and sliding them from the piston. Note the orientation of the rings for reassembly. Remove the circlip and push the gudgeon pin from the piston. 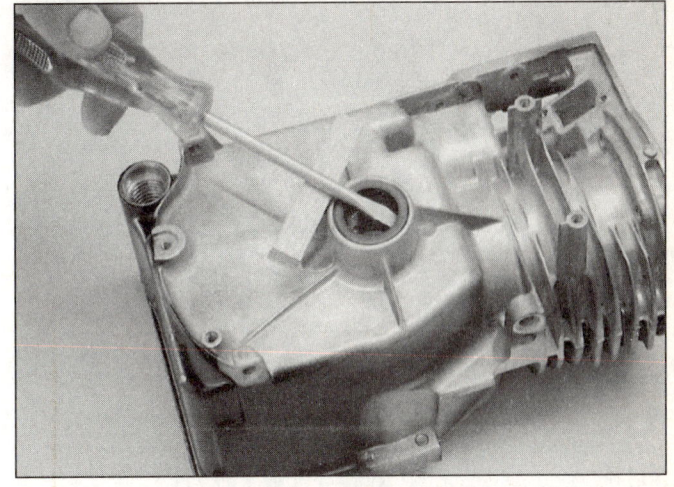
- [ ] Prise the oil seals from the crankcase and sump.
- [ ] Check the condition of the crankshaft bearing, camshaft bearing and cylinder bore for wear, scores or cracks. If the bore is damaged, worn oval or oversized, then professional skills and special equipment will be necessary to restore it. The same applies to worn or damaged bearings. It may be possible to have these reamed out to accept bushes obtainable from spares stockists, but special reaming equipment and knowledge are essential. Check all threaded holes for damaged threads, and repair if necessary by fitting a thread insert of the correct size (*refer to Chapter 2*).

Reassembly

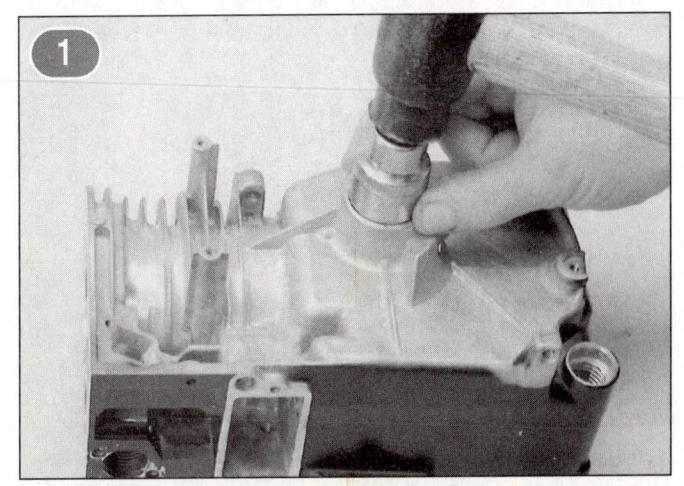

1 Fit new oil seals into the crankcase and sump by carefully pushing them into place using an appropriate sized socket. The seals should be fitted with the sharp rubber edge of the seal towards the inside of the engine.

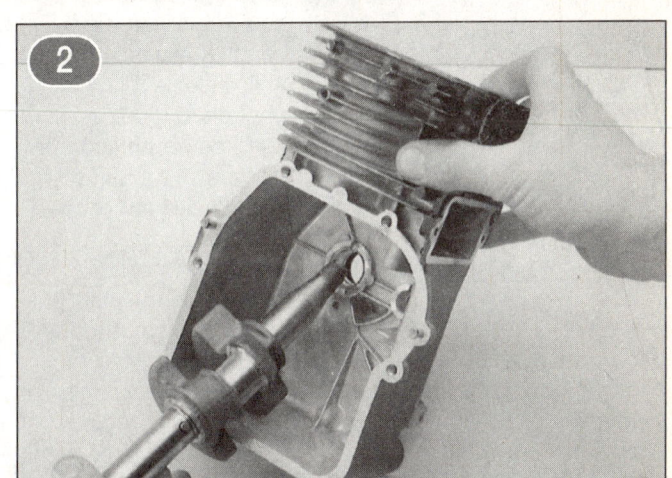

2 Oil the main bearing journal in the crankcase, and insert the crankshaft tapered end first.

Chapter 10

3 If previously removed, fit the gudgeon pin into the piston/connecting rod assembly. The piston is fitted with the circlip groove towards the non-tapered end of the crankshaft, and the 'open' side of the connecting rod towards the camshaft bearing. If the gudgeon pin is reluctant to move, immerse the piston in hot water for a few minutes. This causes the aluminium to expand, and the gudgeon pin to slide easily.

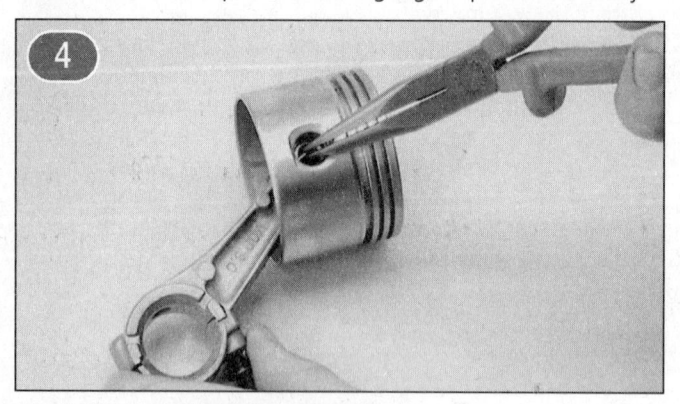

4 Always fit a new piston circlip.

5 Fit the piston rings onto the piston. The oil control (lowest) ring should be fitted first, by carefully expanding the coiled element just enough to slide down over the piston and into its groove. Next fit the second element of the oil control ring in the same manner, positioning it so that the coiled element is inside the second element. Next fit the compression ring into the middle groove. This ring must be fitted with the step in its circumference facing down. The top compression ring is symmetrical in profile. However, if the rings are marked with a dot, fit the rings with the dot facing up. **Beware:** *Piston rings are very brittle. If they are expanded too much, they will break.* Arrange the three ring-end gaps so that they are spaced out around the circumference of the piston at 120° intervals.

6 Smear the piston rings and cylinder bore with oil. Using a piston ring clamp, fit the piston into the cylinder from the top by feeding the connecting rod through first. Make sure that the connecting rod does not scratch the cylinder walls. Press the piston firmly into the cylinder, sliding it out of the clamp as the rings enter the bore. If necessary, using a piece of wood or hammer handle, gently tap the piston out of the clamp and into the cylinder, but stop and investigate any undue resistance.

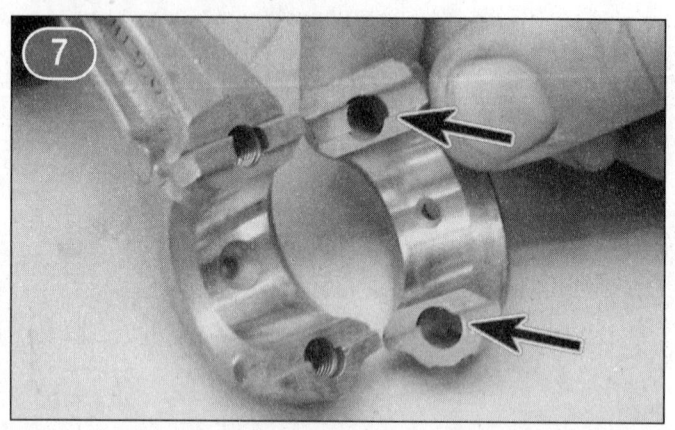

7 Oil the crankshaft journal and engage the big-end onto the journal. Fit the big-end cap. Due to the stepped shape of the cap, it will only fit one way round (arrowed). If you have a suitable torque wrench, tighten the bolts to the torque given in Technical Data. If not, tighten the bolts securely, but do not over-tighten. Rotate the crankshaft to ensure freedom of movement.

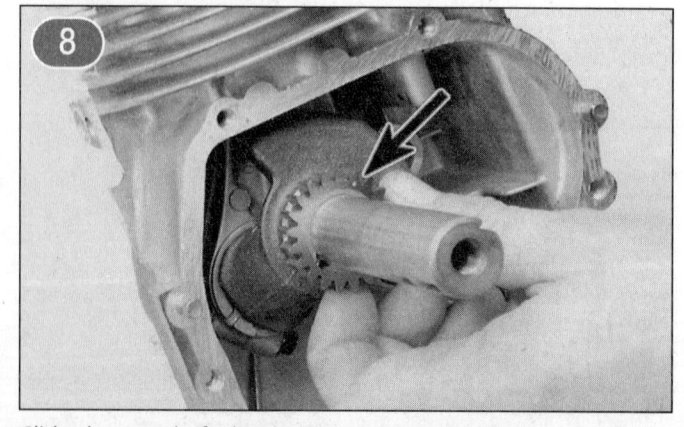

8 Slide the camshaft drive gear over the end of the crankshaft with the timing mark facing outwards (arrowed). The gear locates over a pin in the crankshaft.

10•4

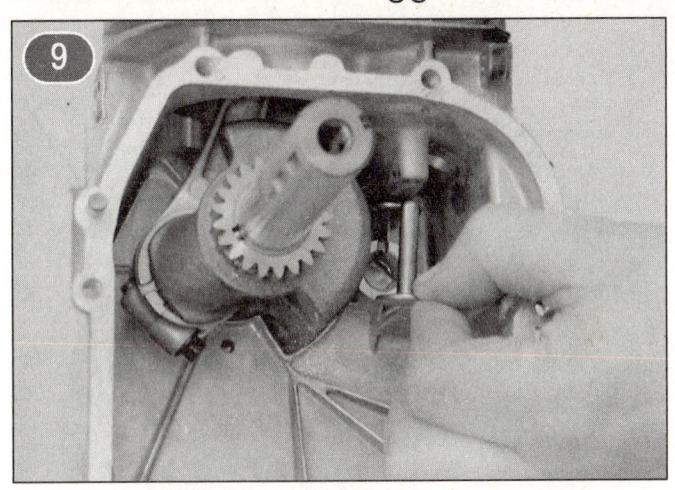

Briggs and Stratton 35 Sprint/Classic 2.6kW 4-stroke engine

9 Oil the cam followers, and refit them to their original locations.

10 Turn the crankshaft until the timing mark on the gear is pointing at the middle of the camshaft bearing hole in the crankcase. Smear some oil on the camshaft bearing journal, and install the camshaft. The timing dimple cast in the camshaft gear must aligned exactly with the mark on the crankshaft gear when the gears are meshed (arrowed). Rotate the crankshaft two revolutions to ensure correct movement.

11 Refit the oil slinger assembly to the end of the camshaft.

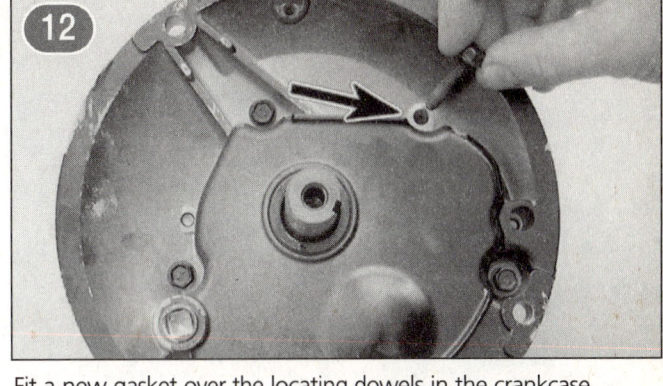

12 Fit a new gasket over the locating dowels in the crankcase gasket face, and carefully refit the sump. Take care not to damage the lip of the oil seal. Secure the sump with the six bolts, using thread sealer on the bolt that enters the engine breather chamber (arrowed). Refit the sump plug and filler/dipstick.

13 Prior to fitting the valve springs, turn the crankshaft until the piston is at TDC on the compression stroke. Slowly continue to turn the crankshaft until the piston has moved down the bore approximately 6 mm. Insert the valves into their respective guides and, with reference to Chapter 4, check both valve clearances. The dimensions are given in the Technical Data. Once the correct clearances have been achieved, remove the valves.

14 Fit the exhaust valve spring and collar into place in the tappet chest, with the close-coiled end of the spring towards the valve head. Ensure that the notch in the rim of the collar is facing out. Insert the exhaust valve. Using a pair of thin-nosed pliers (or similar), compress the valve spring, slide the collar over the end of the valve stem, and move the collar in towards the cylinder. Slowly allow the spring to uncompress, and check that the collar has located correctly on the end of the valve stem. Repeat this procedure for the inlet valve.

Chapter 10

15 Check the fibre disc valve in the engine breather for distortion or cracks. The gap between the disc valve and the body should not exceed 1.1 mm (0.043 in). The valve is held in place by an internal bracket, which will distort if too much pressure is applied to the disc. If the valve is defective, renew the complete breather assembly. Renew the gasket.

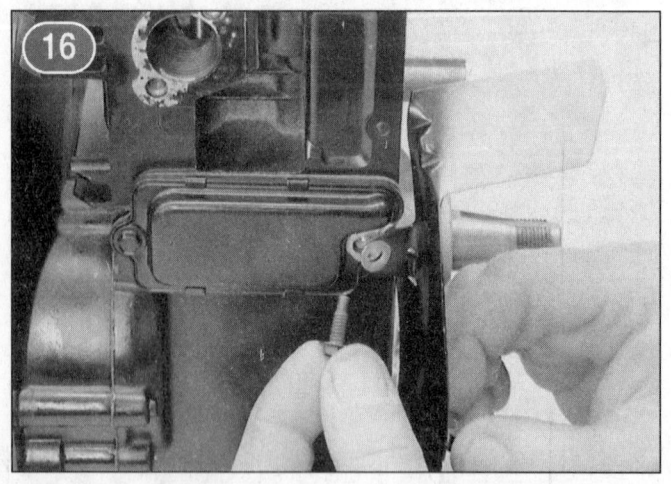

16 Refit the valve/cover and crankcase cowling using the two bolts. Tighten securely.

17 Grease the threads of the engine breather pipe, and screw it into the breather chamber.

18 Place the new head gasket in the correct position. The gasket will only align with the bolt holes one way round. Do not use any jointing compound.

19 Refit the cylinder head and cowling.

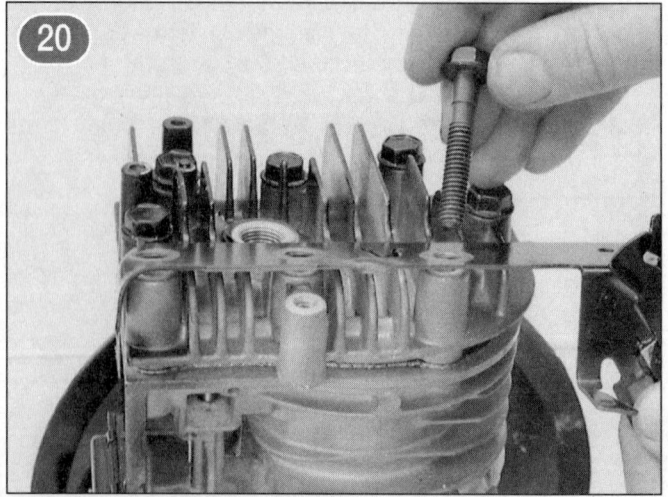

20 Tighten the eight retaining bolts evenly, in a diagonal sequence, to the torque given in Technical Data. Refit the spark plug.

Briggs and Stratton 35 Sprint/Classic 2.6kW 4-stroke engine

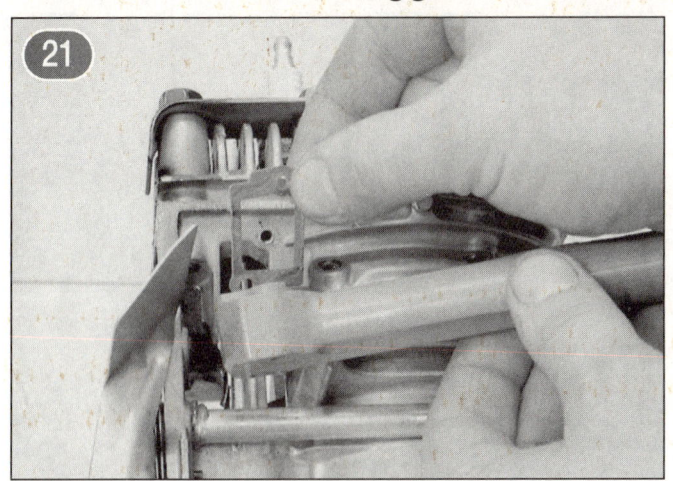

21 Using a new gasket, refit the inlet manifold.

22 Fit the flywheel over the tapered end of the crankshaft, align the keyway, and slide the square sectioned key into place.

23 Refit the screen mesh, starter flange, and retaining nut to the crankshaft. Using a strap wrench to prevent the flywheel from turning, tighten the retaining nut to the torque given in Technical Data. The help of an assistant will be required to steady the engine during this procedure.

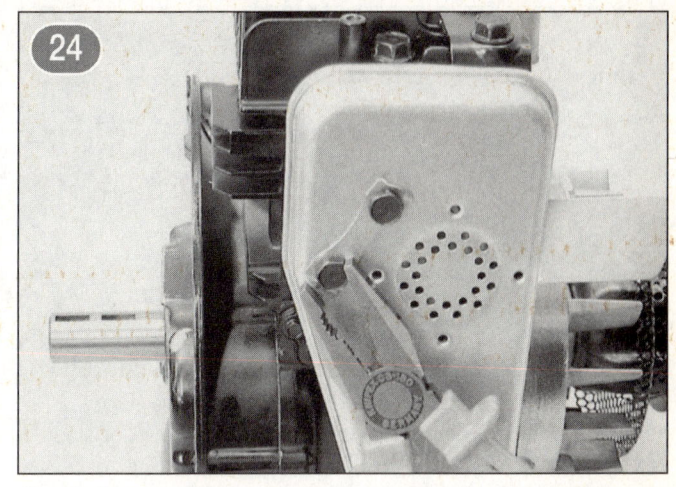

24 Check the condition of the gasket, and refit the exhaust system. The two retaining bolts are locked in place by bending the tabs of the locking washer.

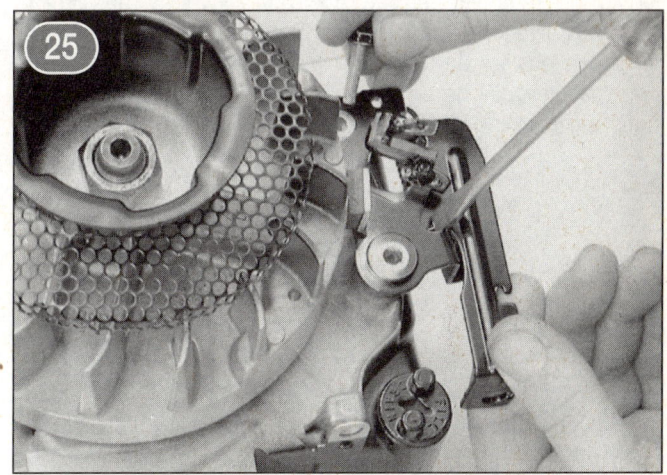

25 Using a screwdriver, wedge the flywheel brake assembly in the 'OFF' position, and refit it to the crankcase using the two retaining bolts. Remove the screwdriver.

26 Route the magneto earthing wire under the engine breather pipe, through the retaining clip, and reconnect it to the engine stop element of the flywheel brake assembly.

Chapter 10

27

Refit the magneto and engine governor using the two retaining bolts. The magneto body is marked 'Cylinder side' on one side, and 'This side out' on the other. Before tightening the two mounting bolts, turn the flywheel so that the magnets are on the opposite side to the magneto, and use a feeler gauge to measure the air gap between the two legs of the magneto's armature and the flywheel. The correct air gap is given in Technical Data. The mounting holes in the armature legs are slotted. Move the armature until the correct gap is achieved. Tighten the bolts securely. Reconnect the magneto earthing wire. Refit the HT cap to the spark plug.

28

Refit the carburettor to the fuel tank using a new gasket. As the carburettor is fitted, ensure that the spring is correctly located in the carburettor body (arrowed). Tighten the six retaining bolts securely.

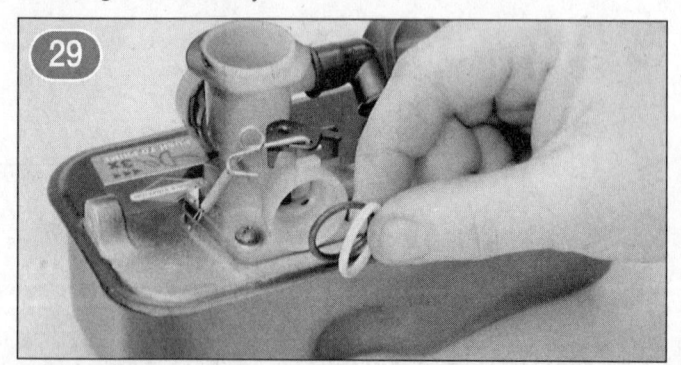

29

The carburettor-to-inlet manifold joint is sealed by an O-ring, retained by a collar in the carburettor outlet. Carefully prise out the collar and check the O-ring for and signs of damage or wear. Fit a new O-ring if in any doubt. Refit the collar by pushing it into place.

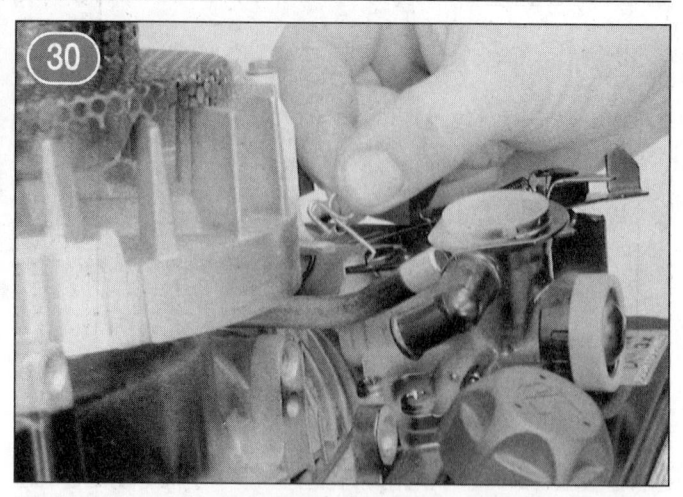

30

As the carburettor and fuel tank assembly is fitted, reconnect the throttle arm-to-governor linkage and reconnect the engine breather pipe. Retain the assembly with the end mounting bolt, but do not tighten.

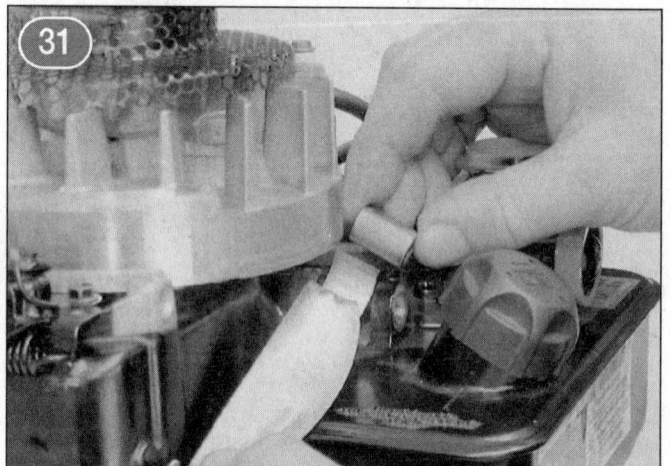

31

Fit the crankcase cowling and spacer, insert the fuel tank-retaining bolt, and tighten both mounting bolts.

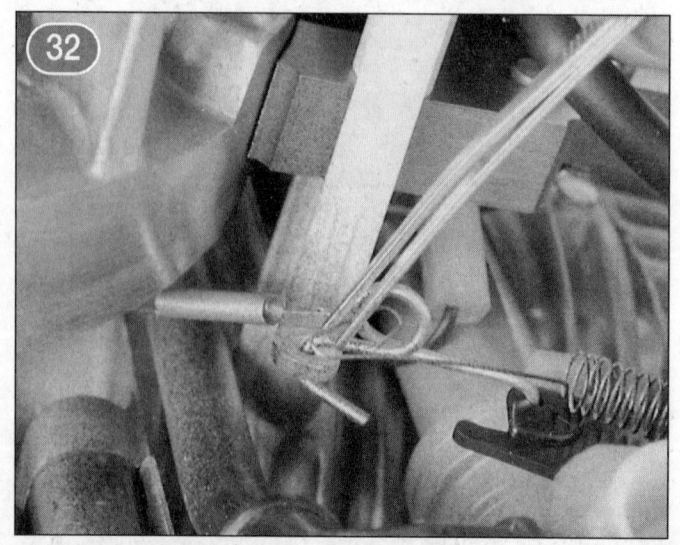

32

Reconnect the governor return spring ...

Briggs and Stratton 35 Sprint/Classic 2.6kW 4-stroke engine

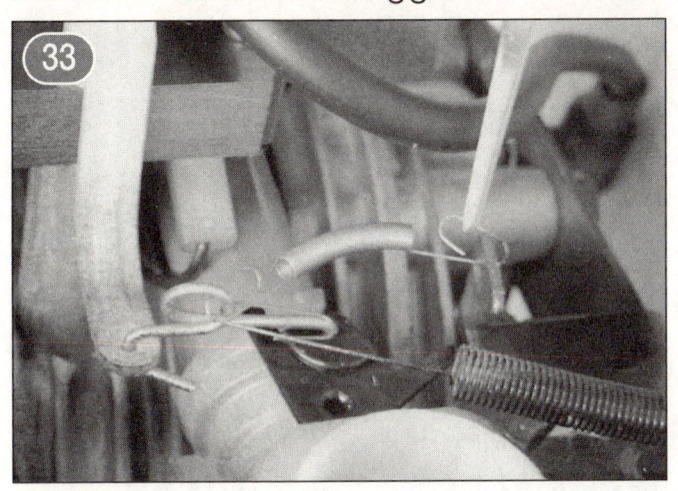

33

... and the throttle spring.

34

Refit the engine cowling/starter using two retaining bolts. One into the top of the cylinder head, and one into the crankcase which also retains the crankcase cowling.

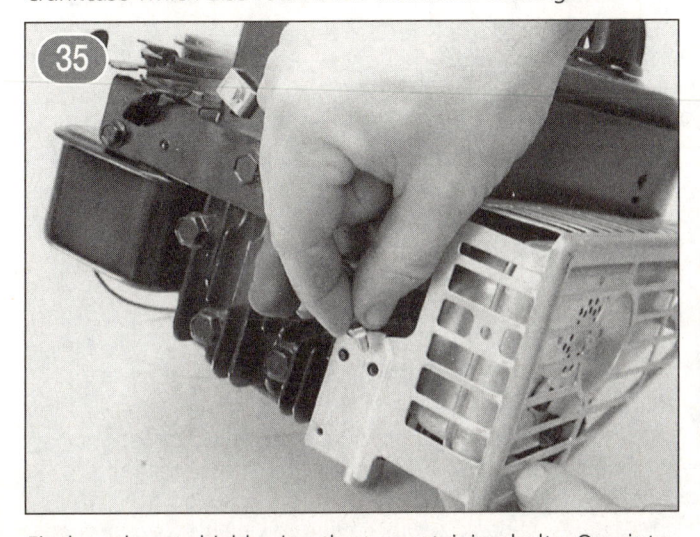

35

Fit the exhaust shield using the two retaining bolts. One into the cylinder head, and the other into the crankcase which also secures the engine cowling.

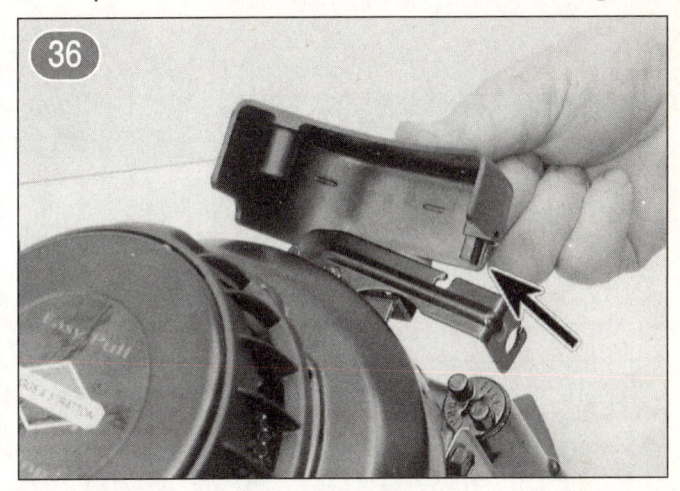

36

Note the locating peg (arrowed), and fit the flywheel brake cover.

37

Refit the air filter assembly, not forgetting the sealing washer between the housing and carburettor.

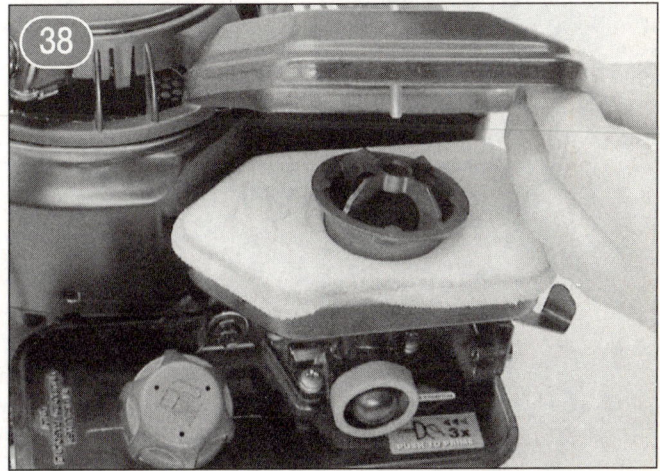

38

If the air filter element is dirty, clean it with fresh petrol, and soak it in clean engine oil. Squeeze the excess oil from the foam and refit it into the housing.

Remember to add the correct quantity and grade of engine oil.

10•9

Chapter 10

Starter repair

With the starter/engine cowling removed, pull the starter rope to its full extension. Lock the rope pulley in this position by inserting a square sectioned piece of wood through the cowling next to the lug on the pulley rim. The lug jams against the wood, and the pulley is held.

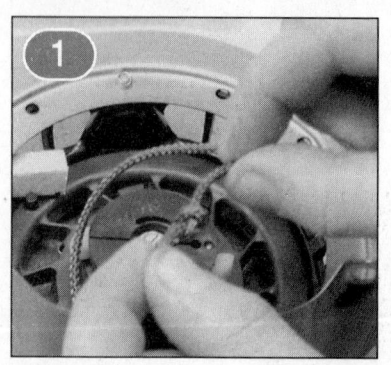

1

To replace the rope: Where the rope goes through the pulley, cut off the knot and pull the rope from the starter. Feed the new rope through the outer hole in the cowling and the inner hole in the pulley. Tie the knot. Then feed the other end of the rope through the hole in the starter handle, again tie the knot. Tension the rope and remove the piece of wood. Be prepared for the spring to violently rewind the starter rope. Refit the starter/engine cowling.

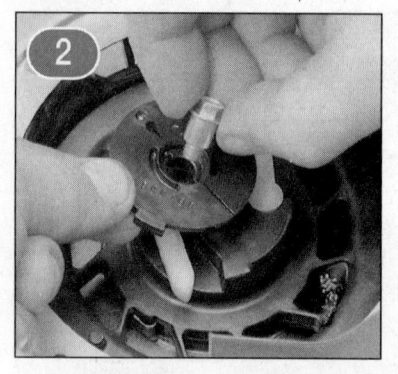

2

To replace the recoil spring: Where the rope goes through the pulley, untie the knot and pull the rope from the starter. Unscrew the central bolt from the pawl mechanism, and lift off the guide plate. Note the position of the pawls, and remove them.

Carefully lift out the pulley, noting the locating slot for the end of the spring. Lift out the spring.

3

Insert the new spring, locating the inner end around the lug on the cowling.

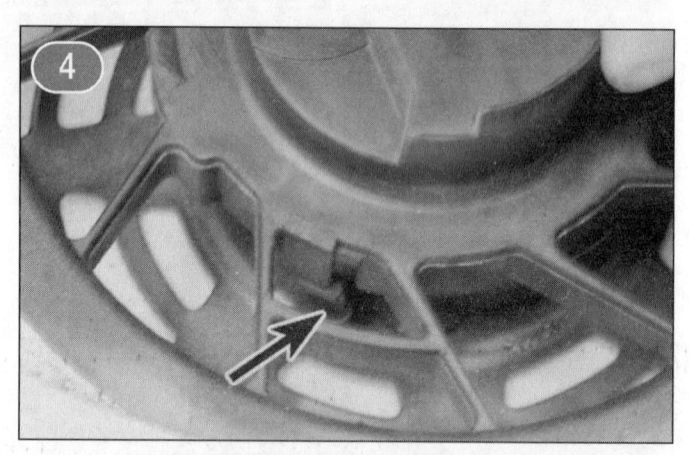

4

Fit the pulley, locating the outer end of the spring in the slot on the pulley (arrowed).

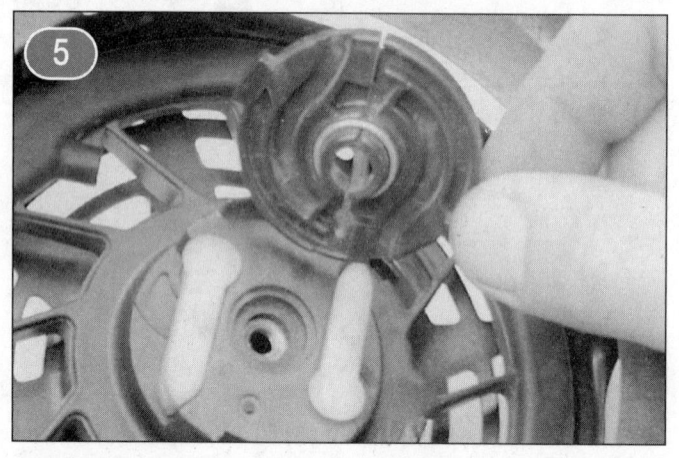

5

Check the starter pawls for damage or excessive wear, and refit them to the pulley. Refit the guide plate onto the pawls, ensuring that the pawl locating pins engage with the slots on the underside of the guide plate. Tighten the central bolt.

Using a screwdriver (or similar), very carefully wind the pulley approximately seven full turns, and align the rope hole in the pulley with the hole in the cowling. The exact number of turns is dependent on the length of rope. Lock the pulley in place by inserting a piece of square sectioned wood through the cowling, jamming the lug on the pulley rim. Exercise extreme caution during this procedure. It will take some effort to wind the spring up, and should the piece of wood slip, the pulley will spin violently.

Feed the rope through the outer hole in the cowling and the hole in the pulley. Tie a knot in the end of the rope. Tension the rope and remove the piece of wood from the cowling. Be prepared for the spring to violently rewind the starter rope. Check for correct operation. Refit the starter/engine cowling.

Honda GXV 120 OHV 4-stroke engine 11

Technical data

Dismantling

Reassembly

Starter repair

Technical Data

Spark plug gap	0.7 to 0.8 mm (0.028 to 0.032 in)
Valve clearances:	
Inlet	0.08 to 0.13 mm (0.003 to 0.005 in)
Exhaust	0.13 to 0.18 mm (0.005 to 0.007 in)
Armature air gap	0.25 mm (0.010 in)
Piston ring gap (standard)	0.23 to 0.525 mm (0.009 to 0.021 in)
Roto-stop brake cable adjustment	
(free play at tip of lever)	5 to 10 mm (0.20 to 0.39 in)
Drive clutch cable (free play at handle bar)	5 to 10 mm (0.20 to 0.39 in)
Speed change cable (free play at tip of lever)	1 to 3 mm (0.04 to 0.12 in)
Oil	SAE 10W-40

Chapter 11

Dismantling

Before starting to dismantle, read Chapter 5. The procedures outlined apply to all engines and if adopted, will ensure an orderly and methodical approach that will make both dismantling and reassembly much easier. The following assumes the engine has been removed from its application.

- [ ] Undo the two nuts securing the air cleaner duct to the carburettor. Remove the bolt securing the air cleaner to the engine. Remove the air cleaner complete with the engine breather pipe.
- [ ] Remove the fuel filler cap.
- [ ] Remove the engine cover.
- [ ] Remove the petrol tank from the engine. Disconnect the fuel pipe from the tank, withdrawing the filter from the tank connector as the pipe is removed. Handle the filter with great care as it is very fragile.
- [ ] Remove the clutch central bolt. Withdraw the cover plate, spring, clutch plate and pressure plate.
- [ ] Make a careful note of the positions of all springs and links to assist reassembly in the same holes.
- [ ] Remove the linkage mounting plate from the engine.
- [ ] Remove the carburettor and the plastic insulator plate. Remove the float chamber, float and needle valve for inspection. Dismantle the fuel tap.
- [ ] Remove the ignition unit.
- [ ] Remove the exhaust muffler assembly (consisting of a shield, muffler box and gasket).
- [ ] Remove the central bolt holding the brake assembly together and lift off the Roto stop brake components.
- [ ] Remove the Woodruff key from the crankshaft.
- [ ] Unscrew the three flange bolts and springs from the brake housing and lift off the housing.
- [ ] Lift the ball retainer from the ball control plate.
- [ ] Remove the Roto-stop return springs and lift off the ball control plate.
- [ ] Remove the circular spacer from the crankshaft.
- [ ] As a precaution, make a permanent mark on the governor lever and the shaft. If the lever ever becomes loose it is then easy to set it to the original datum.
- [ ] Remove the flywheel nut from the crankshaft and lift off the rotating screen/starter hub, and the flywheel and impeller. Remove the key from the crankshaft taper.
- [ ] Remove the overhead valve cover and gasket.
- [ ] Remove the cylinder head complete with valves.
- [ ] Remove the crankcase cover. Make a careful note of where the bolts of differing lengths fit to assist reassembly.
- [ ] Mark the big end of the connecting rod and the cap before removing the latter, as the cap will fit both ways. It must be reassembled the same way round as originally fitted.
- [ ] Withdraw the piston and connecting rod through the top of the cylinder, taking care not to scratch the bore.
- [ ] Withdraw the camshaft and then the crankshaft. Pull the R-shaped clip off the drive shaft. Withdraw the drive shaft from the crankcase cover. To remove and dismantle the final drive unit, remove the right hand rear wheel.
- [ ] Remove the height adjusting plate pivot bolts from both back wheels.
- [ ] Remove the torque reacting bracket.
- [ ] Lift the back axle clear.
- [ ] Disconnect the speed change cable and the drive engage cable.
- [ ] Remove the protector plate from the axle.
- [ ] Remove the final drive case bolts, split the two halves of the casing and remove the internal components.

Note: *If any difficulty is experienced in carrying out these instructions, refer to the photographs in the reassembly instructions that follow. Used in the reverse sequence, these photographs indicate the steps in dismantling and will help to identify the components mentioned above.*

Honda GXV 120 OHV 4-stroke engine

Reassembly

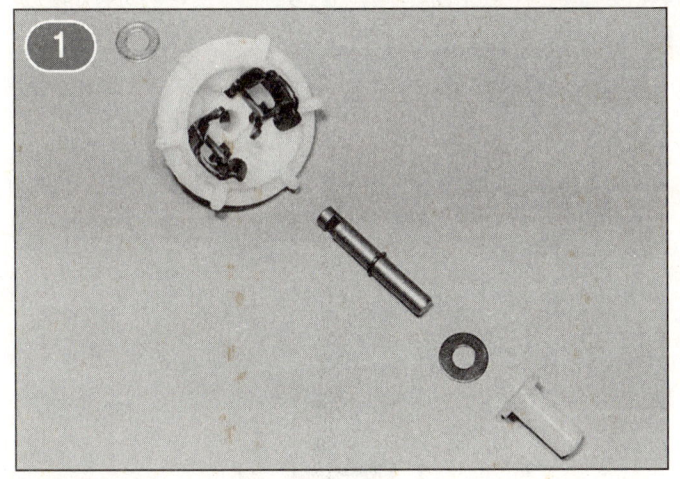

1 The governor components are shown in the photo. Fit the C-clip into the groove in the shaft; it is easier to do this at this stage.

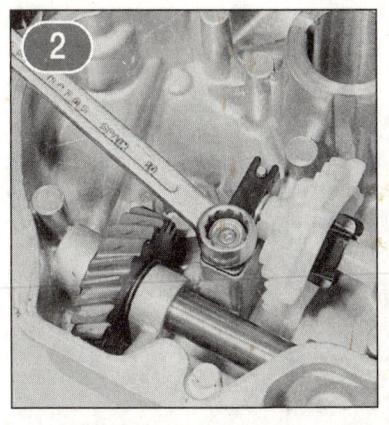

2 Slide the carrier wheel onto the governor shaft from the end with the slot in it. The weights on the wheel must be facing away from the slot. Fit the smaller washer onto the shaft after the wheel, With the wheel and washer as far onto the shaft as they will go, fit the shaft into the crankcase cover. The slot in the shaft mates onto a key machined in the cover casting. Fit the shaft clamp with the fork in the end engaged on the peg on the cover. (The gear seen in the photo will not have been fitted at this stage). Place the larger washer in the shaft, then fit the slider onto the shaft with its flange engaged between the weights.

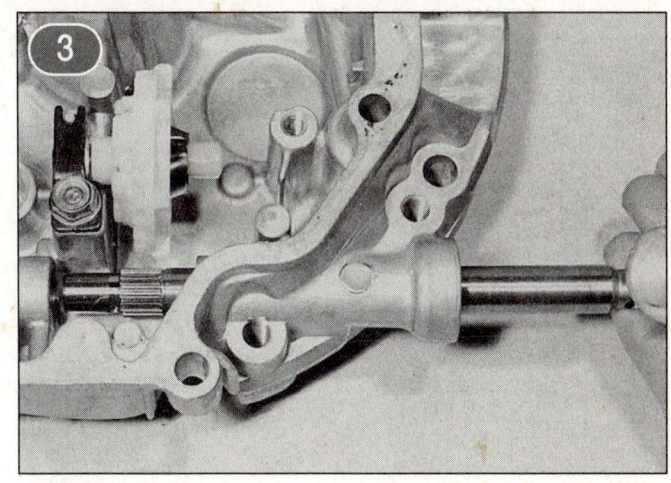

3 Insert the drive shaft into the crankcase cover.

4 The gear and its fixing components are shown in the photo.

11•3

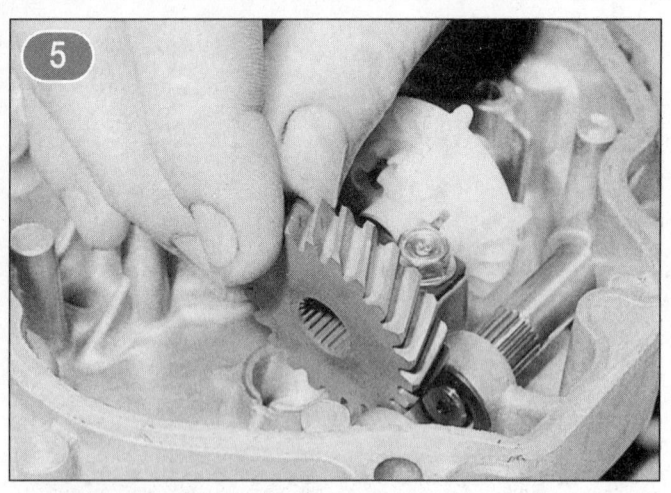

Chapter 11

5 Fit the washer with the smaller hole onto the shaft, so that it will be between the first bearing and the gear. Slide the shaft into the gear.

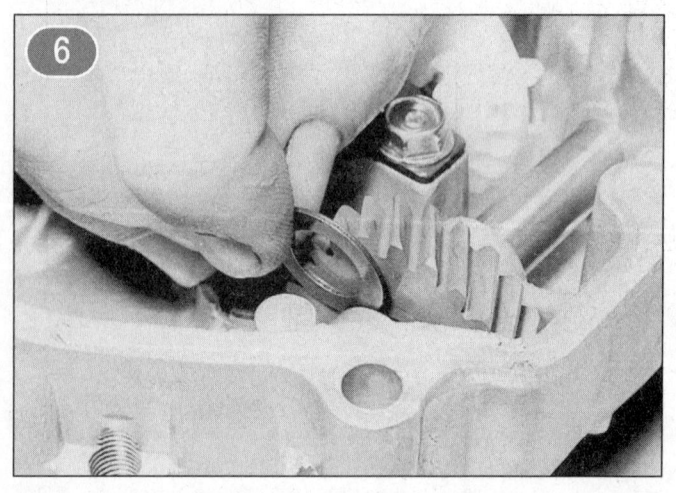

6 Fit the washer with the larger hole onto the end of the shaft then push the shaft into the second bearing.

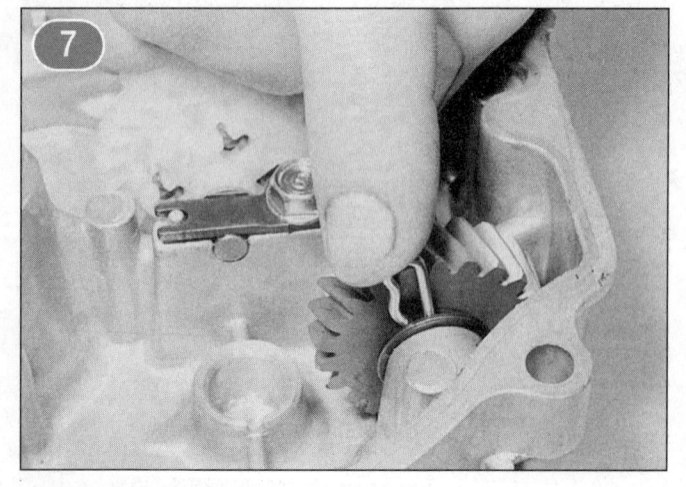

7 Insert the clip between the gear and the washer. Fit the straight leg of the clip into the hole in the shaft and press until it clicks fully home.

8 Fit a new oil seal to the crankcase cover bearing if necessary, in the same way as described previously for other engines.

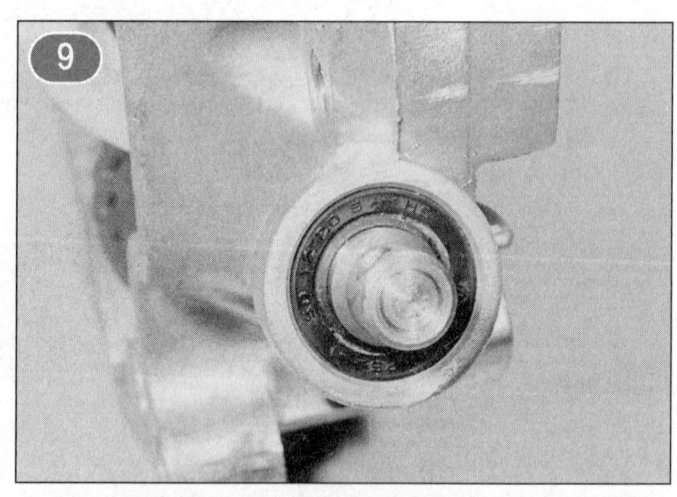

9 The drive shaft is also fitted with an oil seal. If necessary, renew the seal before fitting the drive shaft.

10 Fit a new oil seal to the crankcase flywheel bearing if necessary.

Honda GXV 120 OHV 4-stroke engine

11 The flywheel bearing in the crankcase is a ball bearing. To renew it, remove the oil seal and drive the old bearing in towards the crankcase interior. Fit the new bearing from the interior. Drive it into the housing with a piece of tube that bears on the outer race only. If the ball cage or the inner race are struck, the bearing will be damaged. Keep the bearing square as it is driven into the casting.

12 Smear a little oil on the crankshaft parallel portion at the tapered end. Insert the crankshaft into the crankcase bearing.

13 Assemble the connecting rod to the piston the same way round as when removed i.e. the oil hole on the same side as the arrow on the piston crown. If the gudgeon pin has been removed, fit it in the conventional manner, the same way round as when it was removed, and replace the circlips securely.

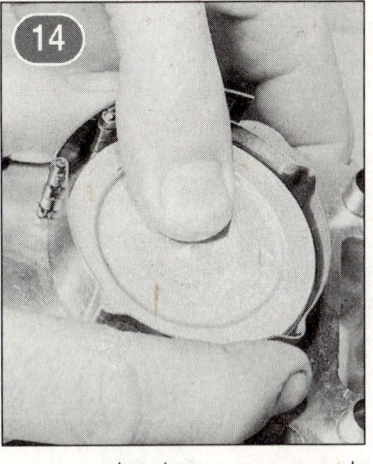

14 Fit a piston ring clamp to the piston. Oil the bore of the cylinder and insert the piston into it, taking care not to scratch the bore with the connecting rod. Press the piston out of the clamp and into the bore. Tap it gently with a piece of wood if necessary, but stop and investigate any obstruction or the piston rings may break. The arrow on the piston crown must be pointing towards the ohv push rod hole in the casting.

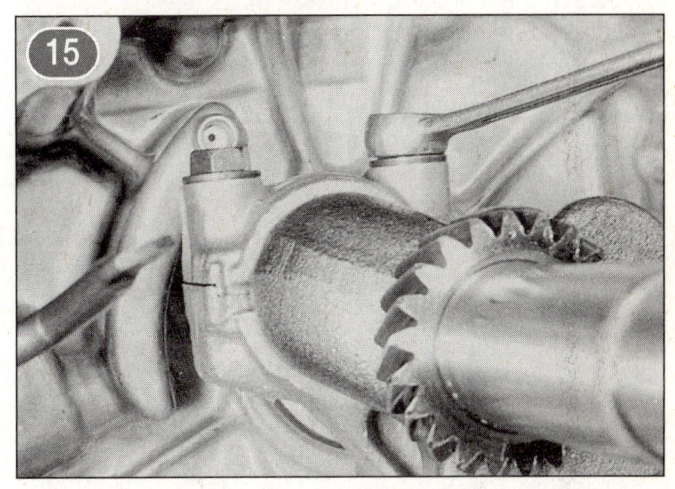

15 Invert the engine and oil the crank pin, engage the big end on it and fit the big end cap the same way round as marked when dismantling. Note that the cap will fit the wrong way round. Tighten the bolts firmly.

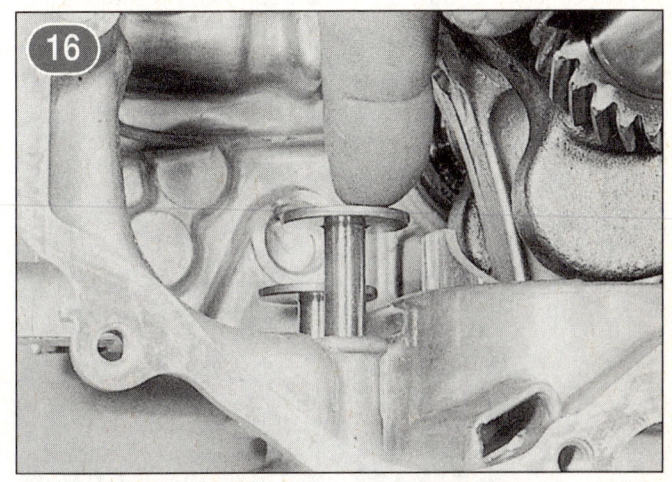

16 Oil the cam followers and fit them into the holes in which they were originally fitted (marked during dismantling).

Chapter 11

17 Check the action of the decompressor on the camshaft gear. Ensure that the spring is undamaged, not stretched, and imparts a positive return action.

18 Check that the toe of the decompressor lever and the two prongs on the weight lever are not worn, and that they remain engaged throughout full travel of the weight lever.

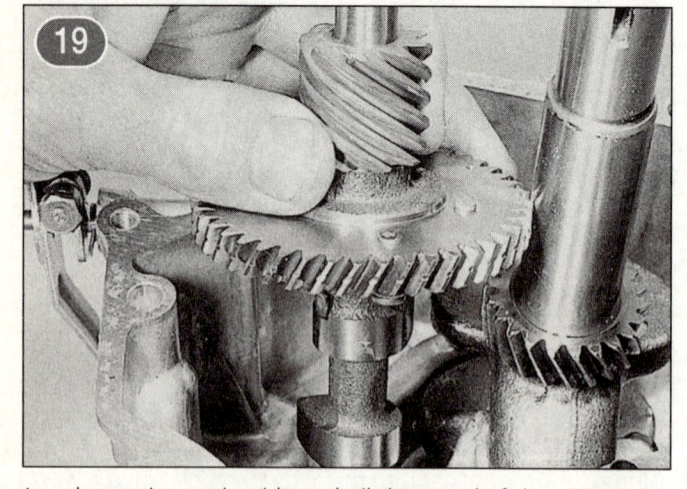

19 Lay the engine on its side and oil the camshaft bearing and insert the camshaft into the crankcase.

20 Mesh the cam gear with the crankshaft gear with the timing marks aligned.

21 Place a new gasket on the crankcase. Oil the camshaft bearing and the crankshaft bearing. Fit the dowel into the crankcase.

22 Fit the ohv oil return pipe into the elongated hole in the crankcase.

Honda GXV 120 OHV 4-stroke engine

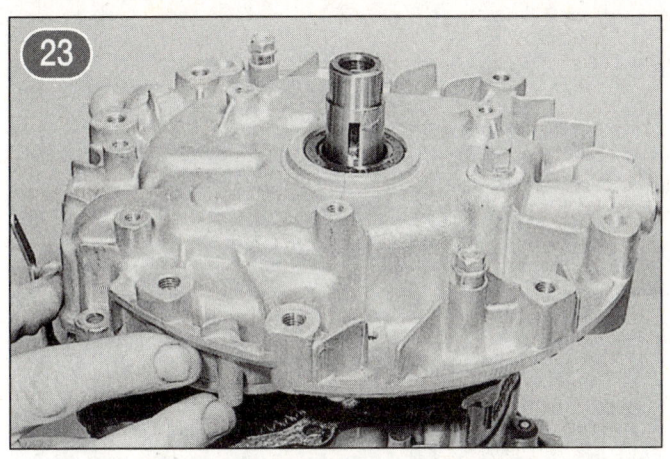

23 Fit the crankcase cover, ensuring that the governor slider and washer do not fall off. Guide the internal governor lever into the space between the governor slider and the side of the crankcase. Engage the cover on the dowel and seat the cover onto the crankcase.

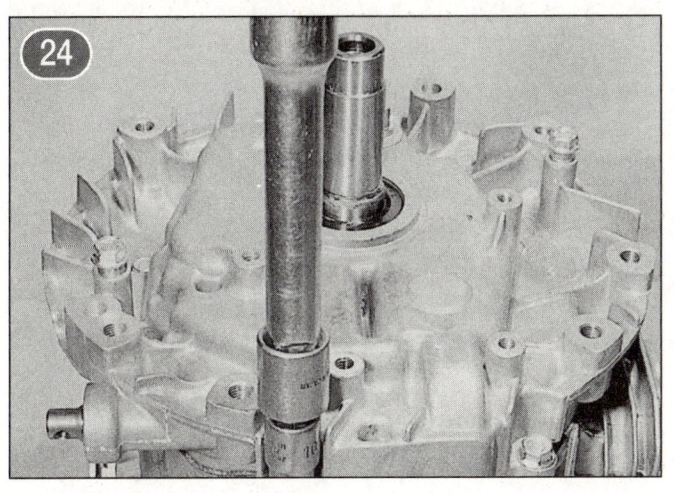

24 Secure the crankcase cover with the six bolts. Tighten diagonally opposite bolts a little at a time to avoid distorting or cracking the cover.

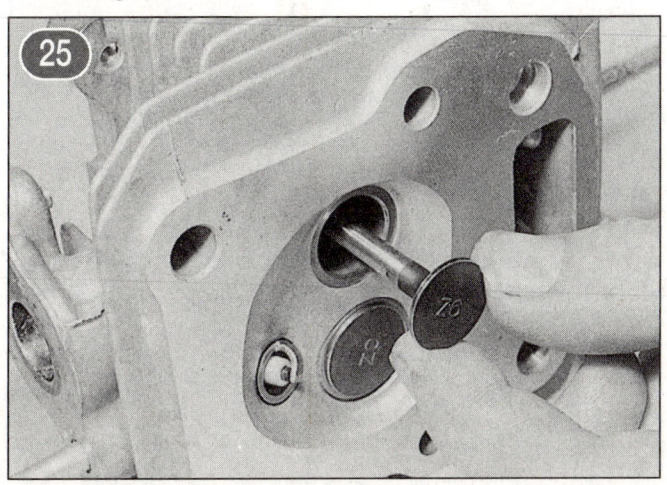

25 Insert the valves into the cylinder head. The exhaust valve has the smaller head of the two.

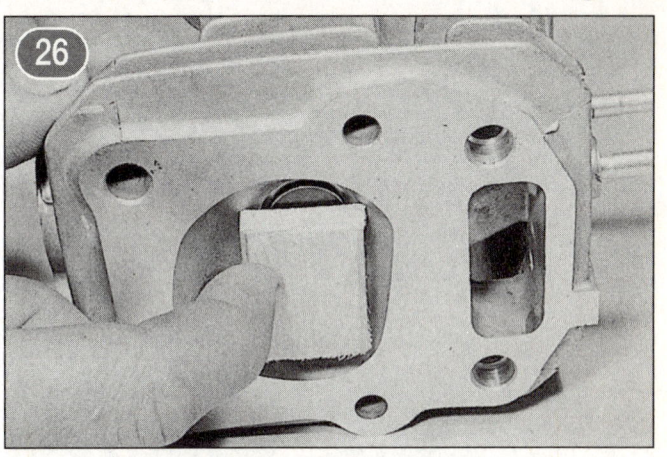

26 Place a small block of wood in the cylinder head to hold the valves on the seats while the springs are fitted. Turn the cylinder head on to its face with the wooden block in position.

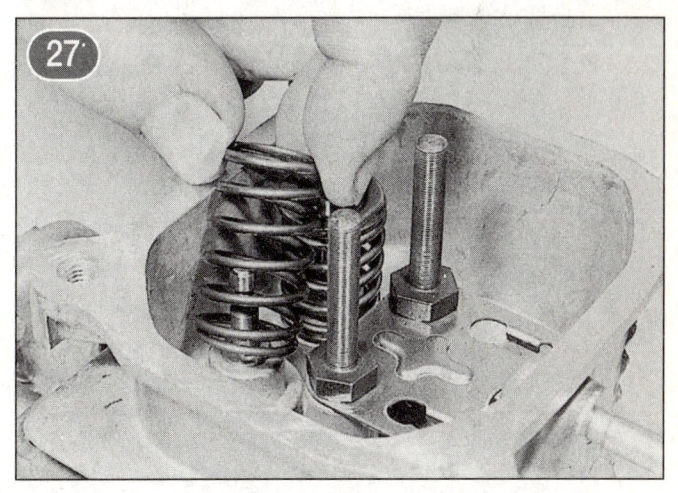

27 Fit the push rod guide plate onto the two studs in the cylinder head and secure with the two nuts. Place the valve spring over the valve stem.

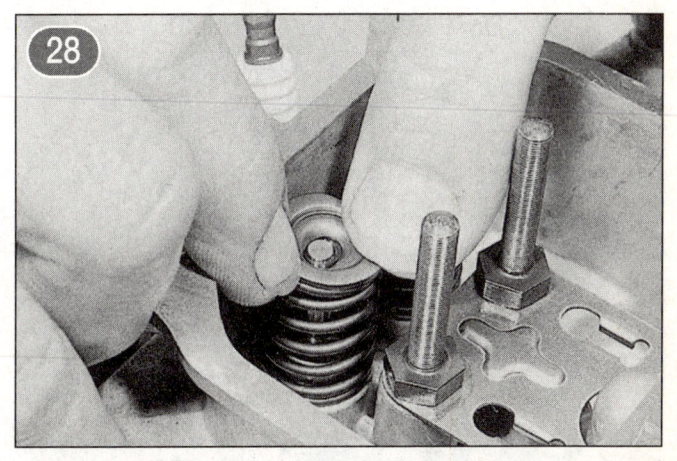

28 Press the collar down onto the spring, slightly off to one side so that the larger, offset hole in the collar can pass down onto the valve stem, then centralise the collar with a sideways movement so that the smaller hole fits under the shoulder near the tip of the valve stem.

Chapter 11

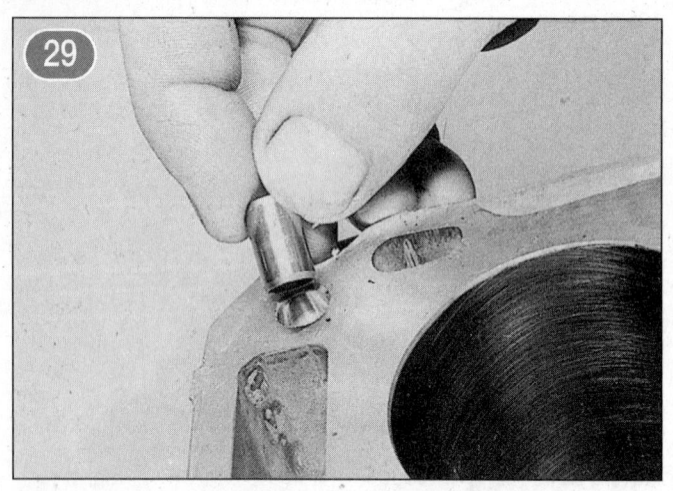

29 Place the two dowels in the top of the cylinder.

30 Place a new gasket on the cylinder. Fit the assembled cylinder head onto the cylinder.

31 Secure the cylinder head with the four bolts, tightening them diagonally to avoid distortion or cracking.

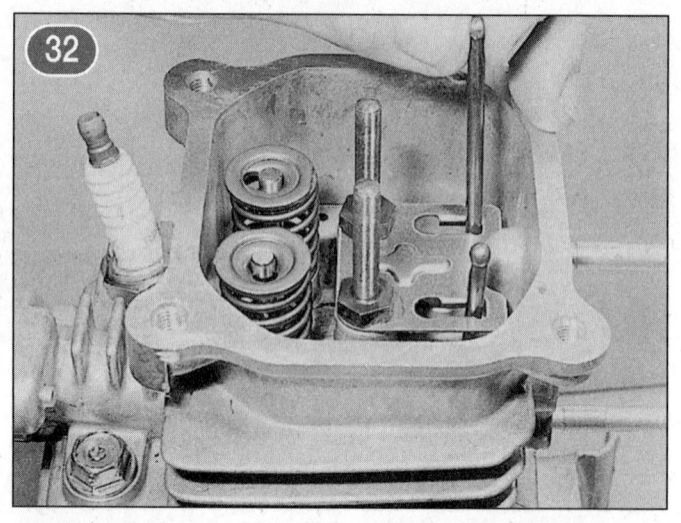

32 Insert the push rods through the retainer plate and locate them in the concave holes in the followers.

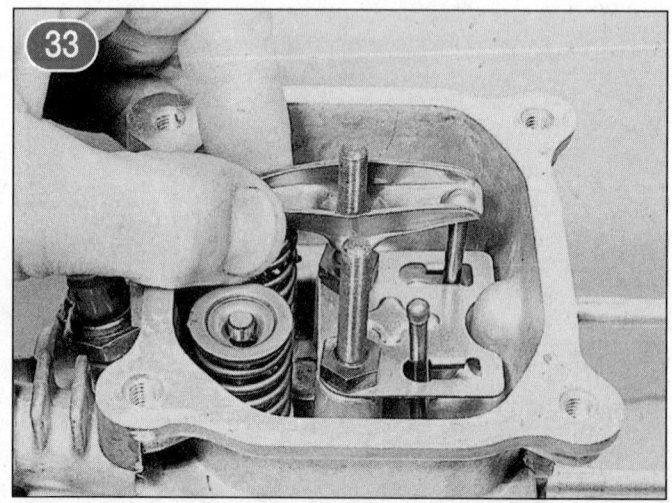

33 Place the rocker arms onto the studs with the smaller dimple seated on the top of the pushrod.

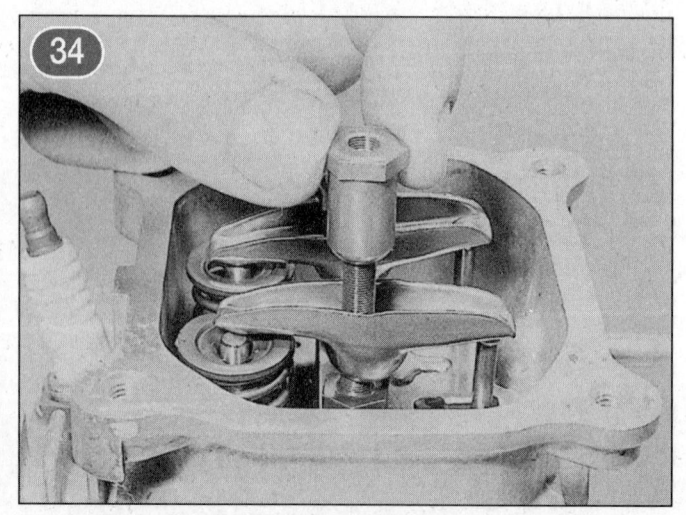

34 Screw the shouldered nuts onto the studs.

Honda GXV 120 OHV 4-stroke engine

35 Fit the locknuts and set the valve clearances as given in Technical Data. Lock the locknuts. This operation must be carried out at Top Dead Centre of the firing stroke.

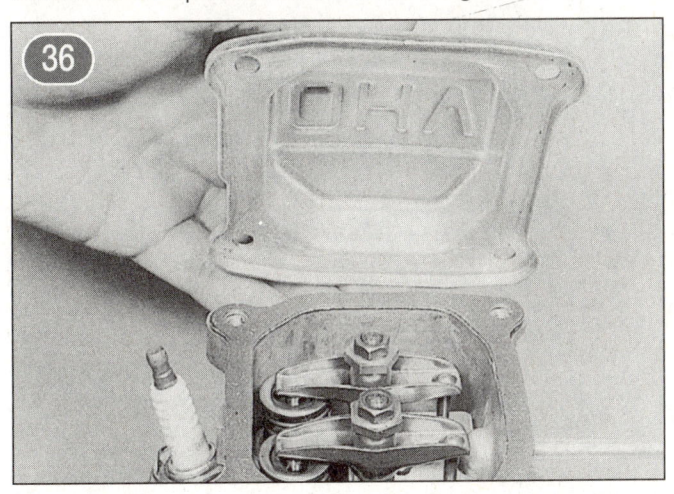

36 Fit a new valve cover gasket, then fit the valve cover but do not tighten down as two of the four bolts are used later to install the cowl.

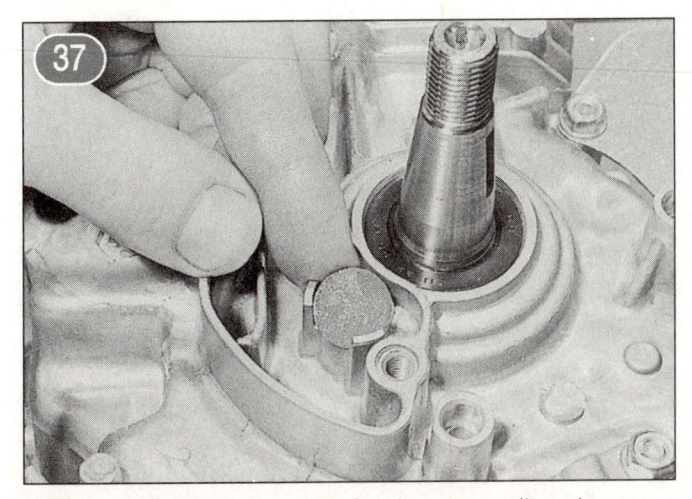

37 Inspect the breather disc valve for damage or distortion. Renew if necessary.

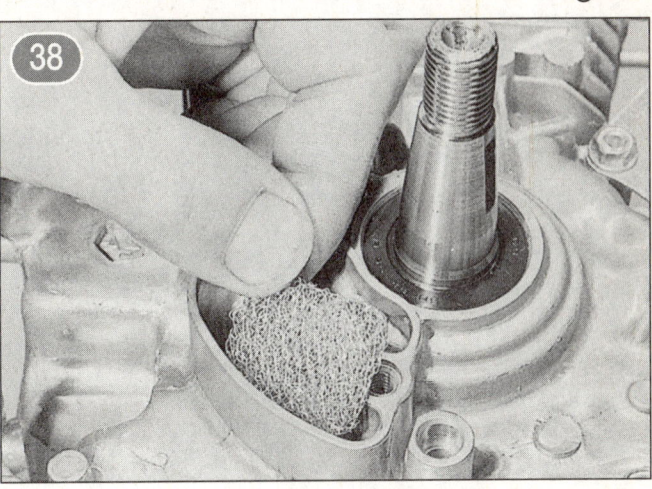

38 Rinse the gauze in solvent, dry thoroughly and insert it into the cavity in the breather housing.

39 Fit a new gasket to the breather cover and secure the cover in position.

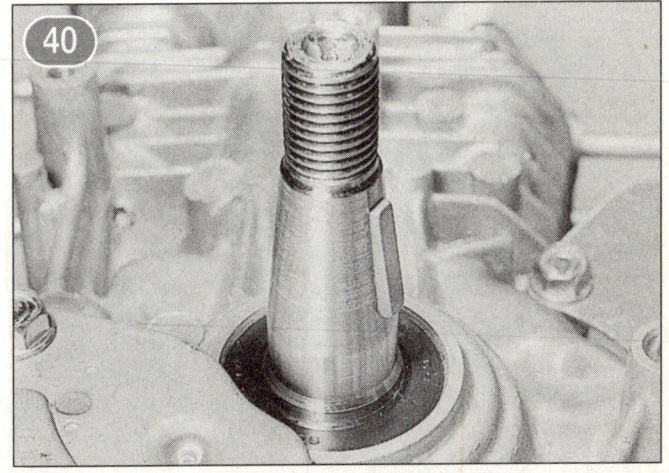

40 Place the Woodruff key in the slot in the crankshaft taper. If there are any shear marks or serious burrs, use a new key.

Chapter 11

41 Install the flywheel and the impeller on the crankshaft, aligned with the key. The impeller has four locating pegs which fit into four holes in the flywheel.

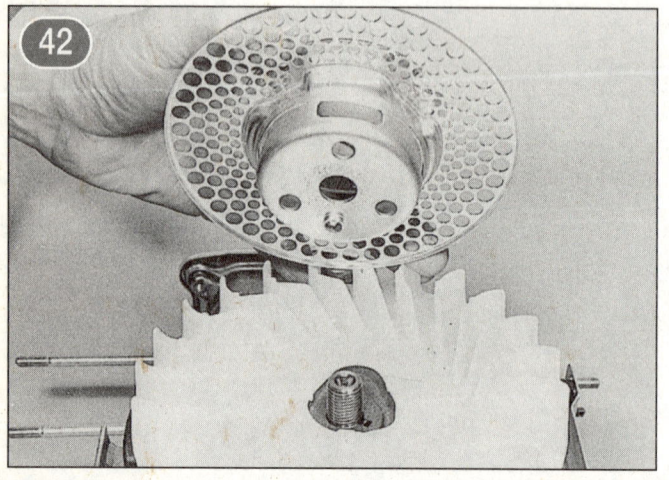

42 Fit the rotary screen and starter hub onto the impeller, with the screen located in the hole in the impeller. The three holes in the hub fit onto three pegs on the impeller. Fit the flywheel nut.

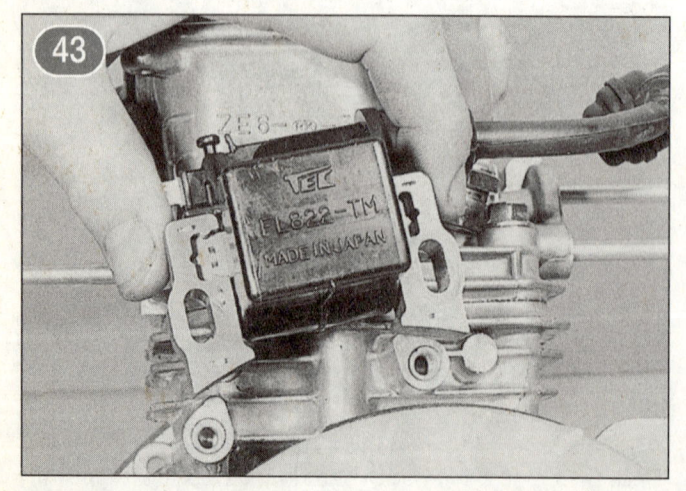

43 Install the ignition unit.

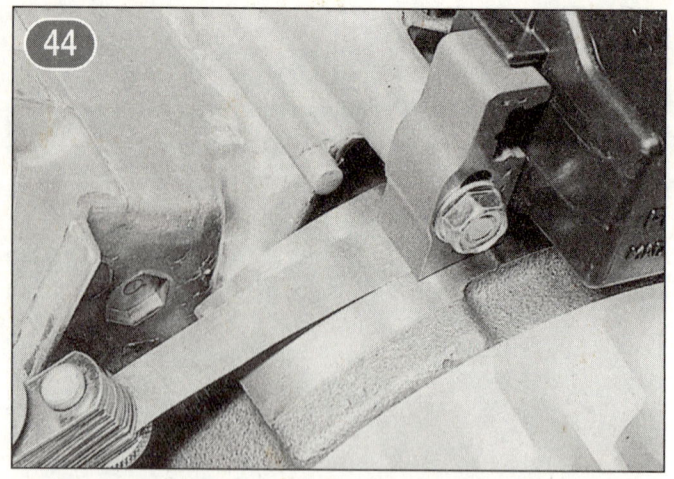

44 Using a non-ferrous feeler gauge, set an air gap as given in Technical Data between the armature legs and the flywheel.

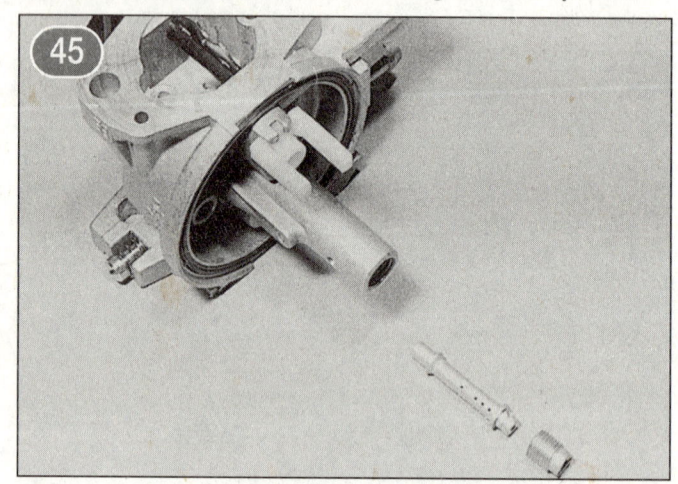

45 Remove the main jet and metering tube and examine them for dirt or gummy deposits. Clean by rinsing and blowing them. Do not poke the openings with a needle or wire, or they may be damaged and the accurate metering lost. Replace the metering tube and the main jet in the carburettor body.

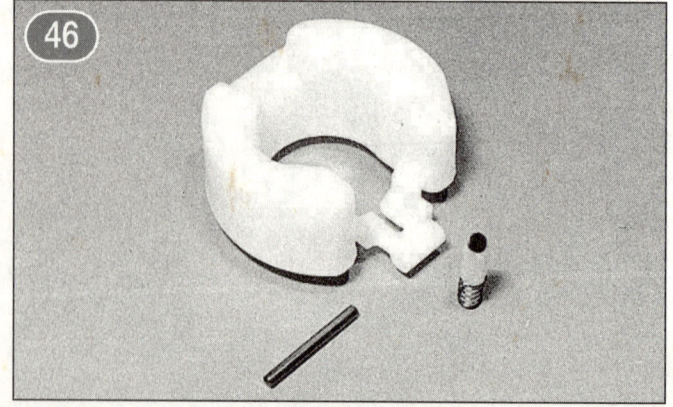

46 To remove the float, pull out the hinge pin. Remove the needle valve by pushing against the coil spring and sliding it out of the slot in the float. Examine the needle head for ridging or wear and renew if necessary.

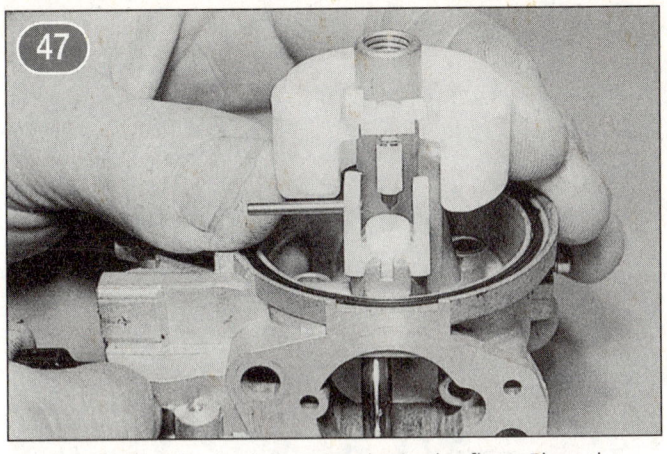

Honda GXV 120 OHV 4-stroke engine

47 Fit the needle valve back into the slot in the float. Place the float hinge in position between the carburettor hinge posts, with the needle in the hole between the posts. Press the hinge pin through the holes and check it for free movement.

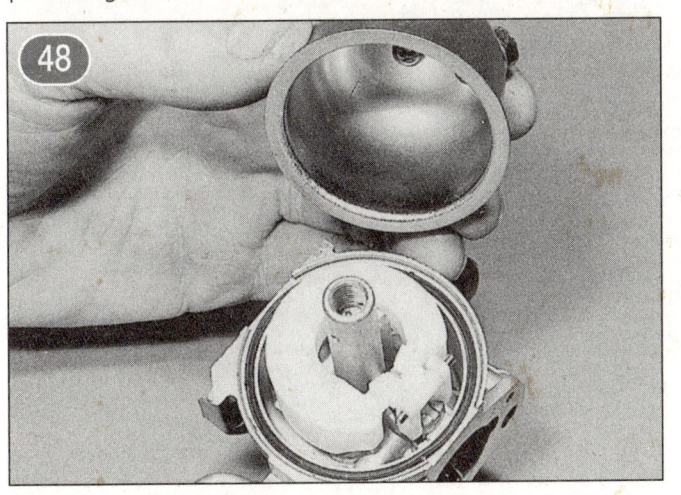

48 Examine the float chamber gasket for distortion or other damage. Renew it if necessary. Ensure that it is properly seated in the groove. Fit the float chamber with the drain plug towards the choke butterfly. Secure it with the bolt and fibre washer.

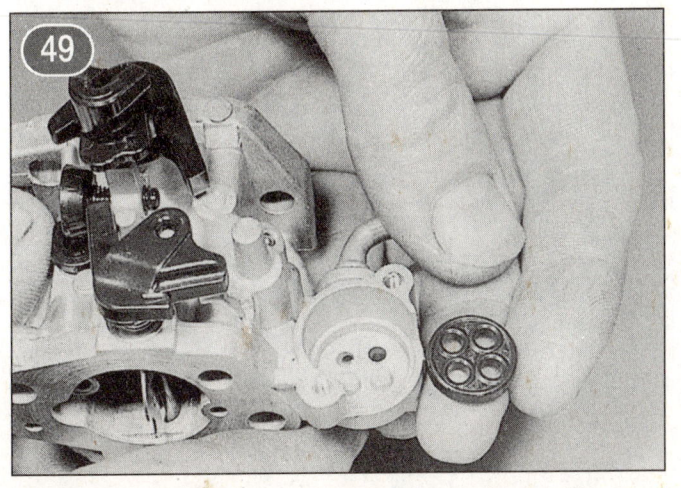

49 Inspect the four hole seal in the fuel tap and renew it if torn, distorted or hardened. Place it on the two shallow studs.

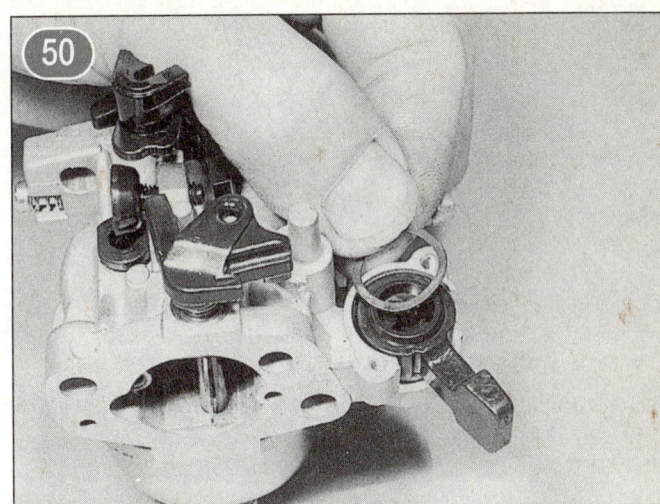

50 Place the lever valve body in the housing. Fit the wave washer on top of the body.

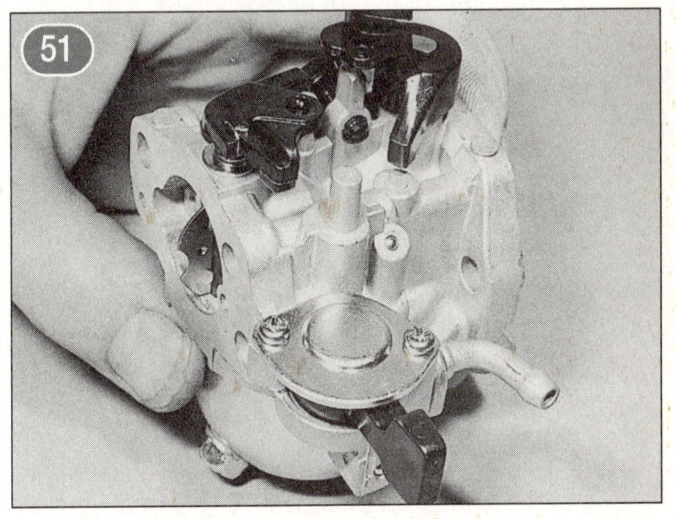

51 Fit the cover plate onto the housing.

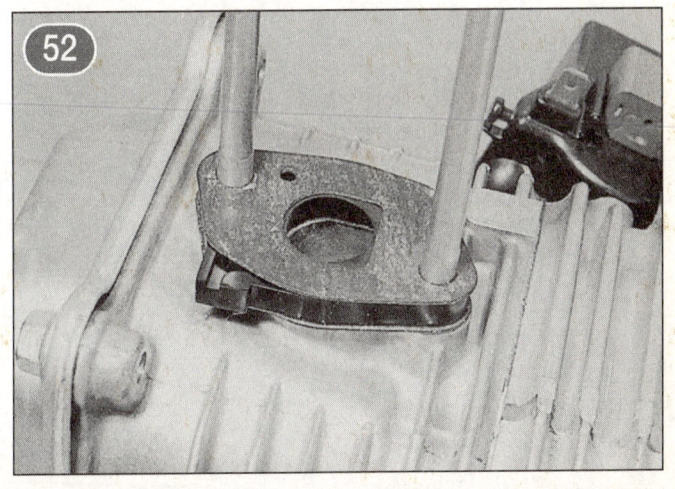

52 Fit a new gasket on the inlet port, place the plastic insulator block on top of it, then fit another new gasket on the insulator block – the small hole in the insulator block must be pointing towards the bottom of the engine.

Chapter 11

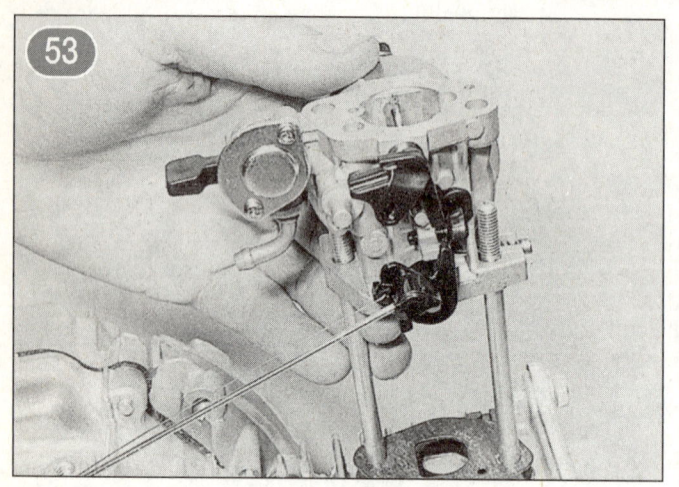

53 Position the carburettor near the studs and connect the governor link to the larger hole in the throttle butterfly lever. Connect the governor spring to the smaller hole in the lever. Slide the carburettor onto the studs.

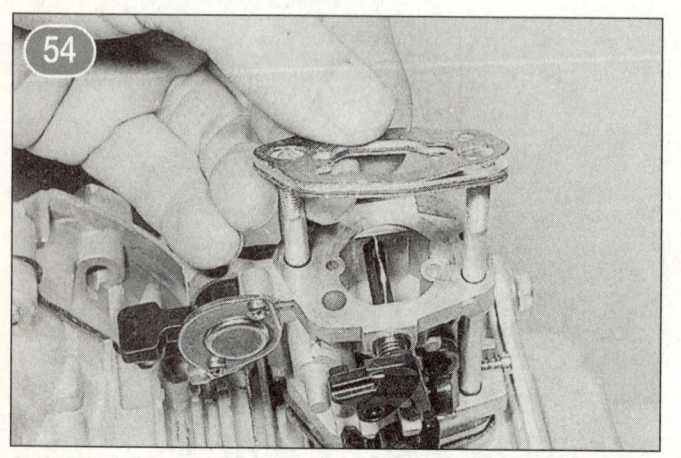

54 Fit the gasket, spacer and second gasket to the carburettor intake.

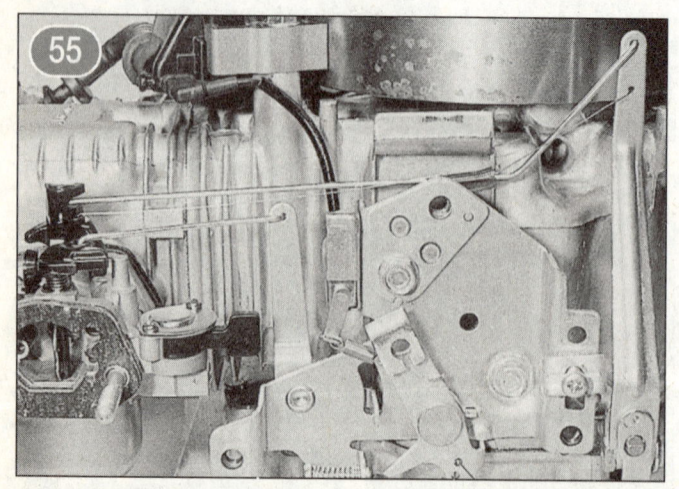

55 Fit the linkage plate to the engine. Connect the short link from the choke butterfly to the lever on the plate. Connect the coil spring from the hole marked STD in the control lever to the small lever at the bottom of the governor lever.

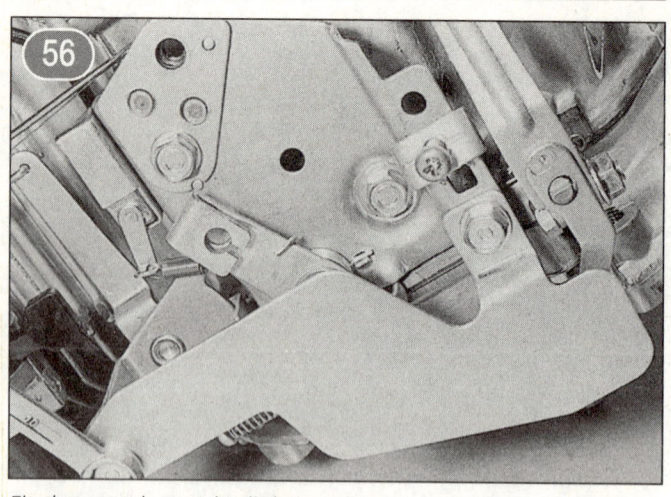

56 Fit the guard over the linkage plate.

57 Place the heat shield gasket on the exhaust port studs with the slanted edge positioned as shown above.

58 Place the muffler on the studs.

11•12

Honda GXV 120 OHV 4-stroke engine

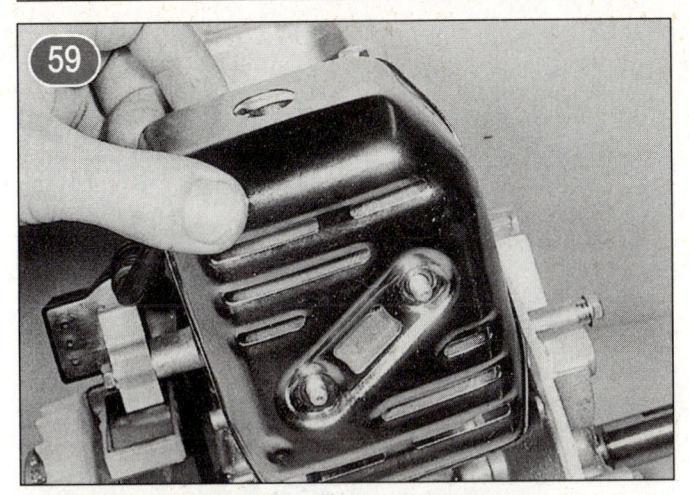

59 Finally, fit the heat shield. Secure with the two nuts.

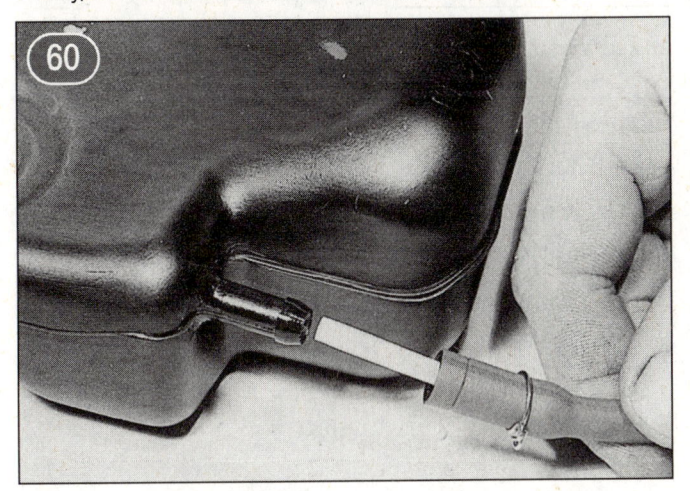

60 Gently rinse the fuel pipe filter mesh in clean petrol. Blow down the pipe from the other end to remove any particles left on the filter. Do not brush or rub it or the mesh will be damaged. Connect the pipe to the tank and secure with the clip.

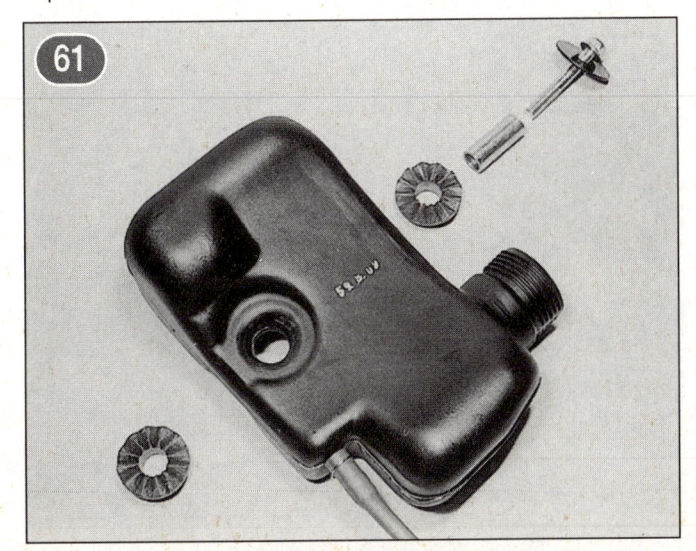

61 The fuel tank attaching parts are shown in the photo.

62 Place the washer on the bolt, then the spacer tube. Fit a rubber grip on the tube. Insert the tube and bolt through the hole in the fuel tank, through the other rubber grip and screw the bolt into the mounting bracket on the crankcase.

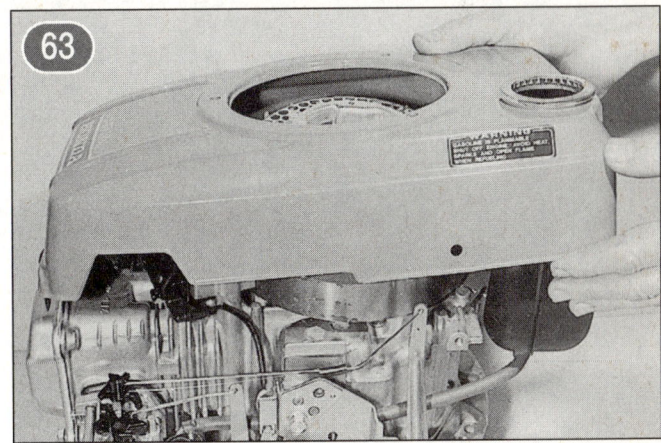

63 Pass the fuel pipe behind the linkage plate and press the pipe support clip into the hole in the linkage plate. Connect the pipe to the carburettor and secure it with the spring clip. Fit the cowl to the engine with the five bolts.

64 Position the air cleaner duct on the carburettor mounting studs.

11•13

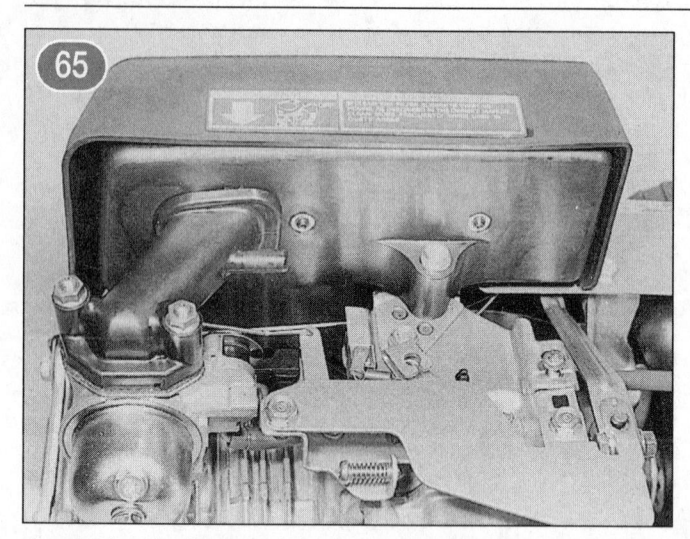

Chapter 11

65 Secure the air cleaner to the studs with the two nuts. Bolt the air cleaner mounting lug to the linkage plate.

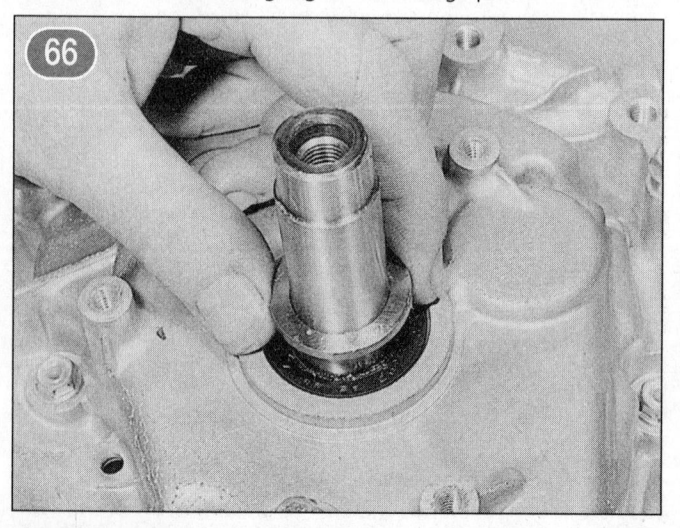

66 Place the spacer on the crankshaft.

67 Fit the Roto-stop ball control plate onto the crankshaft.

68 Connect the two Roto-stop return springs to the two levers and to the anchor bolts.

69 Place the ball retainer on the ball control plate with the balls located in the three concave pressings.

70 Place the brake housing in position with its blisters located on the balls.

Honda GXV 120 OHV 4-stroke engine

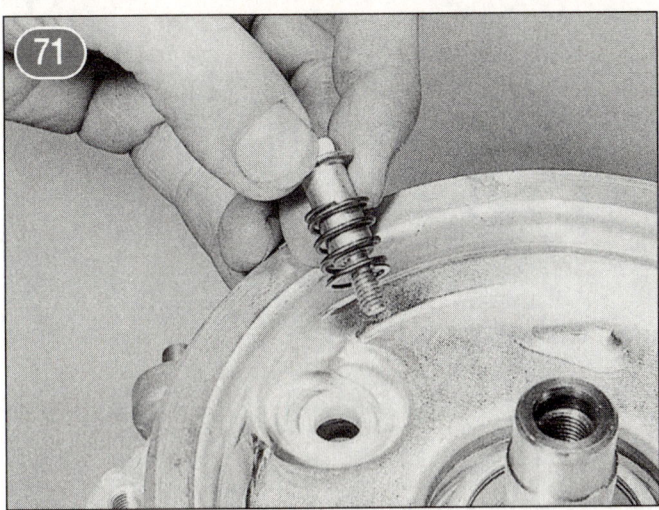

71 Place the brake springs on the flange bolts.

72 Line the brake housing up with its three bolt holes in line with the threaded holes in the crankcase cover. Fit the flange bolts.

73 Tighten them down. Fit the Woodruff key into the crankshaft slot.

74 Fit the drive disc onto the crankshaft, aligned with the key.

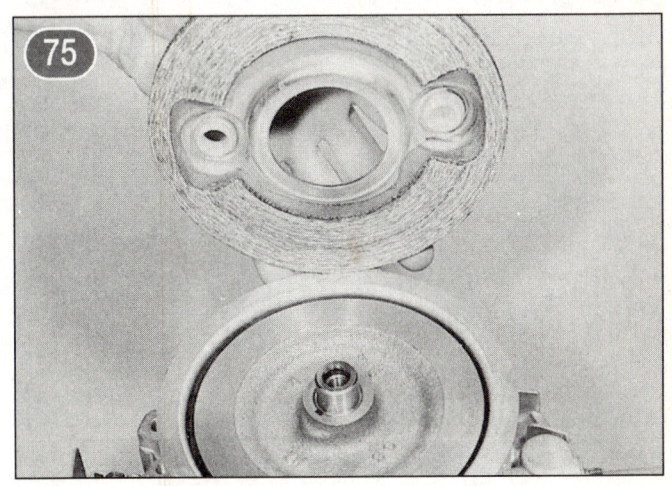

75 Place the brake lining plate on the drive disc.

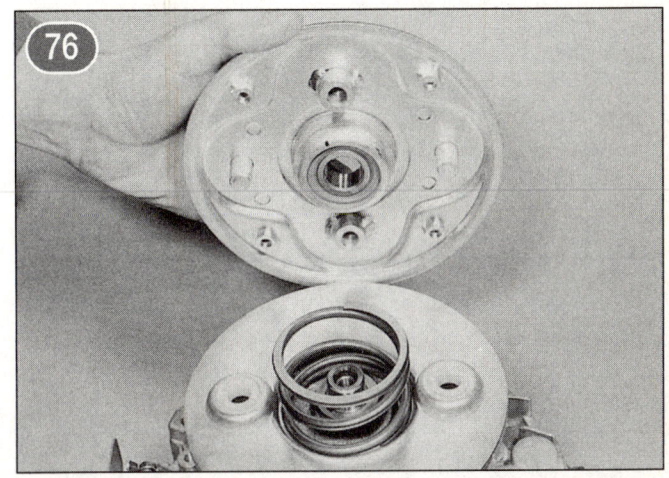

76 Place the clutch spring on the brake lining plate. Fit the driven disc on the brake lining plate with the two pegs in the holes in the brake lining plate. The driven disc has a ball bearing and an oil seal in its centre. Renewal of these is straightforward and the same as for the crankcase bearings described previously.

Chapter 11

77 Fit and tighten the central bolt.

78 Examine the seal in the final drive case for damage or distortion. Ensure that it is properly seated in the groove.

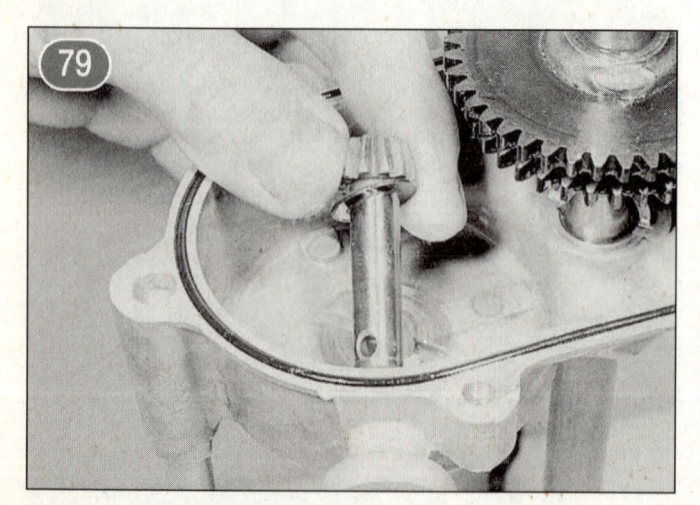

79 Renew the oil seal at the bevel drive shaft bearing if necessary. Insert the bevel drive shaft.

80 Place the thrust washer in the casing.

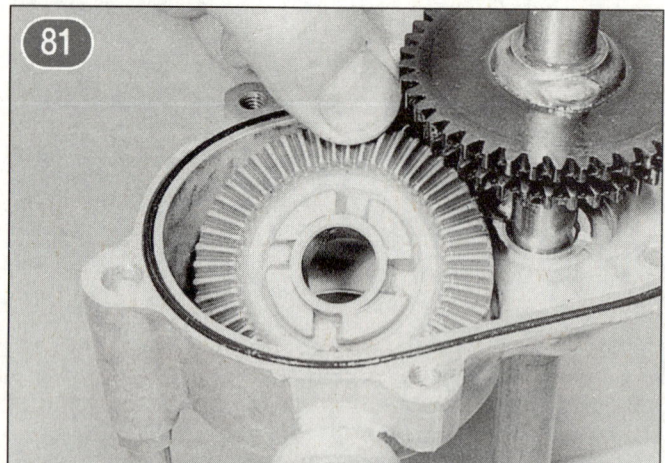

81 Install the bevel gear.

82 Insert the drive selector fork into the bearing in the case.

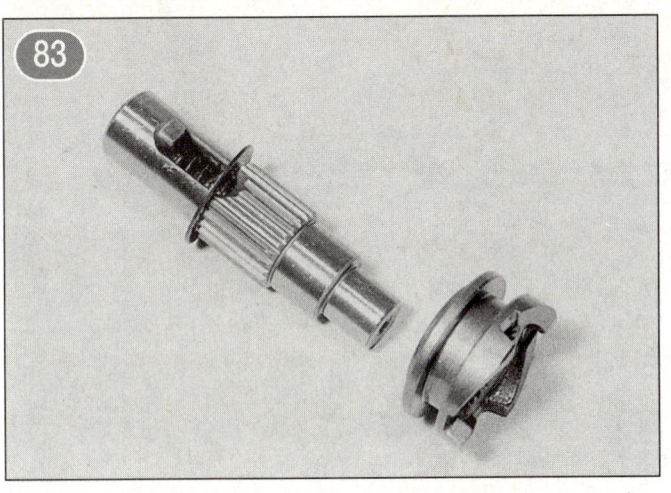

Honda GXV 120 OHV 4-stroke engine

83 The drive gear shaft and clutch ratchet hub are shown in the photo. The internal coil spring can be renewed by withdrawing the cross key from the slots.

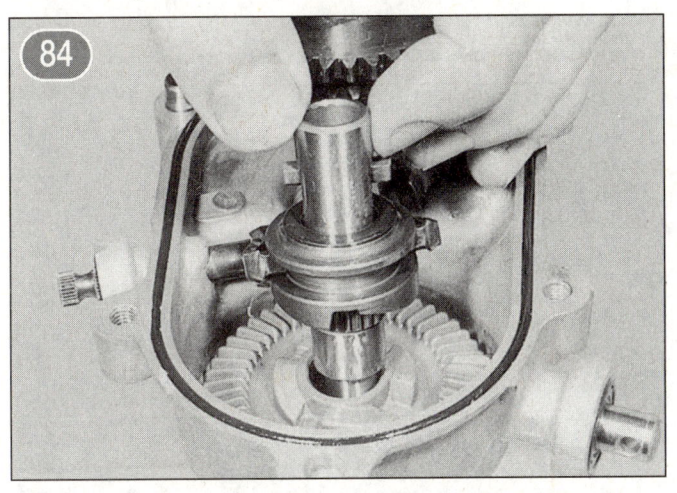

84 Slide the ratchet hub onto the gear shaft splines. Oil the end of the gear shaft and insert it through the bevel gear into the bearing in the case. Engage the hub in the selector fork as the shaft is inserted.

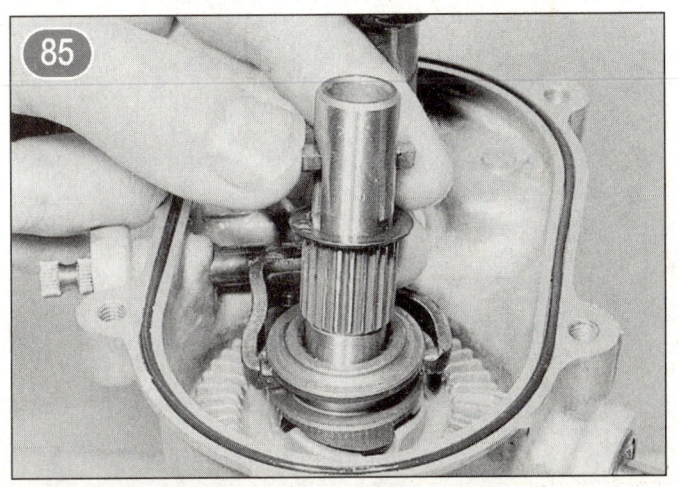

85 Engage the hub ratchet with the bevel gear ratchets.

86 Fit the larger gear flange upwards onto the gear shaft.

87 Fit the smaller gear onto the shaft.

88 Fit the thrust washer. The cross key in the shaft fits into the cross of the small gear.

11•17

Chapter 11

89 Insert the drive actuating plunger into the gear shaft.

90 Insert the hollow dowel in the case lip. Fill the case with a light transmission oil.

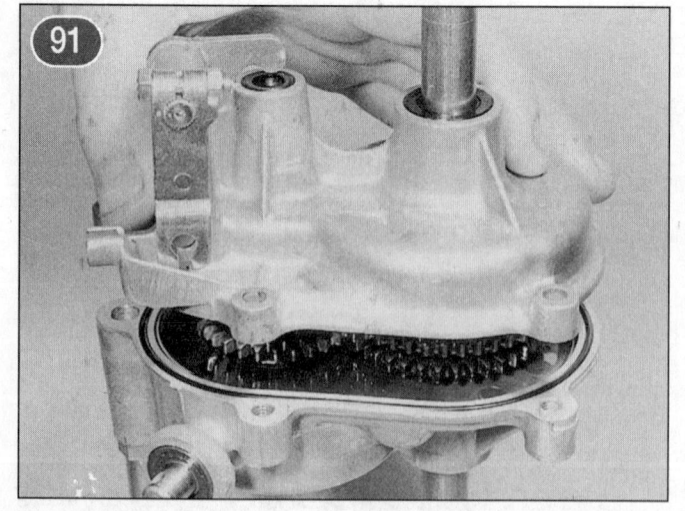

91 Slide the other half of the case onto the axle, engage it on the dowel and mate the two halves together. Secure with the five bolts. Two are longer and are fitted one over the extended torque reactor bolt, and the other at the opposite end of the case.

92 Clamp the speed selector lever to the selector fork shaft. The index mark on the end of the shaft must coincide with the centre pop mark on the lever.

Mount the engine to its application.

Fit the recoil starter onto the engine cowl.

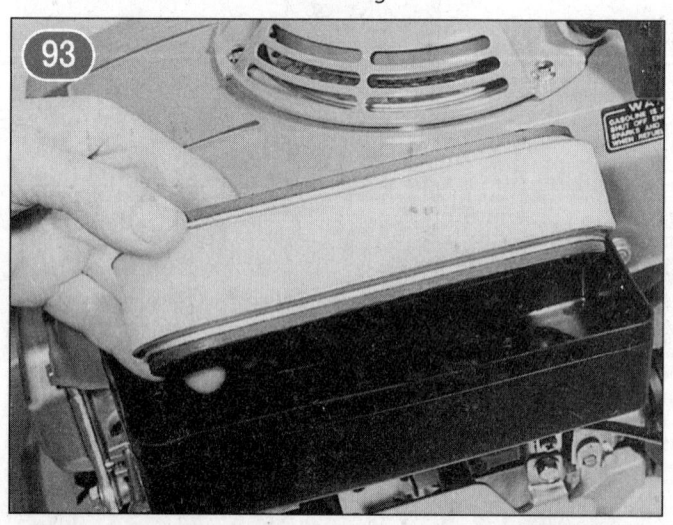

93 Place the element in the air cleaner housing and fit the cover.

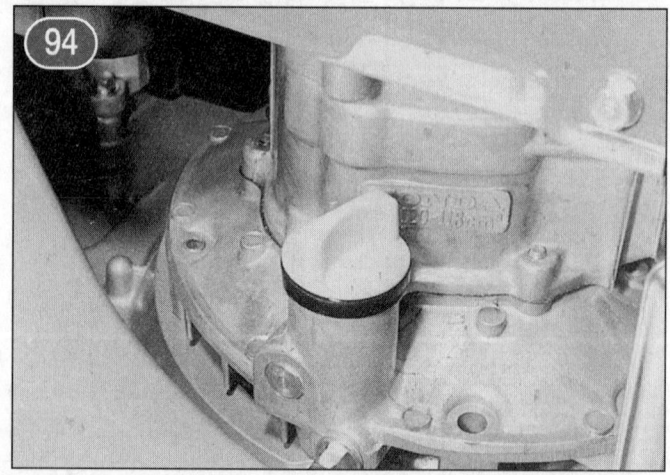

94 Fill the engine with oil to the level shown on the filler plug dipstick.

Honda GXV 120 OHV 4-stroke engine

Starter repair

To fit a new recoil spring or starter cord, proceed as follows:

Remove the recoil starter from the engine cowl.

Bend the tang near the cord exit hole up to allow the rope to be unwound.

Release pulley tension by pulling the cord out about 60 cm (2 ft), holding the pulley and unwinding the cord. Gently release the pulley.

Remove the central bolt and lift off the cover. There is no need to lift the pawls or their spring out unless they need renewing, which is straightforward and can be seen in the following views.

Lift the pulley from the shaft. Remove the recoil spring.

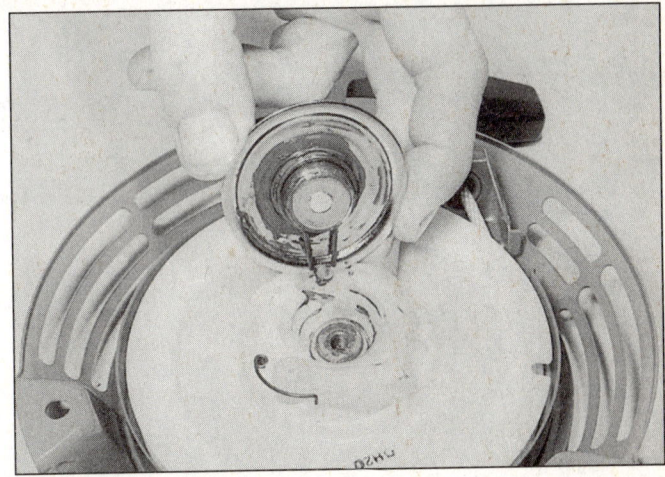

Fit the cover with the two legs of the clip on either side of the peg on the pawl.

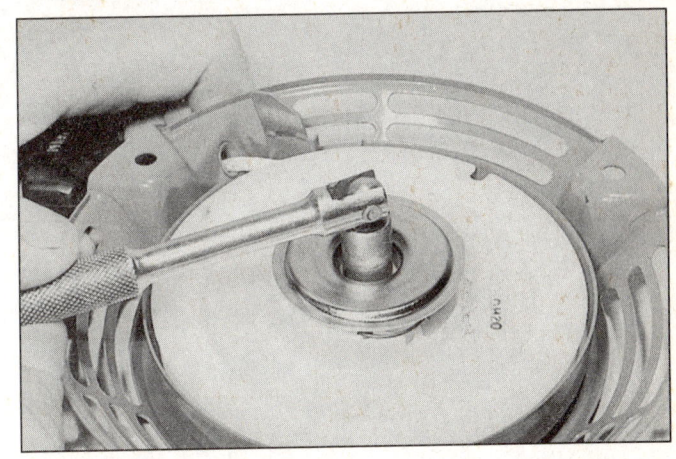

Hook the outer end of the new spring into the slot in the housing. Wind the spring anti-clockwise into the housing, working in towards the middle. Put a blob of grease in the coils. Attach a new cord to the pulley if necessary and wind it anti-clockwise round the pulley. Place the pulley on the stub shaft and turn it gently anti-clockwise until it engages with the hook on the inner end of the recoil spring.

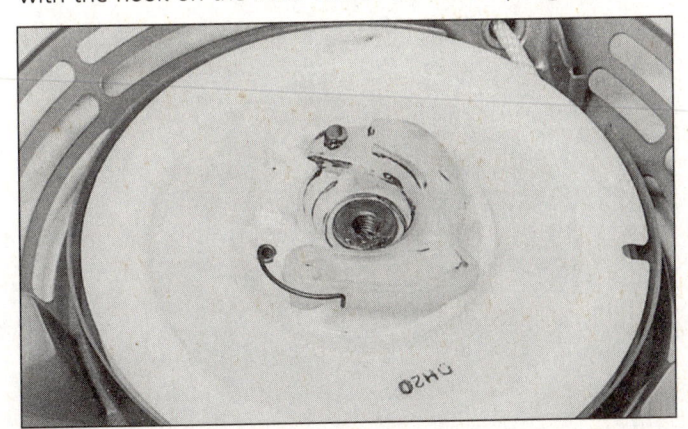

Then fit and tighten the bolt.

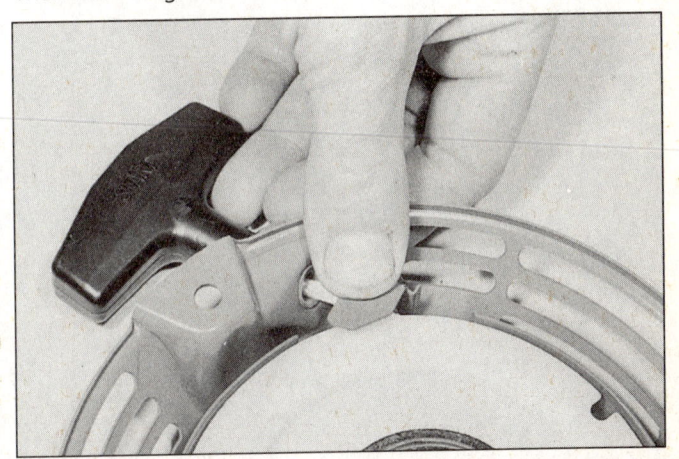

If a new cord was fitted, thread the end through the exit hole and knot the handle in place. Inspect the pawls and their spring, renew if damaged. To tension the pulley, wind it about three turns anti-clockwise, hold it and wind the slack in the cord anti-clockwise onto the pulley, then release the pulley.

Bend the tang down over the cord. Pull the starter handle and check for freedom of movement and a positive return action. Install the starter on the engine cowl with the handle facing the left side of the mower.

11•19

Chapter 11

Honda GCV 135 OHC 4.5 hp 4-stroke engine

12

Technical data
Dismantling

Reassembly
Starter repair

Technical Data

Spark plug type	NGK BPR6ES
Spark plug gap	0.7 to 0.8 mm (0.028 to 0.032 in)
Valve clearances (cold):	
Inlet	0.15 mm ± 0.04 mm (0.006 ± 0.016 in)
Exhaust	0.20 mm ± 0.04 mm (0.008 ± 0.002 in)
Ignition armature air gap	0.254 to 0.355 mm (0.010 to 0.002 in)
Engine oil grade	10W-40
Engine oil capacity	0.55 litres
Torque wrench settings:	
Big-end bolts	12 Nm
Flywheel nut	52 Nm

Chapter 12

Dismantling

Before starting to dismantle, read Chapter 5. The procedures outlined apply to all engines and if adopted, will ensure an orderly and methodical approach that will make both dismantling and reassembly much easier. The following assumes the engine has been removed from its application.

- [ ] Undo the three retaining nuts, and remove the starter assembly. Note the three spacers in the assembly mounting holes.
- [ ] Disconnect the fuel pipe from the fuel tank to the fuel tap. Be prepared for fuel spillage.
- [ ] Remove the oil filler cap/dipstick and drain the engine oil into a suitable container.
- [ ] Unscrew the three retaining bolts, and remove the exhaust shield.
- [ ] Remove the exhaust system.
- [ ] Press down the retaining clips, and remove the air filter cover. Lift out the element.
- [ ] The air filter housing is secured by three bolts. Two silver-coloured bolts, which also retain the carburettor, and one-gold coloured bolt which secures the housing to the linkage plate. Remove the bolts and, as the housing is lifted away, disconnect the engine breather pipe.
- [ ] Disconnect the governor arm-to-linkage plate spring.
- [ ] Undo the mounting screw, disconnect the fuel pipe, and remove the fuel tap.
- [ ] Unscrew the linkage plate mounting bolt. As the plate is lifted away, disengage the choke linkage, and the throttle spring and linkage.
- [ ] Remove the carburettor, heat shield and insulator block.
- [ ] Undo the retaining bolt, and remove the carburettor float bowl. Recover the gasket
- [ ] Push out the pivot pin, and carefully lift away the float with the needle valve attached.
- [ ] Unscrew the main jet, and slide out the emulsion tube.
- [ ] Counting the number of turns required, unscrew the mixture adjustment screw, and the throttle stop screw.
- [ ] Remove the air jet screw.
- [ ] No further dismantling of the carburettor is advised. Clean any fuel/air passages by blowing only.
- [ ] Carefully pull the HT cap from the spark plug.
- [ ] Unscrew the two mounting bolts, disconnect the earthing wire, and remove the ignition magneto.
- [ ] The flywheel retaining nut can be extremely tight. In order to prevent the flywheel from turning, use a strap wrench around the circumference of the flywheel. Disconnect the flywheel brake spring, so that the brake arm can be pushed away from the flywheel, which will give sufficient clearance to fit the strap wrench. The help of an assistant will be needed to steady the engine. Loosen the nut.
- [ ] Leaving the retaining nut flush with the end of the crankshaft, use a two-legged puller to remove the flywheel. The correct location for the puller legs is cast into the rim of the flywheel (arrowed). Whilst the puller exerts pressure on the crankshaft, a gentle tap with a soft hammer on the end of the puller may help to free the flywheel. Recover the Woodruff (half moon) key from the shaft.
- [ ] Unscrew the two retaining bolts, and remove the flywheel brake assembly.
- [ ] Remove the engine breather valve cover, complete with breather pipe.
- [ ] Bend back the tab washer, and unscrew the oil filler spout from the crankcase.
- [ ] Make aligning marks between the governor lever and shaft. Undo the pinch-bolt and remove the lever.
- [ ] Remove the spark plug.
- [ ] Undo the four retaining bolts, and gently prise the cam box cover from the cylinder head.
- [ ] Align the timing marks moulded in to the outside face of the camshaft pulley with gasket face of the cylinder head (arrowed). This should correspond to TDC on the compression stroke.

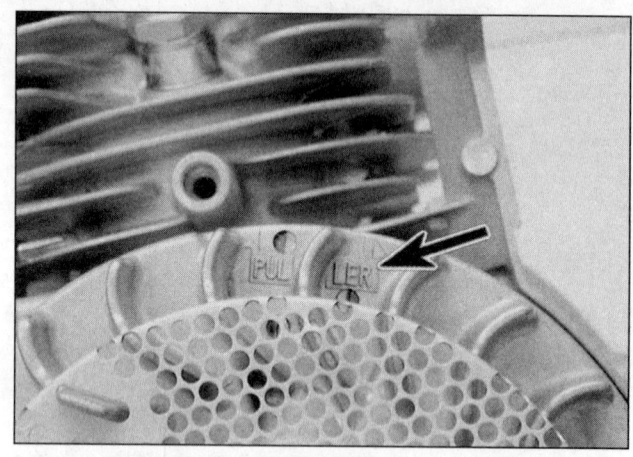

Honda GCV 135 OHC 4.5 hp 4-stroke engine

- ☐ Pull out the rocker arm pivot shafts, and lift the rocker arms away. It is important to label or arrange the components so that, if re-used, they are refitted to their original locations.
- ☐ Slip the belt from the camshaft pulley, pull out the pulley spindle, and remove the camshaft/pulley. Note the O-ring fitted to the pulley spindle.

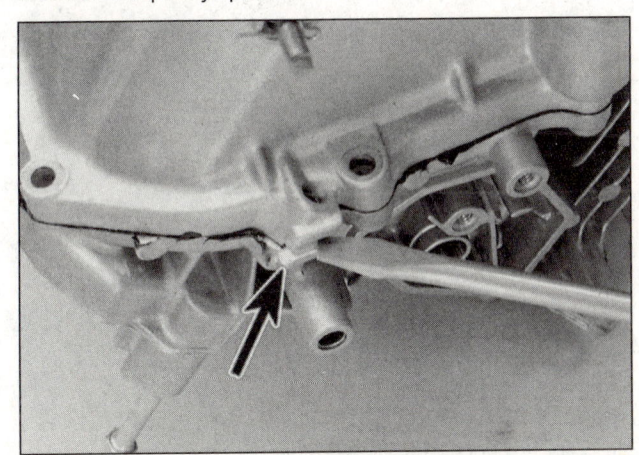

- ☐ Unscrew the eight retaining bolts, and carefully prise the crankcase halves apart. Leverage points are cast into the casings at the locating dowel points (arrowed).
- ☐ Recover the bevelled washer fitted between the crankshaft and crankcase.
- ☐ Undo the retaining bolt and remove the oil slinger/governor assembly.
- ☐ Pull the 'R-clip' from the governor arm, and withdraw the arm and washer from the crankcase.
- ☐ If it is to be re-used, note the direction of rotation, and remove the camshaft drive belt.
- ☐ Undo the retaining bolts, and remove the big-end bearing cap. Gently push the connecting rod up into the cylinder.
- ☐ Carefully lift the crankshaft from the crankcase.
- ☐ Pull the connecting rod down and withdraw the piston from the cylinder.
- ☐ If required, remove the piston rings from the piston by carefully expanding the rings at their ends and sliding them from the piston. Note the orientation of the rings for reassembly.

- ☐ Remove the circlips and push the gudgeon pin from the piston.
- ☐ In order to remove a valve, depress the valve collar and push it towards the flat in the rim of the collar. Due to the size of the spring, it is quite possible to compress them sufficiently by hand. The valve collars have two adjoining holes, one of which is larger than the other. This allows the valve stem to slide through the collar. Remove the spring and slide the valve from the cylinder head. It is important to label or arrange the components so that, if re-used, they are refitted to their original locations.
- ☐ Inspect the valve guides for scoring and excessive wear. Examine the valve seats and renovate as necessary (*refer to Chapter 5*).

- ☐ If required, prise the oil seals from the crankcase halves, noting which way round they are fitted.
- ☐ Check the condition of the crankshaft bearing, camshaft bearing and cylinder bore for wear, scores or cracks. If the bore is damaged, worn oval or oversized, then professional skills and special equipment will be necessary to restore it. The same applies to worn or damaged bearings. Check all threaded holes for damaged threads, and repair if necessary by fitting a thread insert of the correct size (*refer to Chapter 5*).

Chapter 12

Reassembly

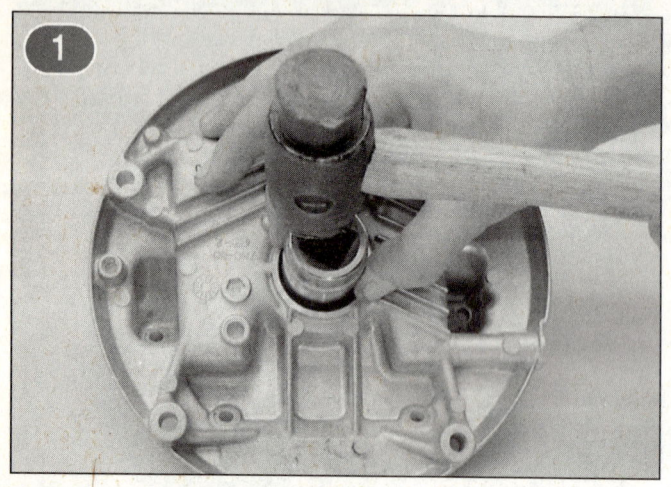

1 If required, fit new oil seals to the crankcase halves using appropriate sized sockets.

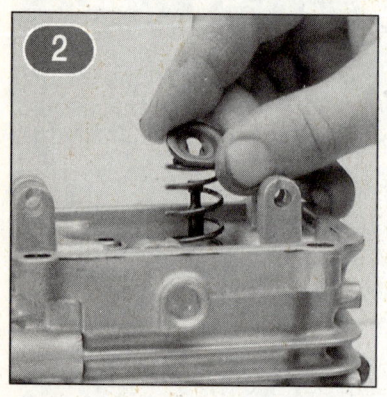

2 Smear the valve stem with oil and refit the exhaust valve into the cylinder head. Fit the exhaust valve spring and collar over the valve stem. As the spring is compressed, slide the valve stem through the larger end of the slot in the collar. Centralise the collar and slowly release the spring. Check that the collar is correctly located. Repeat this procedure for the inlet valve.

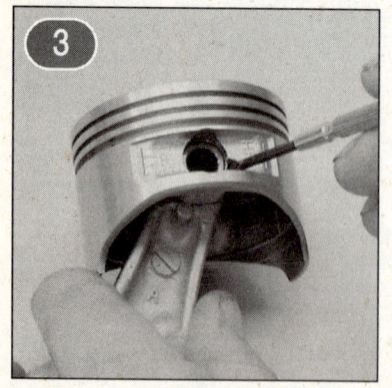

3 If previously removed, fit the gudgeon pin into the piston/connecting rod small end. The piston should be fitted the valve cut-outs in its crown on the timing belt side, and the connecting rod with the cast lug at the big-end towards the inlet port. Always refit the gudgeon pin using new circlips. If the gudgeon pin is reluctant to fit, immerse the piston in hot water for a few minutes. This causes the aluminium to expand, and the gudgeon pin to slide easily.

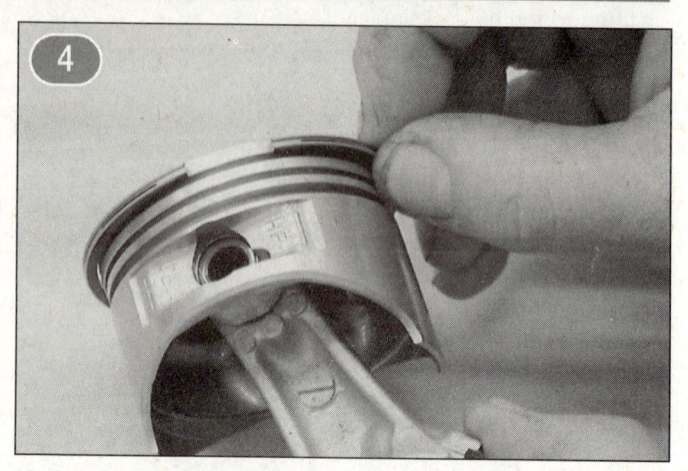

4 Fit the piston rings to the piston. All of the rings have a small letter 'T' stamped into the face that should be fitted towards the piston crown. The oil control ring should be fitted first, by carefully expanding the ring just enough to slide it down over the piston and into its groove. Although a special tool is available to fit piston rings, with care the task is easily accomplished without. However, piston rings are very brittle. If they are expanded too much, they will break. Fit the middle and top compression rings in the same manner. The top ring is identified by its grey-coloured coating on the outside edge. Arrange the three ring-end gaps so that they are spaced out at 120° intervals.

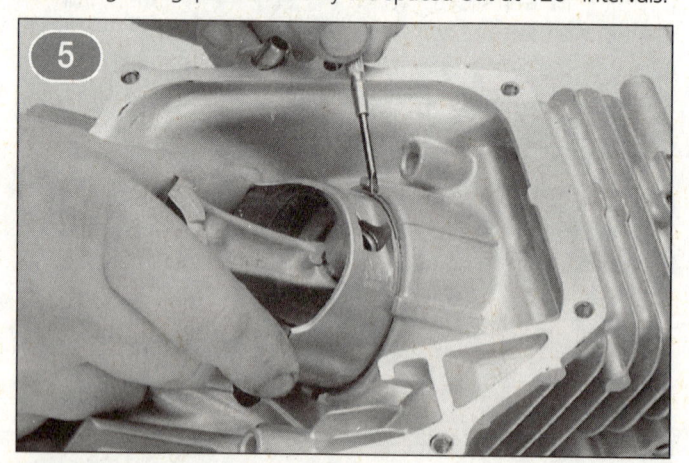

5 Smear the piston rings and cylinder bore with oil. Ensure that the valve cut-outs in the piston crown are on the timing belt side. Insert the piston crown into the cylinder bore. Slowly push the piston into the bore, feeding the piston rings into the lead-in at the lip of the bore. Take great care during this procedure, as the rings are easily broken. Stop and investigate any undue resistance. With the rings successfully engaged in the bore, push the piston/connecting road assembly to the top of the cylinder.

Honda GCV 135 OHC 4.5 hp 4-stroke engine

6 Oil the crankcase bearing journals and insert the crankshaft, tapered end first, into the crankcase. Take care not to damage the oil seal lip.

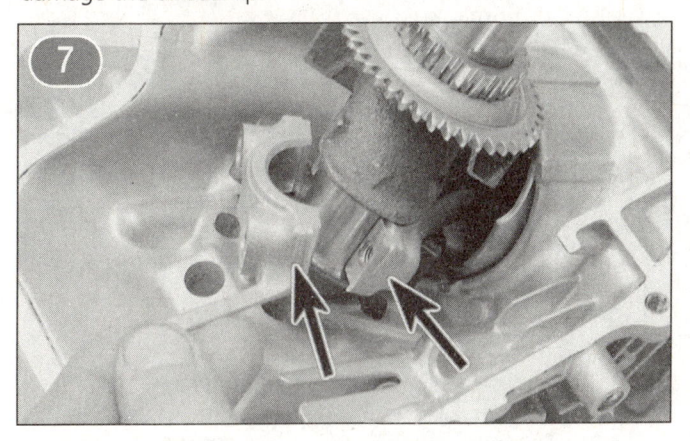

7 Smear the big-end journal with oil, and pull the connecting rod down to engage with the bearing journal of the crankshaft. Fit the bearing cap with the cast lug towards the inlet port side (arrowed). If you have a suitable torque wrench, tighten the bearing cap retaining bolts to the torque given in Technical Data. If not, tighten the bolts securely.

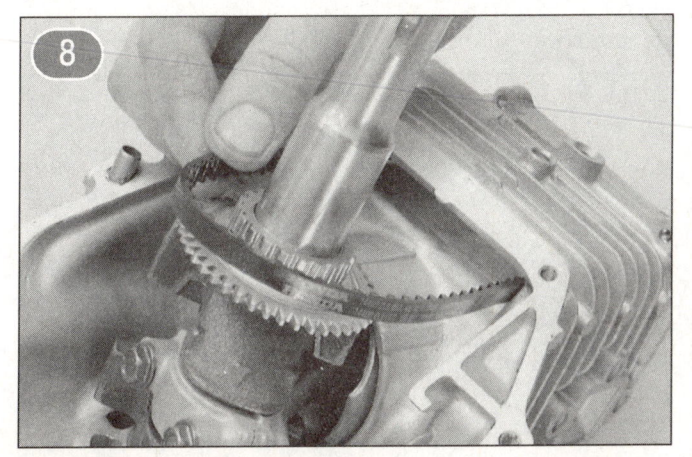

8 Fit the camshaft drive belt over the end of the crankshaft, and up through the tunnel. Engage the belt with the drive pulley teeth. If re-using a belt, ensure that it is refitted in it original direction of rotation.

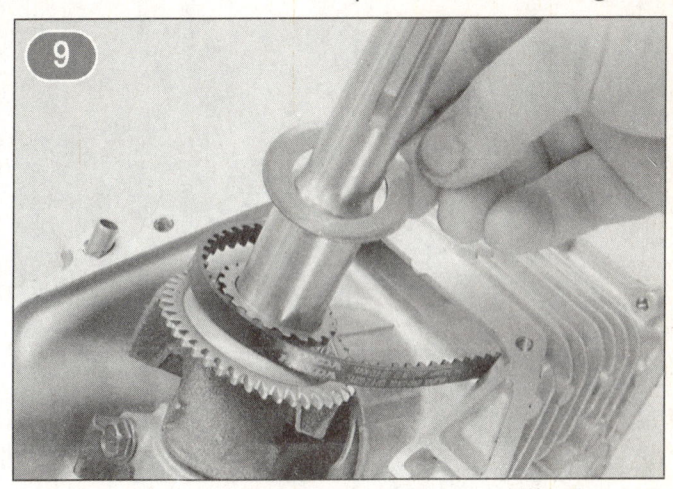

9 Refit the bevelled washer over the end of the crankshaft, concave side facing outwards.

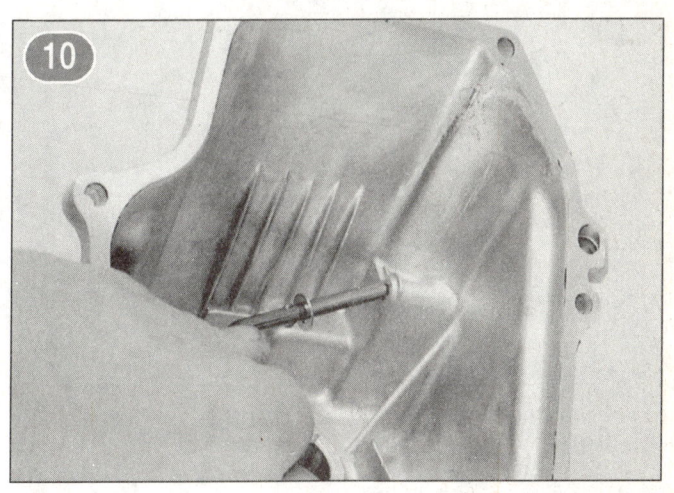

10 Insert the governor arm and washer through the hole in the crankcase.

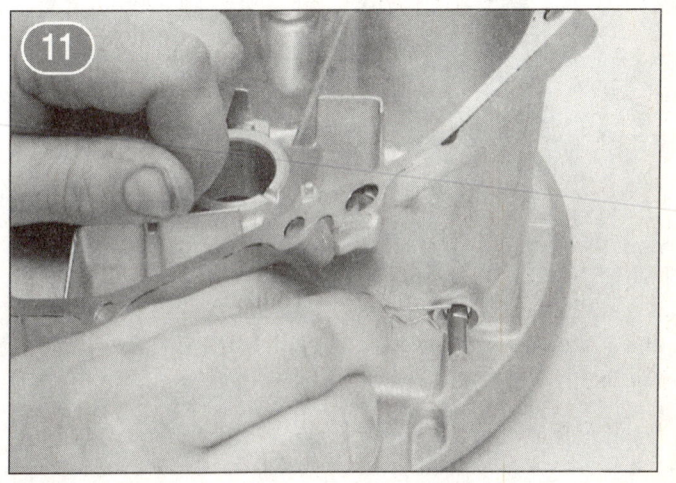

11 The arm is secured with an 'R-clip', which fits into its locating groove in the arm on the outside of the case.

Chapter 12

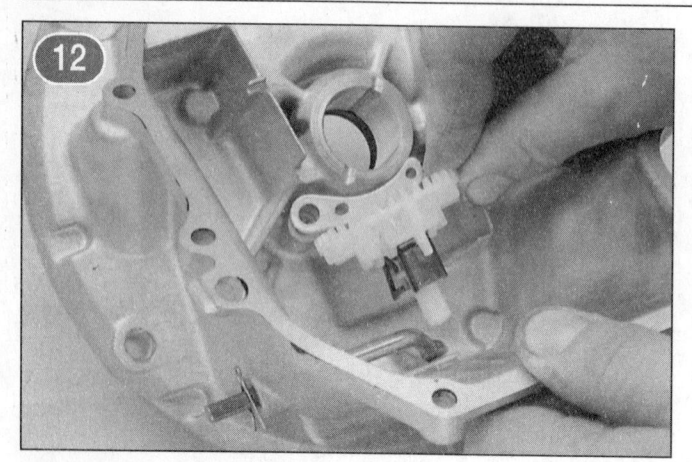

12 Mount the governor/oil slinger assembly over the two locating lugs in the crankcase. Tighten the retaining bolt securely. Ensure that the governor head aligns with the arm.

13 Check that the two crankcase locating dowels are in place (arrowed).

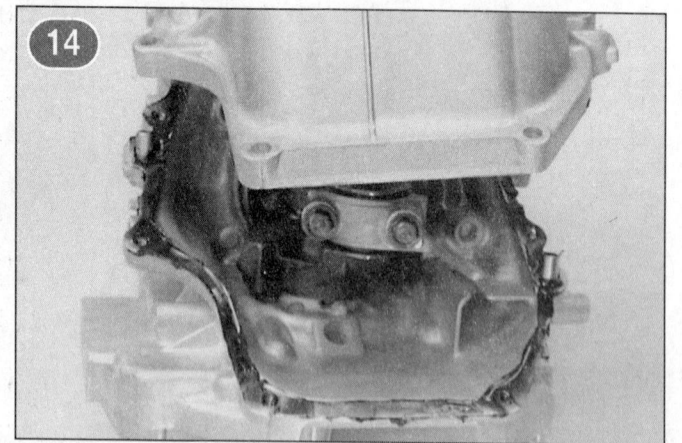

14 Smear the gasket face with non-hardening RTV-type sealant. Oil the main bearing journal, and carefully lower the other crankcase half into place. It may be necessary to turn the crankshaft a little, as the crankcase is fitted, to ensure that the governor gear teeth mesh with the corresponding teeth on the crankshaft. Take care not to damage the oil seal lip. Tighten the eight bolts evenly in a diagonal sequence. Rotate the crankshaft to check for freedom of movement.

15 Turn the crankshaft to Top Dead Centre (TDC). In this position the piston, viewed through the spark plug hole, will be at its highest point, and both crankshaft keyways at the twelve o'clock position (arrowed).

16 Gently push the camshaft drive belt towards the valves, and place the camshaft in position. Check the condition of the O-ring, and insert the pulley spindle so that the flat in the end of the spindle faces up towards, and is parallel with the cam box cover gasket face.

17 Rotate the camshaft pulley until the timing marks align with the cam box gasket face (arrowed).

12•6

Honda GCV 135 OHC 4.5 hp 4-stroke engine

18 Check to ensure that the crankshaft is still at TDC, and slide the belt onto the pulley without turning the camshaft or crankshaft. With the belt fitted, check that the timing marks align and that crankshaft is at TDC. Rotate the crankshaft two full revolutions, and check again. There is no provision for tensioning the belt.

19 Refit the rocker arms to their original locations. The rocker arm pivot shafts must be inserted from the spark plug side.

20 Both valve clearances should be checked with the crankshaft and camshaft at TDC on the compression stroke, as previously set. The clearances are given in Technical Data. If the clearances require adjustment, loosen the relevant tappet locknut, turn the tappet until the correct clearance is obtained, and tighten the locknut. Re-check the clearance.

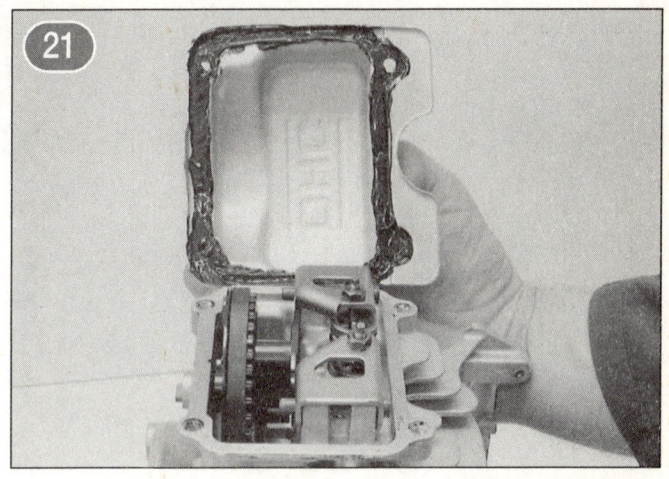

21 Oil the camshaft and followers. Smear some non-hardening RTV-type sealant onto the cam box cover gasket face, and refit the cover. Tighten the four bolts securely. Refit the spark plug.

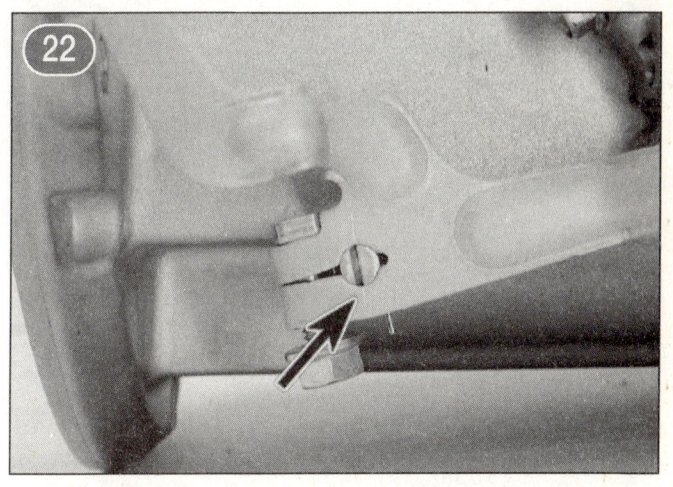

22 Refit the governor lever to the arm, aligning the previously made marks (arrowed). Tighten the pinch-bolt.

23 Check the condition of the engine breather valve, cover and pipe. Refit the cover. Tighten the retaining bolt.

Chapter 12

24 Refit the flywheel brake assembly, and tighten the two retaining bolts securely. Do not reconnect the spring at this stage.

25 Refit the Woodruff (half moon) key and slide the flywheel over the tapered end of the crankshaft.

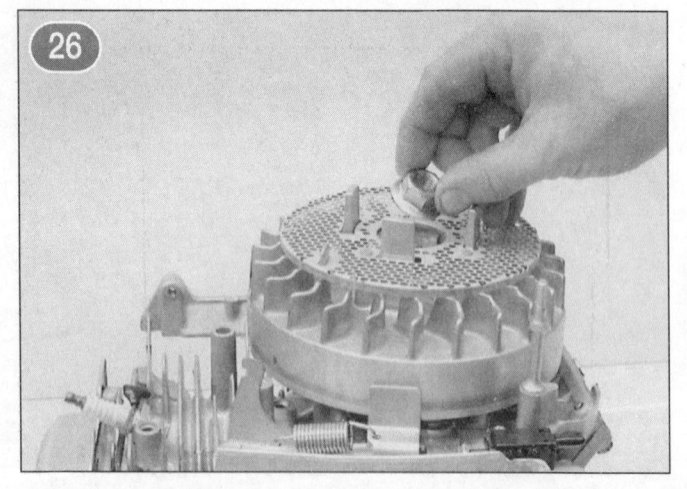

26 Refit the retaining nut.

27 Use a strap wrench to prevent the flywheel from turning. Tighten the retaining nut to the torque given in Technical Data. The help of an assistant may be necessary to steady the engine.

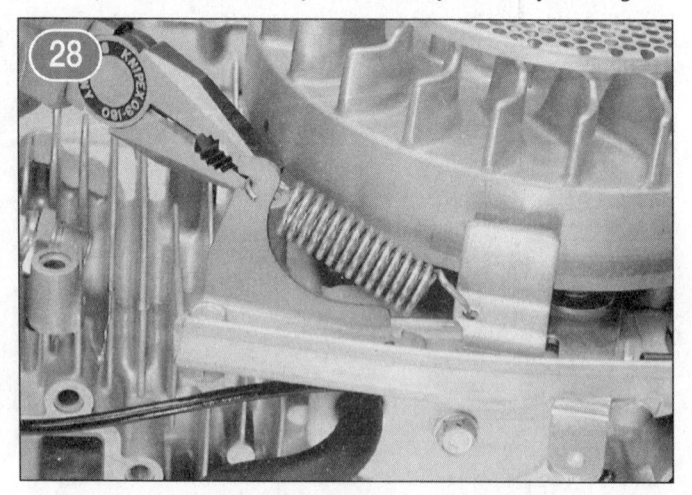

28 Reconnect the flywheel brake spring.

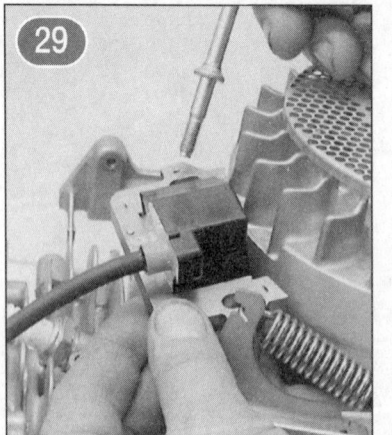

29 Refit the ignition magneto, with the elongated mounting bolt screwed into the hole in the centre of the cylinder, and the earthing wire terminal facing out. Before tightening both mounting bolts, turn the flywheel so that the magnets are on the opposite side to the magneto. Using feeler gauges, check the air gap between the two magneto armature legs, and the flywheel. The correct air gap is given in Technical Data. The mounting holes in the magneto legs are slotted. Move the magneto until the correct air gap is obtained. Tighten the bolts securely, and reconnect the earthing wire. Refit the HT cap to the spark plug.

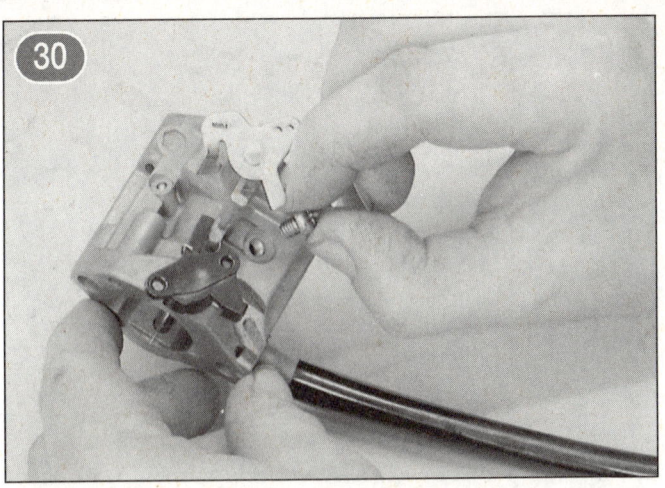

Honda GCV 135 OHC 4.5 hp 4-stroke engine

30 Refit the air jet screw to the carburettor body.

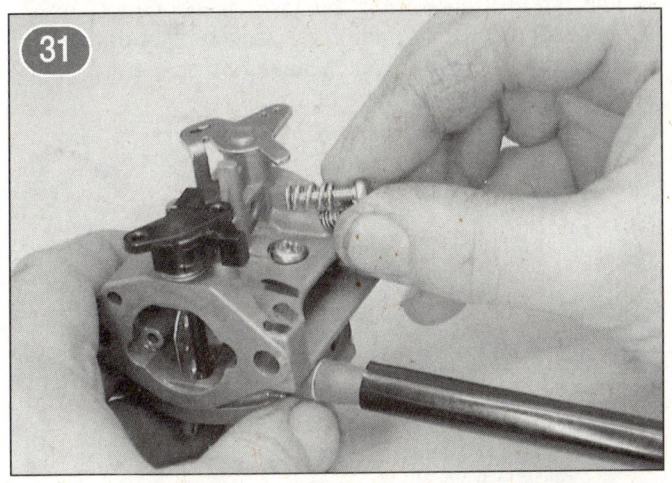

31 Referring to the notes made during their removal, refit the throttle stop and mixture adjustment screws. The base setting for the mixture is to turn the screw in until it seats, then one full turn out.

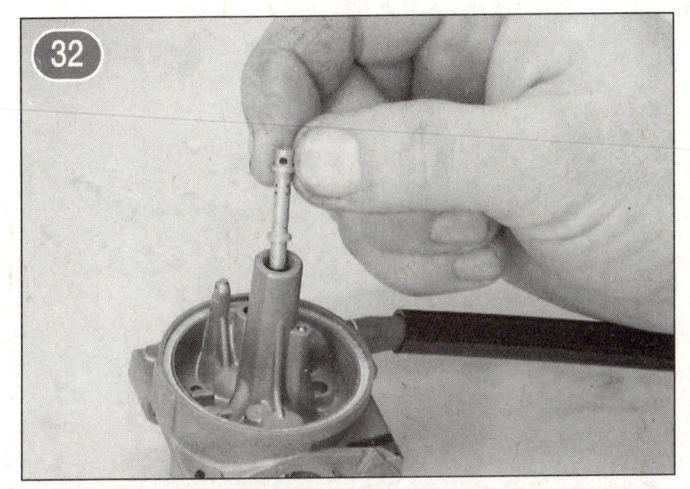

32 Refit the emulsion tube, small holes nearest the carburettor venturi.

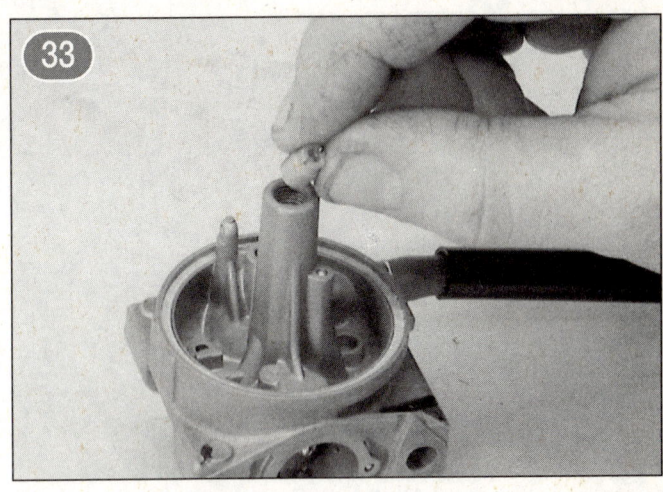

33 Screw in the main jet.

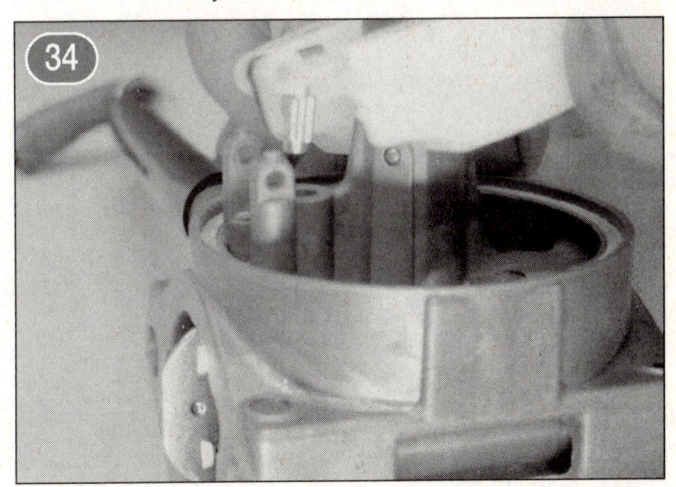

34 Re-attach the needle valve to the float, and insert the valve into its seat.

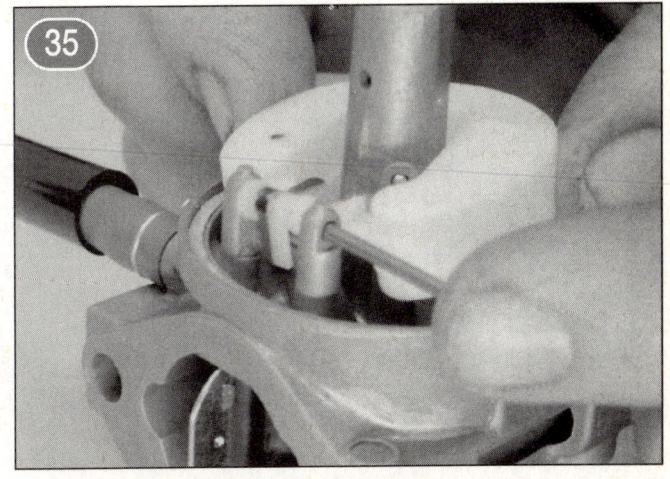

35 Align the float with the pivot hole, and insert the pivot pin. There is no provision for adjusting the float height.

12•9

Chapter 12

36 If necessary, fit a new float bowl gasket, and refit the bowl.

37 Check the condition of the fibre washer, and secure the float bowl with the retaining bolt.

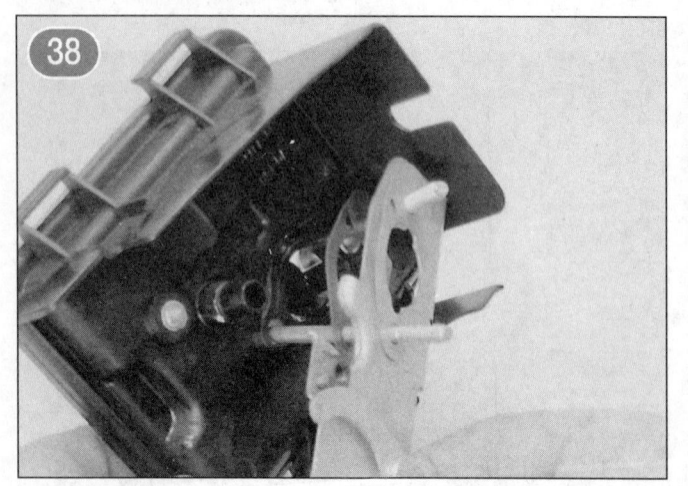

38 The carburettor, linkage plate and air filter housing must be fitted as one assembly. Using a new gasket, fit the air filter housing to the linkage plate, finger tighten the retaining bolt.

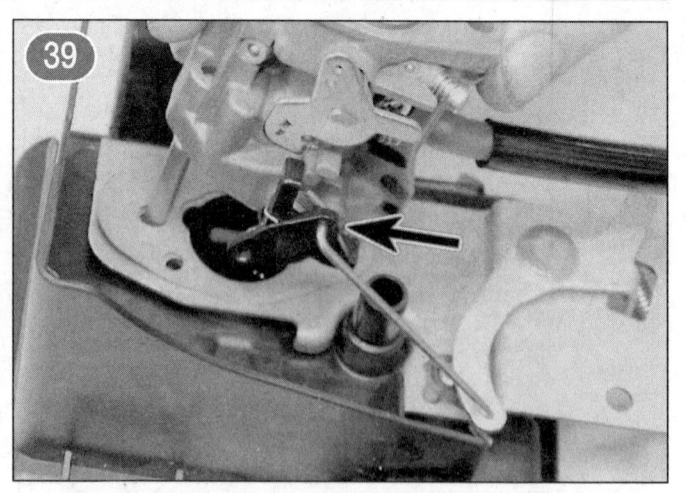

39 Insert the two carburettor mounting bolts through the assembly to assist in aligning the gaskets. Engage the choke linkage with arm on the carburettor (arrowed), and the operating lever on the linkage plate, and slide the carburettor onto the retaining bolts.

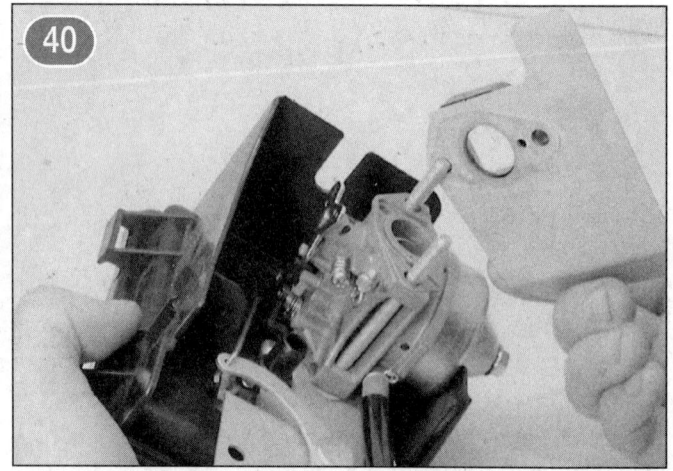

40 Using new gaskets, slide the heat shield and insulator block onto the carburettor retaining bolts.

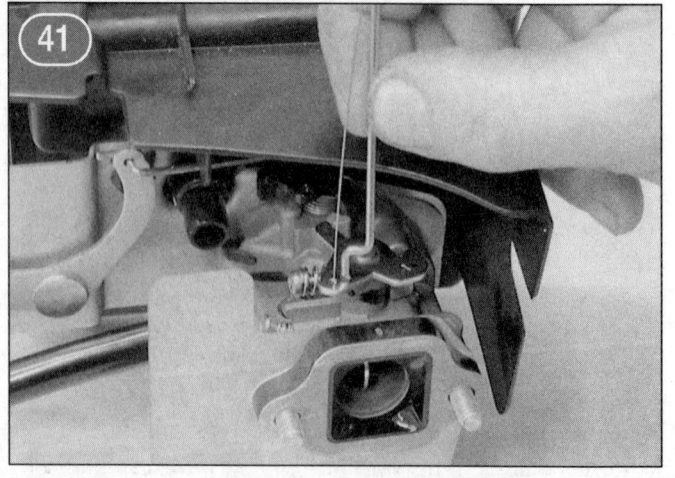

41 Reconnect the governor linkage and spring to the throttle arm and governor lever.

Honda GCV 135 OHC 4.5 hp 4-stroke engine

42 Engage the carburettor mounting bolts with their holes in the cylinder head, but do not tighten at this stage.

43 Fit the linkage plate retaining bolt. Tighten all four carburettor/linkage plate/air filter housing bolts securely.

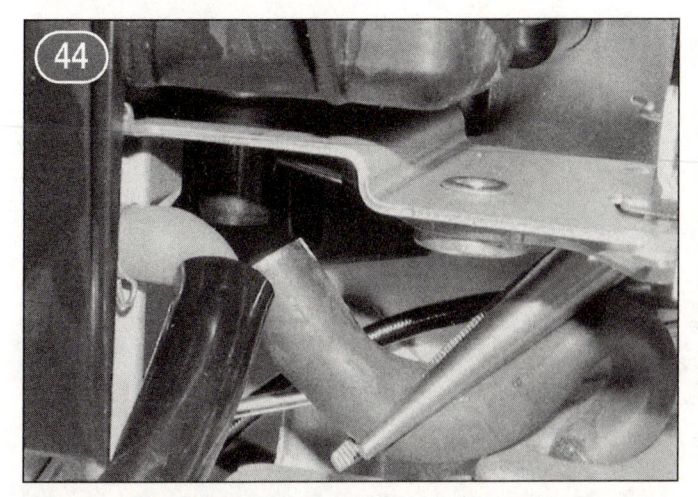

44 Turn the engine on its side, and from underneath, reconnect the engine breather pipe to the air filter housing.

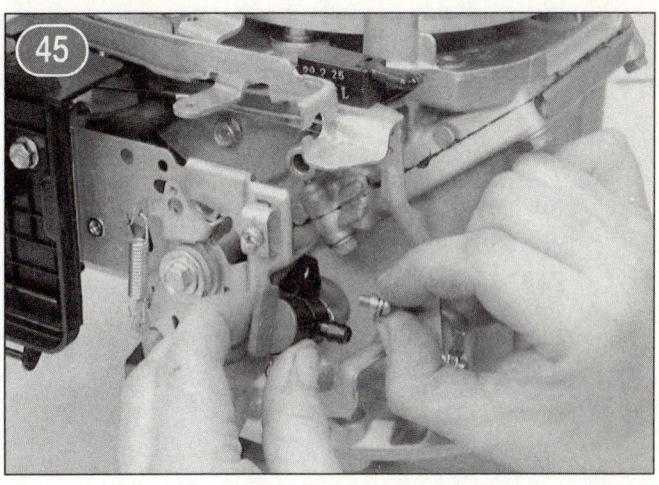

45 Refit the fuel tap to the end of the linkage plate, tighten the retaining screw, and reconnect the carburettor-to-fuel tap pipe. Secure the pipe with the retaining clip.

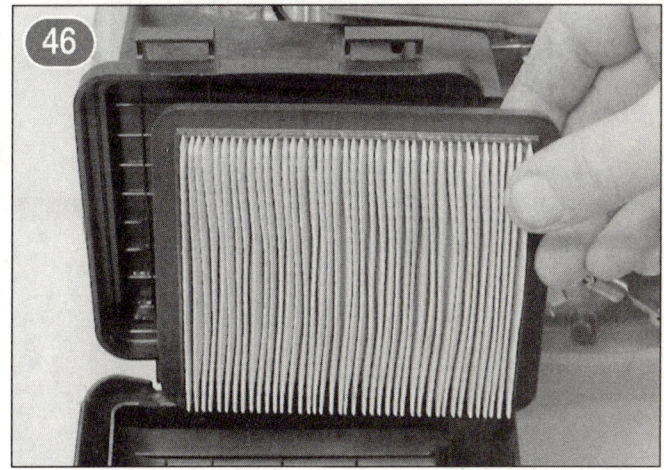

46 Fit the air filter element into the housing, and clip the filter cover into place.

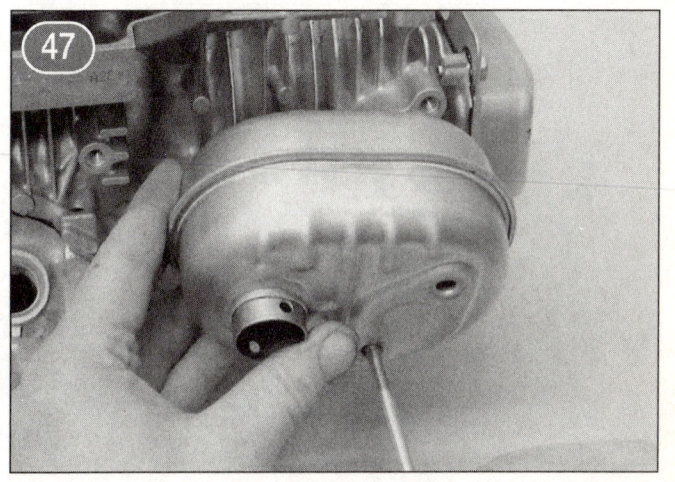

47 The exhaust system mounts onto the cylinder head without a gasket. Fit the system and tighten the two retaining bolts securely.

Chapter 12

48 Refit the exhaust shield. Tighten the three retaining bolts securely.

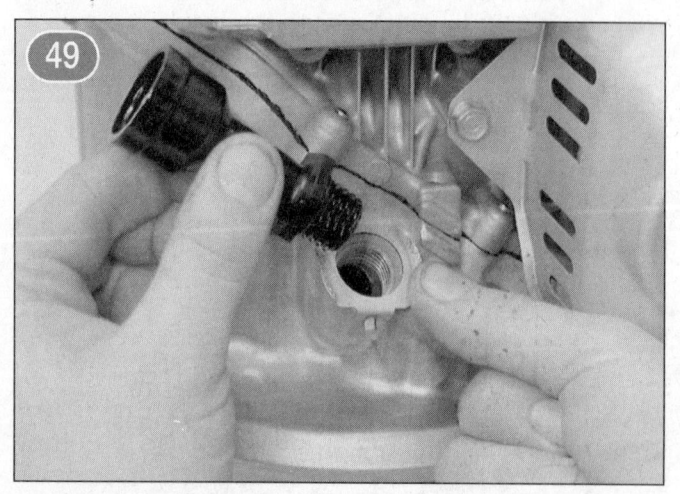

49 Place the tab washer over the oil filler hole in the crankcase, ensuring that the locating lug engages correctly. Screw in the filler spout, and secure it in place by bending the tabs against the nut.

50 Refit the fuel tank/cowling over the mounting studs, ensuring that the HT lead engages with the slot on the underside of the cowling.

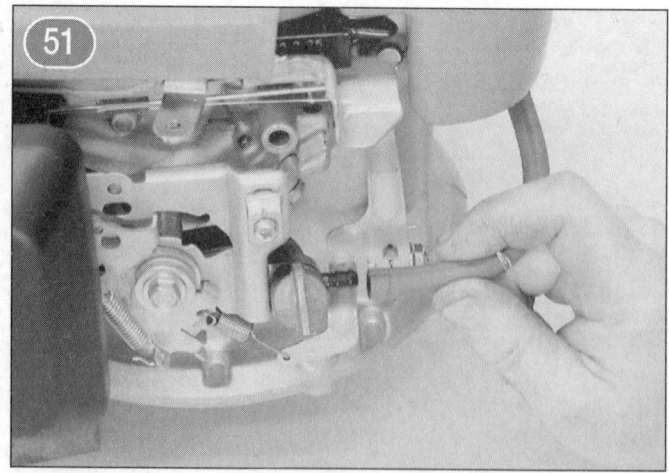

51 Reconnect the fuel tank-to-tap pipe, and secure with the retaining clips.

52 Fit the starter assembly over the mounting studs, and tighten the three retaining nuts securely.
　Refit the engine to its application.
　Remember to add the correct grade and quantity of engine oil.

Honda GCV 135 OHC 4.5 hp 4-stroke engine

Starter repair

Undo the three retaining nuts, and lift the starter assembly from the engine cowling.

Pull the rope to its full extension, and lock the pulley in place by inserting a screwdriver (or similar) through the spokes of the pulley and one of the slots of the outer cover.

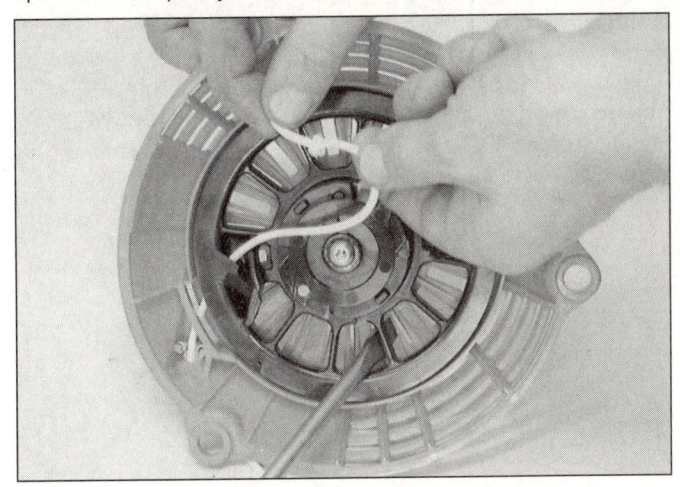

To replace the rope: Where the rope goes through the pulley, cut off the knot and pull the rope from the starter. Feed the new rope through the hole in the outer cover, and through the hole in the pulley. Tie the knot. Feed the other end of the rope through the hole in the starter handle, again tie the knot. Tension the rope and remove the screwdriver from the pulley spokes. Be prepared for the spring to violently rewind the starter rope. Refit the starter assembly to the engine cowling.

To replace the starter spring: Where the rope goes through the pulley, untie the knot and pull the rope from the starter. The Torx screw that secures the guide plate has a **left-hand thread**. Undo the screw, lift off the guide plate, and remove the spring and starter pawls.

Carefully lift out the pulley, noting the locating slot for the end of the starter spring. Lift out the spring.

Fit the new starter spring to the underside of the pulley. Ensure that the outer end of the spring engages correctly with the locating slot in the pulley (arrowed).

Refit the pulley to the outer cover, engaging the inner end of the spring with the locating lug in the centre of the cover (arrowed).

12•13

Chapter 12

Check the starter pawls for damage or excessive wear, and refit them to the pulley. Insert the central spring.

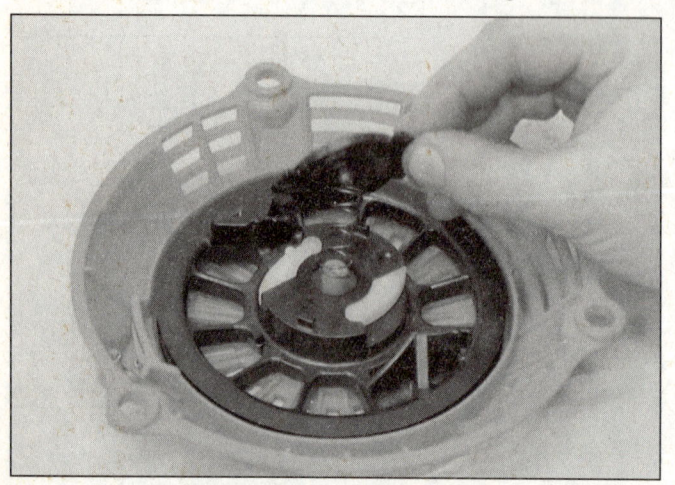

Refit the guide plate onto the pawls, ensuring that the pawls locating pins engage with the slots on the underside of the guide plate. Tighten the retaining Torx screw (**left-hand thread**).

Carefully wind the pulley anti-clockwise approximately six turns, until the rope hole in the pulley aligns with the corresponding hole in the outer cover. The exact number of turns depends on the length of rope. Lock the pulley in this position by inserting a screwdriver (or similar) through the pulley spokes and one of the slots in the outer cover. Exercise extreme caution during this procedure. It will take some effort to wind the spring up, and should the screwdriver slip, the pulley will spin violently.

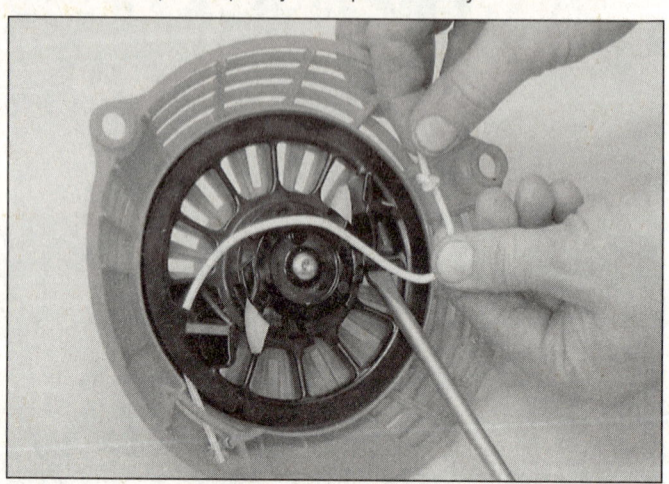

Feed the rope through the hole in the outer cover and the hole in the pulley. Re-tie the knot. Tension the rope and remove the screwdriver from the pulley spokes. Allow the spring to rewind the rope. Check for correct operation. Refit the starter assembly to the engine cowling.

Tecumseh 3.5 hp/Vantage 35 4-stroke engine

13

Technical data
Dismantling

Reassembly

Technical data

Spark plug gap .... 0.8 mm (0.032 in)
Armature air gap .... 0.37 mm (0.015 in)
Valve clearance:
   Inlet and exhaust .... 0.25 mm (0.010 in)
Piston ring gap .... 0.18 to 0.43 mm (0.007 to 0.017 in)
Oil .... SAE 30 or SAE 10W-30

Note: *SAE 10W is an acceptable substitute.* **Do not use SAE 10W-40**

Chapter 13

Dismantling

Before starting to dismantle, read Chapter 5. The procedures outlined apply to all engines and if adopted, will ensure an orderly and methodical approach that will make both dismantling and reassembly much easier. The following assumes the engine has been removed from its application.

- [ ] Disconnect the plug lead. Drain the oil from the engine.
- [ ] Disconnect the fuel pipe from the tank.
- [ ] Disconnect the air cleaner housing from the carburettor inlet.
- [ ] Remove the engine cowling complete with the air cleaner housing, leaving the fuel tank and recoil starter behind on the engine.
- [ ] Remove the recoil starter from the engine. Remove the fuel tank with the starter handle in it.
- [ ] Note the positions of the governor spring and the link from the governor lever to the throttle butterfly lever, so that they can be reassembled in the same holes. Disconnect the spring and the link and remove the carburettor.
- [ ] Grip the engine drive shaft in a soft jaw vice and remove the flywheel nut. Do not overtighten the vice. If the shaft turns while loosening the flywheel nut, replace the cutter sleeve and key on the drive shaft and grip the sleeve in the vice.
- [ ] Remove the flywheel from the taper (see Chapter 2).
- [ ] Remove the offset key from the drive shaft; remove the plastic sleeve from the shaft.
- [ ] Remove the valve cover.
- [ ] Remove the cylinder head.
- [ ] Remove the crankcase cover, disengaging the power drive pinion as it is withdrawn. Remove the oil pump from the camshaft.
- [ ] Remove camshaft.
- [ ] Mark the big end cap for reassembly in the same position, then remove it.
- [ ] Withdraw the piston upwards from the cylinder. Ensure that the connecting rod does not score the bore as it passes through.
- [ ] Mark the cam followers for reassembly in the same holes, then remove them.
- [ ] Remove the valves.
- [ ] Remove the breather assembly from the lower part of the crankcase.

Reassembly

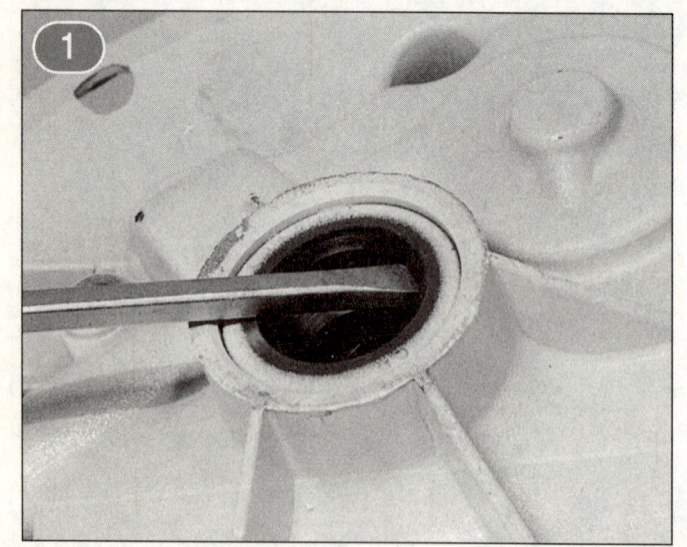

1 Fit new oil seals in the crankcase if necessary, as described for previous engines.

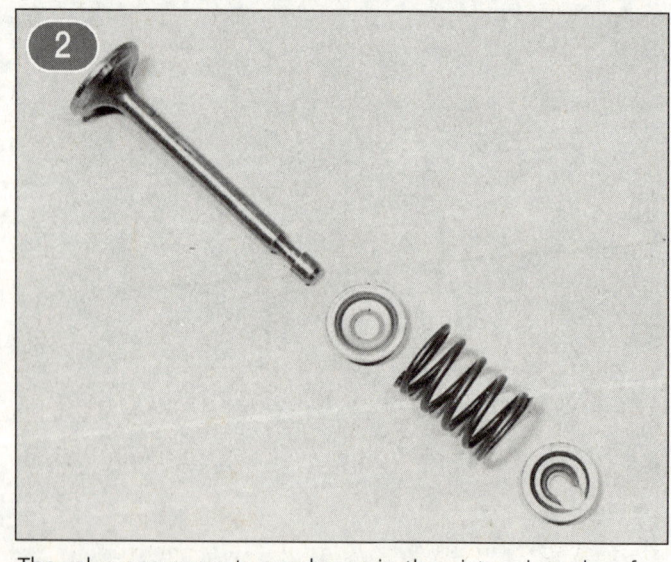

2 The valve components are shown in the picture in order of assembly.

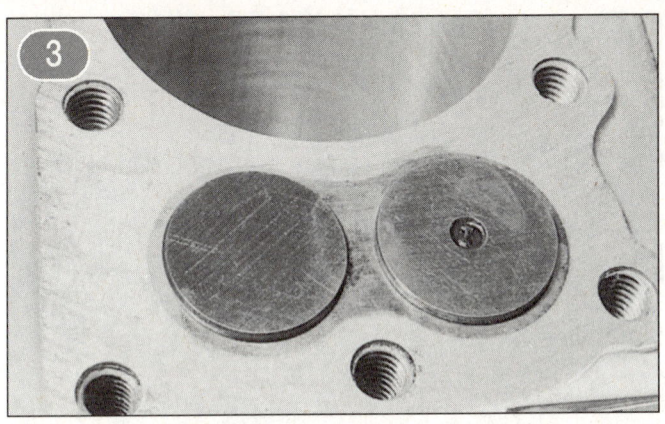

Tecumseh 3.5 hp/Vantage 35 4-stroke engine

3 The valve marked with an I in the centre is the inlet valve. Be careful not to transpose the valves.

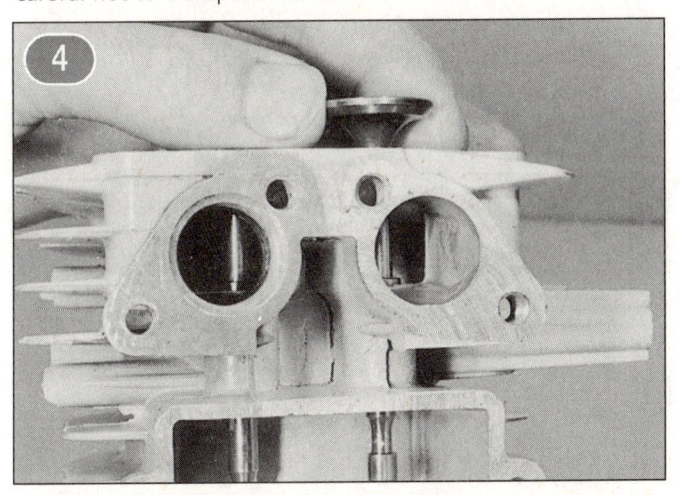

4 Insert the valve into the guide.

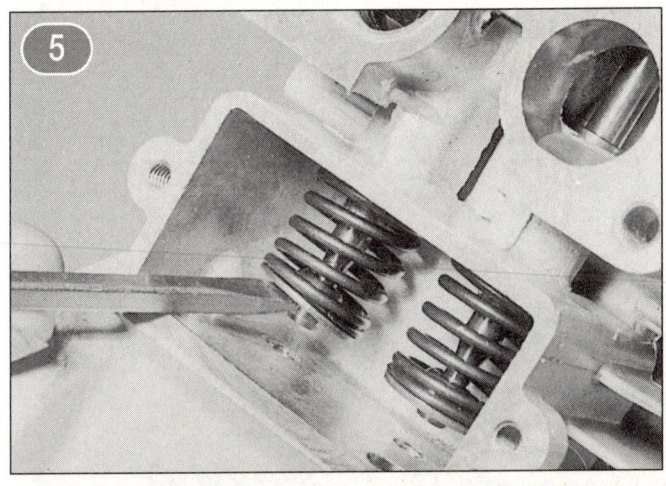

5 Fit the plain hole collar onto the valve stem, dished side to the valve chest. Place the spring against the collar. Fit the slotted collar onto the valve stem, dish into the spring, and offset to allow the valve stem through the wide end of the slot. Lever up the collar and move it sideways so that the narrow end of the slot engages under the shoulder on the valve stem, this locks the spring onto the valve. Fit both valves in an identical manner (this picture shows an exhaust valve).

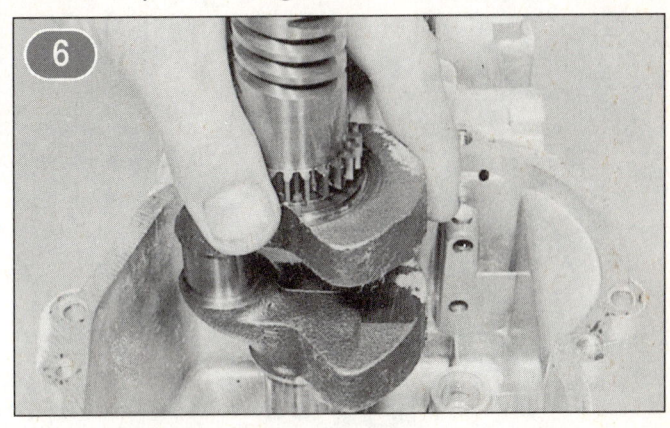

6 Smear crankshaft with oil and insert into the crankcase bearing.

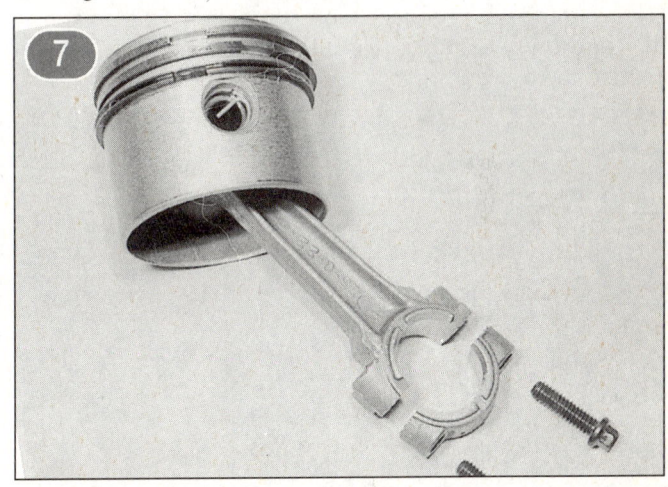

7 Assemble the piston rings and connecting rod on the piston. The rings must be fitted the same way round in the same grooves as when removed. The gudgeon pin and connecting rod must be the same way round as when removed. Ensure circlips are located securely. When assembled in the cylinder, the serial numbers on the connecting rod must face the open end of the crankcase.

8 Fit a piston ring clamp to the piston. Oil the cylinder walls. Insert the piston from the top, taking care not to scratch the bore with the connecting rod. Press the piston out of the clamp, tapping gently with a piece of wood if necessary. If an obstruction occurs, do not force the piston in, stop and investigate.

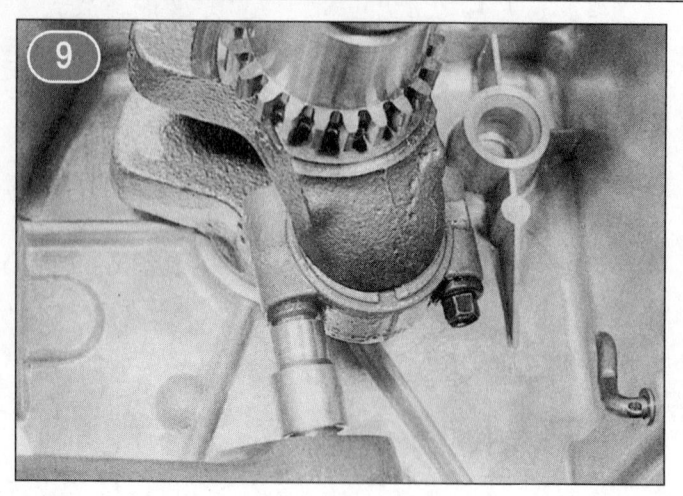

Chapter 13

9 Oil the crankpin and engage the big end on it. Fit the cap the correct way round, as marked during dismantling. Tighten the two bolts firmly.

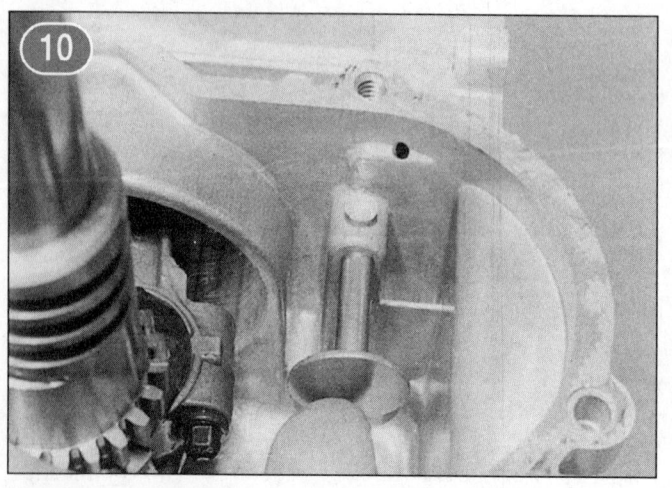

10 Oil the cam followers and insert them in the same holes in which they were originally fitted, as marked during dismantling.

11 Oil the camshaft bearing and insert the camshaft into the crankcase. Mesh the cam gear timing mark in line with the mark on the crankshaft gear.

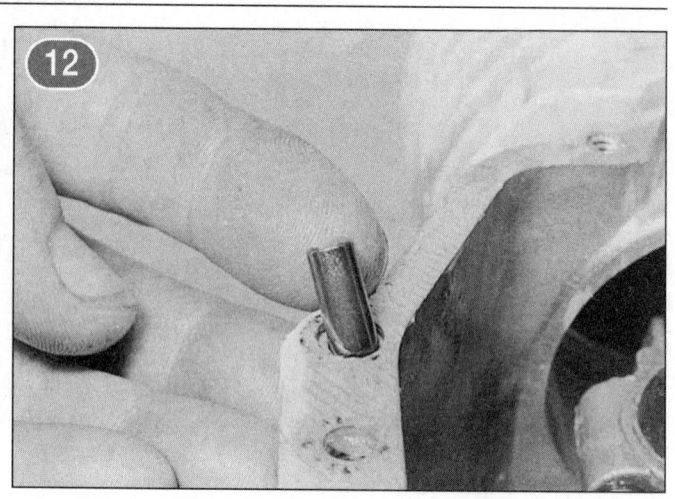

12 Fit the two dowels into the holes in the crankcase. Fit a new crankcase gasket.

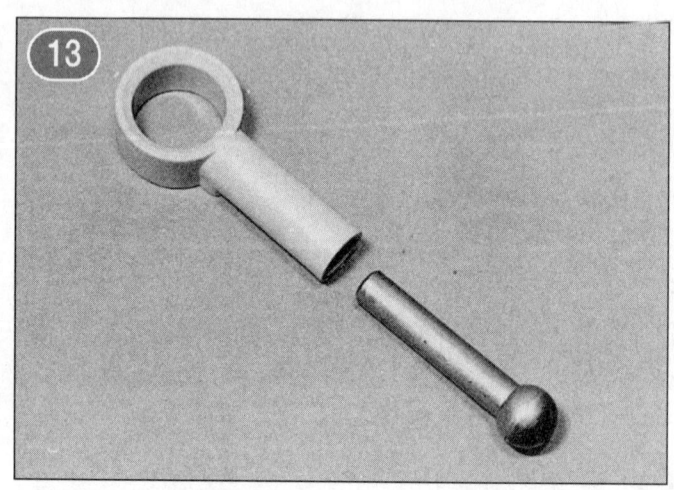

13 Insert the oil pump plunger into the housing.

14 Fit the pump onto the camshaft, with the chamfered side of the hole in the white plastic housing facing down onto the cam gear.

13•4

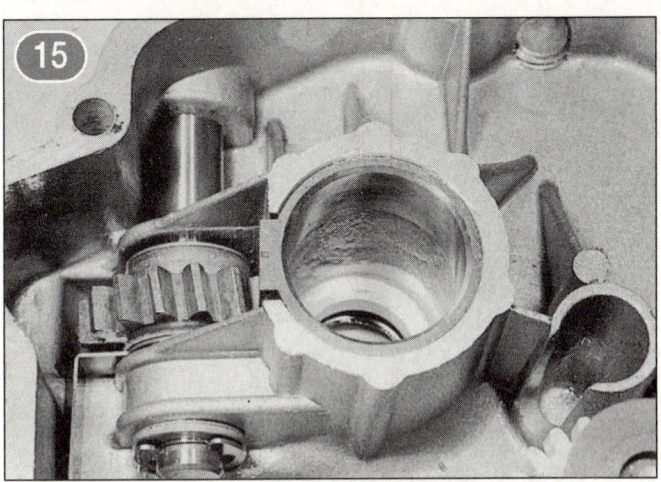

Tecumseh 3.5 hp/Vantage 35 4-stroke engine

15 The final drive shaft and pinion assembly is held in the crankcase by a circlip with a flat washer behind it.

16 The pinion is keyed to the shaft and has a thrust washer on either side of it, one with an anti-spin angled leg. Removal and installation to fit a new pinion or shaft is straightforward and can be carried out from the picture.

17 Check the governor slider and weights for freedom of operation and signs of wear. If faulty, the governor should be renewed as a complete unit. To remove the governor, prise the C-clip out of the groove in the shaft, withdraw the spool, remove the second circlip and lift off the gear assembly and the washer under it. Reassembly is the opposite sequence.

18 The crankcase cover ready for installation is shown in the picture.

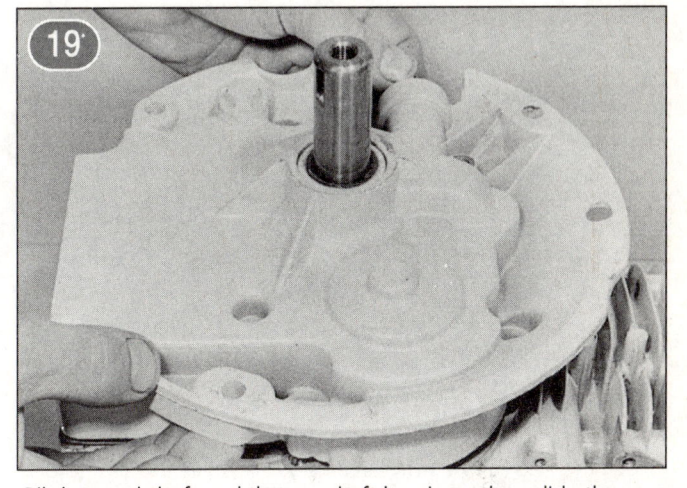

19 Oil the crankshaft and the camshaft bearings, then slide the cover onto the crankshaft. Turn the pinion shaft slightly to engage the pinion with the worm on the crankshaft if necessary. Locate the cover on the dowels. Check through the engine breather hole that the oil pump plunger ball-end is correctly in its housing, and that the governor lever is resting correctly against the governor spindle. Fit and tighten diagonally the six bolts and spring washers that secure the housing.

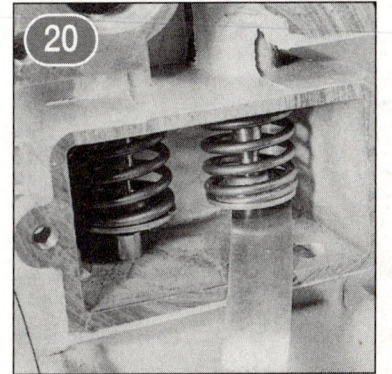

20 Check the valve clearances. Both valves should have a clearance of 0.25 mm (0.010 in). Adjustment of valve clearance is by grinding the tip of the valve stem to increase it or grinding in the valve seat to reduce it, but there are limits to the amount of seat grinding possible. In bad cases, new valves may need fitting. This requires professional attention and the use of special tools.

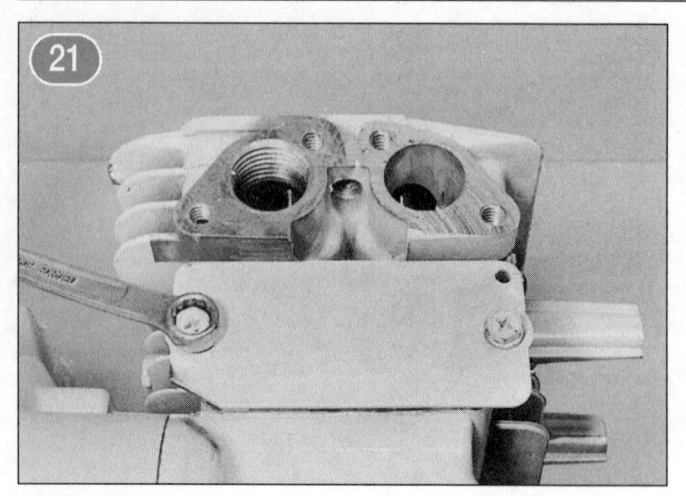

Chapter 13

21 Replace the valve cover with the chamfered corner in the bottom left position.

22 Check the engine breather assembly. The valve in the bottom of the cup must be free, clean and undamaged. Wash the steel wool element in solvent and dry it. Place the circular baffle on the shoulder half way down the cup. Insert the element onto the baffle.

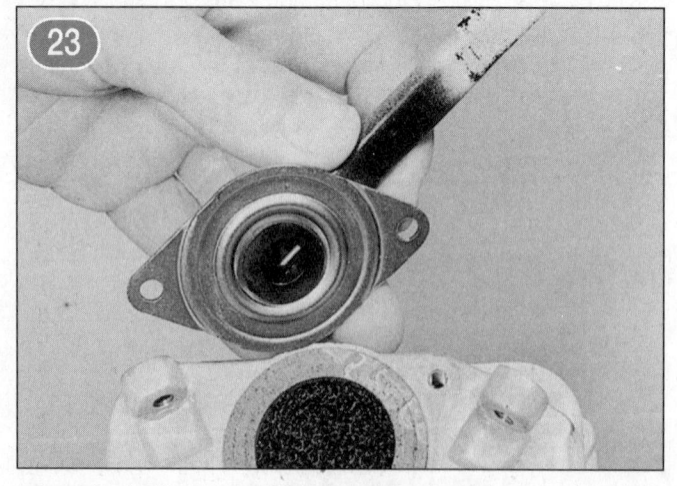

23 Insert the baffle cup assembly into the hole in the crankcase. Fit a new gasket...

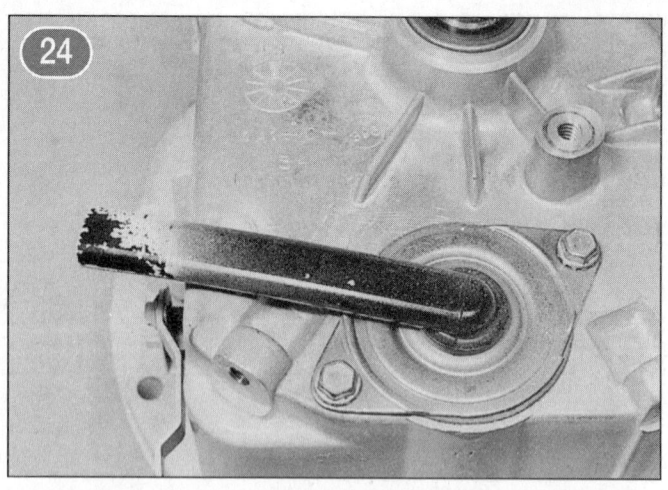

24 ... then fit the cover and tube and secure with the two bolts and shakeproof washers. Ensure that TOP stamped on the cover is towards the top of the engine.

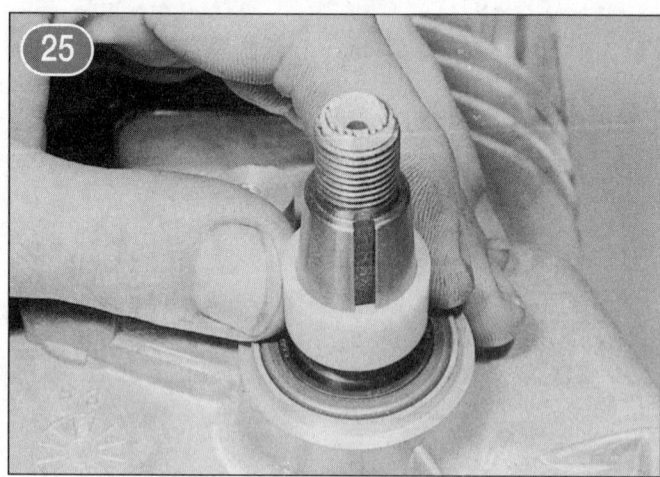

25 Fit the plastic sleeve on the crankshaft with its key in the crankshaft groove.

26 Fit the offset key in the slot as shown in the photo, with the longer offset to the left.

Tecumseh 3.5 hp/Vantage 35 4-stroke engine

27 Fit the flywheel onto the crankshaft aligned with the key...

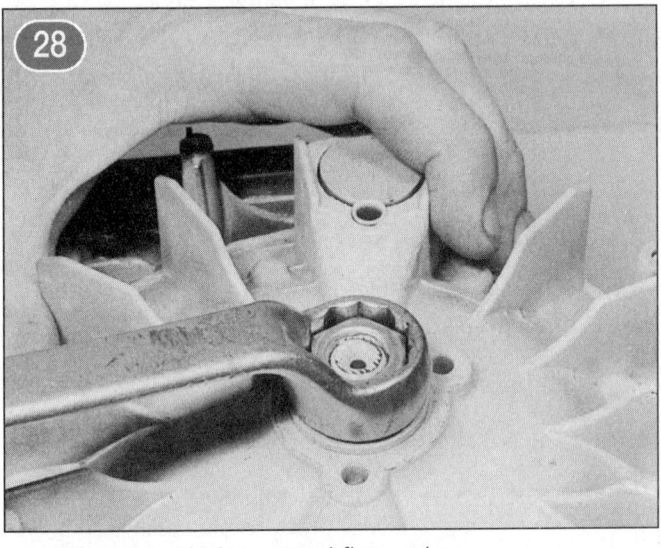

28 ... and secure with the nut and flat washer.

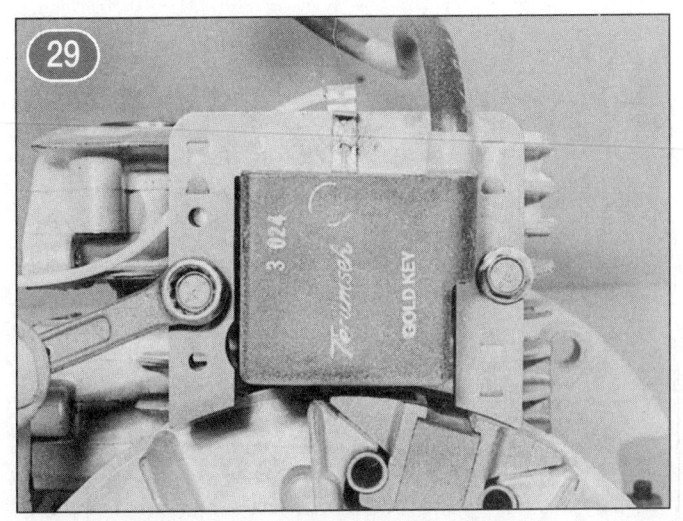

29 Fit the ignition unit and using a non-ferrous feeler gauge...

30 ... set an air gap of 0.37mm (0.015 in).

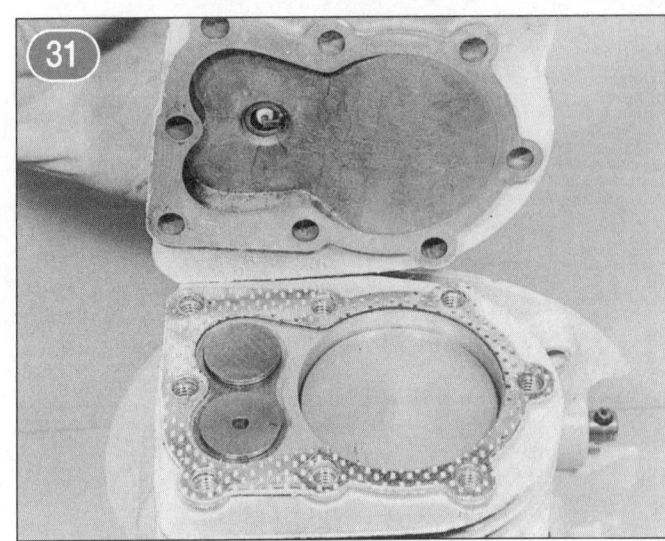

31 Fit a new cylinder head gasket and fit the cylinder head, tightening down a little at a time on each bolt in a diagonal sequence.

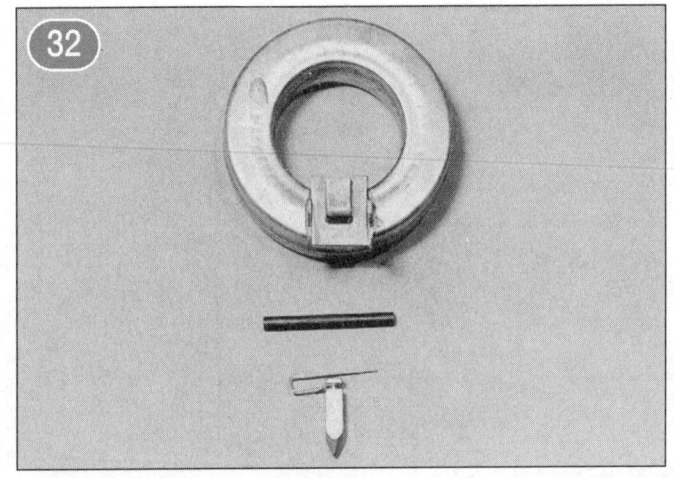

32 The float components are shown in the picture. Check the end of the needle valve for ridging or other damage and renew if necessary.

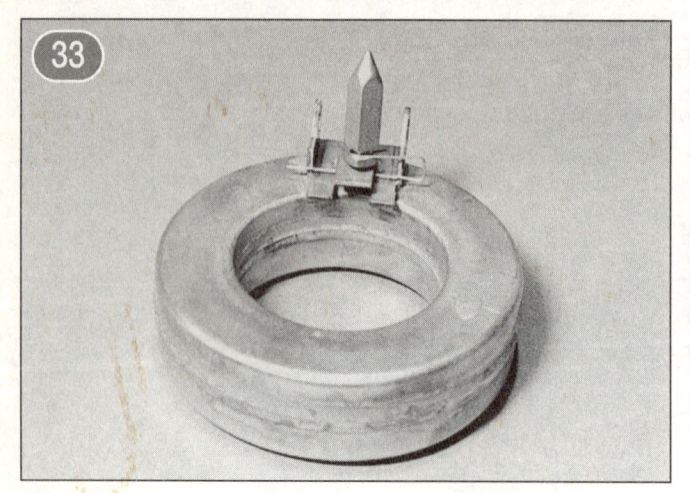

Chapter 13

33 Assemble the needle valve on the float with the clip.

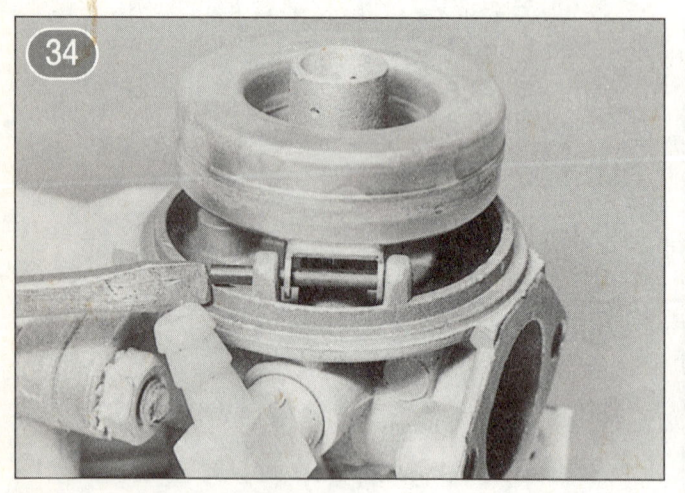

34 Position the float hinge between the carburettor hinge lugs, with the needle valve inserted in the fuel entry hole. Insert the hinge pin.

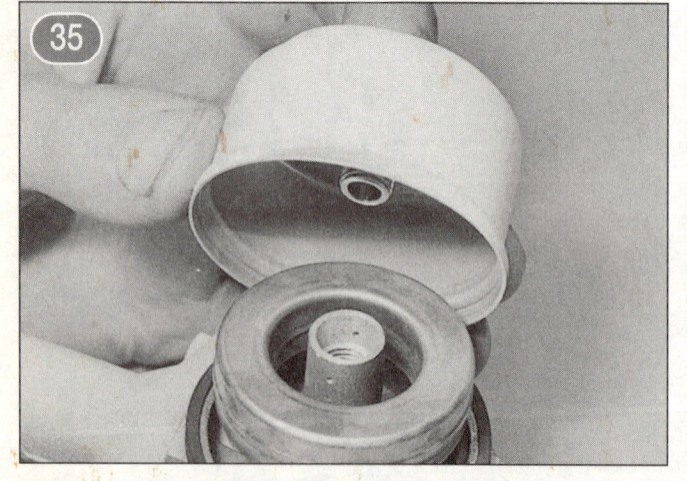

35 Inspect the float bowl seal for damage or distortion and renew if necessary. Fit the bowl onto the carburettor.

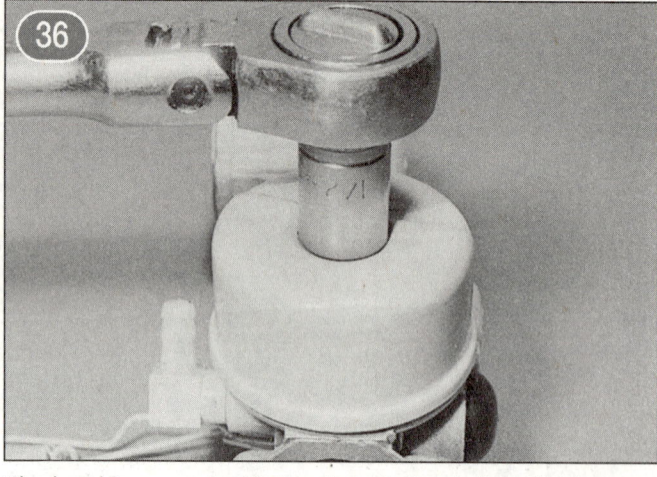

36 The bowl is secured with the threaded main jet. Check the main jet for cleanliness and damage. Rinse and blow to clean it. Do not use a pin or wire on the metered holes or they will be damaged and accurate metering lost.

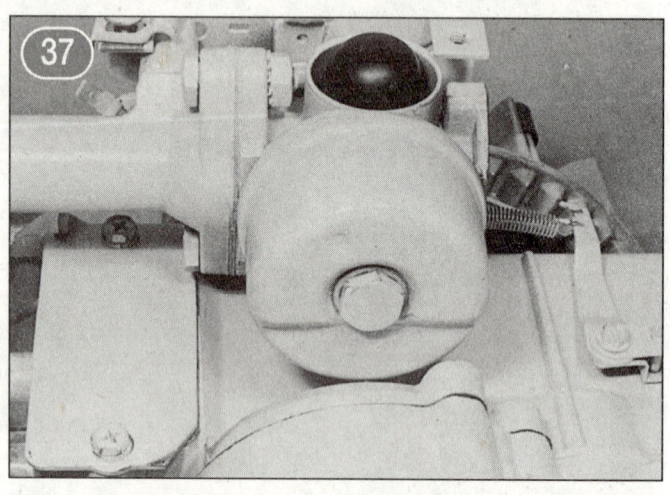

37 The step on the float bowl must be located as shown in the photo to allow full movement of the float.

38 Fit the carburettor and linkage plate to the engine using a new gasket. Two screws and spring washers are used to secure the carburettor.

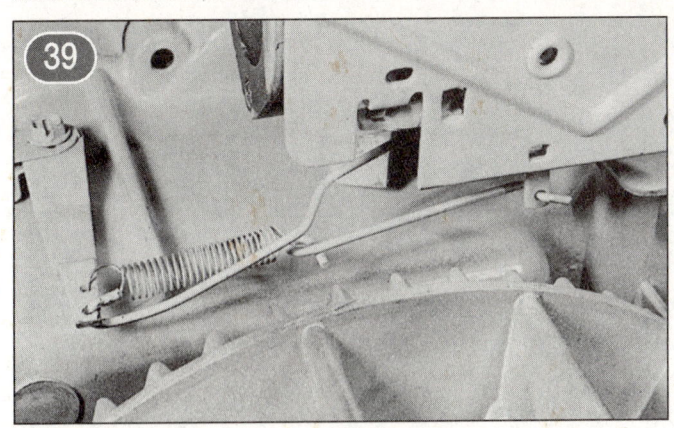

Tecumseh 3.5 hp/Vantage 35 4-stroke engine

39 Connect the link from the throttle butterfly to the hole at the tip of the governor lever. Connect the spring to the next hole in the governor lever, and the link to the lever on the control plate.

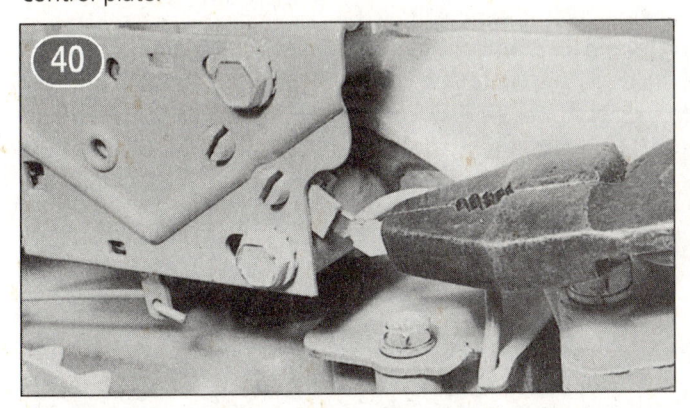

40 Connect the earth lead to the spade connector on the linkage plate.

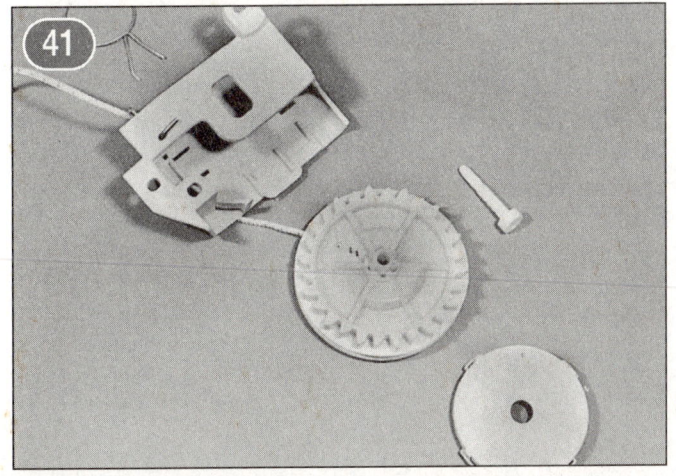

41 Connect the fuel pipe to the carburettor. If the recoil starter needs attention, this should be carried out now as it is difficult to deal with the starter cord after the fuel tank and engine cowl have been installed. The main components of the starter are shown in the picture.

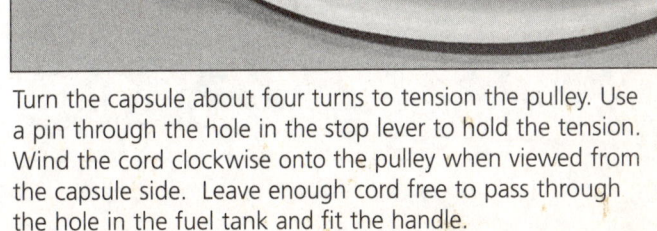

Drive the central pin out by tapping on the chamfered end, then remove the pulley and recoil spring capsule.
Lift the capsule off the pulley.

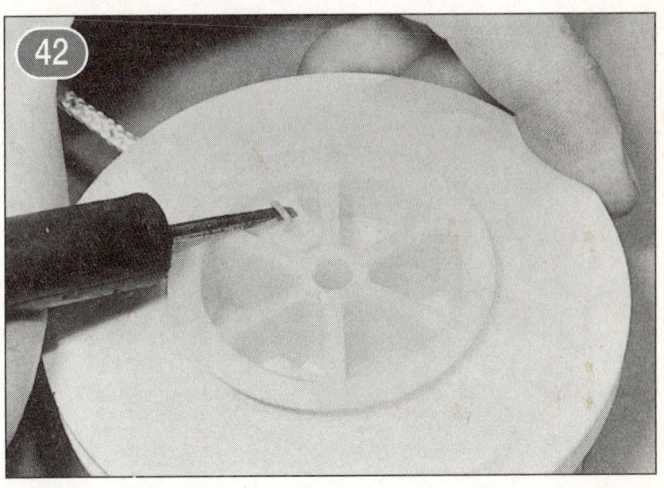

42 To free the cord, prise out the staple in the pulley. Fit the new cord and tap the staple in again.

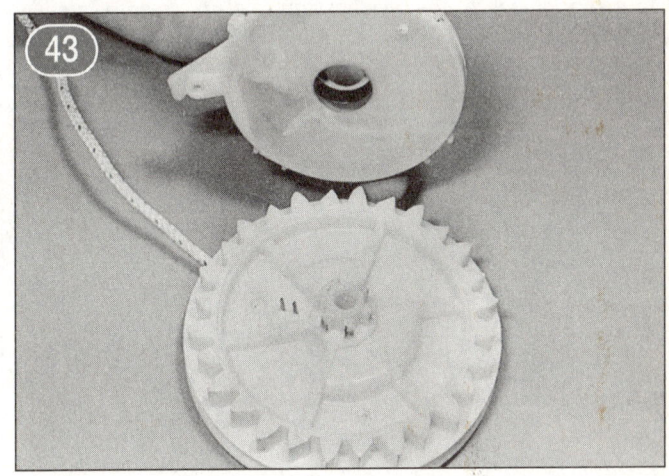

43 Fit the new spring capsule onto the pulley and turn it anticlockwise until the hook on the spring engages in the slot on the pulley hub. This can be verified by increasing tension when turning the capsule.

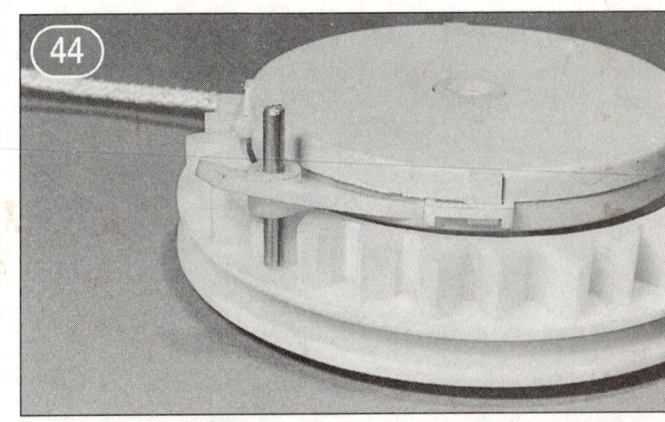

44 Turn the capsule about four turns to tension the pulley. Use a pin through the hole in the stop lever to hold the tension. Wind the cord clockwise onto the pulley when viewed from the capsule side. Leave enough cord free to pass through the hole in the fuel tank and fit the handle.

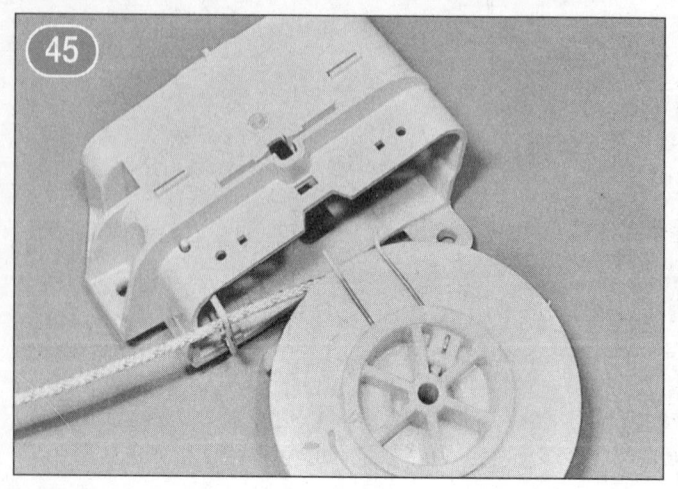

Chapter 13

45 Fit the large clip onto the pulley. Enter the pulley assembly into the housing, ensuring that the legs of the clip are located either side of the divider plate (the tip of the divider plate can just be seen in the picture on the top edge of the housing).

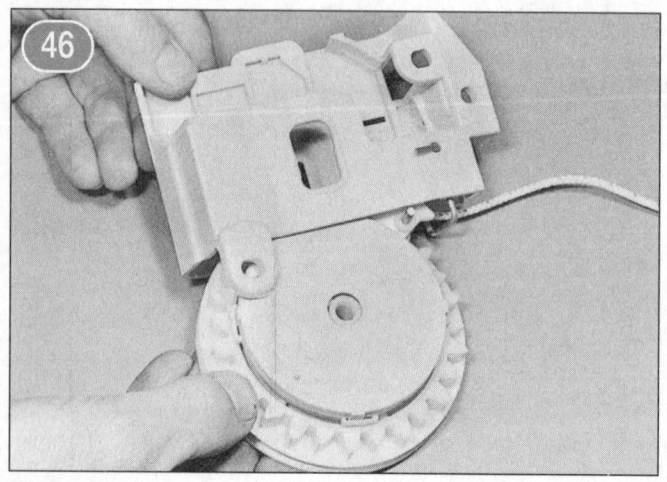

46 Seen from the other side, the photo shows the pulley assembly being entered into the housing with the pin still in the stop lever. Thread the cord under the wire guide.

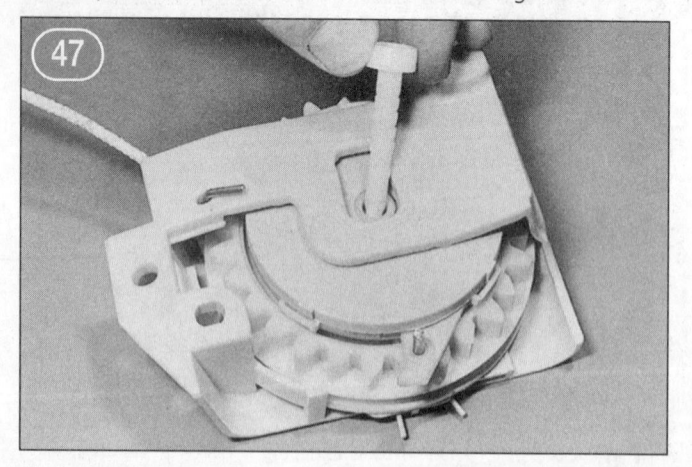

47 Fit the central pin. Do not withdraw the pin from the stop lever yet.

48 Install the recoil starter on the engine with the two bolts and shake proof washers, fitting the engine fairing plate at the same time, as it is secured by the same screws. Take the pulley tension, withdraw the temporary pin from the stop lever. Pull out some more cord then anchor it temporarily.

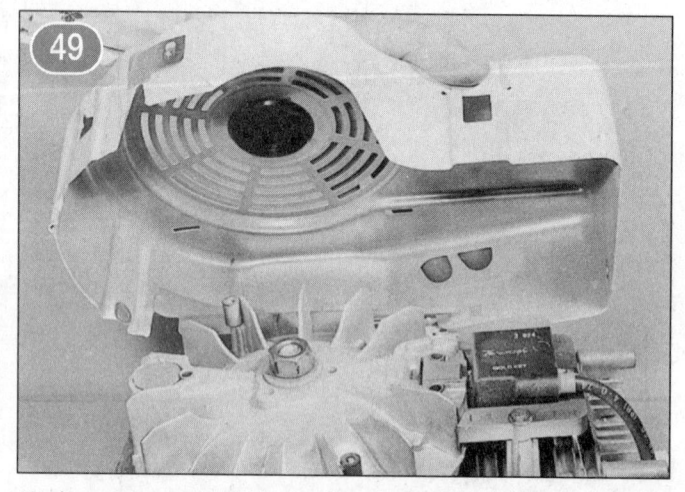

49 Fit the engine cowl with the four bolts and shakeproof washers.

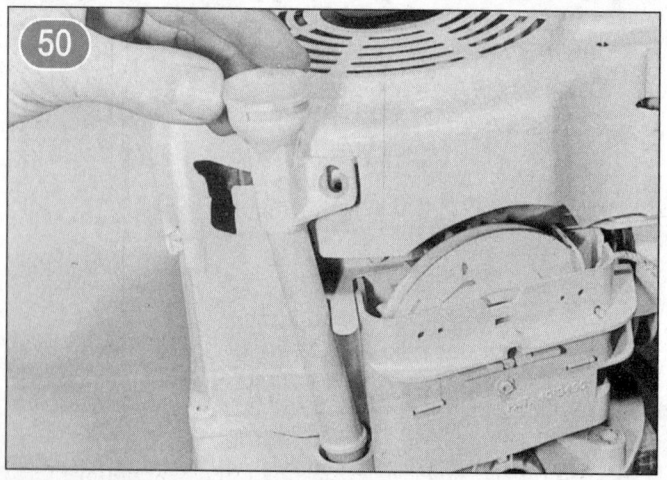

50 Fit the dipstick tube and secure it to the cowling with the bolt.

Tecumseh 3.5 hp/Vantage 35 4-stroke engine

51 Thread the cord through the fuel tank hole...

52 ... slide the fuel tank into the slides on the cowl and secure it with the three bolts. Fit the handle to the cord with the removable staple. Free the cord from its temporary anchorage. Pull the starter handle to check correct operation and a positive return action.

Connect the fuel pipe to the tank and secure it with the spring clip.

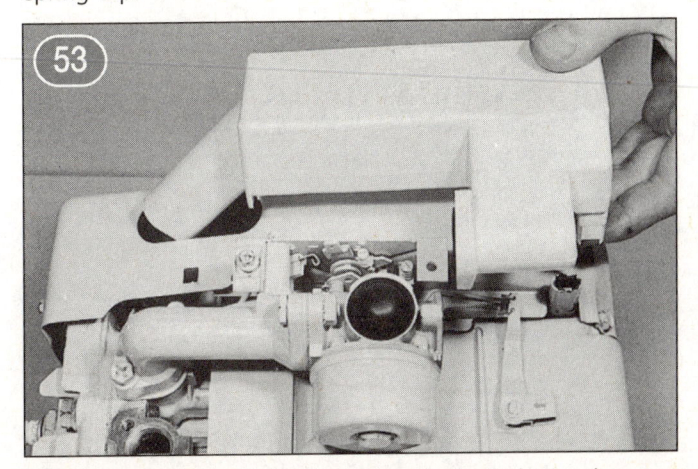

53 Insert the air cleaner inlet duct through the hole in the cowling.

54 Check that the rubber ring is in position on the air cleaner housing elbow duct. Connect the engine breather pipe to the tube on the corner of the air cleaner housing. Position the housing elbow on the carburettor inlet flange and secure with the two screws.

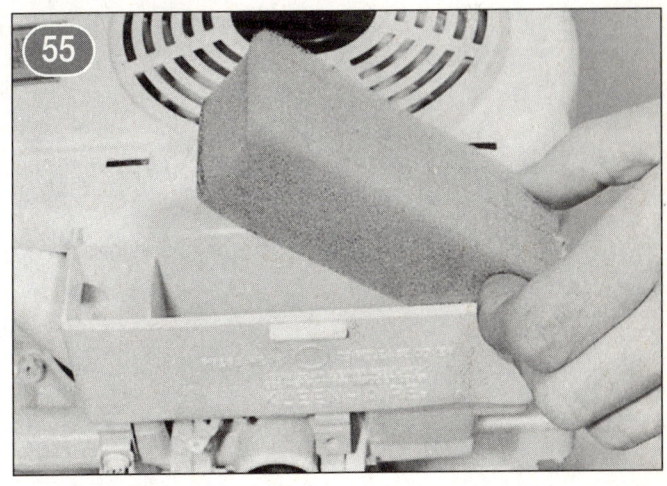

55 Wash the air cleaner foam element in solvent and squeeze it dry. Place it in the housing.

56 Fit the press-on lid.
Don't forget to fill the engine with fresh oil.

Chapter 13

Tecumseh MV100S 2-stroke engine   14

Technical data
Dismantling

Reassembly
Starter repair

Technical Data

Spark plug gap	0.6 to 0.7 mm (0.024 to 0.028 in)
Spark plug type	NGK B4LM
Magneto armature air gap	0.3 to 0.4 mm (0.012 to 0.016 in)
Torque wrench settings:	
Big-end bolts	7 Nm
Cylinder head bolts	11 Nm
Flywheel retaining nut	47 Nm

Chapter 14

Dismantling

Before starting to dismantle, read Chapter 5. The procedures outlined apply to all engines and if adopted, will ensure an orderly and methodical approached that will make dismantling and reassembly much easier.

Remove the engine from its application, and proceed as follows:

- [ ] Turn the fuel tap to the 'Off' position. Release the retaining clip and remove the fuel pipe from the carburettor and fuel tap. Be prepared for fuel spillage.
- [ ] Using pliers, pull the retaining clips up and disengage them from the fuel tank and engine cowling.
- [ ] Slide the fuel tank up and out of its locating slots in the engine cowling.
- [ ] Unscrew the four retaining bolts, and remove the starter assembly from the engine cowling.
- [ ] Remove the engine cowling by unscrewing the four retaining bolts. Note the longer bolt with washer that also secures the exhaust system.
- [ ] Disengage the throttle return spring from the throttle lever and bracket.
- [ ] Unscrew the two retaining nuts, and remove the carburettor.
- [ ] To dismantle the carburettor, undo the float bowl retaining bolt. Be prepared for fuel spillage. Remove the float bowl and rubber gasket.
- [ ] Push out the pivot pin, and carefully lift out the float with the needle valve still attached.
- [ ] The main jet/emulsion tube is located in the centre of the carburettor body. Unscrew the jet/emulsion tube and remove. No further dismantling of the carburettor is advised
- [ ] Check the condition of the needle valve and seat for any damage or wear. Examine the float bowl rubber gasket for any cracks, etc. Check that the holes of the jet/emulsion tube and carburettor body are clear. If necessary, clear the holes by blowing or the use of a thin nylon bristle. Never use a needle or wire to clean a jet. Check the float for damage or cracks.
- [ ] The two exhaust mounting bolts are locked by means of a tab washer. Bend back the tabs, unscrew the bolts, and remove the exhaust system. Recover the gasket.
- [ ] Carefully pull the HT cap from the spark plug.
- [ ] Disconnect the ignition magneto earthing wire, unscrew the two mounting bolts, and remove the magneto. Remove the magneto earthing wire.

- [ ] The flywheel retaining nut is extremely tight. In order to prevent the flywheel from turning, have an assistant jam a large screwdriver (or similar) between the teeth at the back of the flywheel, and the cast lug of the crankcase end plate. Undo the retaining nut, remove the bevelled washer, starter flange and mesh.

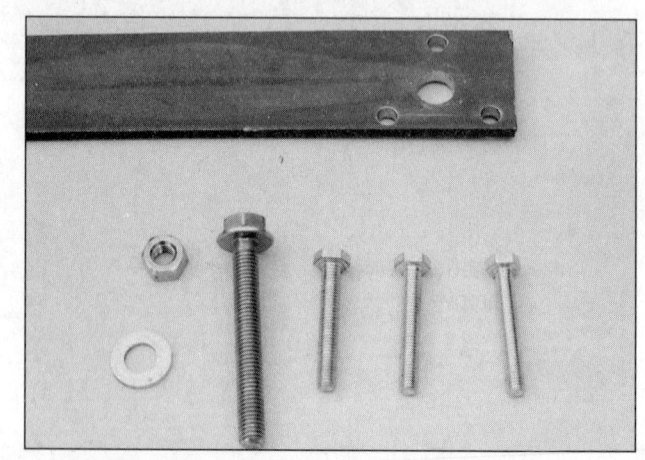

- [ ] To remove the flywheel a puller is required. This can be obtained from a local mower specialist, or one can be fabricated as follows: Using a piece of 6 mm thick mild steel plate, drill three 6.5 mm holes, approximately 38 mm between centres, in the shape of an equilateral triangle. These holes should align with the holes in the centre boss of the flywheel. In the centre of the triangle, drill a 10 mm hole to align with the crankshaft. Assemble the puller using three 6 x 40 mm bolts, and one 8 x 65 mm bolt with nut and washer.

Tecumseh MV100S 2-stroke engine

☐ Regardless of which puller is used, it is necessary tap the centre holes in the flywheel boss to accept the three 6 mm bolts.

☐ Position the flywheel retaining nut flush with the end of the crankshaft, insert the three 6 mm bolts of the assembled puller. Make sure that the centre 8 mm bolt of the puller acts squarely on the end of the crankshaft, and turn the 8 mm nut to apply a strong pulling force. It may be necessary to encourage the flywheel with a light tap from a soft hammer on the on the rim opposite the magnets. Take care to only strike the flywheel on the reinforced section of the rim. Once freed from the crankshaft taper, remove the flywheel, puller, and retaining nut. Recover the nylon collar and square-sectioned key.

☐ Remove the spark plug.

☐ Unscrew the four retaining bolts, and remove the reed valve housing from the base of the crankcase. To remove the reed valves, unscrew the two retaining bolts, lift off the retaining plate, and remove the valves.

☐ In a diagonal sequence, loosen evenly and remove the six cylinder head bolts.

☐ Working through the hole in the base of the crankcase left by the reed valve block, unscrew the big-end bolts. Carefully remove the big-end bearing cap. The big-end bearing is made up of 37 needle rollers, which will fall into the crankcase unless great care is taken when removing the bearing cap. Recover the needle rollers.

☐ Remove any carbon build-up at the lip of the cylinder bore using a soft tool, and gently push the connecting rod and piston assembly up and out of the cylinder bore.

☐ If required, remove the piston rings from the piston by carefully expanding the rings at their ends and sliding them from the piston. Note the orientation of the rings for reassembly. Remove the circlips and push the gudgeon pin from the piston.

☐ Unscrew the four crankcase end plate retaining bolts, but do not attempt to remove the plate at this stage. A hot air gun (or similar) will greatly assist the removal of the crankshaft from the crankcase. Ensure that the crankshaft is free of dirt and rust. Heat up the area of the crankcase that surrounds the main bearing on the drive (parallel) end of the crankshaft. Using a soft hammer, carefully drive the crankshaft (with the bearing still fitted) and end plate assembly from the crankcase.

☐ Heat up the area of the end plate that surrounds the main bearing, and using a soft hammer, drive the crankshaft and bearing from the end plate.

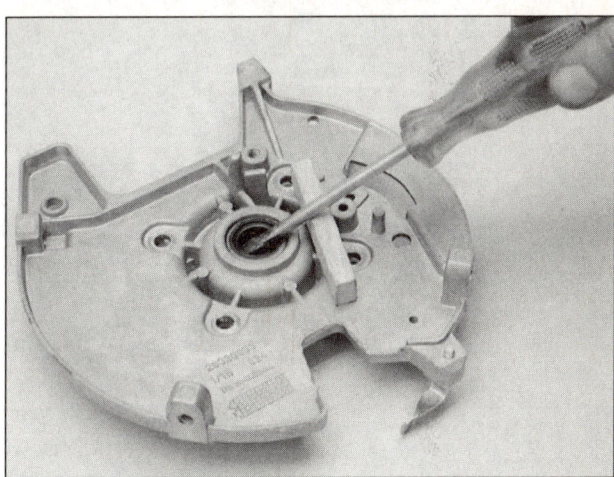

☐ If required, prise the oil seals from the crankcase and end plate, noting which way round they are fitted.

☐ Use a bearing puller, or hydraulic press, to remove the bearings from the crankshaft.

☐ Check the condition of the cylinder bore for wear, scores or cracks. If the bore is damaged, worn oval or oversized, then professional skills and special equipment will be necessary to restore it. Check all threaded holes for damaged threads, and repair if necessary by fitting a thread insert of the correct size (*refer to Chapter 2*).

Chapter 14

Reassembly

If removed, fit new ball bearings to the crankshaft using a hydraulic press. The bearings are fitted with the lettering on the rim facing outwards. Press the bearings right up to the shoulder of the crankshaft webs. The bearing fitted to the drive end (parallel) of the crankshaft is a type 6005, whilst the flywheel end (tapered) is a type 6203.

Fit new oil seals to the crankcase and end plate using appropriate sized sockets. The seals should be fitted with the sharp lip facing inwards.

1 Using a hot air gun, heat up the bearing housing in the end plate. Take care not to damage the oil seal. Smear the inside lip of with two-stroke oil.

2 Fit the crankshaft, tapered end first, into the end plate. Carefully drive the crankshaft and bearing into place using a soft hammer, or hydraulic press.

3 Heat up the bearing housing in the crankcase. Again, take care not to damage the oil seal. Smear the inside lip of the seal with two-stroke oil. With a new gasket in place…

4 … insert the crankshaft/end plate assembly into the crankcase.

5 Position the flywheel retaining nut flush with the end of the crankshaft, and drive or press the bearing into place. Insert and tighten evenly the four end plate retaining bolts. Rotate the crankshaft a few times to check for freedom of movement. Remove the flywheel retaining nut from the end of the crankshaft.

Tecumseh MV100S 2-stroke engine

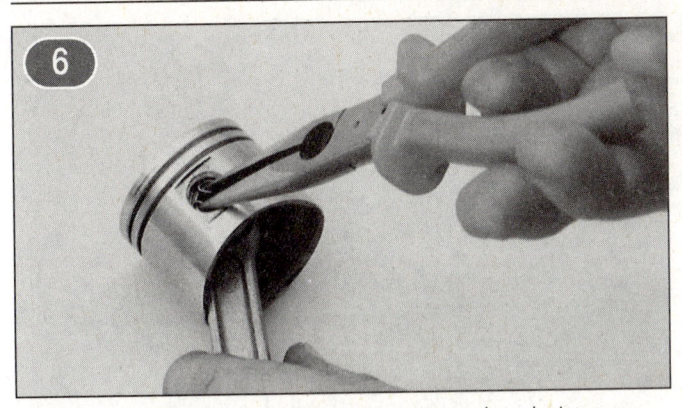

6 Refit the gudgeon pin to the connecting rod and piston using new circlips. Ensure that the notch on the piston crown is on the opposite side to the cast mark at the big-end of the connecting rod.

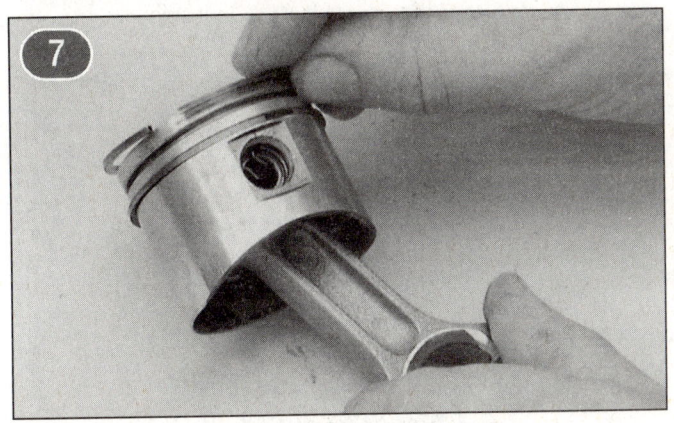

7 Fit the piston rings to the piston. If re-using the old rings, ensure they are fitted to their original locations. The rings are symmetrical in cross section, and can therefore be fitted either way up. Fit the lower compression ring first by carefully expanding the ring just enough to slide it down over the piston, and into the lower groove. Repeat this procedure for the top compression ring. Piston rings are very brittle. If they are expanded too much, they will break.

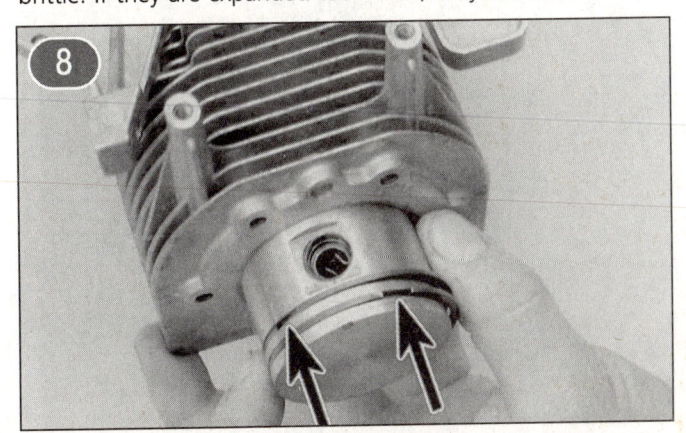

8 Smear the piston rings and cylinder bore with two-stroke oil. Arrange the piston ring end gaps so that they are approximately 30° apart on the notched side of the piston (arrowed). There may be locating pegs in the grooves to keep the rings in this position.

9 Using a piston ring clamp, insert the connecting rod and piston assembly in to the cylinder bore, with the notch in the piston crown towards the tapered end of the crankshaft. Slowly push the piston down into the bore, making sure that the connecting rod does not scratch the cylinder walls. Press the piston firmly into the cylinder, sliding it out of the clamp as the rings enter the cylinder bore. If necessary, use a hammer handle or piece of wood and gently tap the piston out of the clamp and into the cylinder, but stop and investigate any undue resistance.

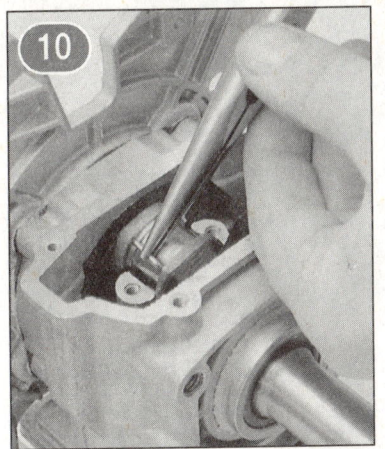

10 Smear the big-end journal with two-stroke oil. Engage the connecting rod big-end with the crankshaft journal, but leave enough room for the needle rollers to be inserted. One at a time, using tweezers (or similar), insert the needle rollers into the gap between the connecting rod and crankshaft journal.

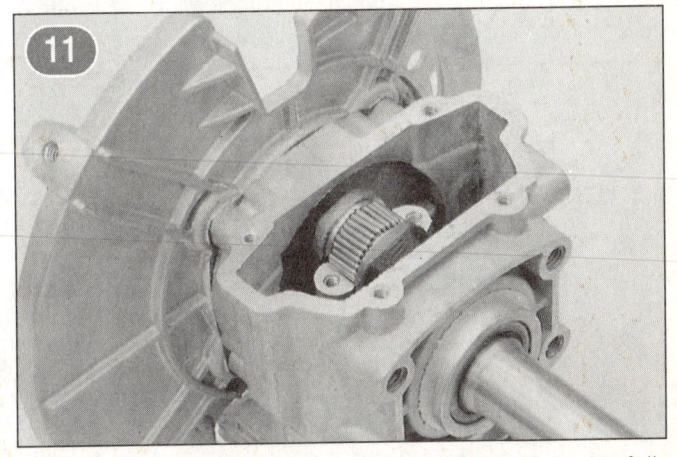

11 Once the gap between the connecting rod and journal is full, carefully add the remaining needle rollers to the journal until all 37 rollers are in place. This is a very delicate operation, and some patience will be required.

14•5

Chapter 14

12 Smear the bearing face of the big-end bearing cap with two-stroke oil and carefully place it over the needle rollers, aligning the cast mark on the cap with the matching mark on the connecting rod (arrowed).

13 With a drop of thread locking compound on their threads, insert and tighten the big-end bolts securely. If a suitable torque wrench is available, tighten the bolts to the torque given in Technical Data. Put a drop of two-stroke oil in to the hole in the end of the big-end cap, and rotate the crankshaft a few times to ensure freedom of movement.

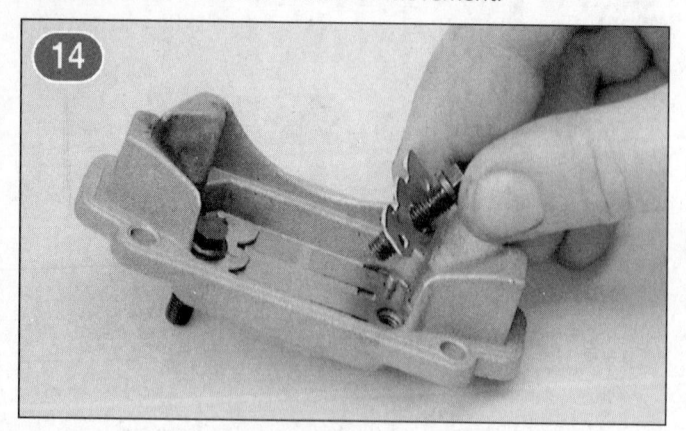

14 If previously dismantled, refit the reed valves in to the housing. Secure each valve in place with the retaining plate, and tighten the retaining bolt securely.

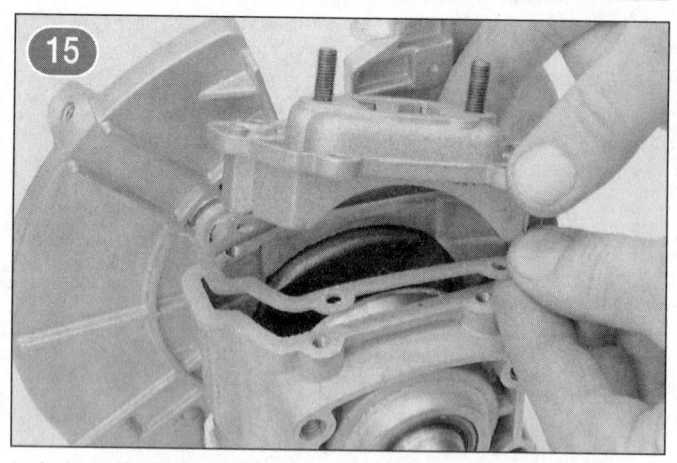

15 Using a new gasket, refit the reed valve housing to the base of the crankcase. Tighten the four retaining bolts securely.

16 Place a new gasket onto the cylinder head, and refit the head to the cylinder. Tighten the six cylinder head bolts evenly, in a diagonal sequence, securely. If a suitable torque wrench is available, tighten the bolts to the torque given in Technical Data. Refit the spark plug.

17 Slide the nylon collar over the tapered end of the crankshaft, ensuring that the nylon tab engages with the keyway of the shaft. Install the square-sectioned key in the crankshaft keyway.

Tecumseh MV100S 2-stroke engine

18 Fit the flywheel over the tapered end of the crankshaft, aligning the keyway in the flywheel with the key previously fitted.

19 Install the starter flange and mesh.

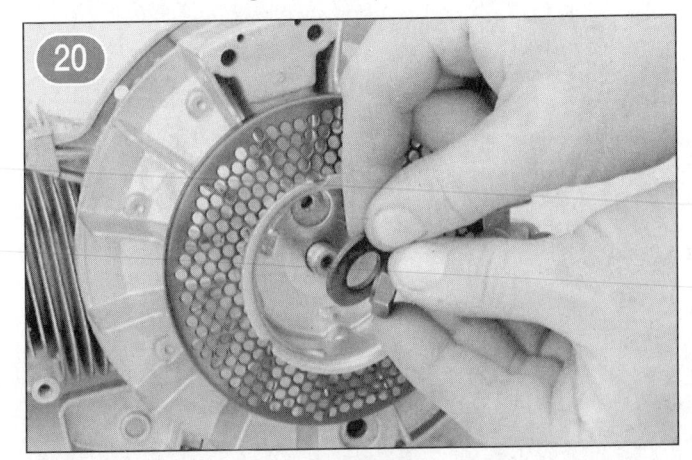

20 Fit the bevelled washer with the concave side against the starter flange. Have an assistant jam a large screwdriver (or similar) between the teeth on the back of the flywheel, and the cast lug of the crankcase end plate. Tighten the flywheel retaining nut, with its shoulder inside the bevelled washer, to the torque given in Technical Data.

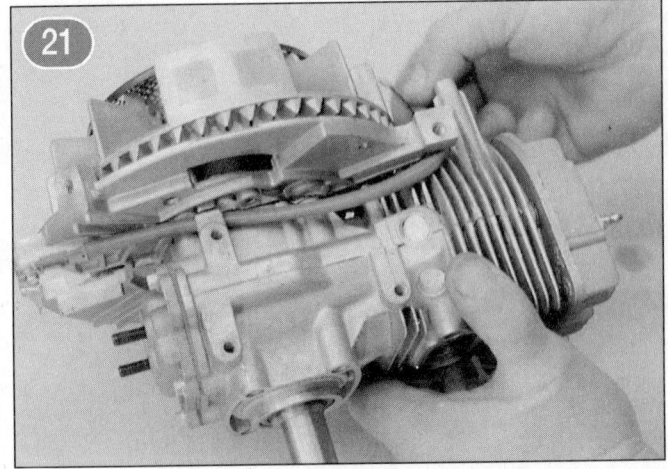

21 Route the ignition magneto earthing wire as shown.

22 Refit the magneto. Before tightening the two mounting bolts, turn the flywheel so that the magnets are next to the magneto. Use non-ferrous feeler gauges to measure the air gap between the magneto's armature legs and the flywheel. The correct gap is given in Technical Data. The holes in the armature legs are slotted. Move the armature until the correct gap is achieved. Tighten the bolts securely. Refit the HT cap to the spark plug.

23 Using a new gasket if necessary, refit the exhaust system. The two retaining bolts fit through a tab washer and reinforcing plate.

14•7

Chapter 14

24 Tighten the bolts securely, and lock them by bending the tabs of the washer. The bracket on the exhaust silencer is secured with an engine cowling bolt at a later stage.

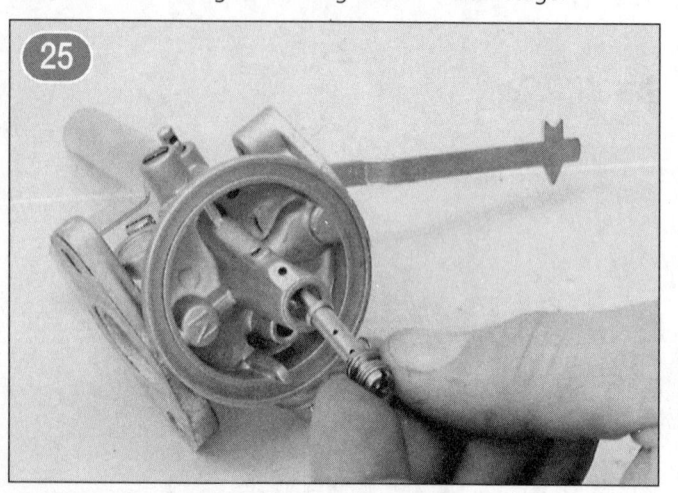

25 Insert the main jet/emulsion tube assembly into the carburettor body. Tighten the jet carefully.

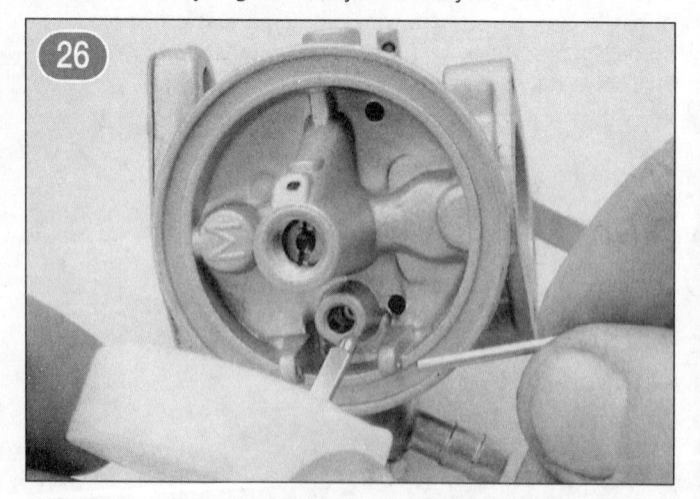

26 Refit the needle valve into its holder in the float, and carefully lower the assembly into place. Align the float with the pivot, and insert the pivot pin. There is no provision for adjusting the float height.

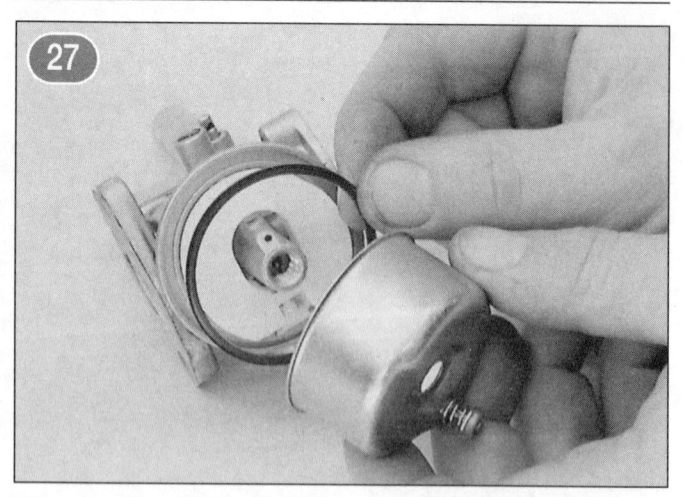

27 Using a new rubber gasket if necessary, refit the float bowl and secure with the retaining nut and fibre washer.

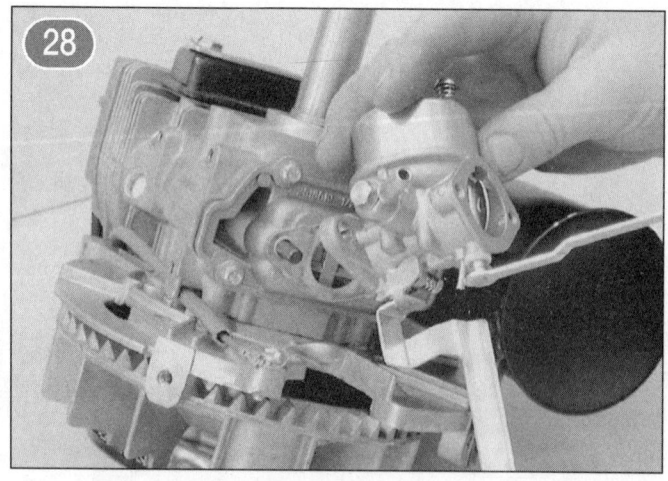

28 With a new gasket in place, refit the carburettor to the reed valve housing. Tighten the two retaining nuts securely.

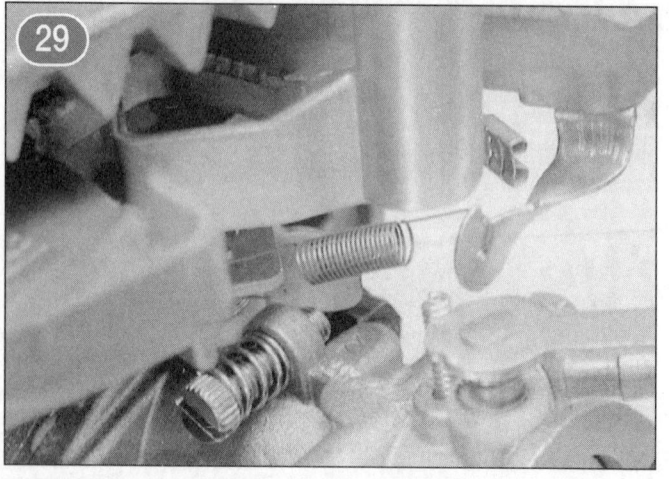

29 Refit the throttle return spring to the throttle arm and bracket.

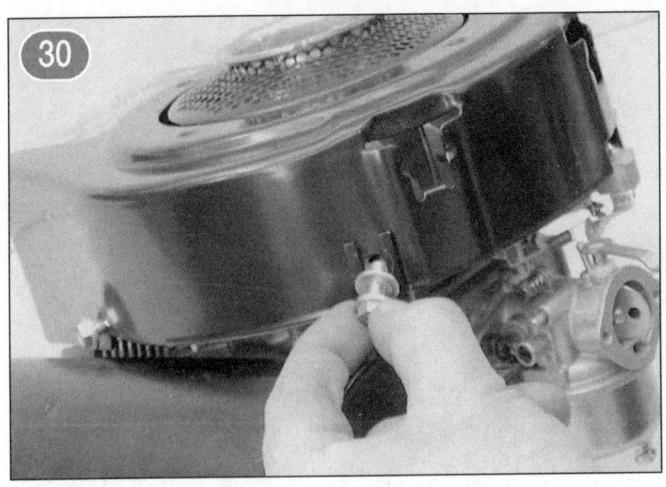

Tecumseh MV100S 2-stroke engine

30 The engine cowling is secured with four bolts. The longer bolt and washer also retains the exhaust silencer bracket.

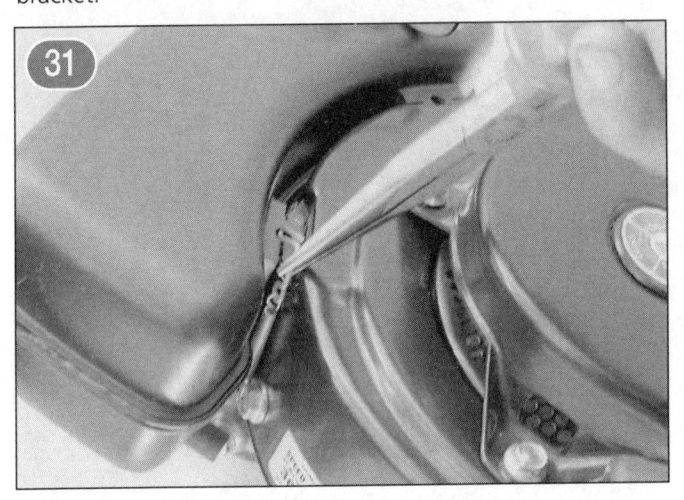

31 Install the starter assembly onto the engine cowling, and tighten the four retaining bolts securely.

32 Slide the fuel tank into its locating slots in the engine cowling. One end of the retaining clips engages with the underside of the cowling, whilst the other end fits into the locating hole in the fuel tank.

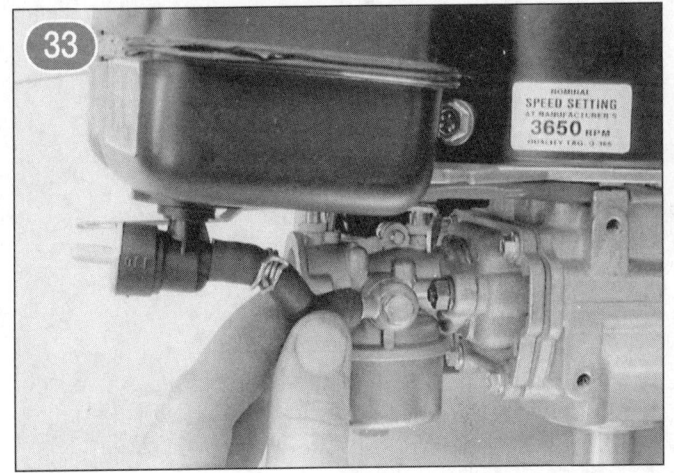

33 Reconnect the fuel pipe to the carburettor and fuel tap. Secure the pipe with the retaining clip.

Chapter 14

Starter repair

Undo the four retaining bolts, and remove the starter from the engine cowling.

Pull the rope to its full extension, and clamp the pulley in place with a self-grip wrench (or similar).

1

To replace the rope: Where the rope goes through the pulley, cut off the knot and pull the rope from the starter. Feed the new rope through the hole in the outer cover, and through the hole in the pulley. Tie the knot.

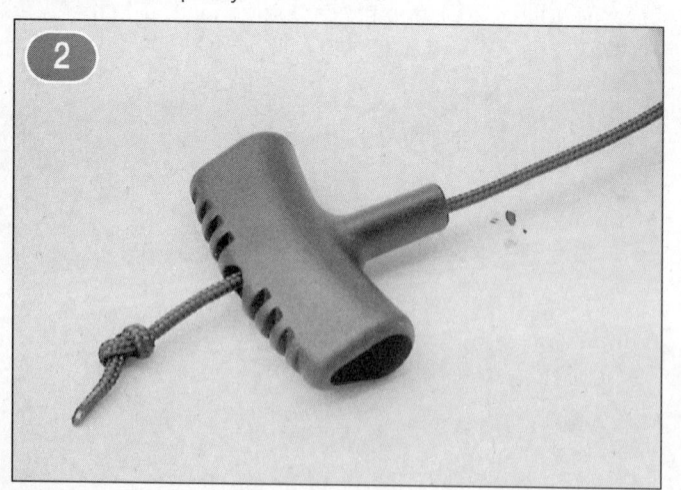

2

Feed the other end through the hole in the starter handle, again tie the knot. Tension the rope, remove the self-grip wrench, and allow the starter spring to rewind the rope.

To replace the starter spring: Where the rope goes through the pulley, untie the knot and pull the rope from the starter.

Unscrew the central screw, and carefully lift off the pawl cover. Note the spring fitted centrally under the cover.

Lift out the starter pawl. Note the 'hair' spring under the pawl. Lift out the pulley. Turn the starter spring retaining cover anti-clockwise to release it from the pulley. Remove the spring.

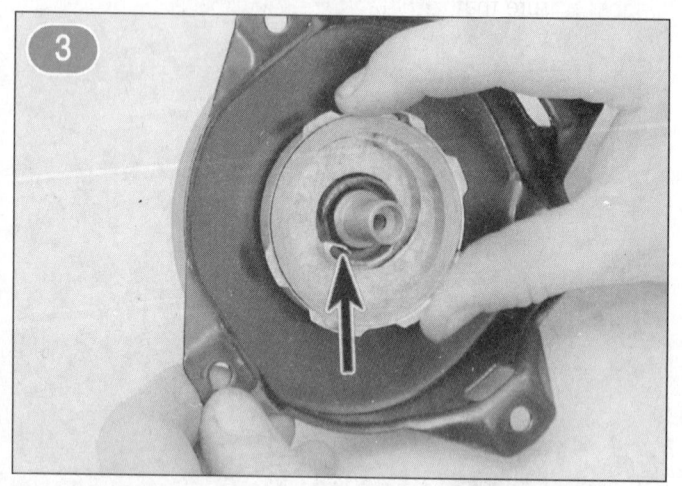

3

The new starter spring should come already fitted into the retaining cover. Place the spring and retaining cover in the starter outer cover, engaging the inner end of the spring with the lug in the outer cover (arrowed).

4

Align the pulley with the spring retaining cover as shown. Fit the pulley over the spring/cover, and twist it anti-clockwise to lock.

Tecumseh MV100S 2-stroke engine

5 Refit the 'hair' spring into the pawl-locating hole and refit the pawl. Ensure that the leg of the spring is on the outside of the pawl (arrowed).

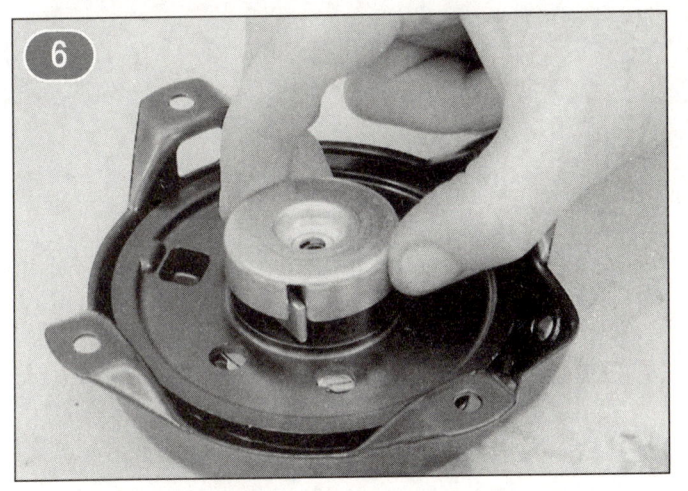

6 Insert the spring into the centre, and fit the pawl cover, engaging the pawl with the slot in the cover. Tighten the screw securely.

Wind the pulley approximately five and a half turns anti-clockwise to tension the starter spring, and align the rope holes in the outer cover and pulley. The exact number of turns is dependent on the length of the rope. Clamp the pulley in place by using a self-grip wrench (or similar).

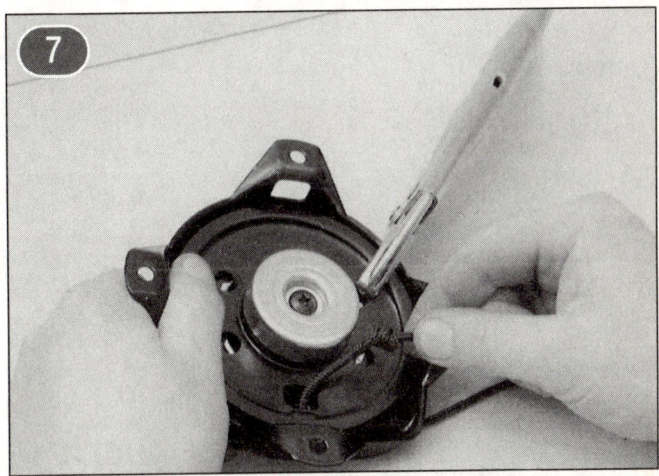

7 Feed the rope through the holes in the cover and pulley, and tie the knot. Tension the rope, remove the self-grip wrench, and allow the starter spring to rewind the rope. Check for correct operation. Refit the starter to the engine cowling using the four retaining bolts.

Chapter 14

Glossary

B

Bellville Washer
A domed spring steel washer used as a locking device.

Breather Valve
Due to the constantly changing pressures in the crankcase whilst an engine is running this valve is needed to equalise the pressure and stop the oil being expelled from the engine.

Bush
A thin tube used to form the outside of a plain bearing. Usually used in soft metal castings to improve the life of the bearing.

C

Cam Followers (Tappets)
Shaped metal rods which fit between the cam lobes of the camshaft and the valves to open the inlet and exhaust valves.

Circlip
A spring steel retaining device located in a groove in a shaft or hole which has lugs at each end to allow compression with special pliers for fitting.

Contact Breaker Points
A set of electrical contacts operated by a cam on the crankshaft to ensure that the fuel-air mixture is ignited at the correct moment in the engine cycle.

Crankcase
The main body of an engine which can consist of two or more parts. The crankcase houses the crankshaft and most internal engine components.

D

Dowels
These are close fitting pegs used to align parts of an engine accurately.

F

Feeler Gauge
Usually a set of steel fingers of specified thickness, for setting gaps between parts i.e. spark plug contacts, ignition contact breaker points.

G

Governor
Most small engines have a speed governing device. This limits the maximum speed of the engine. The two most common types are the pneumatic governor and the mechanical governor.

The pneumatic governor controls the carburettor according to the air flow generated by the cooling fan of the flywheel effecting a vane or paddle placed under the engine.

The mechanical governor is a device inside the crankcase with weights which spin; the centrifugal force pushes the weights into position to control the carburettor.

On both types the speed at which the engine runs is determined by a spring attached to the throttle link.

Gudgeon Pin
The gudgeon pin is a metal pin used to connect the piston to the connecting rod.

Glossary

I

Ignition Coil
An induction coil that supplies the high voltage to the spark plug.

M

Magneto
A combination of coil and flywheel magnets used to generate the electricity to fire the spark plug.

O

Oil Splasher
An internal engine part which disperses oil from the sump around the inside of the crankcase. To lubricate the bearings and the piston.

P

Pawl
A pivoted lever shaped to engage with a ratchet to prevent motion in a particular direction i.e. recoil starter.

Piston Ring Clamp
A tool that consists of a steel band which is tightened up to hold piston rings compressed against piston for assembly purposes.

R

Recoil Starter
A rope based starting device in which the rope is returned onto the pulley by a spring. When the rope is pulled a ratchet engages drive to the engine, drive is disengaged when the rope is returned by the spring.

S

Shim
A thin washer or strip used for adjusting clearances e.g. crankshaft endfloat.

Split Pin
A wire pin with an eye at one end and two parallel shafts making up the pin. When fitted the legs are bent to retain the pin in position.

Spring Washer
A split spring steel washer used to prevent bolts or nuts vibrating loose.

T

Throttle Butterfly
An oval plate in the carburettor which pivots on a shaft to control the air flow through the carburettor and thus the speed of the engine.

Top Dead Centre (TDC)
This is the point when the piston is at the highest point of its travel. It occurs twice in one cycle of a 4-stroke engine. At the top of the compression stroke (when the spark ignites the fuel) and between the exhaust and inlet cycles.

W

Wire Gauge
Usually a set of steel wires of specified thickness, for setting gaps between parts i.e. spark plug contacts, ignition contact breaker points.

Woodruff Key
This is a special type of semicircular key which fits into a slot of the same profile. The slot is in a shaft and is there for locating purposes.

Conversion factors

Length (distance)
Inches (in)	x 25.4	= Millimetres (mm)	x 0.0394	=	Inches (in)
Feet (ft)	x 0.305	= Metres (m)	x 3.281	=	Feet (ft)
Miles	x 1.609	= Kilometres (km)	x 0.621	=	Miles

Volume (capacity)
Cubic inches (cu in; in^3)	x 16.387	= Cubic centimetres (cc; cm^3)	x 0.061	=	Cubic inches (cu in; in^3)
Imperial pints (Imp pt)	x 0.568	= Litres (l)	x 1.76	=	Imperial pints (Imp pt)
Imperial quarts (Imp qt)	x 1.137	= Litres (l)	x 0.88	=	Imperial quarts (Imp qt)
Imperial quarts (Imp qt)	x 1.201	= US quarts (US qt)	x 0.833	=	Imperial quarts (Imp qt)
US quarts (US qt)	x 0.946	= Litres (l)	x 1.057	=	US quarts (US qt)
Imperial gallons (Imp gal)	x 4.546	= Litres (l)	x 0.22	=	Imperial gallons (Imp gal)
Imperial gallons (Imp gal)	x 1.201	= US gallons (US gal)	x 0.833	=	Imperial gallons (Imp gal)
US gallons (US gal)	x 3.785	= Litres (l)	x 0.264	=	US gallons (US gal)

Mass (weight)
Ounces (oz)	x 28.35	= Grams (g)	x 0.035	=	Ounces (oz)
Pounds (lb)	x 0.454	= Kilograms (kg)	x 2.205	=	Pounds (lb)

Force
Ounces-force (ozf; oz)	x 0.278	= Newtons (N)	x 3.6	=	Ounces-force (ozf; oz)
Pounds-force (lbf; lb)	x 4.448	= Newtons (N)	x 0.225	=	Pounds-force (lbf; lb)
Newtons (N)	x 0.1	= Kilograms-force (kgf; kg)	x 9.81	=	Newtons (N)

Pressure
Pounds-force per square inch (psi; lbf/in^2; lb/in^2)	x 0.070	= Kilograms-force per square centimetre (kgf/cm^2; kg/cm^2)	x 14.223	=	Pounds-force per square inch (psi; lbf/in^2; lb/in^2)
Pounds-force per square inch (psi; lbf/in^2; lb/in^2)	x 0.068	= Atmospheres (atm)	x 14.696	=	Pounds-force per square inch (psi; lbf/in^2; lb/in^2)
Pounds-force per square inch (psi; lbf/in^2; lb/in^2)	x 0.069	= Bars	x 14.5	=	Pounds-force per square inch (psi; lbf/in^2; lb/in^2)
Pounds-force per square inch (psi; lbf/in^2; lb/in^2)	x 6.895	= Kilopascals (kPa)	x 0.145	=	Pounds-force per square inch (psi; lbf/in^2; lb/in^2)
Kilopascals (kPa)	x 0.01	= Kilograms-force per square centimetre (kgf/cm^2; kg/cm^2)	x 98.1	=	Kilopascals (kPa)
Millibar (mbar)	x 100	= Pascals (Pa)	x 0.01	=	Millibar (mbar)
Millibar (mbar)	x 0.0145	= Pounds-force per square inch (psi; lbf/in^2; lb/in^2)	x 68.947	=	Millibar (mbar)
Millibar (mbar)	x 0.75	= Millimetres of mercury (mmHg)	x 1.333	=	Millibar (mbar)
Millibar (mbar)	x 0.401	= Inches of water (inH$_2$O)	x 2.491	=	Millibar (mbar)
Millimetres of mercury (mmHg)	x 0.535	= Inches of water (inH$_2$O)	x 1.868	=	Millimetres of mercury (mmHg)
Inches of water (inH$_2$O)	x 0.036	= Pounds-force per square inch (psi; lbf/in^2; lb/in^2)	x 27.68	=	Inches of water (inH$_2$O)

Torque (moment of force)
Pounds-force inches (lbf in; lb in)	x 1.152	= Kilograms-force centimetre (kgf cm; kg cm)	x 0.868	=	Pounds-force inches (lbf in; lb in)
Pounds-force inches (lbf in; lb in)	x 0.113	= Newton metres (Nm)	x 8.85	=	Pounds-force inches (lbf in; lb in)
Pounds-force inches (lbf in; lb in)	x 0.083	= Pounds-force feet (lbf ft; lb ft)	x 12	=	Pounds-force inches (lbf in; lb in)
Pounds-force feet (lbf ft; lb ft)	x 0.138	= Kilograms-force metres (kgf m; kg m)	x 7.233	=	Pounds-force feet (lbf ft; lb ft)
Pounds-force feet (lbf ft; lb ft)	x 1.356	= Newton metres (Nm)	x 0.738	=	Pounds-force feet (lbf ft; lb ft)
Newton metres (Nm)	x 0.102	= Kilograms-force metres (kgf m; kg m)	x 9.804	=	Newton metres (Nm)

Power
Horsepower (hp)	x 745.7	= Watts (W)	x 0.0013	=	Horsepower (hp)

Velocity (speed)
Miles per hour (miles/hr; mph)	x 1.609	= Kilometres per hour (km/hr; kph)	x 0.621	=	Miles per hour (miles/hr; mph)

Fuel consumption*
Miles per gallon, Imperial (mpg)	x 0.354	= Kilometres per litre (km/l)	x 2.825	=	Miles per gallon, Imperial (mpg)
Miles per gallon, US (mpg)	x 0.425	= Kilometres per litre (km/l)	x 2.352	=	Miles per gallon, US (mpg)

Temperature
Degrees Fahrenheit = (°C x 1.8) + 32   Degrees Celsius (Degrees Centigrade; °C) = (°F - 32) x 0.56

It is common practice to convert from miles per gallon (mpg) to litres/100 kilometres (l/100km), where mpg x l/100 km = 282

Notes

Notes

Haynes Manuals – The Complete UK Car List

Title	Book No.
ALFA ROMEO Alfasud/Sprint (74 - 88) up to F *	0292
Alfa Romeo Alfetta (73 - 87) up to E *	0531
AUDI 80, 90 & Coupe Petrol (79 - Nov 88) up to F	0605
Audi 80, 90 & Coupe Petrol (Oct 86 - 90) D to H	1491
Audi 100 & 200 Petrol (Oct 82 - 90) up to H	0907
Audi 100 & A6 Petrol & Diesel (May 91 - May 97) H to P	3504
Audi A3 Petrol & Diesel (96 - May 03) P to 03	4253
Audi A4 Petrol & Diesel (95 - 00) M to X	3575
Audi A4 Petrol & Diesel (01 - 04) X to 54	4609
AUSTIN A35 & A40 (56 - 67) up to F *	0118
Austin/MG/Rover Maestro 1.3 & 1.6 Petrol (83 - 95) up to M	0922
Austin/MG Metro (80 - May 90) up to G	0718
Austin/Rover Montego 1.3 & 1.6 Petrol (84 - 94) A to L	1066
Austin/MG/Rover Montego 2.0 Petrol (84 - 95) A to M	1067
Mini (59 - 69) up to H *	0527
Mini (69 - 01) up to X	0646
Austin/Rover 2.0 litre Diesel Engine (86 - 93) C to L	1857
Austin Healey 100/6 & 3000 (56 - 68) up to G *	0049
BEDFORD CF Petrol (69 - 87) up to E	0163
Bedford/Vauxhall Rascal & Suzuki Supercarry (86 - Oct 94) C to M	3015
BMW 316, 320 & 320i (4-cyl) (75 - Feb 83) up to Y *	0276
BMW 320, 320i, 323i & 325i (6-cyl) (Oct 77 - Sept 87) up to E	0815
BMW 3- & 5-Series Petrol (81 - 91) up to J	1948
BMW 3-Series Petrol (Apr 91 - 99) H to V	3210
BMW 3-Series Petrol (Sept 98 - 03) S to 53	4067
BMW 520i & 525e (Oct 81 - June 88) up to E	1560
BMW 525, 528 & 528i (73 - Sept 81) up to X *	0632
BMW 5-Series 6-cyl Petrol (April 96 - Aug 03) N to 03	4151
BMW 1500, 1502, 1600, 1602, 2000 & 2002 (59 - 77) up to S *	0240
CHRYSLER PT Cruiser Petrol (00 - 03) W to 53	4058
CITROËN 2CV, Ami & Dyane (67 - 90) up to H	0196
Citroën AX Petrol & Diesel (87 - 97) D to P	3014
Citroën Berlingo & Peugeot Partner Petrol & Diesel (96 - 05) P to 55	4281
Citroën BX Petrol (83 - 94) A to L	0908
Citroën C15 Van Petrol & Diesel (89 - Oct 98) F to S	3509
Citroën C3 Petrol & Diesel (02 - 05) 51 to 05	4197
Citroën C5 Petrol & Diesel (01-08) Y to 08	4745
Citroën CX Petrol (75 - 88) up to F	0528
Citroën Saxo Petrol & Diesel (96 - 04) N to 54	3506
Citroën Visa Petrol (79 - 88) up to F	0620
Citroën Xantia Petrol & Diesel (93 - 01) K to Y	3082
Citroën XM Petrol & Diesel (89 - 00) G to X	3451
Citroën Xsara Petrol & Diesel (97 - Sept 00) R to W	3751
Citroën Xsara Picasso Petrol & Diesel (00 - 02) W to 52	3944
Citroën Xsara Picasso (03-08)	4784
Citroën ZX Diesel (91 - 98) J to S	1922
Citroën ZX Petrol (91 - 98) H to S	1881
Citroën 1.7 & 1.9 litre Diesel Engine (84 - 96) A to N	1379
FIAT 126 (73 - 87) up to E *	0305
Fiat 500 (57 - 73) up to M *	0090
Fiat Bravo & Brava Petrol (95 - 00) N to W	3572
Fiat Cinquecento (93 - 98) K to R	3501
Fiat Panda (81 - 95) up to M	0793
Fiat Punto Petrol & Diesel (94 - Oct 99) L to V	3251
Fiat Punto Petrol (Oct 99 - July 03) V to 03	4066
Fiat Punto Petrol (03-07) 03 to 07	4746
Fiat Regata Petrol (84 - 88) A to F	1167
Fiat Tipo Petrol (88 - 91) E to J	1625
Fiat Uno Petrol (83 - 95) up to M	0923
Fiat X1/9 (74 - 89) up to G *	0273
FORD Anglia (59 - 68) up to G *	0001

Title	Book No.
Ford Capri II (& III) 1.6 & 2.0 (74 - 87) up to E *	0283
Ford Capri II (& III) 2.8 & 3.0 V6 (74 - 87) up to E	1309
Ford Cortina Mk I & Corsair 1500 ('62 - '66) up to D*	0214
Ford Cortina Mk III 1300 & 1600 (70 - 76) up to P *	0070
Ford Escort Mk I 1100 & 1300 (68 - 74) up to N *	0171
Ford Escort Mk I Mexico, RS 1600 & RS 2000 (70 - 74) up to N *	0139
Ford Escort Mk II Mexico, RS 1800 & RS 2000 (75 - 80) up to W *	0735
Ford Escort (75 - Aug 80) up to V *	0280
Ford Escort Petrol (Sept 80 - Sept 90) up to H	0686
Ford Escort & Orion Petrol (Sept 90 - 00) H to X	1737
Ford Escort & Orion Petrol (Sept 90 - 00) H to X	4081
Ford Fiesta (76 - Aug 83) up to Y	0334
Ford Fiesta Petrol (Aug 83 - Feb 89) A to F	1030
Ford Fiesta Petrol (Feb 89 - Oct 95) F to N	1595
Ford Fiesta Petrol & Diesel (Oct 95 - Mar 02) N to 02	3397
Ford Fiesta Petrol & Diesel (Apr 02 - 07) 02 to 57	4170
Ford Focus Petrol & Diesel (98 - 01) S to Y	3759
Ford Focus Petrol & Diesel (Oct 01 - 05) 51 to 05	4167
Ford Galaxy Petrol & Diesel (95 - Aug 00) M to W	3984
Ford Granada Petrol (Sept 77 - Feb 85) up to B *	0481
Ford Granada & Scorpio Petrol (Mar 85 - 94) B to M	1245
Ford Ka (96 - 02) P to 52	3570
Ford Mondeo Petrol (93 - Sept 00) K to X	1923
Ford Mondeo Petrol & Diesel (Oct 00 - Jul 03) X to 03	3990
Ford Mondeo Petrol & Diesel (July 03 - 07) 03 to 56	4619
Ford Mondeo Diesel (93 - 96) L to N	3465
Ford Orion Petrol (83 - Sept 90) up to H	1009
Ford Sierra 4-cyl Petrol (82 - 93) up to K	0903
Ford Sierra V6 Petrol (82 - 91) up to J	0904
Ford Transit Petrol (Mk 2) (78 - Jan 86) up to C	0719
Ford Transit Petrol (Mk 3) (Feb 86 - 89) C to G	1468
Ford Transit Diesel (Feb 86 - 99) C to T	3019
Ford Transit Diesel (00-06)	4775
Ford 1.6 & 1.8 litre Diesel Engine (84 - 96) A to N	1172
Ford 2.1, 2.3 & 2.5 litre Diesel Engine (77 - 90) up to H	1606
FREIGHT ROVER Sherpa Petrol (74 - 87) up to E	0463
HILLMAN Avenger (70 - 82) up to Y	0037
Hillman Imp (63 - 76) up to R *	0022
HONDA Civic (Feb 84 - Oct 87) A to E	1226
Honda Civic (Nov 91 - 96) J to N	3199
Honda Civic Petrol (Mar 95 - 00) M to X	4050
Honda Civic Petrol & Diesel (01 - 05) X to 55	4611
Honda CR-V Petrol & Diesel (01-06)	4747
Honda Jazz (01 - Feb 08) 51 - 57	4735
HYUNDAI Pony (85 - 94) C to M	3398
JAGUAR E Type (61 - 72) up to L *	0140
Jaguar MkI & II, 240 & 340 (55 - 69) up to H *	0098
Jaguar XJ6, XJ & Sovereign; Daimler Sovereign (68 - Oct 86) up to D	0242
Jaguar XJ6 & Sovereign (Oct 86 - Sept 94) D to M	3261
Jaguar XJ12, XJS & Sovereign; Daimler Double Six (72 - 88) up to F	0478
JEEP Cherokee Petrol (93 - 96) K to N	1943
LADA 1200, 1300, 1500 & 1600 (74 - 91) up to J	0413
Lada Samara (87 - 91) D to J	1610
LAND ROVER 90, 110 & Defender Diesel (83 - 07) up to 56	3017
Land Rover Discovery Petrol & Diesel (89 - 98) G to S	3016
Land Rover Discovery Diesel (Nov 98 - Jul 04) S to 04	4606
Land Rover Freelander Petrol & Diesel (97 - Sept 03) R to 53	3929
Land Rover Freelander Petrol & Diesel (Oct 03 - Oct 06) 53 to 56	4623

Title	Book No.
Land Rover Series IIA & III Diesel (58 - 85) up to C	0529
Land Rover Series II, IIA & III 4-cyl Petrol (58 - 85) up to C	0314
MAZDA 323 (Mar 81 - Oct 89) up to G	1608
Mazda 323 (Oct 89 - 98) G to R	3455
Mazda 626 (May 83 - Sept 87) up to E	0929
Mazda B1600, B1800 & B2000 Pick-up Petrol (72 - 88) up to F	0267
Mazda RX-7 (79 - 85) up to C *	0460
MERCEDES-BENZ 190, 190E & 190D Petrol & Diesel (83 - 93) A to L	3450
Mercedes-Benz 200D, 240D, 240TD, 300D & 300TD 123 Series Diesel (Oct 76 - 85)	1114
Mercedes-Benz 250 & 280 (68 - 72) up to L *	0346
Mercedes-Benz 250 & 280 123 Series Petrol (Oct 76 - 84) up to B *	0677
Mercedes-Benz 124 Series Petrol & Diesel (85 - Aug 93) C to K	3253
Mercedes-Benz A-Class Petrol & Diesel (98-04) S to 54	4748
Mercedes-Benz C-Class Petrol & Diesel (93 - Aug 00) L to W	3511
Mercedes-Benz C-Class (00-06)	4780
MG A (55 - 62) *	0475
MGB (62 - 80) up to W	0111
MG Midget & Austin-Healey Sprite (58 - 80) up to W *	0265
MINI Petrol (July 01 - 05) Y to 05	4273
MITSUBISHI Shogun & L200 Pick-Ups Petrol (83 - 94) up to M	1944
MORRIS Ital 1.3 (80 - 84) up to B	0705
Morris Minor 1000 (56 - 71) up to K	0024
NISSAN Almera Petrol (95 - Feb 00) N to V	4053
Nissan Almera & Tino Petrol (Feb 00 - 07) V to 56	4612
Nissan Bluebird (May 84 - Mar 86) A to C	1223
Nissan Bluebird Petrol (Mar 86 - 90) C to H	1473
Nissan Cherry (Sept 82 - 86) up to D	1031
Nissan Micra (83 - Jan 93) up to K	0931
Nissan Micra (93 - 02) K to 52	3254
Nissan Micra Petrol (03-07) 52 to 57	4734
Nissan Primera Petrol (90 - Aug 99) H to T	1851
Nissan Stanza (82 - 86) up to D	0824
Nissan Sunny Petrol (May 82 - Oct 86) up to D	0895
Nissan Sunny Petrol (Oct 86 - Mar 91) D to H	1378
Nissan Sunny Petrol (Apr 91 - 95) H to N	3219
OPEL Ascona & Manta (B Series) (Sept 75 - 88) up to F *	0316
Opel Ascona Petrol (81 - 88)	3215
Opel Astra Petrol (Oct 91 - Feb 98)	3156
Opel Corsa Petrol (83 - Mar 93)	3160
Opel Corsa Petrol (Mar 93 - 97)	3159
Opel Kadett Petrol (Nov 79 - Oct 84) up to B	0634
Opel Kadett Petrol (Oct 84 - Oct 91)	3196
Opel Omega & Senator Petrol (Nov 86 - 94)	3157
Opel Rekord Petrol (Feb 78 - Oct 86) up to D	0543
Opel Vectra Petrol (Oct 88 - Oct 95)	3158
PEUGEOT 106 Petrol & Diesel (91 - 04) J to 53	1882
Peugeot 205 Petrol (83 - 97) A to P	0932
Peugeot 206 Petrol & Diesel (98 - 01) S to X	3757
Peugeot 206 Petrol & Diesel (02 - 06) 51 to 06	4613
Peugeot 306 Petrol & Diesel (93 - 02) K to 02	3073
Peugeot 307 Petrol & Diesel (01 - 04) Y to 54	4147
Peugeot 309 Petrol (86 - 93) C to K	1266
Peugeot 405 Petrol (88 - 97) E to P	1559
Peugeot 405 Diesel (88 - 97) E to P	3198
Peugeot 406 Petrol & Diesel (96 - Mar 99) N to T	3394
Peugeot 406 Petrol & Diesel (Mar 99 - 02) T to 52	3982

* Classic reprint

Title	Book No.
Peugeot 505 Petrol (79 - 89) up to G	0762
Peugeot 1.7/1.8 & 1.9 litre Diesel Engine (82 - 96) up to N	0950
Peugeot 2.0, 2.1, 2.3 & 2.5 litre Diesel Engines (74 - 90) up to H	1607
PORSCHE 911 (65 - 85) up to C	0264
Porsche 924 & 924 Turbo (76 - 85) up to C	0397
PROTON (89 - 97) F to P	3255
RANGE ROVER V8 Petrol (70 - Oct 92) up to K	0606
RELIANT Robin & Kitten (73 - 83) up to A *	0436
RENAULT 4 (61 - 86) up to D *	0072
Renault 5 Petrol (Feb 85 - 96) B to N	1219
Renault 9 & 11 Petrol (82 - 89) up to F	0822
Renault 18 Petrol (79 - 86) up to D	0598
Renault 19 Petrol (89 - 96) F to N	1646
Renault 19 Diesel (89 - 96) F to N	1946
Renault 21 Petrol (86 - 94) C to M	1397
Renault 25 Petrol & Diesel (84 - 92) B to K	1228
Renault Clio Petrol (91 - May 98) H to R	1853
Renault Clio Diesel (91 - June 96) H to N	3031
Renault Clio Petrol & Diesel (May 98 - May 01) R to Y	3906
Renault Clio Petrol & Diesel (June '01 - '05) Y to 55	4168
Renault Espace Petrol & Diesel (85 - 96) C to N	3197
Renault Laguna Petrol & Diesel (94 - 00) L to W	3252
Renault Laguna Petrol & Diesel (Feb 01 - Feb 05) X to 54	4283
Renault Mégane & Scénic Petrol & Diesel (96 - 99) N to T	3395
Renault Mégane & Scénic Petrol & Diesel (Apr 99 - 02) T to 52	3916
Renault Megane Petrol & Diesel (Oct 02 - 05) 52 to 55	4284
Renault Scenic Petrol & Diesel (Sept 03 - 06) 53 to 06	4297
ROVER 213 & 216 (84 - 89) A to G	1116
Rover 214 & 414 Petrol (89 - 96) G to N	1689
Rover 216 & 416 Petrol (89 - 96) G to N	1830
Rover 211, 214, 216, 218 & 220 Petrol & Diesel (Dec 95 - 99) N to V	3399
Rover 25 & MG ZR Petrol & Diesel (Oct 99 - 04) V to 54	4145
Rover 414, 416 & 420 Petrol & Diesel (May 95 - 98) M to R	3453
Rover 45 / MG ZS Petrol & Diesel (99 - 05) V to 55	4384
Rover 618, 620 & 623 Petrol (93 - 97) K to P	3257
Rover 75 / MG ZT Petrol & Diesel (99 - 06) S to 06	4292
Rover 820, 825 & 827 Petrol (86 - 95) D to N	1380
Rover 3500 (76 - 87) up to E *	0365
Rover Metro, 111 & 114 Petrol (May 90 - 98) G to S	1711
SAAB 95 & 96 (66 - 76) up to R *	0198
Saab 90, 99 & 900 (79 - Oct 93) up to L	0765
Saab 900 (Oct 93 - 98) L to R	3512
Saab 9000 (4-cyl) (85 - 98) C to S	1686
Saab 9-3 Petrol & Diesel (98 - Aug 02) R to 02	4614
Saab 9-3 Petrol & Diesel (02-07) 52 to 57	4749
Saab 9-5 4-cyl Petrol (97 - 04) R to 54	4156
SEAT Ibiza & Cordoba Petrol & Diesel (Oct 93 - Oct 99) L to V	3571
Seat Ibiza & Malaga Petrol (85 - 92) B to K	1609
SKODA Estelle (77 - 89) up to G	0604
Skoda Fabia Petrol & Diesel (00 - 06) W to 06	4376
Skoda Favorit (89 - 96) F to N	1801
Skoda Felicia Petrol & Diesel (95 - 01) M to X	3505
Skoda Octavia Petrol & Diesel (98 - Apr 04) R to 04	4285
SUBARU 1600 & 1800 (Nov 79 - 90) up to H *	0995

Title	Book No.
SUNBEAM Alpine, Rapier & H120 (67 - 74) up to N *	0051
SUZUKI SJ Series, Samurai & Vitara (4-cyl) Petrol (82 - 97) up to P	1942
Suzuki Supercarry & Bedford/Vauxhall Rascal (86 - Oct 94) C to M	3015
TALBOT Alpine, Solara, Minx & Rapier (75 - 86) up to D	0337
Talbot Horizon Petrol (78 - 86) up to D	0473
Talbot Samba (82 - 86) up to D	0823
TOYOTA Avensis Petrol (98 - Jan 03) R to 52	4264
Toyota Carina E Petrol (May 92 - 97) J to P	3256
Toyota Corolla (80 - 85) up to C	0683
Toyota Corolla (Sept 83 - Sept 87) A to E	1024
Toyota Corolla (Sept 87 - Aug 92) E to K	1683
Toyota Corolla Petrol (Aug 92 - 97) K to P	3259
Toyota Corolla Petrol (July 97 - Feb 02) P to 51	4286
Toyota Hi-Ace & Hi-Lux Petrol (69 - Oct 83) up to A	0304
Toyota RAV4 Petrol & Diesel (94-06) L to 55	4750
Toyota Yaris Petrol (99 - 05) T to 05	4265
TRIUMPH GT6 & Vitesse (62 - 74) up to N *	0112
Triumph Herald (59 - 71) up to K *	0010
Triumph Spitfire (62 - 81) up to X	0113
Triumph Stag (70 - 78) up to T *	0441
Triumph TR2, TR3, TR3A, TR4 & TR4A (52 - 67) up to F *	0028
Triumph TR5 & 6 (67 - 75) up to P *	0031
Triumph TR7 (75 - 82) up to Y *	0322
VAUXHALL Astra Petrol (80 - Oct 84) up to B	0635
Vauxhall Astra & Belmont Petrol (Oct 84 - Oct 91) B to J	1136
Vauxhall Astra Petrol (Oct 91 - Feb 98) J to R	1832
Vauxhall/Opel Astra & Zafira Petrol (Feb 98 - Apr 04) R to 04	3758
Vauxhall/Opel Astra & Zafira Diesel (Feb 98 - Apr 04) R to 04	3797
Vauxhall/Opel Astra Petrol (04 - 08)	4732
Vauxhall/Opel Astra Diesel (04 - 08)	4733
Vauxhall/Opel Calibra (90 - 98) G to S	3502
Vauxhall Carlton Petrol (Oct 78 - Oct 86) up to D	0480
Vauxhall Carlton & Senator Petrol (Nov 86 - 94) D to L	1469
Vauxhall Cavalier Petrol (81 - Oct 88) up to F	0812
Vauxhall Cavalier Petrol (Oct 88 - 95) F to N	1570
Vauxhall Chevette (75 - 84) up to B	0285
Vauxhall/Opel Corsa Diesel (Mar 93 - Oct 00) K to X	4087
Vauxhall Corsa Petrol (Mar 93 - 97) K to R	1985
Vauxhall/Opel Corsa Petrol (Apr 97 - Oct 00) P to X	3921
Vauxhall/Opel Corsa Petrol & Diesel (Oct 00 - Sept 03) X to 53	4079
Vauxhall/Opel Corsa Petrol & Diesel (Oct 03 - Aug 06) 53 to 06	4617
Vauxhall/Opel Frontera Petrol & Diesel (91 - Sept 98) J to S	3454
Vauxhall Nova Petrol (83 - 93) up to K	0909
Vauxhall/Opel Omega Petrol (94 - 99) L to T	3510
Vauxhall/Opel Vectra Petrol & Diesel (95 - Feb 99) N to S	3396
Vauxhall/Opel Vectra Petrol & Diesel (Mar 99 - May 02) T to 02	3930
Vauxhall/Opel Vectra Petrol & Diesel (June 02 - Sept 05) 02 to 55	4618
Vauxhall/Opel 1.5, 1.6 & 1.7 litre Diesel Engine (82 - 96) up to N	1222
VW 411 & 412 (68 - 75) up to P *	0091
VW Beetle 1200 (54 - 77) up to S	0036
VW Beetle 1300 & 1500 (65 - 75) up to P	0039

Title	Book No.
VW 1302 & 1302S (70 - 72) up to L *	0110
VW Beetle 1303, 1303S & GT (72 - 75) up to P	0159
VW Beetle Petrol & Diesel (Apr 99 - 07) T to 57	3798
VW Golf & Jetta Mk 1 Petrol 1.1 & 1.3 (74 - 84) up to A	0716
VW Golf, Jetta & Scirocco Mk 1 Petrol 1.5, 1.6 & 1.8 (74 - 84) up to A	0726
VW Golf & Jetta Mk 1 Diesel (78 - 84) up to A	0451
VW Golf & Jetta Mk 2 Petrol (Mar 84 - Feb 92) A to J	1081
VW Golf & Vento Petrol & Diesel (Feb 92 - Mar 98) J to R	3097
VW Golf & Bora Petrol & Diesel (April 98 - 00) R to X	3727
VW Golf & Bora 4-cyl Petrol & Diesel (01 - 03) X to 53	4169
VW Golf & Jetta Petrol & Diesel (04 - 07) 53 to 07	4610
VW LT Petrol Vans & Light Trucks (76 - 87) up to E	0637
VW Passat & Santana Petrol (Sept 81 - May 88) up to E	0814
VW Passat 4-cyl Petrol & Diesel (May 88 - 96) E to P	3498
VW Passat 4-cyl Petrol & Diesel (Dec 96 - Nov 00) P to X	3917
VW Passat Petrol & Diesel (Dec 00 - May 05) X to 05	4279
VW Polo & Derby (76 - Jan 82) up to X	0335
VW Polo (82 - Oct 90) up to H	0813
VW Polo Petrol (Nov 90 - Aug 94) H to L	3245
VW Polo Hatchback Petrol & Diesel (94 - 99) M to S	3500
VW Polo Hatchback Petrol (00 - Jan 02) V to 51	4150
VW Polo Petrol & Diesel (02 - May 05) 51 to 05	4608
VW Scirocco (82 - 90) up to H *	1224
VW Transporter 1600 (68 - 79) up to V	0082
VW Transporter 1700, 1800 & 2000 (72 - 79) up to V *	0226
VW Transporter (air-cooled) Petrol (79 - 82) up to Y *	0638
VW Transporter (water-cooled) Petrol (82 - 90) up to H	3452
VW Type 3 (63 - 73) up to M *	0084
VOLVO 120 & 130 Series (& P1800) (61 - 73) up to M *	0203
Volvo 142, 144 & 145 (66 - 74) up to N *	0129
Volvo 240 Series Petrol (74 - 93) up to K	0270
Volvo 262, 264 & 260/265 (75 - 85) up to C *	0400
Volvo 340, 343, 345 & 360 (76 - 91) up to J	0715
Volvo 440, 460 & 480 Petrol (87 - 97) D to P	1691
Volvo 740 & 760 Petrol (82 - 91) up to J	1258
Volvo 850 Petrol (92 - 96) J to P	3260
Volvo 940 petrol (90 - 98) H to R	3249
Volvo S40 & V40 Petrol (96 - Mar 04) N to 04	3569
Volvo S40 & V50 Petrol & Diesel (Mar 04 - Jun 07) 04 to 07	4731
Volvo S60 Petrol & Diesel (01-08)	4793
Volvo S70, V70 & C70 Petrol (96 - 99) P to V	3573
Volvo V70 / S80 Petrol & Diesel (98 - 05) S to 55	4263

DIY MANUAL SERIES

Title	Book No.
The Haynes Air Conditioning Manual	4192
The Haynes Car Electrical Systems Manual	4251
The Haynes Manual on Bodywork	4198
The Haynes Manual on Brakes	4178
The Haynes Manual on Carburettors	4177
The Haynes Manual on Diesel Engines	4174
The Haynes Manual on Engine Management	4199
The Haynes Manual on Fault Codes	4175
The Haynes Manual on Practical Electrical Systems	4267
The Haynes Manual on Small Engines	4250
The Haynes Manual on Welding	4176

* Classic reprint

All the products featured on this page are available through most motor accessory shops, cycle shops and book stores. Our policy of continuous updating and development means that titles are being constantly added to the range. For up-to-date information on our complete list of titles, please telephone: (UK) +44 1963 442030 • (USA) +1 805 498 6703 • (Sweden) +46 18 124016 • (Australia) +61 3 9763 8100

CL24.08/09

Preserving Our Motoring Heritage

The Model J Duesenberg Derham Tourster. Only eight of these magnificent cars were ever built – this is the only example to be found outside the United States of America

Almost every car you've ever loved, loathed or desired is gathered under one roof at the Haynes Motor Museum. Over 300 immaculately presented cars and motorbikes represent every aspect of our motoring heritage, from elegant reminders of bygone days, such as the superb Model J Duesenberg to curiosities like the bug-eyed BMW Isetta. There are also many old friends and flames. Perhaps you remember the 1959 Ford Popular that you did your courting in? The magnificent 'Red Collection' is a spectacle of classic sports cars including AC, Alfa Romeo, Austin Healey, Ferrari, Lamborghini, Maserati, MG, Riley, Porsche and Triumph.

A Perfect Day Out

Each and every vehicle at the Haynes Motor Museum has played its part in the history and culture of Motoring. Today, they make a wonderful spectacle and a great day out for all the family. Bring the kids, bring Mum and Dad, but above all bring your camera to capture those golden memories for ever. You will also find an impressive array of motoring memorabilia, a comfortable 70 seat video cinema and one of the most extensive transport book shops in Britain. The Pit Stop Cafe serves everything from a cup of tea to wholesome, home-made meals or, if you prefer, you can enjoy the large picnic area nestled in the beautiful rural surroundings of Somerset.

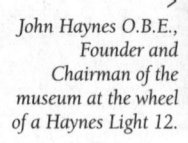

John Haynes O.B.E., Founder and Chairman of the museum at the wheel of a Haynes Light 12.

Graham Hill's Lola Cosworth Formula 1 car next to a 1934 Riley Sports.

The Museum is situated on the A359 Yeovil to Frome road at Sparkford, just off the A303 in Somerset. It is about 40 miles south of Bristol, and 25 minutes drive from the M5 intersection at Taunton.
Open 9.30am - 5.30pm (10.00am - 4.00pm Winter) 7 days a week, *except Christmas Day, Boxing Day and New Years Day*
Special rates available for schools, coach parties and outings Charitable Trust No. 292048